The City and the Railway in Europe

Historical Urban Studies

Series editors: *Richard Rodger* and *Jean-Luc Pinol*

Titles in this series include:

Capital Cities and their Hinterlands in Early Modern Europe
editors: Peter Clark and Bernard Lepetit

*Power, Profit and Urban Land: Landownership in Medieval and
Early Modern Northern European Towns*
editors: Finn-Einar Eliassen and Geir Atle Ersland

Advertising and the European City
editors: Clemens Wischermann and Elliot Shore

*Cathedrals of Urban Modernity:
The First Museums of Contemporary Art, 1800–1930*
J. Pedro Lorente

*Body and City:
A Cultural History of Urban Public Health*
editors: Helen Power and Sally Sheard

The Artisan and the European Town, 1500–1900
editors: Geoffrey Crossick

*Urban Fortunes:
Property and Inheritance in the Town, 1700–1900*
editors: Jon Stobart and Alastair Owens

*Urban Governance:
Britain and Beyond since 1750*
editors: R. J. Morris and R. H. Trainor

Printed Matters
editors: Malcolm Gee and Tim Kirk

*Identities in Space:
Contested Terrains in the Western City Since 1850*
editors: Simon Gunn and Robert J. Morris

*Young People and the European City:
Age Relations in Nottingham and Saint-Etienne, 1890–1940*
David M. Pomfret

The City and the Railway in Europe

Edited by

RALF ROTH
and
MARIE-NOËLLE POLINO

ASHGATE

Published by
Ashgate Publishing Limited
Gower House
Croft Road
Aldershot
Hants GUl 1 3HR
England

Ashgate Publishing Company
Suite 420
101 Cherry Street
Burlington, VT 05401-4405
USA

Ashgate website: http://www.ashgate.com

British Library Cataloguing in Publication Data
The city and the railway in Europe. - (Historical urban
    studies)
    1.Railroads - Europe - History 2.Cities and towns - Europe
    - History - 19th century 3.Cities and towns - Europe -
    History - 20th century 4. Cities and towns - Growth
    I.Roth, Ralf II.Polino, Marie-Noëlle
    303.4'832'094

Library of Congress Cataloging-in-Publication Data
The city and the railway in Europe / edited by Ralf Roth and Marie-Noëlle Polino.
    p. cm. -- (Historical urban studies series)
    Includes bibliographical references and index.
    ISBN 0-7546-0766-6 (alk. paper)
    1. Railroad stations--Europe. 2. City planning--Europe. I. Roth, Ralf. II. Polino,
Marie-Noëlle III. Historical urban studies

TF302.E85 C58 2003
307.76'094'09034--dc21   2002028173

ISBN 0 7546 0766 6

Printed and bound in Great Britain by Biddles Ltd *www.biddles.co.uk*

Contents

PART I: LINE, REGION, CITY-SYSTEM

List of Figures and Tables

Figures

Tables

List of Abbreviations

AEG	Allgemeine Elektrizitäts-Gesellschaft
AFR	Association of the Friends of Railways
AHICF	Association pour l'Histoire des Chemins de Fer en France
BLHA	Brandenburgisches Landeshauptarchiv, Berlin
BVG	Berliner Verkehrsgesellschaft
CBD	Central Business District
CCC	Correspondence Consulaire Commerciale, Archives du Ministère des Affaires Etrangères, France.
CGO	Compagnie Générale des Omnibus
CMP	Compagnie du Chemin de Fer Métropolitain de Paris
CP	Companhia dos Caminhos de Ferro Portugueses
CRNS	Centre National de la Recherche Scientifique
EAUH	European Association of Urban Historians
EEC	European Economic Community
FO, CCR	Consular Commercial Reports, Public Record Office, London
FO, CR	Consular Reports, Public Record Office, London
GIProMeZ	Gosudarstvennyi Institut po Proektirovaniiu Novykh Metallurgicheskikh Zavodov (State Institute for the Projecting of New Metal Works)
GDR	Groupe de Recherche
GIS	Geographical Information System
GWR	Great Western Railway
HSM	Hollandsche IJzeren Spoorweg Maatschappij (Amsterdam-Haarlem-The Hague-Rotterdam line)
ICE	Inter City Express
IfSG	Institut für Stadtgeschichte, Frankfurt am Main
INRETS	Institut National de Recherche sur les Transports et leur Sécurité
KPD	Kommunistische Partei Deutschlands
Kuzbass	Kuznetskij ugol'nii bassein (Kuznetsk coal basin)
KVZhD	Kitaisko-Vostochnaia Zheleznaia Doroga (Chinese Eastern Railway)
LAB	Landesarchiv Berlin
LATTS	Laboratoire Techniques, Territoires et Sociétés
MAO	Moskovskoe Arkhitekturnoe Obshchestvo (Moscow Architectural Society)
MAV	Magyar Államvasutak (Hungarian Railways)
NRS	Nederlandsche Rhijnspoorweg-Maatschappij (Amsterdam-Utrecht-Arnhem and Rotterdam-Utrecht line)
NSDAP	Nationalsozialistische Deutsche Arbeiterpartei

OSA	Ob'edinenie Sovremennykh Arkhitektorov (Union of Contemporary Architects)
RATP	Régie Autonome des Transports Parisiens
RB	Reichsbanner
RER	Réseau Express Régional
RFB	Roter Frontkämpferbund
SNCF	Société Nationale des Chemins de fer Français
TGV	Train à Grande Vitesse
Transsib	Transsibirskaia Zheleznodorozhnaia Magistral (Trans-Siberian Railway)
UIC	Union Internationale des Chemins de Fer
USSR	Union of Socialist Soviet Republics

Historical Urban Studies
General Editors' Preface

Density and proximity are two of the defining characteristics of the urban dimension. It is these that identify a place as uniquely urban, though the threshold for such pressure points varies from place to place. What is considered an important cluster in one context may not be considered so elsewhere. A third defining characteristic is functionality – the commercial or strategic position of a town or city which conveys an advantage over other places. Over time, these functional advantages may diminish, or the balance of advantage may change within a hierarchy of towns. To understand how the relative importance of towns shifts over time and space is to grasp a set of relationships which is fundamental to the study of urban history.

Towns and cities are products of history, yet have themselves helped to shape history. As the proportion of urban dwellers has increased, so the urban dimension has proved a legitimate unit of analysis through which to understand the spectrum of human experience and to explore the cumulative memory of past generations. Though obscured by layers of economic, social and political change, the study of the urban milieu provides insights into the functioning of human relationships and, if urban historians themselves are not directly concerned with current policy studies, few contemporary concerns can be understood without reference to the historical development of towns and cities.

This longer historical perspective is essential to an understanding of social processes. Crime, housing conditions and property values, health and education, discrimination and deviance, and the formulation of regulations and social policies to deal with them were, and remain, amongst the perennial preoccupations within towns and cities. No historical period has a monopoly of these concerns. They recur in successive generations, albeit in varying mixtures and strengths; the details may differ.

The central forces of class, power and authority in the city remain the organisers. If this was the case for different periods, so it was for different geographical entities and cultures. Both scientific knowledge and technical information were available across Europe and showed little respect for frontiers. Yet despite common concerns and access to broadly similar knowledge, different solutions to urban problems were proposed and adopted by towns and cities in different parts of Europe. This comparative dimension informs urban historians as to which were systematic factors and which were of a purely local nature: general and particular forces can be distinguished.

These analytical frameworks, considered in a comparative context, inform the books in this series.

Université de Tours   Jean-Luc Pinol
University of Leicester   Richard Rodger

Notes on Contributors

François Caron, Professor emeritus at *Université Paris-Sorbonne (Paris IV)*, France, is a recognised specialist in economic history, business history and history of technology. His wide-ranging publications in railway history include two major books: *Histoire de l'exploitation d'un grand réseau: la Compagnie du chemin de fer du Nord 1846–1937* (Paris and The Hague 1973) and *Histoire des chemins de fer en France*, 2 vols. (Paris 1997).

Hugh Campbell is a lecturer at the *School of Architecture, University College Dublin*, Ireland. He has written extensively on Irish architecture and urban history including Irish Identity and the *Architecture of the new State in Twentieth Century Architecture: Ireland* (Dublin 1997), and 'The Emergence of Modern Dublin: reality and representation', *Architectural Research Quarterly*, no. 8, 1997 and 'Irish Architecture 1800–2000' in the forthcoming *Cambridge Companion to Modern Irish Culture*.

Diane Drummond is a senior lecturer in Victorian Studies and History at the *Faculty of Arts and Humanities, Trinity and All Saints' College, the University of Leeds*, United Kingdom. She is author of *Crewe: Railway Town, Company and People, 1840–1914* (Aldershot 1995) and co-authored with E. W. Ives and L. D. Schwarz, *The First Civic University: Birmingham 1880–1980 - An Introductory History* (Birmingham 2000).

Andrea Giuntini is professor at the *Faculty of Economics of Modena and Reggio Emilia*, Italy. He is author of *Leopoldo e il treno. Le ferrovie nel Granducato di Toscana, 1824–1861* (Napoli 1991), and has collaborated with A. Bellinazzi on the book, *In treno a Firenze. Stazioni e strade ferrate nella Toscana di Leopoldo II* (Florence 1998).

Vilma Hastaoglou-Martinidis is Associate Professor of Urban History and Design at the *Faculty of Technology, Aristotle University of Thessaloniki*, and at the *Department of Urban and Regional Planning and Development, School of Architecture*, Greece. The present article is based on her extensive on-going research on the urban transformation of major Levantine port-cities in the end of the 19th century. She has already published the following articles: 'Les villes-ports du bassin oriental de la Méditerranée à la fin du XIXe siècle: travaux portuaires et transformations urbaines', in C. Vallat, ed., *Petites et grandes villes du bassin méditerranéen* (Rome 1999), and 'The harbour of Thessaloniki, 1896–1920', in A. Jarvis, and K. Smith, eds., *Albert Dock: Trade and Technology* (Liverpool 1999).

Alena Kubova is professor at the *Ecole d'architecture* in Lyon, France. Her main contribution to the field is *L'Avant-garde architecturale en Tchécoslovaquie 1918– 1939* (Liège 1992).

Neil McAlpine is a researcher at the *Transport Research Institute, Napier University of Edinburgh*, United Kingdom. His contribution to this book is the result of his ongoing research which uses the Geographical Information Systems (GIS) as a visual tool to map out new railway lines and their structures as well as showing the development of the urban form in London.

Anja Kervanto Nevanlinna is Senior Research Fellow at the *Academy of Finland* and at the *Department of Art History, University of Helsinki*, Finland. She is author of 'Classified Urban Spaces: Who Owns the History of Helsinki South Harbor?', in Simon Gunn and Robert J. Morris, eds., *Identities in Space: Contested Terrains in the Western City since 1850* (Aldershot 2001), and *Interpreting Nairobi: The Cultural Study of Built Forms* (Helsinki 1996).

Ivan V. Nevzgodine is a lecturer at the *Faculty of Architecture, Delft University of Technology*, Netherlands, and at the *Novosibirsk State Academy of Architecture and Fine Arts* in Novosibirsk, Russia. He has written 'Experiments in Siberian Constructivism during the 1920s', in M. Botta, ed., *Vision and Reality: Proceedings of the Fifth International Docomomo Conference* (Stockholm 1998), 194–8.

Magda Pinheiro is professor at the public university institution *Instituto Superior de Ciéncias do Trabalho e da Empresa* in Algés nearby Lisbon, Portugal. She has written *Chemins de Fer, Structure Financière de L'État et Dépendance Extérieure au Portugal, 1852–1890*, 3 vols., University Paris I Ph.D. thesis, 1986, and co-authored the anthology *Para a História do caminho de Ferro em Portugal* (Lisbon 1999), with Maria Filomena Mónica, Fernanda Alegria, and José Barreto.

Marie-Noëlle Polino, ancienne élève de *l'Ecole Normale Supérieure*, is managing director of the *Association pour l'histoire des chemins de fer en France in Paris*, France, and senior editor of the *Revue d'histoire des chemins de fer.*

Ralf Roth is Lecturer of History at the *Historische Seminar, Johann Wolfgang Goethe-Universität* in Frankfurt am Main, Germany. His numerous articles published in German journals are focused on the social and cultural history of cities and communication networks. After his research on the development of urban elites he completed the project entitled 'The Overcoming of Space and Time. The Impact of the Railways on German Society 1800 until 1914 (*Die Verkürzung von Raum und Zeit. Der Einfluß der Eisenbahn auf die deutsche Gesellschaft 1800 bis 1914*)'. He co-authored with Lothar Gall, *Die Eisenbahn und die Revolution 1848* (Berlin 1999).

Henk Schmal is Lecturer in Geography and Planning at the *University of Amsterdam*, The Netherlands. He is the author of 'Patterns of de-urbanisation in the Netherlands between 1650 and 1850', in H. van der Wee, ed., *The Rise and Decline of Urban Industries in Italy and in the Low Countries* (Leuven 1988), and *Den Haag of 's-Gravenhage. De 19de-eeuwse gordel, een zone gemodelleerd door zand en veen* (Utrecht 1995).

Austin Smyth is Professor of Transport Economics at the *Transport Research Institute* in Edinburgh. He leads the *TRI – Transport Policy and Economics Group* and is Convenor of the *Transport Planning and Policy Cluster*. Present research interests include urban transportation modelling, stated preference and attitudinal research techniques, appraisal, evaluation and assessment procedures. He is also interested in transport planning and operations analysis, demand forecasting, investment appraisal, corporate planning and policy development.

Pamela E. Swett is Assistant Professor in the *Department of History, McMaster University* in Ontario, Canada. She has written *Neighborhood Mobilization and the Violence of Collapse: Berlin Political Culture, 1929–1933*, Brown University Providence Ph.D. thesis, 1999.

Michel Tanase, received his Ph.D. in Urban Studies, and is teaching assistant at the *Université Paris I - Pantheon-Sorbonne* in Paris, France. His numerous papers published in French and Romanian journals are focused on transport networks developement in both countries.

Preface

This book has its origin in the fruitful discussions in the Fifth International Conference on Urban History: 'European Cities – Networks and Crossroads' which were hold in Berlin in September 2000, hosted by the *European Association of Urban Historians* (EAUH). The session 'The Railway and the City', chaired by Karen Bowie (*l'École d'architecture*, Versailles), Ralf Roth (*Johann Wolfgang Goethe-Universität*, Frankfurt am Main), and Marie-Noëlle Polino (*Association pour l'histoire des chemins de fer en France*, Paris), opened new perspectives on railway and city history and we thank the EAUH for having included it in the programme as a main session.

All papers presented there have been extensively rewritten and enlarged for inclusion in this book. We thank the authors for having answered our questions and for the fruitful dialogues about their work. We added several contributions, which broadened the book's European perspective to twelve countries, from Greece to Finland, from Russia to Ireland. We believe that some breakthroughs in comparative railway and urban history may result from what is still a first step in a very promising field.

We wish to renew our thanks to professors Jean-Luc Pinol and Richard Rodger for having included this book in the Historical Urban Studies series, to *Ashgate publishers* and to Thomas Gray for his patient help.

The translations from the French (chapters I.3., II.1, and II.2,) have been provided by V. O. Paris, and the translation from the Italian (chapter I.7) by Cathleen Compton. Above all we would like to thank Diane Renfordt for her resourceful and indispensable contributions to the editing process.

The edition has been made possible by a special grant of 6.500 Euros from the *Association pour l'histoire des chemins de fer en France* (French Railway Historical Society).

Paris and Offenbach am Main

Marie-Noëlle Polino
Ralf Roth

Introduction
The city and the railway in Europe

Ralf Roth and Marie-Noëlle Polino

The relevance of the theme

In 1965, the German city planner, Professor Wilhelm Wortmann proposed his vision of a local and commuter traffic system to the city assembly of Offenbach. During this time he was responsible for the infrastructural development of the region south of Frankfurt (*Unteres Maingebiet*). This region included Offenbach, a city of 110.000 inhabitants situated near Frankfurt. Wortmann had proposed the construction of a modern underground line just below the old tracks which had originally been built in 1848 for the *Lokalbahn*. If his vision had become reality, this line would have not only connected the cities of Frankfurt, Offenbach, and Hanau together, but would also have linked them to the regional railway system (*S-Bahn*) which covered a region of four to five million people.[1] As it turned out however, his idea was rejected by the city government because of the prevailing attitudes towards motor traffic at that time. The general tendency was to pour money into improving and enlarging roads for motor cars, rather than investing in rail traffic. This rejection resulted in the replacement of the rusty and decaying tracks with a main street to accommodate the increasing car traffic. Street construction followed the flood of car traffic in every city of Europe.

Although personal mobility does have clear advantages, there is a growing feeling that its advantages are quickly being outweighed by its disadvantages. One disadvantage is that when cars are not being driven they take up valuable public urban space. This means that a vast amount of public space is not available for other uses. Secondly, the permanent stream of motor cars cuts cities and towns up into a thousand little pieces that block the routes of pedestrians. As a result of the increasing devastation of public space, people have been forced back into smaller pedestrian precincts. This growing emphasis on improving and enlarging the traffic system has meant a serious reduction of the space available for pedestrians. The motor car pollutes the air one breathes. It causes noise. It diminishes the quality of life for every resident.[2] In the past several decades the advantages have always

---

[1] See 'Schnellbahnen in den Stadtkern', *Offenbach Post*, June 18, 1965.
[2] See Winfried Wolf, *Eisenbahn und Autowahn. Personen und Gütertransport auf Schiene und Straße* (Hamburg 1986); Peter M. Bode, Sylvia Hamberger, and Wolfgang Zängl, *Alptraum Auto. Eine hundertjährige Erfindung und ihre Folgen* (München 1986), and Till Bastian and Harald Theml, *Unsere wahnsinnige Liebe zum Auto* (Weinheim 1990).

more or less balanced the disadvantages. Nowadays however, the number of complaints about noise and motor-car emissions in all major cities is on the rise. In spite of this fact, the tremendous increase in motor-traffic and the reduction of railway networks all over the world is a conspicuous sign that the motor car has indeed replaced train traffic.

But the so-called 'motor car society' (*Automobilgesellschaft*) will probably only survive for a relatively short period of time. All in all, it stretches over four or five decades which is a brief period in the history of urbanisation. Although motor traffic is currently the predominant mode of transport throughout the world, it has become a growing burden in the densely populated metropolises or city agglomerations in Europe. Unrestricted private vehicle traffic collides more and more with the limited capacity of streets.

The older terms of *traffic jam*, *Stau*, or *embouteillage* of the nineteenth century have being used once again as this phenomenon has become widespread throughout societies in the modern world. These expressions came into existence because of the crowds of coaches and carriages in places such as *Ludgate Hill* in London, at *Place de l'Opéra* in Paris, or at *Leipziger Straße* in Berlin. None of the current efforts in street construction have been able to solve the problem of traffic jams. This problem intensified in the case of Offenbach when the actual space available on the streets around the city rapidly reached their capacity. This was the reason why thirty years after Wortmann's vision, the city of Offenbach returned to his ideas of 1965 and constructed an underground railway in a short period of time.

Since 1995 the city has been connected with Wiesbaden, Frankfurt and Hanau via a system of modern electric local trains. It has also been successfully integrated into the regional S-train system. It is now possible to commute between the cores of half a dozen cities in a region of 3,000 square kilometres within fifteen to thirty minutes. Millions can use the trains without having to worry about where to park their cars in a densely crowded city like Frankfurt. They also avoid contributing more noise to an already noisy city and air-pollution to a highly polluted city.

Another interesting aspect of public transport is that one can witness a diverse cross section of humanity travelling together side-by-side in these train compartments. There are the young and old, the poorer residents together with the wealthy bankers on their way to work in the heart of the financial district as well as the wide and varied spectrum of all those who come in between. It is a colourful, sometimes picturesque scene. People from 140 nations are living today in Frankfurt as well as in Offenbach, most of whom, interestingly enough, have only just immigrated in the last decade. Everyone is mixed together in this dynamic prosperous region of Europe. In ten or fifteen years the cities and towns of this region will probably have grown together into a metropolis of six to ten million people.

Growing city agglomerations, metropolises, or megalopolises seem to be the most likely form that urban living will take, not only in the Rhein-Main-region of Germany but throughout the entire world. If we follow projections on the future of cities, such as Peter Hall's and Ulrich Pfeiffer's study *Urban 21*, one can imagine that what we are experiencing at the moment is only the beginning of a second phase of urbanisation.[3] In the last four decades mankind has doubled. Within every continent people have been migrating to big cities and metropolises. Another striking development is that of people making their way by air from anywhere in the world to the centres of the global economy. These gigantic streams of migration are extremely mobile and transcontinental.[4] The consequences of this could either be an extremely high density of living space, or a further spreading outward into the surrounding region, or both. In either case this new dynamic in urbanisation in the near future will require new means of efficient and rational traffic systems for cities. The capacity of these new systems of transport has to be high and in addition, quieter and almost emission free. They must also be so well constructed as to minimally encroach upon the already limited city space in which 80 per cent of the European population will live.

It is precisely because of this current situation at the beginning of the twenty-first century that the question of efficient traffic systems in such densely populated living spheres and the role of railways as linking networks in and between cities reappears. The requirement for the urban future demands that we re-examine the urban past with its nineteenth century densely constructed cities in a new light. It is from there that fruitful theoretical discussions can harvest a richness of practical experiences about the current problem of how to solve traffic problems in a more and more crowded world. Furthermore, nineteenth-century cities were not dominated by private vehicle traffic, but by systems of railways, which were adapted in several steps to be used comfortably in urban spheres.

Looking back nearly 150 years ago to the middle of the nineteenth century, it is extremely interesting that the problem of limited city space and traffic being discussed at that time, possessed an uncanny and perceptive grasp of a problem we undoubtedly must deal with today. The prefect of Paris in the time of Napoleon III, Georges-Eugène Haussmann, not only planned a system of boulevards and squares laid out on a grand scale, but also tackled the question of which traffic systems would best suit this space.[5] He doubted the efficiency of private vehicle traffic and feared the wasting of space. To avoid this, he preferred a monopoly by horse-omnibuses for the public passenger traffic. For this reason, the *Compagnie Générale des Omnibus* (CGO) was founded in 1855. They were more efficient than coaches, transported more passengers per car than private carriages and saved the

---

[3] See Peter Hall and Ulrich Pfeiffer, *Urban 21. Der Expertenbericht zur Zukunft der Städte* (Stuttgart 2000), 12.

[4] See Klaus J. Bade, *Europa in Bewegung. Migration vom späten 18. Jahrhundert bis zur Gegenwart* (München 2000), 378–82. In Germany conurbation increased significantly in the last decade and its six city-regions could develop to metropolises in a relatively short period of time. See Saskia Sassen, *Metropolen des Weltmarkts. Die neue Rolle der Global Cities* (Frankfurt am Main 1997), 63–5.

[5] It was this public space for the use of the new citizen that we remember from the novels and paintings of impressionist artists. See Juliet Wilson-Bareau, *Manet, Monet: La gare Saint-Lazare*, exhibition catalogue (Paris 1998).

public street space. The idea caused a sensation and spread to many European and North American cities in the 1860s. It was the beginning of a series of further innovations, especially in the case of the railways that conquered the urban space. In the 1880s horse omnibuses were replaced by more efficient horse-trains and then followed by electric trams.[6] Around 1900 modern high-speed trains (*Schnellbahnen*) finally appeared. Built as elevated trains or undergrounds, they left the streets, thereby leaving more space available for other uses. In addition to this, modern railways were regarded unanimously as being indispensable for real modern cities. Based on the model of London's underground, the *Compagnie du Chemin de Fer Métropolitain de Paris* (CMP), succeeded in presenting its system as the most successful mass traffic system for the new twentieth century at the World Fair of 1900 in Paris.[7]

Whatever their specific form was, these new traffic systems which were electric, almost emission-free, quiet, and compatible with city space, fulfilled the pre-conditions for easing the traffic jams in the metropolises of London, Paris, Berlin and elsewhere in Europe. They had realised a new vision of urban living in the twentieth century. Le Corbusier's sunny and glassy solitaire high-rise buildings were connected by subways and separated from each other by 500 metre green spaces.

At the beginning of the twentieth century the electrified means of mass-traffic freed up the streets and created space for a new, noisy and smellier piece of equipment, the motor car. Its triumphant progress after World War II was caused by many factors and had many consequences. As a result of the motor car, we have experienced an extreme reconstruction of our cities. The urban sphere spread out into the region with enormous side effects upon our social and cultural lifestyle.[8] It is due to the proliferation of millions of commuters that the volume of traffic has increased so tremendously in recent years. Therefore, it can be safely said that car traffic is the main perpetrator responsible for the more negative phenomena occurring in our modern day cities. The next logical question to be asked is, whether these problems will give birth to a renaissance in rail construction in cities?

The answer is probably yes, especially when we take into consideration another factor that would support such a development. There is no large city within Europe today that can exist without either a modern system of railways or the traffic

---

[6] See Anthony Sutcliffe, 'Die Bedeutung der Innovation in der Mechanisierung städtischer Verkehrssysteme in Europa zwischen 1860 und 1914', in Horst Matzerath, ed., *Stadt und Verkehr im Industriezeitalter* (Köln 1996), 231–41, and Theo C. Barker and Michael Robbins, *A History of London Transport. Passenger Travel and the Development of the Metropolis*, 2 vols. (London 1963–1975).

[7] See the latest contribution to the history of Paris urban transport Dominique Larroque, Michel Margairaz, and Pierre Zembri, *Paris et ses transports, XIXe–XXe siècles* (Paris 2002).

[8] See lately Mathieu Flonneau, *L'Automobile à la conquête de Paris, 1910–1977. Formes urbaines, champs politiques et représentations*, 3 vols., Université de Paris I Ph.D. thesis, 2002.

networks that link them together. This development clearly signals the end of the reduction of railways that we have been experiencing since World War II. Supported by the *European Commission*, more and more old railway networks will be restructured to solve the problems motor traffic has caused.[9] Meanwhile in some countries, high-speed trains are successfully competing with air traffic. To illustrate this, we will cite four examples from the twelve countries that are reviewed in this book.

In 1991, the *Inter City Express* (ICE) was introduced in Germany. It not only covers the distance between the most important cities in a shorter time than planes need, but it also allows managers working in the centre of Frankfurt to live 200 kilometres away in the cities of Mannheim or Kassel.[10] The same can be said about the new high-speed line between Frankfurt and Cologne as well as a planned connection between Frankfurt and Stuttgart.[11] The lines linking these cities to each other will reduce commuter travelling time to less than one hour. Could it really happen that Mannheim, Kassel or even Cologne and Stuttgart become the future suburbs of Frankfurt?

Leaving Germany to concentrate on France, we see that an identical process has occurred. French cities have wanted to be associated with what was presented by the *Train à Grande Vitesse* (TGV) as a 'new mode of transport' and thus acquiring the title and being recognised as 'TGV cities'.[12] However, twenty years after the opening of the first stretch of the new line there is still no consensus concerning the tools for measuring the effects these have had on the cities themselves. In June 2001, *Le Monde* published an article on the occasion of the opening of a new TGV railway-track between Lyon and Marseilles. It pointed out that this new connection combined with the Paris-Lyon section allows passengers to cover the distance between Paris and Marseilles within a mere three hours. Will Marseilles eventually become a suburb of Paris? The manner in which the media covered the June 7, 2001 inauguration of the new Valence-Marseilles line clearly shows to what extent the debate surrounding the new line has sparked discussion about the hierarchy of

---

9 See 'Eisenbahn soll EU vor Verkehrskollaps retten – EU-Kommission fordert Richtungswechsel in der Verkehrspolitik', and 'Szenarien für eine neue europäische Verkehrspolitik', both articles *Frankfurter Allgemeine Zeitung*, June 18, 2001.

10 'Zusammenrücken der Regionen durch neue "Massen"-Verkehrsmittel (ICE). Wohnen in Karlsruhe, Mannheim oder Limburg und Arbeiten in Frankfurt wird eine gewöhnliche Sache sein, die Zeit zum Überwinden der Distanz nicht höher als heute von den Wohnstandorten in der Region.' Albert Speer, 'Frankfurt am Main: eine kleine Stadt und keine Metropole', in Albert Speer, *Die intelligente Stadt* (Stuttgart 1992), 162.

11 See Christian Siedenbiedel, 'Pendeln im ICE mit Tempo 300. Montabaur und Limburg rüsten auf', and 'In 60 Minuten von Frankfurt nach Stuttgart', both articles in *Frankfurter Allgemeine Zeitung*, December 23, 2001, and January 25, 2002.

12 The association of *Les villes européennes de la grande vitesse* or 'TGV-cities' was founded in 1991. An influential lobby, it has been presided over since then by a prominent elected official, the mayor and parliamentary representative of one of the member cities. This association lobbies government, launches studies and organises conferences and meetings.

cities, the reconfiguration of their relationships to one another, the creation of new passenger traffic flow patterns and the emergence of new behaviours whose real impact cannot be measured yet. It does not however, touch upon the impact of the new structures or the modification of the century-old railway land holdings on the cities themselves.[13] On the other hand, we can note the transformation, even inversion, of the values attached to public transport in general and to the train in particular. The recent network of new lines being constructed is encouraging urban development projects which are regarded as being positive. This is because these projects increase the financial worth of those urban areas that had been tainted by the development of railway zones a century earlier and left out of planning projects which would have projected them as cities being 'turned toward the future'. The TGV has successfully shown that railways, as a means of mass transport, can still be a modern and effective mode of transport. It is perhaps for this reason that, in the past ten years, public transportation has systematically been proposed as a solution in all of the urban development proposals from which it had hitherto been systematically excluded in favour of the automobile. French cities are building metro systems or tram systems that often follow the routes or re-use the tracks of old tramways or secondary rail lines abandoned during the 1930s. Just as the TGV has become instrumental to the weekend breaks of the residents of the greater Paris area, so has the *Réseau Express Régional* (RER) to their daily working life. Any break in the service provided by the Metro or RER creates insurmountable problems of congestion for the 'capital region' and its ten million inhabitants. It is the balance between the 'private' automobile and 'public' transport with regard to peoples' behavioural patterns and existing infrastructures, that seems to be the challenge facing cities during the next decade in France.[14] To the important decision-makers, these work stoppages regularly prove the importance of rail transport for cities as well as the inevitability of their development in the future of public transport. In the history of this transport system the question is raised regarding the constraints which it has carved into the urban fabric and surroundings of cities.

---

[13] The media have reported the cases of people – rare, with high revenues and unusual occupations – who have said they are looking forward to retiring in the South of France even while maintaining their activities in the Paris region, which concentrates the greater part of France's economic activity and in particular its role as 'beach-head' toward foreign countries. On the other hand, the reduction in travel time which puts the South at 'three hours from Paris' and the reduction in the length of the working week to 35 hours between 1998 and 2002 has made this region one of the primary weekend leisure destinations, much as Normandy became for Parisians in the nineteenth century. See Luc Leroux and Marcel Scotto, 'Hi-tech train link to boost Marseille's fortunes', *Guardian Weekly*, June 14, 2001 (original: *Le Monde*), and Gerald Braunberger, 'Der neue TGV lehrt Air France das fürchten', *Frankfurter Allgemeine Zeitung*, June 6, 2001.

[14] In the history of this transport system the question is raised regarding the constraints which it has carved into the urban fabric and surroundings of cities.

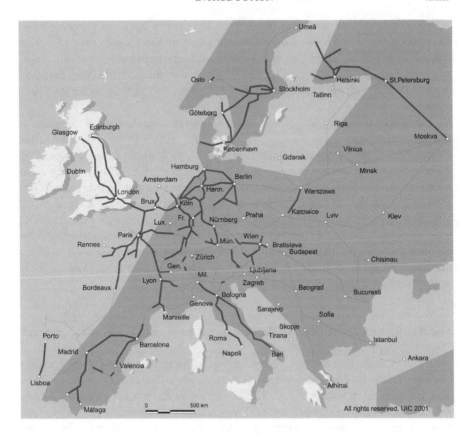

Figure 1   European high-speed network, 2010

Source: © Daniel Tessèdre, courtesy of UIC, Paris.

What is so obviously apparent in the Rhein-Main region of Germany and the Île-de-France is even more so for regions on the periphery of Europe such as the area around Lisbon in Portugal or Helsinki in Finland. In Helsinki the most interesting developments are the plans to improve its international rail connections to St. Petersburg and Moscow. One will be able to reach Moscow within five hours, less than half the time it takes today. The rail traffic in metropolitan Helsinki and within a 100 kilometre radius has been improved, extended and now seriously competes with car traffic. Everywhere else in the country, including the other major cities, the local railway traffic has been dramatically reduced or even entirely discontinued. The local railway traffic that was established in the 1880s, is an intrinsic part of the mass transportation systems of the metropolitan area. It is still popular, reliable and relatively cheap. The impact of railways in cities can also be felt in Italy as well. This was due in part, not only to the construction of high-speed lines, the well-known *Direttissime*, but also by the second wave of station construction. Similar plans for improvements in high-speed railways traffic, inter-city lines and modern railway systems for the regions around large cities currently exist in Poland, Austria, Spain, the United Kingdom, and in many other European countries.

Furthermore, on the basis of analogous suggestions, the *European Commission* and the *Union Internationale des Chemins de Fer* (UIC) in 1997 developed the project of a 'Pan European Transport Network', that would link European and Asian cities within a broad corridor from the West to the East. However, the signs for a renaissance of the railway systems of large cities cannot be overlooked. The relationship of the city and the railway has currently generated quite a bit of interest in Europe, it has also entailed a rediscovery of its historical experiences as well. Although the history of this more than 150 year old relationship with its economic, social, political, and cultural consequences is clearly a wide field for historical research, it is interesting to note that it has been an astonishingly neglected research topic in the past.

The relationship of the city and the railway: a desiderata in historical research

Firstly, it is important for us to consider that a European historical study on the question, 'How railways affected cities?' does not in fact, really exist. In Allan Mitchell's recent scholarly study, *The Great Train Race*, the problem is barely touched upon when he compares the railway networks of Germany and France and then only returns to the role of the capital from time to time.[15] It is however, on the national level that the study of the achievements in railway history seems to be more convincing. But the quality of these achievements do not only differ from country to country they barely cover the many 'blank spaces' on the map of historical research as can be seen in the case of Germany. Although we can note some impressive improvements in railway history since the 1970s many aspects of the development of railways still remain unknown.[16] In none of these works about

---

[15] Allan Mitchell, *The Great Train Race: Railways and the Franco-German Rivalry* (New York and Oxford 2000).

[16] In these decades Rainer Fremdling's or Dieter Ziegler's studies about economic and political consequences of railways had been published. See Rainer Fremdling, *Eisenbahnen und deutsches Wirtschaftswachstum 1840–1879. Ein Beitrag zur Entwicklungstheorie und zur Theorie der Infrastruktur*, 2nd edn. (Dortmund 1986), and Dieter Ziegler, *Eisenbahnen und Staat im Zeitalter der Industrialisierung. Die Eisenbahnpolitik der deutschen Staaten im Vergleich* (Göttingen 1996). Additional recent researches on the field of regional, local, and social history brought to light not only detailed information about specific developments of the network but also about railway workers and railway employees. An impressive account by James M. Brophy for example treated the role of railways for the burgher (*bürgerlich*) milieu in the new era after the revolution of 1848. See James M. Brophy, *Capitalism, Politics, and*

German railway history has the diverse aspects of the relationship between city and railway been sufficiently reflected upon. This is strikingly true for most local studies. Many authors have only provided an overview of the history of the railway network itself. The studies deal with the foundation of local railway companies, the construction of the tracks and stations inside the city and surrounding area. In others, we find long-winded tales about the expansion of the system with all its facilities. In the main, many accounts were dominated by technical details, and the key interest focused on trains, special locomotives, wagons, and other technical material. Due to the lack of easily available and reliable traffic statistics being in some cases, a *circonstance atténuante*, it is hardly surprising that most writers did not turn their attention towards the consequences of railways for the city and vice versa.[17]

Apart from the architectural history of stations and the debate on their picturesque styles, nothing exists which is comparable to the scholarly achievements of Anglo-American historians such as John R. Kellett in *The Impact of Railways on Victorian Cities*, Jack Simmons in *The Railway in Town and Country*, or William Cronon in *Nature's Metropolis* about the rise of Chicago. Horst Matzerath made some critical remarks about this deficit in German history in his anthology, *Stadt und Verkehr im Industriezeitalter* (City and Traffic in the Age of Industrialisation).[18] Although his book failed to generate more active interest in the topic, it did however, presents a mosaic of interesting contributions about the history of railways in Ulm, Konstanz, Stuttgart, Berlin and a few cities in Saxony. It also picks up the subject of our volume, 'The City and the Railway'. One of the

---

Railroads in Prussia 1830–1870 (Columbus/Ohio 1998), and Volker Then, *Eisenbahnen und Eisenbahnunternehmer in der industriellen Revolution. Ein preußisch/deutsch-englischer Vergleich* (Göttingen 1997). At the end of this period of innovations in railway history a lucid summary was undertaken by Lothar Gall and Manfred Pohl, eds., *Die Eisenbahn in Deutschland. Von den Anfängen bis zur Gegenwart* (München 1999).

[17] Examples for this literature are Gerd Bergmann, *150 Jahre Eisenbahn in Eisenach*, (Eisenach 1997); Kurt Kaiss, *Dresdens Eisenbahn 1894–1994* (Düsseldorf 1994), or Peter Lisson, ed., *Drehscheibe des Südens. Eisenbahnknoten München* (Darmstadt 1991). Only regarding stations we do find a progress in analytical debate insofar as history of art and architecture was brought together. Under the influence of Carroll Meeks and Mihály Kubinszky, Ulrich Krings worked on a general revision on the interpretation of style and forms of railway architecture. His art historical achievements influenced many local monographs on stations in some important cities in Germany – for example the works of Heinz Schomann and Helmut Maier about the main stations of Frankfurt and the Anhalter station in Berlin. See Carrol L. V. Meeks, *The Railroad Station. An Architectural History* (New Haven 1956); Mihály Kubinszky, *Bahnhöfe Europas. Ihre Geschichte, Kunst und Technik* (Stuttgart 1969); Ulrich Krings, *Bahnhofsarchitektur: Deutsche Großstadtbahnhöfe des Historismus* (München 1985); Heinz Schomann, *Der Frankfurter Hauptbahnhof* (Stuttgart 1983), and Helmut Maier, *Berlin Anhalter Bahnhof* (Berlin 1984).

[18] See John R. Kellett, *The Impact of Railways on Victorian Cities* (London and Henley 1979); Jack Simmons, *The Railway in Town and Country, 1830–1914* (London 1986); William Cronon, *Nature's Metropolis. Chicago and the Great West* (Chicago 1992), and Horst Matzerath, ed., *Stadt und Verkehr im Industriezeitalter* (Köln 1996), VIII.

most important issues dismissed in many of the contributions was how railways changed from being city-developers into obstacles for city-planning. Another issue concerned the different systems of railways for urban traffic. Something similar can be said about the scholarly work of Elfi Bendikat *Öffentliche Nahverkehrspolitik in Berlin und Paris* (Public Traffic Policy in Berlin and Paris), which highlighted the role of inner urban traffic in the development of these two metropolises and compared them in an ambitious study. In *Die Vernetzung der Stadt* (The Networked Cities), Dieter Schott integrates the railway network into a wider and more expansive perspective when considering how cities work. He illustrates how the growth of economic and social needs in the cities was responsible for the spread of different networks for water, gas and electricity supplies as well as for railways. We are also provided insights into the role of railways in the development of these regions.[19] Although there has been a multitude of observations concerning the relationship between city and railways and achievements in railway history in Germany there is still no work to this day, that is comparable to *Berlin und seine Eisenbahnen* (Berlin and its Railways). Written on the occasion of an exhibition fair in 1896, the study is quite sobering in its conclusion that until now, only a few aspects of the relationship between city and railway have come under closer scrutiny.[20] Many of the variables that seriously influenced the widespread economic, social, political and cultural facets of the topic still remain open questions today.

A similar conclusion can be drawn for many European countries and especially for France which has experienced a similar situation. For the past twenty years people have spoken more of 'The Railway and Cities' than of 'The Railway and the City', although French urban studies have become a growing field.[21] It is

---

[19] See Elfi Bendikat, *Öffentliche Nahverkehrspolitik in Berlin und Paris 1890–1914. Strukturbedingungen, politische Konzeptionen und Realisierungsprobleme* (Berlin/New York 1999). Connected with the expansion of these networks was a public engagement of citizens, who tried to influence the railway system in directions they preferred. This engagement appears not only in detailed discussions in the press but also in protest meetings and permanent complaints about unpleasant consequences of railways in the surrounding spaces. This protest served as an important corrective to decisions of city assemblies or mayors. It is also remarkable that railways were incorporated into deliberate strategies to prevent medium-sized cities like Mannheim, Darmstadt and Mainz from becoming larger metropolises with all their attendant social problems. See Dieter Schott, *Die Vernetzung der Stadt. Kommunale Energiepolitik, öffentlicher Nahverkehr und die 'Produktion' der modernen Stadt. Darmstadt – Mannheim – Mainz 1880–1918* (Darmstadt 1999).

[20] See Königl.-preußischen Minister der öffentlichen Arbeiten, ed., *Berlin und seine Eisenbahnen 1846–1896*, 2 vols. (Berlin 1896).

[21] See the Foundation in 1999 of the *Société française d'histoire urbaine* (Jean-Luc Pinol, chairman), which publishes the journal *Histoire urbaine*. Urban studies are in France also an interdisciplinary field of research. Among many other publications, see *Enquête - anthropologie - histoire - sociologie*, no. 4 (special issue: La ville des sciences sociales) 1996, which collects essays falling in the fields of history, sociology,

extremely surprising that the experience of the high-speed train in today's French cities, with its contrasts and hopes, its enthusiasts and its detractors, has not attracted the attention of researchers as much as one would have expected. There has been little interest toward the founding experience of the nineteenth century in the field of 'railways and cities'. Just ten years ago, the history of these relationships was a mosaic of disciplines and monographic studies that were only held together by mostly modernist presuppositions which acted as a sort of 'screen' between the researcher and his or her subject.[22] Art historians have traditionally regarded 'industry' as being non-art and it was only in the wake of Carroll Meeks that railway stations were finally recognised as part of this field of research.[23] Urban history in the same manner, regarded railway land holdings as 'breaks', 'constraints' or 'brown fields', something whose effects had to be cancelled out before erasing it entirely from the urban fabric. It is not easy to evaluate ten years of research in the time of a theoretical renewal and considerable activities for new railway construction. This integration and spread of the very high-speed networks into the European transport systems, has caused some new political and commercial consequences in western Europe. The subsequent developments of massive investments, the creation of complex intermodal stations, and especially the systematic renewal of commercial and interconnecting spaces, have clearly influenced the ways in which we perceive the subject of study.[24] Looking at it from this perspective, we can see today that rail travel, rail stations and rail heritage all benefit from a certain type of fashionableness. The architectural and urban analysis of railway stations viewed as exchange nodes continues to develop. Comparing the impacts of the present to the past during the construction of the first network and the siting of railway functions, is rich not only in theoretical lessons but also in practical ones for current operations. The reality of a world wide technical heritage and its landscape is increasingly being taken into account by historians, town planners and municipal office-holders who are responsible for the management of our historical and cultural heritage and to a lesser degree, by those building the new structures. Railway land holdings change very quickly because their development follows that of technological and economic activity, increases in the

---

[22] geography, anthropology by Bernard Lepetit, Michel Agier, Marcel Roncayolo, Jean-Luc Pinol, Isaac Joseph et al.

[23] Local historians have produced reliable and well documented 'stations monographs', although not related to the issues of urban history. See for instance Paul Génelot, *La Gare de Montpellier à travers le temps* (Montpellier 1993).

[24] See the pioneering study of Jean Dethier, ed., *Le Temps des gares*, exhibition catalogue (Paris 1978), and Karen Bowie, *L'Éclectisme pittoresque et l'architecture des gares parisiennes au XIXᵉ siècle*, 3 vols., université de Paris I Ph.D. thesis, 1985, and Karen Bowie, ed., *Les Grandes Gares parisiennes au XIXᵉ siècle*, exhibition catalogue (Paris 1987).

See the numerous publications edited by the main railway companies in Europe on stations renewal and new buildings, and for example Bund Deutscher Architekten and Deutsche Bahn AG, eds., *Renaissance der Bahnhöfe. Die Stadt im 21. Jahrhundert* (Stuttgart 1996), and Agence des Gares AREP, ed., *Parcours 1988–1998* (Rome 1998).

volume of goods transported and the emergence of new types of rail traffic and needs. The study of their history familiarises us with their continual extensions and re-workings and commits us to taking care of them.

Economic and sociological studies of transport systems often aim to determine the impact of infrastructures and new services. Even more interestingly, they study the decisions that made them possible, their workings and their procedures, modifications of behaviour and the mobility of people and goods.[25] Geography highlights morphology and the development of transport networks in urban networks, the space created by the relationship between cities and railways and their representations.[26] Architecture and planning ensure the re-use of nineteenth-century railway land holdings by inserting new infrastructures. The studies of the 'GDR' (*Groupe de Recherche*) 'Networks' of the *Centre National de la Recherche Scientifique*, which is now being continued by the group '*LATTS Réseaux, institutions et territoires*', underline the integration of the network as a whole in the analysis of urban planning. This has now become a primary issue for the new century.[27] Many questions have been raised today with respect to other sites and

[25]   See the collection of the *Institut National de Recherche sur les Transports et leur Sécurité* (INRETS) reports, esp. Jean-Michel Fourniau, *La Genèse des grandes vitesses à la SNCF, de l'innovation à la décision du T.G.V. Sud-Est*, INRETS report no. 60 (Paris 1988). See also Isaac Joseph et al., eds., *Gare du Nord: mode d'emploi, programme de recherches concertées Plan Urbain-SNCF-RATP*, INRETS report no. 96 (Paris 1994), and Isaac Joseph, ed., *Les Lieux-mouvements de la ville*, seminar proceedings, 5 vols. (Paris), enlarged for publication as Isaac Joseph, ed., *Villes en gares* (La Tour d'Aigues 1999).

[26]   See Jean Ollivro, *Essai de modélisation d'une implantation ferroviaire. L'exemple du T.G.V. Méditerranée*, Université de Haute-Bretagne Ph.D. thesis, Geography, 1994 and this author's numerous papers. See for instance the contribution Jean Ollivro, 'Le réseau des lignes à grande vitesse: prégnance centralisatrice ou redéfinition de l'espace français?', *Revue d'histoire des chemins de fer* 12–13, 1995, 195–219. See also Valérie Mannone, *L'Impact régional du TGV Sud-Est*, 2 vols., Université d'Aix-Marseille II Ph.D. thesis, 1995.

[27]   See LATTS (*Laboratoire Techniques, Territoires et Sociétés*) Réseaux, institutions et territoires, one volume of collected papers published by the members of the research group each year, 1997–2001, and the journal (published in French and in English) *FLUX, International Scientific Quaterly on Networks and Territories*. For a general introduction to 'networks studies', including urban transport in this perspective, see Gabriel Dupuy, *L'Urbanisme des réseaux, Théories et mé-thodes* (Paris 1991). The 'Architecture and Planning' group of the *Association pour l'histoire des chemins de fer en France* (AHICF) has aimed since 1989 to study the impact of the arrival of the railway in several French cities and in particular the consequences of the construction of a station, a cut, or workshops on real estate activity, the use and value of land, the siting and specialisation of economic activities. Studies by Karen Bowie and Annie Térade are examples. Further studies may rely now on the methodological breakthrough achieved by Juliet Wilson-Bareau, who combined the methods of art history with those of urban history to evoke convincingly and surprisingly the uses and images of the area around the Saint-Lazare station which became a creative centre for artists to meet and work. The studies of Michèle Lambert on the arrival of the railway in Nîmes and Avignon retrace for their part the debates which determined the siting of the stations in those

other players, questions whose answers will permit us to measure the role of the railway in the city. The strategic, economic and social issues that it has raised now determine the developmental constraints of historic city centres and have created a legacy that is increasingly being regarded as a heritage.

Aside from these general descriptions of the situation in many countries there are many aspects which are not even being looked at. In Russia, for example, the enormous influence of railways on colonisation and the reorganisation of vast territories of land into an urban landscape with numerous brand new cities had been neglected.[28] The railway in Europe was a successful revolution in the development of communication structures. The advent and spread of railways during the nineteenth century not only contributed to industrialisation and urbanisation but also transformed the meaning of space and time, perceptions and experiences of distance and geography. Although we have invested in serious research and harvested fruitful yields of scholarly debate about this topic, the detailed causes and consequences of mobility as well as their differentiation and complexity, are rarely mentioned in the main historical studies of all European countries.

Travel and goods-traffic was a complex social occurrence with different dimensions such as business travel, migration, commuter traffic, family visits of relatives, cultural and tourist trips as well as the transport of all kinds of goods. The mobility that resulted caused tremendous changes in the departure and arrival points in both villages and cities. This is of great importance especially for the hubs of the railway network. That is why it is so important to bridge the wide gap that existed between railway and urban history. Because of these numerous 'missing tracks' in railway history we offer this collection of essays on the topic: 'The City and the Railway in Europe'. The series of well-documented case studies presented here allows us to make comparisons of the ways that railways have impacted modern cities and in which ways they have developed along with them. These fourteen studies, situated at the intersection of social, cultural, urban,

---

cities. See Karen Bowie, ed., *Polarisation du territoire et développement urbain: les gares du Nord et de l'Est et la transformation de Paris au XIXe siècle. Une étude sur l'instauration et l'évolution des rapports entre les acteurs des grands aménagements ferroviaires urbains, première étape (1830–1870)*, 2 vols. (Paris 1999); Michèle Lambert, *Les Voies ferrées et les gares dans les villes*, 2 vols. (AHICF, Paris 1992 and 1994); Annie Térade, *La Formation du quartier de l'Europe à Paris: lotissement et haussmannisation (1820–1870)*, 2 vols., Université de Paris VIII Ph.D. thesis, 2001; Annie Térade, 'Le nouveau quartier de l'Europe et la gare Saint-Lazare', *Revue d'histoire des chemins de fer*, vol. 5–6, 1991/1992, 237–260, and Juliet Wilson-Bareau, *Manet, Monet: La gare Saint-Lazare* (Paris 1998).

[28] One reason was that the history of the construction of the Trans-Siberian railway was not welcomed by the former Communist Party. The successes and the scale of its construction was obviously not a pleasant comparison of the later achievements of the soviet regime in Siberia. So we have the astonishing situation that – similar to the German railway researches on Berlin – the best book on the subject is still today S. V. Sabler and I. V. Sosnovskii, *Sibirskaia zheleznaia doroga v ee proshlom i nastoyaschem* (St. Petersburg 1903).

architectural, art and transport history, permit clarification of issues that we feel are fundamental to the history of cities and territories, but which are insufficiently brought into focus unless the different approaches are combined.

The relationship of the city and the railway in Europe

The following articles are based on a multitude of questions: 'What role did the railway networks play and continue to play for the cities? What side-effects do the infrastructure and points of access to this system have inside the city? Beyond their influence on topography, what part in the evolution of the city do railways determine? What can be said about the economic, social, political and cultural consequences of railways in cities and what role do they play in the preservation of this heritage? These articles attempt to provide some insights into these questions.

The anthology is divided into two parts consisting of seven articles each. In the first part, 'Line, Region, City-system' the articles concentrate on the relationship of railway networks and their implications for cities in regions or explicitly city-systems, which were connected together by a common railway network. Ralf Roth's contribution, 'Interactions between Railways and Cities in Nineteenth-Century Germany' begins this general thematic with a short sketch on the visions and hopes of the railway era and discusses the role cities played in these visions. He presents an overview of the multitude of economic, social, political, and cultural effects railways had upon cities. He developed his theses using the German cities of Berlin, Frankfurt, Oberhausen, Offenbach, and the sea spa Sassnitz as his examples. From his analysis, he draws the conclusion that railways not only had serious repercussions on German cities, but that they were also forced to metamorphose because of the requirements of these cities. In general, railways and cities formed a complex relationship and influenced each other in many ways. The degree and type of influence depended on the type of city, its magnitude, its geographic location as well as its specific situation in a rapidly changing social environment. Looking back at what the visionaries had foreseen at the beginning of the railway age, we see that, step by step, it has in fact come to pass. Railways were of tremendous importance for trade cities, municipalities that were the seats of governments, the mobility of people, the rise of industrial cities, the change of fishing and farming villages into flourishing tourist cities and the urbanisation of Germany.

In 'Cities and Railways in the Netherlands between 1830 and 1860' Henk Schmal also focuses on the development of a national railway network that linked cities. He describes the serious rivalry that existed between the railways and a fully-developed canal-system. This rivalry set Holland apart from other European countries and would prove to be a major factor in the railway history of this country over several decades. Another striking particularity to Holland was the relatively late connection of the Dutch lines to other European networks that isolated the Dutch railway companies from the trans-national flow of goods-traffic.

On the basis of his lucid analysis of the role railways played in Delft, Amsterdam, Utrecht, Leiden, Rotterdam and Haarlem, the author raises the problems of the initial development of conurbations in the main cities of Amsterdam and The Hague. He concludes that the first tentative steps towards a spreading out into the region and the subsequent segregation became visible around 1860. This was at a relatively early stage of a phenomenon that was common in Europe and made Amsterdam comparable with London and Paris.

In contrast, Michel Tanase uses an entirely different approach to the topic in his article 'Railways, Towns and Villages in Transylvania (Romania): Impact of the Railways on Urban and Rural Morphology'. His plausible and innovative approach to railway history first begins with a discussion of the role of urban morphology and then develops the possibilities of his research method by applying it to a lesser known region in Europe. He shows quite impressively how this morphology affected railway planning using the example of certain Romanian villages which shared a common history that lasted over centuries. With this analytical interpretation Tanase would like to encourage researchers to use his approach for a more in-depth study of the material of unexplored archives and especially of cadastral maps. He expresses the opinion that this would provide a clearer picture of the decision-making process involved in the choice of railway routes and their impact on rural and urban morphology.

Whereas Henk Schmal stresses the historical significance of canals being the competitors of railways in his contribution, Vilma Hastaoglou-Martinidis in her article 'The Advent of Transport and Aspects of Urban Modernisation in the Levant during the Nineteenth Century' directs our view to the importance of port cities as an essential part of the railway networks. She not only sheds light on the lesser known development of railways in Greece and the Levante, consisting today of Lebanon, Egypt, Syria, and Turkey, but also re-examines the remarkable interdependency between rail traffic and the shipyard. She further provides new insights into the famous railway to Bagdad. In her impressive contribution, which is based on in-depth research covering the entire region, she also demonstrates what consequences the railways had in the longer-range regions of the southeastern parts of Europe and the Middle East. She also provides a rich analysis of what modernisation in such a widespread region means, as well as fundamental explanations for the urban development of many big cities like Alexandria, Cairo, Beirut, Istanbul, Smyrna, Salonica, Piraeus, and Athens.

As we leave Hastaoglou-Martinidis' contribution on the South of Europe we then touch upon Europe's Eastern region with Ivan V. Nevzgodine's essay. Here we are presented with an impressive body of research on the remarkable topic of 'The Impact of the Trans-Siberian Railway on Architecture and Urban Planning of Siberian Cities' which, for the first time, analyses what up to now had only seriously been discussed within the example of North America: the colonisation of a territory from a continental dimension. He strikingly introduces the function of railways as city-founders on a very large scale and as the means for the colonisation of vast territories. His article is of great importance to the historical debate and sharpens our understanding of the multidimensional consequences of railways. It also contributes to our understanding of the development of numerous cities and villages like Cheliabinsk, Krivoschekovo, Irkutsk, Vladivostok, Baykal, Kuznetsk, Barnaul, Novosibirsk, and Krasnoyarsk. Today each of these cities is a metropolis with several million inhabitants.

Another blank space on the map of railway history in Europe is of course Portugal. Magda Pinheiro, however, succeeds in shedding some light on the region in her contribution, 'Portuguese Cities and Railways in the Nineteenth and Twentieth Century'. She not only provides us with some insight into the lesser known development of railways in Portugal, but also into the interdependencies of railways and the two major cities of Lisbon and Porto. Her analysis focuses on the construction of the main lines of the national railway network over a long period of time. At the end of her research she concludes that the railways appear to have played a positive role in urban modernisation and expansion during the nineteenth century. She also points out that although the nineteenth century rail infrastructures built in these two cities had positive effects on twentieth century suburban development as well, its network was limited in many areas.

Following after Vilma Hastaoglou-Martinidis' and Magda Pinheiro's studies, Andrea Giuntini completes the series of articles on Southern Europe by directing our attention to Italy with his contribution, 'Downtown by the Train: The Impact of Railways on Italian Cities in the Nineteenth Century – Case Studies'. He begins his essay with the problem of the arrival of the railways in the Italian cities of Milan, Florence, and Rome. He raises the question of railways and town planning, their aesthetic dimension and political implications as well as the role of symbolic ornaments on the façades of railway stations. He further discusses the meaning of traditions today and the problem of new urbanism in the latter part of the twentieth century. In his very ambitious overview of more than one and half centuries he concludes that, 'Today the railway can once again carry out an essential role in the restructuring of the city based on the renewed integration among connecting spaces, open spaces and built-up spaces brought together as an organic unit, playing a decisive role in the present complex relations in the urban development model' (p. 127). It is indeed a suitable contribution to end the first part of our anthology.

Leaving the series of articles which have focused on the question of railway networks and city systems, our following set of articles in the second part move on to the topic of 'The metropolis and the railway' expounding the problems of the role of railways for the metropolises and capitals. François Caron begins the second part with the capital of France, Paris. In his contribution, 'Railway Development in the Capital City: The Case of Paris', he stresses the importance of a capital for the national railway network. The city of Paris however, was not only a centre for a high-speed railway system and many regional lines, the structure of the capital was also formed by these railways at the same time. The author developed this thesis along the lines of the general developments of the railway network. Just as the debate about conurbation had begun at the end of the nineteenth century in the Dutch cities the same had occurred in Paris. Aside from describing the many aspects of interdependencies between a big city and a complex railway network, his lucid piece of research is of particular importance because his essay follows the line over a long period of time (*longue durée*) and is comparable to Magda Pinheiro's analysis on Portugal.

This is also true for Alena Kubova's historical study 'Railway Stations and Planning Projects in Prague, 1845–1945' which follows the debate and construction process over a period of no less than one hundred years. Her main topic is the role of a railway station for the image of a capital city. She provides us with detailed information about the construction programme, its aesthetic dimension, and its political implications. She also draws our attention to the surrounding area of the railway station of Prague and finally, its competition with the airport of the capital. Most importantly, Kubova shows us that the debate over the aesthetic dimension of railway buildings inside the city was linked to the concept of modernisation and to the image of a capital. 'It is when, in 1918, Prague became a national capital that the previous conception of urban railway developments is judged to be incompatible with the idea one has of the "modern" city' (p. 168).

We return once again to using a new methodological approach to railway and city history in Neil McAlpine's and Austin Smyth's study of London: 'Urban Form, Social Patterns and Economic Impact arising from the Development of Public Transport in London, 1840–1940'. Using the *Geographical Information System* (GIS) as the basis of their research, both authors discuss the influence of railways to the urban form, social patterns and the economic effects which resulted from the development of public transport in London. Similar to Magda Pinheiro, François Caron and Alena Kubova, they endeavour to develop their arguments on the basis of long-range studies covering the decades between 1840 and 1940. Their study is highly informative regarding the many aspects of the railways and their competition with other transport systems as well as their social effects and social costs. They conclude that the railways were not only an important factor in the growth and development of London but that together with the trams, omnibuses and underground they helped to develop the pattern of London both in terms of its physical form and socio-economic conditions.

Using the preceding articles that surveyed the meaning of railways for the capitals of France, Czechia, and the United Kingdom as a point of reference, we are thus able to make comparisons to the capital of the Republic of Ireland, Dublin. Hugh Campbell delivers a remarkable study about 'Railways Plans and Urban Politics in Nineteenth-Century Dublin'. He effectively shows us how railway construction was shaped by many interest groups each of whom possessed very contrary perspectives for developing railways sites in different forms. In the beginning of his article he describes the protest against railways because of the prevailing fear that they would destroy the aesthetic beauty of the capital city. Thereafter came the fight for modernisation waged by certain elite groups such as the brewers. The struggle within the city and the hotly debated controversies that erupted in the national parliament clearly demonstrates to what extent this debate was influenced by the national conflict between Ireland and Great Britain. A large number of monumental dreams failed to materialise and ambitious plans were crippled because of the current political atmosphere and its implications. Hugh Campbell's outstanding study is based on a systematic analysis using unconventional sources for railway history. He evaluates political conflicts that have been documented and preserved in newspapers and in thus doing, stands alongside Tanase or McAlpine and Smyth in contributing to a new and interesting methodological approach in the field of railway and city history.

Another ambitious study evolving from an extremely well-developed theoretical framework is Anja Kervanto Nevanlinna's, 'Following the Tracks – Railways in the City Centre of Helsinki: Bygone Past or Unwritten Urban History?'. She begins her article by pointing out that modern architects have been projecting the future of the capital of Finland without railways because of their belief that they had lost their importance in the era of postmodern cities and were relegated as diminished remnants of an old tradition. She would like her article about the railways in Helsinki to be understood as an act of memory and emphasises the fact that railway relicts should be regarded as a field for further historical research activities. It is on this basic assumption that she reconstructs the long period of time when railways were of great importance for the city. In spite of the fact that the railway made a late arrival in Helsinki in contrast to other European capital cities, it then went on to dominate the development of the capital for more than one hundred years. During this time railways played an important role for the image of the capital. They effected changes in the morphology of Helsinki, a result which is also noted in both Kubova's and Campbell's conclusions. Rather than merely referring to them as remnants of a bygone past she pleads for the preservation of railway heritages in the capital and argues: 'We may read the histories of built forms only if traces of all of its time layers exist, not just the one which in a particular era is seen as valuable and aesthetically coherent. If we only preserve what we appreciate today, other equally authentic, but less understood remains will be destroyed. Railways in the city centre contain our memory. They are invaluable to us as documents of a bygone past but they are possible for us to understand, if we follow the tracks' (p. 219).

In Pamela E. Swett's essay which is also based on new theories and methodological accesses to the railway and city, the author examines what is both a fundamental and extremely important question for historians: How to form a monument in mind? In her contribution 'Political Networks, Rail Networks: Public Transportation and Neighbourhood Radicalism in Weimar Berlin' she presents detailed research about the political battlefield around underground and streetcar stations in Germany's capital of Berlin, during the 1930s. She describes them as flash points of violence and political action. Her main thesis is that between 1900 and 1930 the rail system meant something more to the working class than a gateway to the city, a monument to the modern age, or a means of commuting to their work. 'In those years, rail stations, especially the small, local rail, tram, and underground stations, became central to the social and political life of Berlin's neighbourhoods, in ways that challenged the very definition of these transportation sites as public spaces' (p. 224). Her description of railways in Weimar Berlin is indeed an impressive piece of research that sheds new light not only on her general starting point, but also on what have hitherto been the more neglected aspects of the effects railways had on cities.

Last but not least, we have Diane Drummond's article, 'The Impact of the Railway on the Lives of Women in the Nineteenth Century-City'. After a multitude of articles which strive to explore the various aspects of railways and cities, such as in Schmal's and Hastaoglou-Martinidis' on the economic effects, the political and cultural implications in Giuntini's, Nevanlinna's, Kubova's and Campbell's and the social consequences in Roth's and McAlpine and Smyth's we finally arrive at Drummond's article which touches upon the different uses of railways in the city space by men and women. Although this field of research has not yet been explored in depth, this article presents a very thorough and systematic study that discusses the different dimensions of the topic. Using the example of the 'slum clearance' and the consequences it had for poor families, especially for women, Diane Drummond begins her argumentation on the consequences of railway building. She then continues with a description of the effect railways had on the structure of a metropolis like London; the differentiation into city quarters with certain characteristics, the phenomena of segregation, the division of business districts and quarters for housing and finally how all of these factors together determined the labour market which in turn resulted in the use of railways by different sexes. Another dimension of the railway, the city and the gender aspect, is her analysis of the wider discussion on 'security' in railway sites and railway facilities and how this impacts the decision of lone women to travel on the train. Although she concludes that women frequent railways less than men, she emphasises the liberating effect railways had for women. Drummond points out that it was a woman who first raved enthusiastically about the new travelling machine: 'You can't imagine how strange it seemed to be journeying on thus, without any visible cause of progress other than the magical machine, with its flying white breath and rhythmical, unvarying pace' (p. 255).

City and railway as understood in our anthology means interdependencies between both sides. It also means a metamorphosis of the city as well as of the technical system. As we witness the different types of railway networks spreading out from city centres to suburbs, from metropolises into the region and from city to city, it is clear that the repercussions are many. In two examples, the primary function of the railway was the colonisation of vast areas. Railways speeded up dynamic processes; they divided prosperous cities from those that were forced into stagnation, they stimulated competition between cities and as a result, a new hierarchy of the city-system evolved, they were also used as symbols for modernity and the modernisation of cities and especially for capitals. Because of their importance, we find discussions on railway construction in many cases overlapped by general political debates. Finally, the railways, trains and stations were places that held a different meaning for both sexes.

The different articles bring together many pieces of a jigsaw that illustrate the European dimension of the relationship between cities and railways. We not only learn about the interdependencies of the railway question between Ireland and the United Kingdom, Finland and the Russian empire, but also of the tremendous repercussions the transport and communication network had on the entire Mediterranean world. Thus railways did not only influence the urban development in Portugal, Italy, Romania or Greece but also the countries of the former Levante – Turkey, Lebanon, Syria and Egypt. At the core of Europe we have multidimensional interdependencies between France, Holland, Germany and even the northern parts of the former Habsburg Empire, a part of which later evolved into the Czech Republic. In the East the railway network is extensive and far reaching, dramatically affecting the rise of an urban world stretching outwards from Europe to Asia. The Pan-European network of railways and its hubs, the cities, were built by a European-wide elite consisting of engineers, railway entrepreneurs and bankers. The web had been woven in many countries but the network as a whole is more than the sum of its national parts.

In conclusion we can say that cities and railways have formed and continue to form a complex relationship with many dimensions and many facets. Seen in this light, the impact of railways on cities in the past, present and future is a wide field for historical research. We would like this collection of essays on the topic of 'The City and the Railway in Europe' to be an occasion to discuss current research and we hope it will initiate further national and international comparisons.

Line, Region, City-system

I, the rain

I've always been a source of
Inventive imagination –
Fascination, admiration,
Wonder and delight
In this maze of rails
Ever since the first royal salute was fired
And my steam engine succeeded
All those memorable chariots
And I became a never ending inspiration
In design and development.

I race through the immensity of speed and sound
To operate in perfect safety
In an Earthly network
Linking together regions within regions,
Cities within countries,
Countries within continents,
In systems of callous priorities
Imposing inalterable forces
Of bonding and co-ordination
Beyond cosmic principles-
Within the WEB of Time...

By Arlette Abrahamian

CHAPTER ONE

Interactions between railways and cities in nineteenth-century Germany: some case studies

Ralf Roth

In the nineteenth century, railways shaped the face and structure of cities. This is well known and well documented. But this was only one side of the process. There was also a backlash: Cities, i.e. the conditions of city life, shaped the railway network and the railways as well. This was a conflicting process and accompanied by mass protests against railways as a source of noise and smoke and against their aesthetic appearance. The opposition supported a metamorphosis of the technical structure of this facility, which led from steam-driven trains to electrical fast-speed railways for short-distance travel and later on for long-distance travel. This paper aims to discuss some of these interactions.[1]

First visions – The age of innocence

In the beginning of the Railway Age, between 1820 and 1840, many suggestions and expectations arose concerning the advantages which this facility might bring for the future of German society. The ensuing debate – between several dozens of local committees over the introduction of railway lines – touched upon economic, political, social and cultural questions.[2] On the one hand, the lowering of transportation costs was expected to benefit economic progress in commercial

---

[1] The article is part of a more detailed study about cultural aspects of railway history. The manuscript: '*Die Herrschaft über Raum und Zeit. Kulturgeschichte der deutschen Eisenbahn im 19. Jahrhundert*' will be published in 2003.

[2] One of the most important railway pioneers in Germany, Friedrich List, had argued for example: 'What in former days was steamshipyard for sea- and river-traffic, that will be railways and transport by steam coaches for land-traffic. It is a Hercules in the cradle, which will free the nations from the plague of war, national hate and unemployment, ignorance and laziness. It will fertilize fields enliven manufactures and mines, and it will give strength to the lowest to educate himself through the visiting of foreign countries, to find employment in far regions and health in distant baths and spas.' Friedrich List, *Das deutsche National-Transport-System in volks- und staats-wirtschaftlicher Beziehung* (Berlin 1988), 6.

cities. On the other hand, railway lines between capital cities and cities in the province were supposed to make government work much easier.[3] A third theme in promotional literature (*Denkschriften*) revolved around the mobilisation of labour; growing labour markets would contribute to an enormous rise in industrial cities.[4] In addition to this, by the 1830s, promoters were already drawing sketches of mass tourism, and as a consequence they foresaw a new type of city, which would attract masses of people. This would occur either because of the city's cultural attraction, its function as a spa (*Heilbad*), or due to the beautiful landscape.[5] Furthermore, this literature contained a very clear picture of future development in urban living. Some foresaw 'mega cities', while others predicted a decentralisation of cities. This latter prediction was because railways would allow people to escape from the noisy and densely-populated city centres into the countryside's healthier environment of fresh air, clean water and where there was less social control of the neighbourhood.[6] In this respect railways were seen as a means for urban dwellers to access large open spaces, thus contributing to breaking down the contrast between city and rural life.

These visions gave hope to many. Every German city could now envisage themselves as being the 'centre' of an European communication network, thus leading them to praise the advantages their new geographical position would bring in the future. Johannes Scharrer, the initiator of the first German railway envisaged that a rail link between Nuremberg and Fürth, together with their resulting union 'will become the central point for inner German trade between river Main and Danube and on to a main location of transit trade between the West and East of Europe'.[7] Someone holding a very similar perspective wrote anonymously in a

---

[3]   As one author of such a promotional literature put it: 'By the influence of railways the country become more concentrated, the dense population more dense – exactly seven times.' Von Traitteur, *Gutachten über die Anlage einer Locomotiv-Eisenbahn zwischen Mannheim (resp. Frankfurt), Straßburg und Basel* (Mannheim 1837), 24–5.

[4]   With a railway network 'thousands of workers will take a long journey of many miles to get more useful or more profitable jobs than at home.' David Hansemann, *Die Eisenbahnen und deren Aktionäre in ihrem Verhältnis zum Staat* (Leipzig and Halle 1837), 35.

[5]   'Railways will be the means to travel just for pleasure.' Ludwig Newhouse, *Vorschlag zur Herstellung einer Eisenbahn im Großherzogtum Baden von Mannheim bis Basel und an den Bodensee* (Karlsruhe 1833), 99.

[6]   On the problem of land use alongside railway lines and free settlement in the region see David Hansemann, *Die Eisenbahnen und deren Aktionäre in ihrem Verhältnis zum Staat* (Leipzig and Halle 1837), 132, and Ludwig Newhouse, *Vorschlag zur Herstellung einer Eisenbahn im Großherzogtum Baden von Mannheim bis Basel und an den Bodensee* (Karlsruhe 1833), 125–6.

[7]   Johannes Scharrer, *Deutschlands erste Eisenbahn mit Dampfkraft oder Verhandlungen der Ludwigs-Eisenbahn-Gesellschaft in Nürnberg: von ihrer Entstehung bis zur Vollendung der Bahn* (Nürnberg 1836), 8. He drew sketches of a new transcontinental transportation line, which led from the Netherlands, Rhenisch Prussia, Bavaria and Austria to Hungary, Serbia, Wallachay and Bessarabien. Alongside this line the cities of 'Amsterdam, Rotterdam, Cölln, Mainz, Frankfurt, Würzburg, Nürnberg, Regensburg,

Frankfurt newspaper: 'If someone could be today in Paris and tomorrow in Vienna, then nobody – neither in Paris nor in Vienna – needs a Frankfurt salesman for intermediate trade. Our wholesale trade will suffer an important diminution.'[8] Therefore, the local railway committee, mainly consisting of bankers who, while longing for a licence to build a railway towards the Rhine River, argued that:

> our father city (*Vaterstadt*) located in the middle of Germany where streets crossed from North to South and East to West, must fight for this means of connecting (*Verbindungsmittel*) without delay. The railway from Hamburg, Leipzig, Augsburg, Nuremberg, Basel, and Mainz have to come together in Frankfurt. When this aim is achieved, the wealth of our city is once again saved.[9]

Thuringian cities such as Weimar, Eisenach, or Gotha followed suit and pursued the same goal. Similarily to Frankfurt and Nuremberg, they were already seeing themselves in the centre of the European flow of traffic. Indeed, in 1833 Friedrich List had proposed a German railway network the length of 600 German miles (ca. 4,500 kilometres), in which Thuringia was crossed by a railway line, thus connecting Leipzig with Frankfurt am Main.[10] In addition to this, Carl Joseph Meyer, the famous editor of one of the most important German encyclopaedias and born in Gotha, proposed a plan for a German railway system for Thuringia. He hoped to push his fatherland, with its mineral resources, into the centre of the German railway industry. But Meyer's plans were in direct competition with two other proposals. One being an extensive North-South connection between Hamburg and Munich and the other, a Prussian initiative, which aimed to concentrate all lines from West to East on its own territory. It was because of this last competitor that Meyer failed.[11]

This failure of Meyer's plans clearly shows the inherent illogicality and physical impossibility for all German cities to be at the 'hub' of the new railway

---

Passau, Linz, Wien, Ofen, Pest etc.' would have been brought into close contact. See ibid. 44.

[8] Anonymous, 'Ist es für Frankfurt nothwendig, Eisenbahnen anzulegen', *Frankfurter Jahrbücher*, 7, no. 16, 1836, 95–6.

[9] 'Antrag auf Erlaß eines milden und zweckmäßigen Expropriationsgesetzes', Institut für Stadtgeschichte (IfSG), Eisenbahnakten H. 12, Nr. 11, Enteignung. Quoted by Peter Orth, *Die Kleinstaaterei im Rhein-Main Gebiet und die Eisenbahnpolitik, 1830–1866* (Limburg a. d. Lahn 1938), 31–2, or Richard Schwemer, *Geschichte der freien Stadt Frankfurt am Main, 1814–1866*, 3 vols. (Frankfurt am Main 1910–15), vol. 3/1, 12–5.

[10] See Friedrich List, 'Über ein sächsisches Eisenbahnsystem als Grundlage eines allgemeinen deutschen Eisenbahnsystems und insbesondere über die Anlegung einer Eisenbahn von Leipzig nach Dresden', in Erwin Beckerath and Otto Stühler, eds., *Friedrich List: Schriften zum Verkehrswesen*, 2 vols. (Berlin 1929), vol. 1, 155–95. On further plans concerning Thuringian railways see Gerd Bergmann, *150 Jahre Eisenbahn in Eisenach* (Eisenach 1997), 10–11.

[11] Meyer founded the *Deutsche Eisenbahnschienen-Compagnie* and built a rolling mill and further factories in Neuhaus and near Sonneberg furnaces between 1845 and 1847. See Hans Allekotte, *Carl Josef Meyer als Eisenbahnunternehmer in Mitteldeutschland um die Mitte des vorigen Jahrhunderts* (Steinheim 1931), 20.

system. How difficult this was is shown by the example of Frankfurt. This small, but independent, city republic was surrounded by the states of Nassau, Hesse-Darmstadt, and Kur-Hesse and further afield but still nearby lay Prussia, Baden, Palatine and Bavaria. Frankfurt was forced to negotiate with all of these countries over its railway interests. The Hessian states in particular were opposed to Frankfurt's wish to become the main railway hub between the North and South of Germany. They coveted this role for their own respective capitals: Kassel, Darmstadt and Wiesbaden. Nevertheless, the delegation of Frankfurt succeeded in exploiting the dissensions among the Hessian states to its own advantage. In addition to this, the city could depend upon the capital of their bankers, in particular, the Frankfurt Rothschild family. Without this capital, a project of such dimensions could never have been realised otherwise. Although the Frankfurt plans were opposed by the neighbouring states the first line between Frankfurt, Mainz and Wiesbaden had already been built in 1840. It was one of the first eight lines to be constructed in Germany. Six years later, the Main-Neckar railway to the South was opened, followed by the Main-Weser Railway to the North in 1852. Shortly before this time a connecting line to the Bavarian Ludwig Railway had been built. The goal of becoming a main railway hub together with Leipzig, Cologne, and Munich had been reached.[12] Frankfurt's success was a victory of capital over political power, whereas Berlin, as the biggest hub in Germany, owed its position instead to the political role it was playing in Prussia. It was in Berlin that the many advantages of the railway network could be fully appreciated.

First solutions – Cities in a new network

As the visionaries had predicted, the German railway system in the nineteenth century, was, above all, a network linking cities. This network would certainly have enormous consequences. But the interactions between railway and city were complex and differed from city to city. In fact we can note a variety of influences. Berlin, the isolated capital of Prussia and later of Germany as a whole, was separated by long distances from other political centres and commercial regions of Germany. Therefore, railways were a necessary prerequisite for its further development. Already in the 1840s, the system with its original five railway lines, later extended to twelve, connected this political centre not only to the distant provinces in the West and the East, but also with the most industrialised regions of Germany between the Rhein and Ruhr, in Saxony and in Silesia. At first the Berlin

---

[12]   On the different projects and the political controversies see Peter Orth, *Die Kleinstaaterei im Rhein-Main Gebiet und die Eisenbahnpolitik, 1830–1866* (Limburg a. d. Lahn 1938), 48–58, Ludwig Brake, *Die erste Eisenbahnen in Hessen: Eisenbahnpolitik und Eisenbahnbau in Frankfurt, Hessen-Darmstadt, Kurhessen und Nassau bis 1866* (Wiesbaden 1991), 78, and Ralf Roth, *Stadt und Bürgertum in Frankfurt am Main: Ein besonderer Weg von der ständischen zur modernen Bürgergesellschaft, 1760–1914* (München 1996), 301–8.

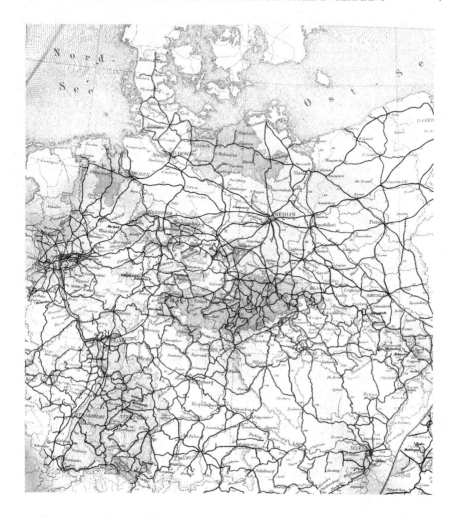

Figure 1.1   The German railway network of 1880

Source: Ernst Kühn, *Die historische Entwicklung des Deutschen und Deutsch-
                 Oesterreichischen Eisenbahn-Netzes* (Berlin 1882), map 1880.

Potsdam Railway connected the capital with the king's court and a garrison in
1838. Its extension to Magdeburg reduced the distance to a flourishing industrial
city. In the forties this line was extended to the industrial region in the West of
Prussia and connected to the trade routes between Cologne and Aachen and further
on to Antwerpen and Paris. The Anhalter Railway directed to Jüterbog with its
garrison and onward to the industrial region of Saxony. This line connected Berlin
to the southern part of Germany and tourist regions in Bavaria, the Alps and Italy.

Since 1846 the Hamburg Railway gave direct access to the biggest port at the North Sea and constructed a further line to Cologne and the Ruhr region. Finally, the Niederschlesisch-Märkische Railway with its Görlitz Station connected Berlin with Frankfurt/Oder and on to Breslau, Poland and coal and industrial regions in Silesia between Görlitz and Oppeln.[13] The Stettin Railway went through the region of Brandenburg in the Northeast of the city to the port of Stettin and further on to Königsberg. A second line, the *Ostbahn* (Eastern Railway), connected the provinces in the East with the capital as well. As Traitteur had predicted, its extension to Königsberg brought the distant provinces closer to the capital and linked the German to the Russian network together. Finally, the Northern Railway, built in the 1860s, created a direct connection to the Brandenburg region in the North and the port of Stralsund at the Baltic sea. This network served various different purposes. Alongside the rapid increase in the numbers of passenger, military, and mail transport, the railways established processing industries such as machine construction and later, electrical manufacturing on a large scale. This was made possible through the cheap transport of raw materials. The railways created another precondition for industrial progress in Berlin, that of importing cheap energy, especially coal. It came via railways from the coal mines of Silesia. In this respect, railways were intrinsic in making Berlin a very important industrial centre in Germany and later after the middle of the nineteenth century, its only Metropolis.

Parallel to, and interacting with this development were the big migration movements. The eastern part of Germany was especially distinguished by mass emigration, in particular the great exodus to the West. In mid-century the infrastructural preconditions for this movement, that of several railway lines to the East, had already been created. The construction of the Eastern Railway had in particular been broadly discussed. It was one of the most controversial infrastructural projects in German history.[14] The revolution caused a delay and the railway was not built until the 1850s. The consequences of this delay were

---

[13] On the importance of this line see Volker Then, *Eisenbahnen und Eisenbahn-unternehmer in der industriellen Revolution: Ein preußisch/deutsch-englischer Vergleich* (Göttingen 1997), 69.

[14] The planning by the Prussian State in the years before the 1848 revolution coincided with the rise of the liberal movement. For the Rhenish bourgeoisie in the western parts of Prussia this railway was uneconomical and therefore of no importance. For the government in Berlin, it had a military rationale and would also serve the better integration of far distant provinces with the capital region. The attempt to enforce the construction of that railway led directly to the revolution of 1848. See Lothar Gall and Ralf Roth, *Die Eisenbahn und die Revolution 1848* (Berlin 1999), 2–4. Moreover, the Prussian state hoped that it might be possible, with the help of the railway, to develop Prussia's original eastern provinces and to build up an economic power in the East to balance the flourishing regions in the West, which it had acquired in 1815. On the different purposes of the East Railway see Born, 'Die Entwicklung der Königlich Preußischen Ostbahn', *Archiv für Eisenbahnwesen*, 34, 1911, 879–939, 1125–72, and 1431–61.

momentous because the opening of the railway coincided with the final stage of peasant emancipation and with further liberal reforms such as the introduction of the freedom of domicile (*Freizügigkeit*). In the late 1850s, hundreds of thousands of migrants from the East and Southeast took the railway and, because of the structure of the Prussian railway network, they were forced to travel through Berlin. Many stayed in the city, accounting for the dramatic increase of its population from 340,000 in 1850 to more than three million people in 1910. This demographic development affected social and political life in the city. But there were many who continued on towards the industrial regions of the Rhein and Ruhr and even further on to America.[15] This was an impressive confirmation of what Hansemann had foreseen in his study written in 1837 on the consequences which railways might bring for the future.[16]

These few remarks, we mentioned above, illustrate the great importance of railways for a city like Berlin. Railways shaped cities in other ways too. Thus, for example, their monumental railway stations contributed to the overall image of a city. This fact was closely connected to the self confidence of the mighty railway companies and their private entrepreneurs. Their growing influence was especially felt on the economic and political life of Berlin manifesting itself in a large building programme. In this respect Berlin and its railway companies were in close competition with Paris and London. On the model of these two metropolises, old railway stations were replaced by new structures between the 1860s and the 1870s. The most prominent of these was the new Anhalter Station by Franz Schwechten in Berlin. During a ten-year planning stage, the dimensions of this building were constantly being expanded because of the growing traffic and also because of

---

[15]   In the 1850s, the eastern provinces of Prussia lost a little more than 40,000 people through migration. Most of them emigrated to other parts of Germany. In the 1860s, the number rose to more than 270,000 and in Prussia as a whole to more than 350,000. By 1907, nearly 2 million people had left the provinces of East Germany. See Wolfgang Köllmann, ed., *Quellen zur Bevölkerungs-, Sozial- und Wirtschaftsstatistik Deutschlands 1815–1875*, 3 vols. (Boppard 1980), vol. 1, 153–5. At first, many of them arrived in Berlin at Frankfurt Station, Silesia Station or East Station either to stay in the city or to move on toward the industrial regions at Rhein and Ruhr via the Berlin-Magdeburg Railway Company at Potsdam Station or towards the ports of the North Sea like Bremen and Hamburg via the Hamburg Railway at Hamburg Station and later at Lehrter Station. See Ralf Roth, 'Metropolenkommunikation: Einige Überlegungen zum Zusammenhang von Migrationsbewegungen und Ideentransfer am Beispiel von Berlin und Chicago im 19. Jahrhundert', *Rheinisch-westfälische Zeitschrift für Volkskunde*, 46, 2001, 291–318. Around 1890, a special emigration station in Ruhleben was built nearby Berlin. See Karin Schulz, 'Der Auswandererbahnhof Ruhleben: Nadelöhr zum Westen', in Dieter Vorsteher, ed., *Die Reise nach Berlin* (Berlin 1987), 237–41, esp. 237. To prevent immigration of Eastern European emigrants the Prussian state only allowed stops of extra trains (*Sonderzüge*) at Ruhleben. See Michael Just, 'Transitland Kaiserreich: Ost- und südosteuropäische Massenauswanderung über deutsche Häfen', in Klaus J. Bade, ed., *Deutsche im Ausland – Fremde in Deutschland: Migration in Geschichte und Gegenwart* (München 1992), 295–302, esp. 297.

[16]   See David Hansemann, *Die Eisenbahnen und deren Aktionäre in ihrem Verhältnis zum Staat* (Leipzig and Halle 1837), 35.

suggestions on how to make it more representative. It became important that the building symbolised the might of the company and the power of the newly created national capital. In the end, the company wanted to build the biggest railway station in Europe. Through the import of French and British know-how in station construction Schwechten succeeded in building the Anhalter Station with a vaulted hall (*Hallengewölbe*) of basilica-like crosscut, a barrel formed (*tonnenförmigem*) roof and a width of 65 metres. During the opening ceremony on June 10, 1880, 'the representatives of the Berlin-Anhalter Railway Company were very proud (...) they had not only built the most impressive railway station in Berlin and Germany but also a prominent symbol of the economic and political power of the railway company.'[17]

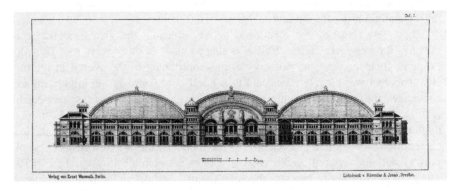

Figure 1.2   The first prize of the architectural competition for Frankfurt's new main station designed by A. Eggert, 1881

Source: *Empfangs-Gebäude für den Central-Bahnhof zu Frankfurt am Main. Sammelmappe hervorragender Concurrenz-Entwürfe*, 2 vols. (Frankfurt am Main 1881), plate 2.

However, in the same year, when the widely admired Anhalter Station was being opened, a relatively minor provincial city, just recently annexed by Prussia, wanted to compete with the German capital for the largest railway station. To demonstrate its economic power as a trade and banking centre, the city of Frankfurt am Main also undertook building a main station. Indeed, in 1888 a colossus was erected, which exceeded the station of Schwechten by more than one hundred metres.[18]

---

[17]   Helmut Maier, *Berlin Anhalter Bahnhof* (Berlin 1984), 237. See also Ulrich Krings, *Bahnhofsarchitektur: Deutsche Großbahnhöfe des Historismus* (München 1985), 97–9.

[18]   In an architectural competition the given order was ambitious: 'The aim was to build something unique, a new type of a central station, which should excel through its massive size all existing railway stations.' Anonymous, 'Die Concurrenz für den Centralbahnhof zu Frankfurt am Main', *Wochenblatt für Architekten und Ingenieure*, 1881, 69–82. The engineers achieved the enormous dimensions of the hall by three mighty vaults with a width of 56 metres each. In order to achieve this, they made use of

This success opened the way for further competition. A series of commercial and state capitals like Bremen, Dresden, Hamburg, Cologne, Leipzig and Munich followed Frankfurt's example. The new type of railway station was not only big, it was lavishly shaped by an extensive aesthetic programme. This included a canon of architectural forms, which stood for power and prestige. The railway stations were unique symbols for the might of the German middle-class in these old commercial cities. Berlin lost this competition. At the end of the nineteenth century its railway stations were only mediocre in size and form by comparison. This indeed was a remarkable deficit for a capital city in Europe.[19] This deficit was also mirrored in the structure of the German railway network. In contrast to France with its Paris centred railways, Germany possesses a dozen railway hubs in the West. Only East Berlin was, similar to Paris, the dominant hub.[20]

---

a new type of girder. This was a prototype for a similar construction of the famous *salle des machines* at the 1889 World Fair in Paris. See Alfred Gotthold Meyer, *Eisenbahnbauten: Ihre Geschichte und Ästhetik* (Esslingen 1907), 146–50; Ralf Roth, 'Weltausstellung und Eisenbahn: Versuchsfelder der Moderne', *Damals*, 32, no. 6, 2000, 36–42, esp. 40–1, and Heinz Schomann, *Der Frankfurter Hauptbahnhof* (Stuttgart 1983), 125–35.

[19] The canon of typical achitectural forms included vaulted halls of Roman baths, arched windows of Renaissance and Baroque styled cathedrals or basilicas and arcades of castles. Looking at Frankfurt Main Station the parallel to Dresden Castle (*Zwinger*) is striking. In the 1950s and 1960s Carroll Meeks and Mihály Kubinszky provided international comparisons of the architectural history of stations. See Carrol L. V. Meeks, *The Railroad Station: An Architectural History* (New Haven 1956), 2, and Mihály Kubinszky, *Bahnhöfe Europas. Ihre Geschichte, Kunst und Technik* (Stuttgart 1969). Both described the aesthetic forms of stations, in particular the Picturesque Style, as a common phenomenon with similar tendencies all over the world. Schivelbusch picked up this topic but developed a conflicting view. See Wolfgang Schivelbusch, *Geschichte der Eisenbahnreise: Zur Industrialisierung von Raum und Zeit im 19. Jahrhundert* (München and Wien 1977), 152–4. He considered the international bourgeoisie, especially the German one of the Kaiserreich, as conservative and premodern. This was in his view the main reason to hide the modern construction of stations behind Picturesque façades. This thesis was heavily inspired by views of architects from the beginning of the twentieth century. See Siegfried Giedion, *Raum, Zeit und Architektur* (Ravensburg 1965). In the 1980s, Ulrich Krings undertook a fundamental critique of this position and stressed the role of architectural and art history for the interpretation of railway stations. See Krings, Ulrich Krings, *Bahnhofsarchitektur: Deutsche Großbahnhöfe des Historismus* (München 1985), 54–77.

[20] On the structure of the network see Allan Mitchell, *The Great Train Race. Railways and the Franco-German Rivalry, 1815–1914* (New York and Oxford 2000), 37–67. On the role of Berlin see Gerhard Brunn, 'Berlin (1871–1939) – Megalopolis Manqué', in Theo Barker and Anthony Sutcliffe, eds., *Megalopolis: the Giant City in History* (Hampshire and London 1993), 97–115, esp. 107–9.

The complaints – The darker side of an industrial facility

The aspects discussed so far, architectural forms which symbolised power and prestige had not played any role in industrial cities. As in all countries of Europe, the rise of this type of city could not be envisioned without railways. They were of tremendous importance for the transportation of the key mass goods of industrialisation – coal. The transportation of coal was in the beginning of the railway age one of the main reasons for the construction of railway lines. Many projects were based on this aspect. The plan for a railway between Elberfeld, the centre of German textile industry, and Witten, a region with coal mines was 'calculated preferably for coal transportation'.[21] And Friedrich Harkort who was one of the most prominent railway enthusiasts of the 1830s, stated in a key project of the German railway network, that a rise of German industry would not be possible, 'if coal and ore are not brought together via railways.'[22] Indeed, as his keen vision foresaw, the railways delivered the ore to the furnaces and transported the raw materials for further processing not only into different industrial regions of Germany but also to the capital of Prussia – Berlin. Furthermore, in industrial areas in the West like the Ruhr region the railway stations were arrival stations for hundreds of thousands of immigrants from the German and Polish East. Therefore, many of the smaller towns of the Ruhr region grew into big cities with hundred of thousands and more inhabitants between 1880 and 1900.[23]

It was especially in these industrial cities that the darker side of the railway age could be seen. This rapid surge in the growth of the railway networks was regarded as being largely responsible for hindering city planning. For several decades, their rank growth prevented a rational urban building programme for these rapidly expanding cities. A very good example of this is the industrial city of Oberhausen, which did not exist before the middle of the century and came into being as a railway station on a railway crossing near a furnace and a coal mine. The coal mines alongside this railway line were in fierce competition with those along the river Ruhr, which distributed their coal by ships. The coal mines with access to the railway network were able to deliver their product to all the regions of Germany during winter and summer, independent of the river tides or weather conditions.

---

[21] Ludwig Henz, *Bericht über Project und Vorarbeiten zu der Anlage einer Eisenbahn von Elberfeld über Hagen nach Witten* (Elberfeld 1836), 110.

[22] Friedrich Harkort, *Die Eisenbahn von Minden nach Cöln* (Hagen 1961), 16.

[23] See David Crew, 'Modernität und soziale Mobilität in einer deutschen Industriestadt: Bochum 1880–1901', in Hartmut Kaelble, ed., *Geschichte der sozialen Mobilität in der industriellen Revolution* (Königstein im Taunus 1978), 139–85; Karin Schambach, *Stadtbürgertum und industrieller Umbruch in Dortmund, 1780–1870* (München 1996), 257–262; Jürgen Reulecke, *Geschichte der Urbanisierung in Deutschland* (Frankfurt am Main 1985), 68–72, and Jürgen Reulecke, 'Verstädterung und Binnenwanderung als Faktoren soziokommunikativen Wandels im 19. Jahrhundert', in Dieter Cherubim and Klaus Mattheier, eds., *Voraussetzungen und Grundlagen der Gegenwartssprache: Sprach- und sozialgeschichtliche Untersuchungen zum 19. Jahrhundert* (Berlin 1989), 43–56.

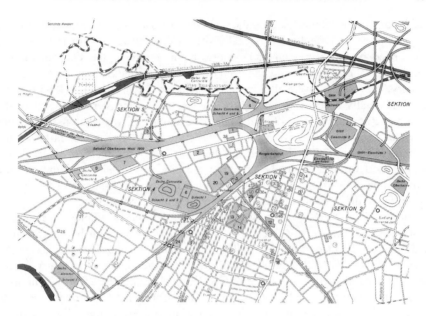

Figure 1.3   Map of Oberhausen, 1914

Source: Heinz Reif, *Die verspätete Stadt: Industrialisierung, städtischer Raum und*
              Politik in Oberhausen, 1846–1929 (Oberhausen 1993), map 5.

Because of this advantage they were able to compete successfully with their rivals.
The intended purpose of developing commercial activities was the basis for the rise
of Oberhausen. Numerous railway lines increased as the city grew. Around 1900,
this rapidly expanding city was divided by many railway tracks, which led
sometimes to a total obstruction of inner urban traffic.[24] A similar development to
that of Oberhausen can be observed in the industrial city of Offenbach for it too
had been been directly dependent economically on the new nationwide railway
system. In this case however, it was not the distribution of coal or steel, but the
leather production for the rapidly growing tourism market: leather briefcases,
ladies' handbags and leather suitcases for railway travel. But in direct contrast to
Oberhausen and other cities which had functioned as railway hubs, Offenbach's
strength to centralise the flow of traffic on its own territory had failed. The reason
for that was its close distance to Frankfurt. The old trade city dominated the
railway structure in the Rhein-Main region, and 'absorbed like a gigantic

---

[24]   See Heinrich Foerster, *Von oeder Heide zur Industrie-Großstadt: Eine wirtschaftliche*
      Studie und Schilderung des Werdens und der Entwicklung der Stadt Oberhausen/
      Rheinland, Johann Wolfgang Goethe-Universität Frankfurt am Main Ph.D. thesis, 1922,
      18–23, and Heinz Reif, *Die verspätete Stadt: Industrialisierung, städtischer Raum und*
      Politik in Oberhausen, 1846–1929 (Oberhausen 1993), 177–208.

maelstrom all the labour forces and commercial resources of the region'.[25] After a delay of 15 years Offenbach had finally got his first railway line in 1848. But the line ended in Frankfurt and had no direct connection to the German railway network. Furthermore, the city had been excluded from regional railways for half a century, because they were all focused on Frankfurt. It was not until 1895 that the city had finally succeed in building a line in the Southeastern direction to the region of Rodgau. From 1848 on it would take another 25 years before the citizens of Offenbach would achieve a direct connection for long-distance traffic on the Bebra-Railway in 1875. However, this line was built on a piece of undeveloped land a short distance from the city. But the city was rapidly growing and the railway line with its embankments later proved to be an obstacle to Offenbach's expansion to the South in the last decades of the nineteenth century.[26]

Both cities, Oberhausen as well as Offenbach, were examples of a general problem which beset many cities. Everywhere railways and their buildings, which had been constructed from the 1840s to the 1860s on the edges of the cities, became a problem to the further urban growth at the end of the century.[27] This problem became particularly acute in Germany, when the process of urbanisation accelerated, after the middle of the century. Most German cities were now growing more rapidly than cities in other European countries, encircling railway stations and rail tracks, and this divided city districts and was hindering street traffic. This dysfunctional aspect of the railway system was aptly expressed, when Otto Bismarck complained: 'These railways, they only impede the traffic!'.[28] It was a burden for city planning in general and especially for Berlin. A prominent town planner complained about the numerous crossings of street and railways in the following summary: 'From which (increase in railway traffic and growing of cities, Ralf Roth) resulted dissensions, which should be set aside – as well in the interest of the railways as well as of the cities. But the abolition of these disadvantages is always connected with great difficulties and enormous costs.'[29]

---

[25] Heinz Christian Göbel, *Verkehrslage und wirtschaftliche Entwicklung der Stadt Offenbach*, Universtität Heidelberg Ph.D. thesis, 1912, 14.

[26] See Jens Freese and Michael Hofmann, *Der Äbbelwoi-Express: Auf den Spuren der Lokalbahn von Frankfurt nach Offenbach* (Schweinfurt 1995), 16, Kurt Glück and Hermann Görlich, *150 Jahre Industrie- und Handelskammer Offenbach a. M., 1821–1971* (Offenbach 1971), 54, and Christina Uslular-Thiele, 'Die leidigen Bahnangelegenheiten', in Winfried S. Sahm and Christina Uslular-Thiele, eds., *Offenbach: Was für eine Stadt* (Offenbach 1998), 150–56, esp. 152.

[27] For many examples of this problem see Horst Matzerath, ed., *Stadt und Verkehr im Industriezeitalter* (Köln 1996), and Dieter Schott, *Die Vernetzung der Stadt: Kommunale Energiepolitik, öffentlicher Nahverkehr und die 'Produktion' der modernen Stadt. Darmstadt-Mannheim-Mainz, 1880–1918* (Darmstadt 1999).

[28] Quoted by Peter G. Kliem and Klaus Noack, *Berlin Anhalter Bahnhof* (Frankfurt am Main et al. 1984), 23. See similar complaints about railways in Berlin by James Hobrecht, *Entwicklung der Verkehrsverhältnisse in Berlin* (Berlin 1893), 33–4.

[29] Otto Most, *Die deutsche Stadt und ihre Verwaltung: Eine Einführung in die Kommunalpolitik der Gegenwart*, 3 vols. (Berlin and Leipzig 1912), vol. 3, 47–8. See Horst Matzerath, 'Verkehr und Stadtentwicklung. Stand und Möglichkeiten historischer

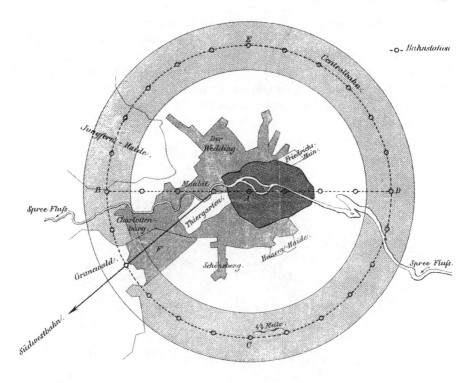

**Figure 1.4   Sketch with Berlin's City and Circle line and built-up area from a
petition of 1871**

Source: Hermann Schwabe, *Berliner Südwestbahn und Centralbahn, beleuchtet vom
                 Standpunkt der Wohnungsfrage und der Industrie Gesellschaft* (Berlin 1873),
                 34–5.

Ironically, the burdens of the railways were the consequence of the increase in
mobility, which was made possible by railways. The railways had further
unpleasant consequences for cities, because they accelerated the problems of big
cities. This was especially true of Berlin where the social consequences of
industrialisation were compounded, forming a huge bundle of severe political
problems as well. The rapid immigration and the demand for cheap housing
provided an enormous boom to the building trade, and resulted in the construction
of tenement blocks (*Mietskasernen*) in vast built-up areas in the new suburbs

---

Forschung', in Horst Matzerath, ed., *Stadt und Verkehr im Industriezeitalter* (Köln
1996), VII–XXI, esp. XVIII.

(*Vorstädte*). Nevertheless, construction lagged behind the pace of immigration. This resulted in overcrowding with all its social problems. Since the 1870s reformers complained about living conditions and demanded that vast areas should be set aside for residential building. They suggested using railways to open new areas and they precipitated a far-ranging debate about the structure and goals of urban traffic, including a first and gigantic attempt in 1871 to get a grip on the growing housing problem.

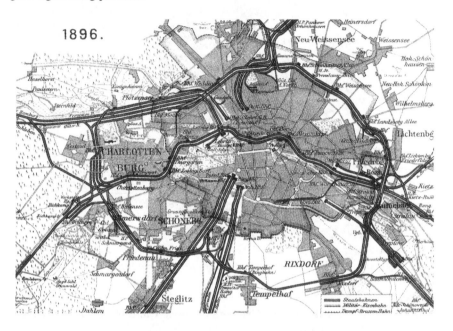

Figure 1.5   Map of Berlin, 1896

Source: Königl.-preußischer Minister der öffentlichen Arbeiten, ed., *Berlin und seine
              Eisenbahnen 1846–1896*, 2 vols. (Berlin 1896), vol. 1, plate 8.

In a petition to the Ministry of Trade, Industry and Public Works of October 23, 1871, the magistrate demanded a circle line around the city with a connection to the city centre. This was justified by the need for urban passenger traffic and for the opening of the region for development. The purpose was to make possible healthy and inexpensive housing for all classes 'with all amenities of country living and the incomparable joys of Mother Nature.'[30]

---

[30] Petition of the magistrate from October 23, 1871, quoted by Hermann Schwabe,
      *Berliner Südwestbahn und Centralbahn, beleuchtet vom Standpunkt der Wohnungsfrage
      und der Industrie Gesellschaft* (Berlin 1873), 7–9. The intention was 'to colonise on a
      big scale'. For the petitioners, it was obvious 'that only railways (...) were able to serve
      all demands of a frequent mass passenger-traffic for all classes of the population.' Ibid.

One result was the 'City and Circle line' (*Stadt- und Ringbahn*) built between 1873 and 1882. But the ambitious goal of healthy spacious living in natural surroundings was not reached. The developers made use of the maximum density allowed by the building code and built six storey high tenements for lower middle and working class people which again became rapidly overcrowded due to the permanent immigration into the poorer districts of the city. As a result of the large scale traffic planning in the 1880s and 1890s, the Wilhelminian ring of settlement was developed, between the older district and the Circle line. Critics of city planning would later call this area, a 'sea of stone' (Hegemann). Despite the gigantic building programme of the land developers, the city administration did not get a handle on the social problems and criticism continued. Berlin inherited the negative reputation of being the 'biggest tenement city of the world' (*größte Mietskasernenstadt der Welt*), sometimes being worse than that of industrial cities in the Ruhr region.[31]

Anti-urbanism – the escape to suburbia and beyond

This negative image was intensified by critical reflections about the metropolis that came from its own cultural milieus. Literary and artistic movements were deeply influenced by the unsolved social problems, the changes in living conditions, and the appearance of the city. This was a general phenomenon in many big cities in Germany. This was especially true in Berlin with its many interconnected sociocultural milieus, where these critical movements were very intense.[32] Many

---

This line of argumentation shaped the bulk of the public debate in which leading members of the railway and city administration participated. The different projects developed in this context envisaged a ring of settlement, ten kilometres in diameter, for no fewer than 200,000 households, i.e. a million people. See also E. Engel, 'Die Wohnungsnoth: Ein Vortrag auf der Eisenacher Conferenz am 6. Oktober 1872', *Zeitschrift des kgl. Statistischen Bureaus*, 1872, 392–4. On the social background and on the fear of a 'coherent Berlin mass of stone' see Dieter Radicke, 'Öffentlicher Nahverkehr und Stadterweiterung: Die Anfänge einer Entwicklung beobachtet am Beispiel von Berlin zwische 1850 und 1875', in Gerhard Fehl and Juan Rodriguez-Lores, eds., *Stadterweiterungen, 1800–1875: Von den Anfängen des modernen Städtebaues in Deutschland* (Hamburg 1983), 345–57, esp. 350.

[31] See Werner Hegemann, *Das steinerne Berlin: Geschichte der grössten Mietkasernenstadt der Welt* (Berlin 1922), 2; Karl Scheffler, *Wandlungen einer Stadt* (Berlin 1931), 24–6; Christoph Bernhardt, *Bauplatz Groß-Berlin: Wohnungsmärkte, Terraingewerbe und Kommunalpolitik im Städtewachstum der Hochindustrialisierung, 1871–1918* (Berlin/New York 1998), 33, 43–4, 51–3, and 135–7; Fritz Neumeyer, 'Massenwohnungsbau', in Jochen Boberg, Tilman Fichter, and Eckhart Gillen, eds., *Exerzierfeld der Moderne: Industriekultur in Berlin im 19. Jahrhundert*, 2 vols. (München 1984), vol. 1, 224–31, and Harald Bodenschatz, *'Platz frei für das Neue Berlin!' Geschichte der Stadterneuerung in der 'größten Mietskasernenstadt der Welt' seit 1871* (Berlin 1971).

[32] Around 1900, there spread a general uneasiness about big cities as a 'Moloch'. This was a form of cultural pessimism of the *fin de siècle*. See Christian Engeli, 'Die Großstadt

literary works of the naturalists showed the same uneasiness about the metropolis as did many paintings by expressionist artists. In novels and poems as well as in paintings, literary figures and artists put into pictures what they observed, cities that were being more and more shaped by industry and that city life was quite remote from the dream of a beautiful life in nature. Many artists used the motif of the railways to convey their critique of the Berlin metropolis. Julius Hart, for example, described in 'On a railway journey to Berlin' (*Auf der Fahrt nach Berlin*), all the roars, groans and hollow sounds of the journey and the city itself was seen through steam, 'smoke in black veils', and flames as 'a hell in shadows and mouldering pale'.[33]

Even more impressive were paintings from impressionist and expressionist artists. Around 1895, Franz Skarbina in his impressionist painting 'Railway-tracks' (*Gleisanlage*) portrayed an an old worker and his wife crossing the rail-yards of Anhalter Station in Berlin in the dawn. Skarbina shows a landscape shaped by the lights of living quarters and the steam of passing trains and smoke. The haggard faces of the couple mirror the gloomy unreality and desertedness of the city. Twenty years later the expressionist artist Ernst Ludwig Kirchner created his painting 'Railway bridge' (*Eisenbahnbrücke*) with the same intention. Parts of the City and the Circle line at Grunewald are depicted and like Skarbina he drew

---

um 1900: Wahrnehmungen und Wirkungen in Literatur, Kunst, Wissenschaft und Politik', in Clemens Zimmermann and Jürgen Reulecke, eds., *Die Stadt als Moloch? Das Land als Kraftquell? Wahrnehmungen und Wirkungen der Großstädte um 1900* (Basel et al. 1999), 21–51. This movement was intermingled with a general discontent about the cultural and socioeconomic reality of this time. With 20 and 24 per cent of all German literary figures and artists, Berlin was the German centre of this discussion. See Gerhard Brunn, 'Berlin (1871–1939) – Megalopolis Manqué', in Theo Barker and Anthony Sutcliffe, eds., *Megalopolis: the Giant City in History* (Hampshire and London 1993), 97–115, esp. 104.

33 See Julius Hart, 'Auf der Fahrt nach Berlin', in Waltraud Wende, ed., *Großstadtlyrik* (Stuttgart 1999), 45–6. A similar piece of literature is Jakob van Hoddis, 'Morgen', in ibid. 96. Hart and Hoddis were important members of the naturalists. Both authors, influenced by Zola, show some remarkable peculiarities. They were astonishingly weak in descriptions of the labour conditions in modern industry and the living conditions of workers. Very often they offered middle class prejudices about the life of the poor and confused the life of workers and sub-proletarians. See Klaus Michael Bogdal, *Schaurige Bilder: Der Arbeiter im Blick des Bürgers* (Fankfurt am Main 1978), 72, and Martin Halter, *Sklaven der Arbeit – Ritter vom Geiste: Arbeit und Arbeiter im deutschen Sozialroman zwischen, 1840–1880* (Fankfurt am Main and Bern 1983), 105. Otherwise they were more convincing in their general critique about the dark side of urban living such as nervousness, noise, or air pollution. See Christoph Perels, 'Vom Rand der Stadt ins Dickicht der Städte: Wege der deutschen Großstadtliteratur zwischen Liliencron und Brecht', in Cord Meckseper and Elisabeth Schraut, eds., *Die Stadt in der Literatur* (Göttingen 1983), 57–80; Wolfgang Sofsky, 'Schreckbild Stadt: Stationen der modernen Stadtkritik', *Die alte Stadt*, 13, 1986, 1–21, and Dirk Schubert, 'Großstadtfeindschaft und Stadtplanung: Neue Anmerkungen zu einer alten Diskussion', ibid. 22–41.

Figure 1.6   Franz Skarbina, *Railway-tracks*
(*Gleisanlage des Güterbahnhofs Weißensee*), 1895

Source: Bildarchiv Preußischer Kulturbesitz (bpk).

sketches of an unreal and deserted landscape in the heart of the metropolis of Berlin.[34]

These literary and artistic groups not only complained about the inhumanity of big cities in general and Berlin in particular, they actively showed their dissatisfaction by leaving the city, and founding artist colonies on the outskirts of Berlin, such as the naturalists in Friedrichshagen, or Gerhard Hauptmann in Erkner, and Heckel and Kirchner at the coast of the Baltic Sea. In spring and

---

[34]   On Franz Skarbina see Wibke Andresen, *Die Darstellung des städtischen Lebens in der deutschen Malerei des späten 19. Jahrhunderts* (München 1987), 179. On the development of the motif of railways and city landscapes in art see Renate Weinhold, *Die Eisenbahn als Motiv der Malerei: Eine Studie zur Bildinhaltskunde des 19. und 20. Jahrhunderts*, Universität Leipzig Ph.D. thesis, 1955, 95–106. On the intellectual positions of Brücke artists like Kirchner see Horst Jähner, *Kuenstlergruppe Brücke* (Berlin 1996), 19, 39, 65, and 172, and Wieland Schmied, 'Ausgangspunkt und Verwandlungen: Gedanken über Vision, Expressionismus und Konstruktion in der deutschen Kunst, 1905–1985', in Christos M. Joachimides, Norman Rosenthal, and Wieland Schmied, eds., *Deutsche Kunst im 20. Jahrhundert: Malerei und Plastik, 1905–1985* (München 1986), 21–41, esp. 23.

summer, they escaped to these localities and in autumn and winter they would come back to the city using the modern railway system. But in this respect, the avant-garde was only part of a broader movement of the escape from Berlin to 'suburbia and beyond' (Lewis Mumford). In the beginning of the 1880s, exclusive residential areas (*Villenkolonien*), with villas or country-houses for the upper middle-class, were erected in great number. These quarters had been established in areas distant from the city and on the outside of the Circle line. As the visionaries had predicted about the use of railways for the decentralisation of settlement in the beginning of the railway age, there was a drift towards the western and southwestern parts of the city, in the direction of the Wannsee and Grunewald.[35] Exclusive residential colonies built directly in unspoiled natural surroundings flourished there. This development was closely connected with the railway system of the city. Soon there grew a string of such colonies along the railway lines, leading out from the Circle line to different suburbs.[36] All those who could not afford this expensive housing 'in the green' (*im Grünen*), escaped on sun and

---

[35] See Ludwig Newhouse, *Vorschlag zur Herstellung einer Eisenbahn im Großherzogtum Baden von Mannheim bis Basel und an den Bodensee* (Karlsruhe 1833), 125–6. Already in the 1860s land developers such as Carstenn founded several exclusive residential areas southwest of Berlin with less success. At this time the railway companies showed less interest in the meager traffic. This changed radically with the construction of the City and Circle line in 1882 and the opening of some short distance lines to various suburbs. On the development of the suburb Lichterfelde see Thomas Wolfes, *Die Villenkolonie Lichterfeld: Zur Geschichte eines Berliner Vorortes, 1865–1920* (Berlin 1997), 44–7, and 73. For the success of such colonies a railway connection to the centre of the city was absolutely necessary. Indeed Carstenn established a station on the Anhalter Railway for his colony in Lichterfelde. Also Steglitz and Friedenau had a station and a railway line at their disposal. See Dieter Radicke, 'Öffentlicher Nahverkehr und Stadterweiterung: Die Anfänge einer Entwicklung beobachtet am Beispiel von Berlin zwische 1850 und 1875', in Gerhard Fehl and Juan Rodriguez-Lores, eds., *Stadterweiterungen, 1800–1875: Von den Anfängen des modernen Städtebaues in Deutschland* (Hamburg 1983), 345–57, esp. 347–9. On the negotiations between Carstenn and the Anhalter Railway see Peter Bley, *150 Jahre Berlin-Anhaltische Eisenbahn* (Düsseldorf 1990), 57–8, and Königl.-preußischer Minister der öffentlichen Arbeiten, ed., *Berlin und seine Eisenbahnen 1846–1896*, 2 vols. (Berlin 1896), vol. 2, 121–5.

[36] Most of the inhabitants were businessmen, entrepreneurs, bankers, officials and freelancers. On housing in exclusive residential areas see Goerd Peschken, 'Wohnen in der Metropole', in Jochen Boberg, Tilman Fichter, and Eckhart Gillen, eds., *Exerzierfeld der Moderne: Industriekultur in Berlin im 19. Jahrhundert*, 2 vols. (München 1984), vol. 1, 132–37. On the different uses of short distance travel see Ernst R. Höwer, 'S-Bahn-Verkehr und Siedlungsentwicklung im Berliner Raum am Bsp. der Zossener Vorortstrecke', in Wolfgang Ribbe, ed., *Berlin-Forschungen* (Berlin 1989), vol. 4, 179–234, esp. 179–83, and 194–6. On the increase of short distance travel see Peter Bley, 'Eisenbahnknoten Berlin', in Jochen Boberg, Tilman Fichter, and Eckhart Gillen, eds., *Exerzierfeld der Moderne: Industriekultur in Berlin im 19. Jahrhundert*, 2 vols. (München 1984), vol. 1, 114–25, esp. 121.

holiday trips via excursion trains to the nearer environs.[37] But the most important new phenomenon was the rise of mass tourism, at least for the middle class.[38] By the 1830s promotional literature about railways were already praising the possibility of journeys to beautiful landscapes and spas. They had foreseen how much the prosperity of villages in such regions would be affected by railways. Fifty years later, the escape from Berlin in summer, the wish to 'live in the allure of a modern spa or anywhere else in rural silence, only for one's own health', achieved a mass scope, 'against which the dimension of the "völkerwanderung" appears small'.[39] This escape developed in parallel to the construction and extension of the 'steinernes Berlin'.

With the construction of the Northern Railway between Berlin and Stralsund and on to the Isle of Rügen began the rise of many seaside resorts at the Baltic Sea.[40] Beside older ones such as Bad Doberan, there soon flourished Pölitz, Sassnitz and Binz on Rügen, Wolgast, Zinnowitz, Koserow, Swinemünde, Wollin, Dievenow, or Polzin. Many small fishing villages were transformed by tourism into bigger towns and even smaller cities. The phenomenon was astonishing. A closer look at the rise of the Wilhelminian 'emperors' spa (*Kaiserbad*) Sassnitz brings further details to light. Because of its popularity during the 1890s, the former fishing and farming village of Sassnitz grew extensions in the form of exclusive residential districts, which were financed largely from Berlin's wealthy middle class.[41]

---

[37]   The railway companies took that into consideration and for that reason they offered special stations for excursions in their urban railway. On the use of excursion trains see Gustav Schimpff, 'Wirtschaftliche Betrachtungen über Stadt- und Vorortbahnen', *Archiv für Eisenbahnwesen*, 35, 1912, 597–643, 849–73, 1167–1201, 1456–82, and *Archiv für Eisenbahnwesen*, 36, 1913, 20–53, 383–416. In the 1890s the excursion traffic rose to unknown quantities. See Königl.-preußischer Minister der öffentlichen Arbeiten, ed., *Berlin und seine Eisenbahnen 1846–1896*, 2 vols. (Berlin 1896), vol. 2, 121–3.

[38]   See Ludwig Newhouse, *Vorschlag zur Herstellung einer Eisenbahn im Großherzogtum Baden von Mannheim bis Basel und an den Bodensee* (Karlsruhe 1833), 99.

[39]   Königl.-preußischer Minister der öffentlichen Arbeiten, ed., *Berlin und seine Eisenbahnen 1846–1896*, 2 vols. (Berlin 1896), vol 2, 47–8.

[40]   On the construction of the Northern Railway see Peter Bley, '100 Jahre Berliner Nordbahn 10.7.1877 – 10.7.1977', *Berliner Verkehrsblätter*, 24, 1977, 110–72, esp. 111–4. Since the forties initiatives for the construction of a northern railway between Berlin and Stralsund had existed. After the Danish-Prussian War in 1863 the Prussian State supported these plans too in connection with a project for a naval port at the North of the Isle of Rügen (Arkona). See Königl.-preußischer Minister der öffentlichen Arbeiten, ed., *Berlin und seine Eisenbahnen 1846–1896*, 2 vols. (Berlin 1896), vol. 1, 274–6. But a concrete project did not succeed until the 1870s. At the end of the 1870s the railway reached Stralsund and in 1891 Sassnitz on Rügen.

[41]   In the 1860s, at the beginning of the rise of this village into an exclusive sea spa resort town, the inhabitants tried to hide the simplicity of the façade of their Pomeranian fishery and farmhouses with carved wooden balconies. Even until today, this factor continues to shape the appearance of many seaside resorts at the Baltic Sea. See Egon Weber, 'Die Entwicklung des Ostseebades Saßnitz bis zum ersten Weltkrieg',

Another highlight of the seaside resort Sassnitz was the building of the castle named *Dwasieden* for four million Marks by Adolf von Hansemann. He was the former director of the main Prussian bank, the Disconto-Gesellschaft. His father, David Hansemann – one of the most important railway visionaries – had been Prime Minister of Prussia in 1848. The elder Hansemann had acquired his wealth by financing railway construction in the western parts of Prussia. Adolf von Hansemann had planned and built the Lehrter Railway from Berlin to Lehrte in 1863. In 1871 he, together with Bismarck's private banker Gerson Bleichschröder, succeeded over Bethel Henry Strousberg, the uncrowned railway king of Germany in this decade, and of Jewish origin. Because of the war between Germany and France, Strousberg had come into serious troubles with his ambitious railway plans in Germany, Russia, and Romania. Bleichschröder and Hansemann made use of this advantageous situation and took over most parts of his railway empire. From the profits he gained from this transaction Hansemann bought, as did many of the big entrepreneurs of his time, the Lancken Manor on Rügen in the neigbourhood of Sassnitz. Furthermore, he engaged the architect Friedrich Hitzig to erect a castle on the periphery of Sassnitz – later called *Dwasieden*. Hitzig was the man who had realised many of Strousbergs construction projects, and he reproduced in this building many features of the Görlitz Station in Berlin, which was built by Strousberg in the 1860s. In this respect, *Dwasieden* was a monument which illustrated the victory over Strousberg.[42] In the 1890s, the emperor's family stayed at this castle several times during their summer vacation on the Baltic coast. This laid the ground for the city's reputation as a emperor's spa and stimulated a further rise of the former fishing village.

Soon financiers like Hansemann, the rising elite of the sea spa and railway administrators developed far-reaching visions in the 1890s. They planned a port and a train ferry to Sweden to open up the Scandinavian market and to develop the tourism to the northern countries. They succeeded, with the help of Hansemann, in getting Wilhelm II engaged in that project. Making use of the emperor's enthusiasm about the Scandinavian countries, their project was realised in an astonishingly short time.[43] By 1896 the port and by 1909 a train ferry were built. Perhaps not on this large scale, but on many locations along the coast, hundreds of hotels and tens of thousands of exclusive summer residences were built in a similar way. A total distance of several hundred kilometres along the Baltic coast from the capital had now been totally transformed by the railways. After developing the West, South and East, north of Berlin lay a region that offered far-reaching

---

Greifswald-Stralsunder Jahrbuch, 4, 1964, 117–80, and *Greifswald-Stralsunder Jahrbuch*, 5, 1965, 45–92.

[42] On the competition between Hansemann and Strousberg see Ralf Roth, 'Der Sturz des Eisenbahnkönigs Bethel Henry Strousberg: Ein jüdischer Wirtschaftsbürger in den Turbulenzen der Reichsgründung', *Jahrbuch für Antisemitismusforschung*, 10, 2001, 86–112.

[43] See Birgit Marschall, *Reisen und Regieren: Die Nordlandfahrten Kaiser Wilhelm II.* (Heidelberg 1991), 13–6 and 134–6.

potential for economic and political development.[44] The Berlin scenario was only one of many that had been played again and again in many other regions of Germany. Such phenomena could be observed in the surroundings of Hamburg and the coast of the North Sea near Munich and the Alps or near Breslau and the mountains of Silesia. On the basis of railways, beautiful landscape and cultural attractions even Thuringian cities like Eisenach or Weimar changed their appearance from small and backward farming towns (*Ackerbürgerstädte*) to wealthy centres of tourism.[45]

New visions – the electric city

All in all we had at the end of the nineteenth century several different but mighty movements away from big cities and a growing fondness for living in unspoiled nature. Important signs of this were cultural trends like the *fin de siecle*, 'Reform of Living' (*Lebensreform*), and 'Enthusiasm for the European North' (*Nordland-begeisterung*). All these tendencies were directly or indirectly supported and sometimes initiated by the expanding railway network with its tremendous opportunities for mobility. This widespread socio-cultural movement had enormous side-effects on the urbanisation of provincial regions and it increased the pressure for the renewal of a city. Not only was there a growing tendency to escape from big cities, but there were equally signs for their modernisation as well. Berlin was also, in this respect, a centre of discussion. Around 1900, architects and town planners began developing comprehensive plans for the reconstruction of the city as well as for the development of vast areas for a continuously growing population. Striking were the plans for new traffic infrastructure, which played a more important role than in the previous decades. Again the railways attracted the most attention. Now the idea was that they should be thoroughly adapted to the conditions of cities. City planners looked for traffic systems which enabled the expansion of cities to a diameter of twenty or forty kilometres. They sought to bypass the more negative elements of smoke, noise, street traffic intersections and the cutting off of neighbourhoods caused by conventional railways. Since the 1880s an intense search had been started to look for new technical solutions that would resolve these problems.

The magic word was electrification and the efforts of Werner von Siemens were a milestone in the spread of electrical railways. At the World Fair of 1867 in Paris and 1878 in Vienna he offered technical solutions, and in 1879, he presented a train at a commercial fair in Berlin. Arising from this experimental framework

---

[44] On the dream of living in suburbia and the dialectical revolve into conurbation see Lewis Mumford, *The City in History: Its Origins, Its Transformations, and Its Prospects* (San Diego et al. 1961), 482–90.

[45] See Reinhold Brunner, '*...die dem Armen hilft, das Wenige, was er besitzt, zu Rathe zu halten...*': *Die Geschichte der Sparkasse Wartburgkreis 1822 bis 1997* (Stuttgart 1999), and Jensen Zlotowicz, *Villen in Eisenach* (Weimar 1999).

the first tramway had been created in Berlin-Lichterfelde two years later. An entrepreneur from Offenbach, Kommerzienrat Weintraut would several months later take up this idea. He founded the *Frankfurt-Offenbach Trambahn Gesellschaft*, which was completed in 1884, making it the second tramway line in Germany.[46] Both tramways in Berlin and Offenbach heralded a new railway age in cities. But before this could be fully achieved, the problem of electrical power supply had to be solved. In this respect the International Electrical Exhibition in Frankfurt am Main in 1891, which supported systems of urban electrification was a further milestone. An important event was the transmission of alternating current over a distance of 173 kilometres. Indeed, after many urban power plants had been built, electrical tramways rapidly spread into many German cities at the end of the 1890s.[47] But in a metropolis like Berlin, tramways were only half of the solution. To avoid the conflict with the street traffic and to overcome space by speed, railways needed their own traffic level.

Concrete proposals for the building of an electrically elevated train in Berlin existed since the 1880s, but they were not accepted by the King of Prussia. A breakthrough was finally brought to the World Fair of 1893 in Chicago. An international audience observed with great excitement what had been tested in practice in the elevated trains of New York or in the undergrounds of London before.[48] In Berlin, city developers and traffic specialists tentatively regarded the success of these traffic systems and many drew the conclusion that, 'elevated trains were responsible for an enormous rise in traffic', for a 'change in living conditions' and for a fundamental 'revolution in city traffic'. Furthermore, they 'were suitable to be accepted by the people'.[49] With the help of the World Fair in Chicago, Siemens' original project was making good progress and in the same year, his plan was confirmed by the king. Nevertheless, a quick implementation failed because of administrative delay and citizens' protest.

The Berlin magistrates preferred electrical tramways so they did not support the Elevated Train Company (*Hochbahngesellschaft*) of Siemens. Construction work did not begin until 1897. But once again, Siemens and his engineers under-estimated

---

[46] See Jürgen Steen, *Frankfurt am Main und die Elektrizität, 1800–1914. Die zweite industrielle Revolution* (Frankfurt am Main 1981), 106, and Jens Freese and Michael Hofmann, *Der Äbbelwoi-Express: Auf den Spuren der Lokalbahn von Frankfurt nach Offenbach* (Schweinfurt 1995), 46.

[47] On the exhibition of 1891 see Jürgen Steen, *'Eine neue Zeit ...': Die Internationale Elektrotechnische Ausstellung 1891* (Frankfurt am Main 1991). On the spread of tramways see Karl Heinrich Kaufhold, 'Strassenbahnen im Deutschen Reich vor 1914: Wachstum, Verkehrsleistung, wirtschaftliche Verhältnisse', in Dietmar Petzina and Jürgen Reulecke, eds., *Bevölkerung, Wirtschaft, Gesellschaft seit der Industrialisierung* (Dortmund 1990), 219–37.

[48] See Ralf Roth, 'Weltausstellung und Eisenbahn: Versuchsfelder der Moderne', *Damals*, 32, no. 6, 2000, 36–42, esp. 41.

[49] Gustav Kemman, 'Schnellverkehr in Städten mit besonderer Berücksichtigung von London und Newyork', *Archiv für Eisenbahnwesen*, 16, 1893, 263–72 and 455–71, esp. 466–7.

Figure 1.7 Sketch of an elevated train at *Friedrichstraße* in Berlin, 1880

Source: Bildarchiv Preußischer Kulturbesitz (bpk).

the opposition of Berlin's citizens. Although the system of electrical trains had made great progress compared with steam engines, the citizens – especially the landlords – feared the noise, the shadow of the iron construction in the streets and a drastic diminishing of the quality of life. As a result of this they predicted a devaluation of their properties, an exodus of wealthy tenants away from the city and the endangerment of health. The more the construction of the train moved forward to the West and into wealthier quarters of the city the louder the protest became. In addition to this fear, there was also an outcry about the aesthetic appearance of this elevated train and how it would appear afterwards in Berlin's streets.[50] Opposition centring around these issues continued. The citizens drew comparisons to other cities and were reminded of the experiences of other European metropolises. Indeed in London, Budapest, and Paris the traffic companies and city administrations preferred subways and undergrounds in contrast to the American model. The Elevated Train Company was forced by the movement to follow these examples as well. It was only after a general revision of

---

[50] See Sabine Bohle-Heintzenberg, *Architektur der Berliner Hoch- und Untergrundbahn: Planungen, Entwürfe, Bauten bis 1930* (Berlin 1980), 33; Ralf Roth, 'Ab in den Untergrund: Zur Geschichte der Berliner Schnellbahnen', *Damals*, 32, no. 11, 2000, 36–42, and Elfi Bendikat, *Öffentliche Nahverkehrspolitik in Berlin und Paris 1890–1914: Strukturbedingungen, politische Konzeptionen und Realisierungsprobleme* (Berlin 1999), 112–15.

the plans for this facility and its change into an underground railway that the construction of the line between *Warschauer Straße* and *Bahnhof Zoo* was finished in 1902. Following that, enthusiasm about the new, clean, quiet and fast traffic system gradually began appearing. This new form of a railway not only solved the problem of distance in the city area, it also opened space for a new dimension of the city, and it made cheap housing possible. It was in this way that the electrified trains contributed to alleviating the social question. It also solved the aesthetical and environmental problems of the old railways. The electrical railway was a good deal quieter. In addition, there was no longer conflict with the street traffic and it did not cut the communication between the cities' districts. All in all, it was a serious attempt to reduce the conflicts between railways and cities.[51] In the new form, underground railways contributed in solving the traffic problems in Berlin, the most rapidly growing metropolis of Germany. The modern electric trains were seen as the traffic facility of the new century. This was the keen hope at the dawn of the automobile age.

On the basis of this metamorphosis of railways, tremendous visions for the renewal of Berlin sprang up around 1900. The bearers of these visions were not only land developers, but remarkable entrepreneurs like Werner von Siemens and Emil Rathenau, supported by important financial institutions like *Deutsche Bank*, *Dresdner Bank* or *Berliner Handelsgesellschaft*. Above all, they planned a radial system of a dozen fast speed railways after looking closely at other countries' experiments in the same field. This system would allow passengers to enter the centre from all the points on a circle with a diameter of forty kilometres within half an hour. This would have revolved the geographical structure of the region and given ten or twelve million people access to land for housing development. But around 1900, contrary to this assumption of a permanent immigration towards Berlin, the wave of migration actually slowed. The vision of Berlin as one of the biggest cities in the world had been based on a statistical estimation of demographical tendencies after the middle of the nineteenth century. But the migration lost its momentum in the decade before World War I, when the birth rate dropped, and the region in the East was deserted. This desertion was the result of more than three million people having emigrated to America between 1873 and 1893. The underestimation of this change caused a serious crisis in the building trade as well as in the banking system. Many construction projects collapsed.[52] Then World War I broke out.

---

[51] The electrical fastspeed trains were described as 'one, the special conditions of cities fully adapting and with cities intermingling (*verwachsendes*) element of modern time'. Paul Wittig, *Die Weltstädte und der elektrisch Schnellverkehr* (Berlin 1909), 6–7.

[52] See Bernhardt Christoph, *Bauplatz Groß-Berlin: Wohnungsmärkte, Terraingewerbe und Kommunalpolitik im Städtewachstum der Hochindustrialisierung, 1871–1918*, 145–8, 267–9, and 296–300.

Conclusions

As we have seen, railways and cities formed a complex relationship and influenced each other in many ways. The degree and type of influence depended on what kind of city it was, its magnitude, its geographic location and the specific situation in a rapidly changing social environment. But this relationship especially shows the variety of influences which railways had on German society in general and on cities in particular. That which the visionaries had foreseen from the beginning of the railway age had in reality come to pass. Railways were of tremendous importance for trade and government cities, for the mobility of people and the urbanisation of Germany, for the rise of industrial cities, for the change of fishing and farming villages into flourishing tourist cities, and for many other city types as well, which could not be mentioned in this article. The metropolis Berlin brought to light many of these aspects. It was in this city in particular that economic and political progress, social consequences and cultural movements can be observed as part of one intermingled process which was, in many cases, influenced by the interactions between the railways and the city.

CHAPTER TWO

Cities and railways in The Netherlands between 1830 and 1860

Henk Schmal

Introduction

The introduction of the railway brought dramatic changes to the relationship between cities as well as between the city and the countryside. This was not only because the train had a far higher speed than previous modes of transport but also because, in contrast to its predecessors, it bypassed the countryside and stopped only in cities. These developments had profound ramifications. In The Netherlands the railway age started in 1839 with the opening of the railway line between the cities of Amsterdam and Haarlem. Despite this relatively early start, the formation of a national network took a long time. By the end of the 1850s two companies had run 255 kilometres of track that linked most of the important cities within The Netherlands. Until 1856 both lines were not extended beyond the borders of The Netherlands. Dutch historians devote considerable attention to the question of why it took such a long time to realise a national network.[1] It was not until the 1860s that the government took the initiative to construct a national railway network, which was finally completed in 1880.

This chapter explores the relationship between the railway and the city in the early period i.e. 1830–1860. The main discussion focuses on the way the cities reacted to the birth of the railway age and the geographical effects of the railway on the cities. The chapter starts with a brief history of the infrastructure in The Netherlands in the opening decades of the nineteenth century. It then discusses the motives of entrepreneurs, cities and others to create a railway line and the resulting geographical design of the lines and stations. Finally, it examines some of the direct and indirect effects of the early railway on the cities.

---

[1] See for instance I. J. Brugmans, *Paardenkracht en Mensenmacht, Sociaal-economische geschiedenis van Nederland 1795–1940* (Den Haag 1961), 102; J. G. van Dillen, 'De economische ontwikkeling van Nederland', in J. A. Bartstra and W. Banning, eds., *Nederland tussen de natiën*, 2 vols. (Amsterdam 1948), vol. 2, 80–120, esp. 104; R. T. Griffiths, *Industrial retardation in The Netherlands, 1830–1850* (Den Haag 1979), 71–74; J. H. van Stuyvenberg, 'Economische groei in Nederland: een terreinverkenning', in P. W. Klein, ed., *Van Stapelmarkt tot Welvaartsstaat: economisch-historische studiën over groei en stagnatie van de Nederlandse volkshuishouding, 1600–1970* (Rotterdam 1970), 52–74.

Roads and traffic in The Netherlands in the first decades of the nineteenth century

Since 1600 people in the economic centres of The Netherlands made use of frequent and cheap passenger transport through a network of canals. Barges connected cities at some times with even hourly services. The facilities for the transportation of goods were less efficient. Although waterways extensively covered The Netherlands, they were far from being a single well-integrated network. For each area of natural water a particular type of vessel had evolved that was unsuited to local conditions in other areas. Moreover, many of the canals had been built primarily for drainage purposes and were only seldom used as connecting links.[2]

In the first decades of the nineteenth century water-transport links were transformed. New links were built and existing links were improved. The construction of new canals at the ports of Amsterdam and Rotterdam provided better connections to the sea. The North Holland Canal, measuring eighty kilometres, was laid between Amsterdam and the North.[3] Several new waterways were built, reaching into what hitherto had been the unserved regions of the eastern provinces. The new canals were equipped with towpaths and led to the establishment of several new barge services, the first since the mid-seventeenth century.

In this land of barge transport, roads were neglected until Napoleonic times. Before 1800 the roads were in a shocking state, amounting to little more than unpaved tracks across marshy swamps or boggy sands. Under Napoleon, and later, more effectively under William I, a series of broad, paved, toll-maintained highways were built. Although the new communication network was far from ideal, it did create however, new possibilities for the peripheral rural areas. Wagon and coach services increased and prospered as the highways were improved. Hence, in the 1820s and 1830s, the two centuries of barge transportation had to yield considerable ground to coaches using the expanding network of paved roads. The new mode of transport was particularly popular among the higher income groups and the traditional barge became a facility that was used more and more by the lower classes.[4]

---

[2] See H. C. Kuiler, *Verkeer en vervoer in Nederland. Schets eener ontwikkeling sinds 1815* (Utrecht 1949), 2–4.

[3] See W. M. Zappey, 'Het Kanaal door Holland op zijn langst', *Ons Amsterdam*, 28, no. 8/9, 1976, 234–41.

[4] Information about the types of travellers using various modes of transportation just prior to the coming of the railroad is conveyed in Hildebrand (Nicolaas Beets) in Camera Obscura. In the 'Verslag van den toestand der provicie Noordholland over het jaar 1851 (The Provincial Report 1851)', 500–501, the traditional barge is called a *volksschuit*, a ship for ordinary men.

The introduction of the railway

The railway was introduced to Holland in 1839, the same year that Assen, the provincial capital of Drenthe, received its first barge. The Dutch Iron Railroad Company (*Hollandsche IJzeren Spoorweg Maatschappij*, HSM) opened the first railway track between Amsterdam and Haarlem. Four years later the Dutch Rhine Railroad Company (*Nederlandsche Rhijnspoorweg-Maatschappij*, NRS) started a line from Amsterdam to Utrecht and, two years later, to Arnhem. In 1847 the HSM track was extended to Rotterdam. The construction of the railways progressed slowly in The Netherlands. Although 255 kilometres of track were opened in 1855 it neither formed a single network nor connected the country with the existing European network. In the 1860s the state finally began to promote and build railways in various parts of the country. A National Railroad Company (*Staats Spoorwegen*) was formed to operate the lines then opened. A few decades later the Dutch railway network would be completed.[5]

During the nineteenth century the Rhine trade to the industrialised regions of Germany grew rapidly. Rotterdam was in a particularly advantageous position for the transport of bulk goods to and from the 'Rhineland'. Amsterdam's water links were no match for those of Rotterdam, even though the waterway from Amsterdam to the Rhine was enlarged in the 1820s. But the passage to Cologne still took a lot of time. Amsterdam's share of the Rhine trade slowly diminished.

In 1831 the Amsterdam Chamber of Commerce strongly supported plans to create a railway line from Amsterdam to Cologne. This support underlined the expectation that the railway would attract a large share of the trade and that Amsterdam would be able to compete with Rotterdam. The interest in this project waned when the financing fell through.[6] In 1836 the plans attracted new attention when a railway line was laid between Antwerp and Cologne.[7] Rotterdam, which had excellent water links, showed almost no interest in a railway line, but Amsterdam found itself in another position. A National Committee feared the Belgian design and alternatively supported the plans for a railway heading East from Amsterdam to Arnhem. The committee even suggested that the project be funded by the government, but the Lower House rejected the bill in 1838. Within a month King William I responded by granting a loan with guaranteed interest. The railway track between Amsterdam and Utrecht was opened in 1843 and was extended to Arnhem in 1845. It took another eleven years to build a connection with the German network and it was not until four years later, in 1860, the railway link to Arnhem could finally solve the problems of the Amsterdam–Rhine trade.

---

[5] See J. H. Jonckers Nieboer, *Geschiedenis der Nederlandse spoorwegen, 1832–1938* (Rotterdam 1938), 337–42.

[6] See W. Fritschy, 'Spoorwegaanleg in Nederland van 1831 tot 1845 en de rol van de staat', *Economisch en Sociaal-Historisch Jaarboek* 46, 1983, 180–246, esp. 188.

[7] See J. de Vries, *Barges and Capitalism; passenger transportation in the Dutch economy, 1632–1839* (Utrecht 1981), 76.

Figure 2.1 The principle railway lines in The Netherlands, 1860

Source: I/O-Graph, Utrecht.

The Rhine Railroad was no competitor in the international Rhine trade. The railway derived its revenue from passenger traffic rather than freight traffic.

In the 1830s some initiatives had also emerged to develop a railway line from Amsterdam to Rotterdam via The Hague. The Amsterdam Chamber of Commerce and the city council showed little interest in these plans. The Chamber of Commerce did not even want this connection, as it would merely prove the inferiority of the Amsterdam connection with the 'Rhineland' compared with that of Rotterdam. The city council was also afraid that well-to-do citizens would migrate *en masse* to the area of Haarlem. The introduction of the train would change one's concept of distance-to-time and might prompt people to move house to the more attractive region of the dunes. Only a few manufacturers situated along the projected line however supported the plan.

In 1836 the National Committee that had assessed the request for the Amsterdam-Haarlem railway line displayed very little confidence in the project. Thinking only in terms of goods traffic, it concluded that the market demand was not great enough to warrant such an infrastructure as the one proposed. The entrepreneurs, however, who had introduced the railway to The Netherlands had other intentions. They, in contrast to the National Committee, wanted to develop a railway line exclusively for passenger transport. What is even more interesting is that, despite the lack of government interest, the entrepreneurs still succeeded in finding the necessary funding to establish and open the first railway line of The Netherlands in 1839. The venture was successful and within a few years the line was extended to Leiden (1842), The Hague (1843) and Rotterdam (1847).

The difference in orientation between the NRS and the HSM is reflected in the profile of the shareholders shortly after the opening. The list of shareholders of the NRS contains a relatively high number of merchants, and a relatively low number of manufacturers. The distribution is reversed in the HSM list.[8]

Trains for passengers

The entrepreneurs who introduced the railway to The Netherlands faced a rather unique situation. The early investors had the one great advantage of being very well-informed about the market. Whereas elsewhere the potential market was based solely on guesswork, in The Netherlands it was based on more accurate projected estimates of the traffic that could be expected in the first years of operation. This explains why the first railway track was constructed parallel to the most heavily-used barge canal between Amsterdam and Haarlem.

A few years later, trains appeared alongside other successful barge canals in Holland. When railway construction finally began in the Northern Provinces in 1863, the first route, once again, ran parallel to the most important barge canal in that region, the route between Harlingen and Leeuwarden.

Better information seemed to be the only advantage that the railway promoters reaped from the existence of the barge network. The remaining implications all tended to raise obstacles to railway development. The majority of the canals were owned by the municipalities of the cities that were connected together in this network. To them, the construction of the railway meant that the value of their

---

[8] See S. Boom and P. Saal, 'Spoorwegaanleg en het beeld van de eerste helft van de negentiende eeuw', *Economisch en Sociaal-Historisch Jaarboek*, 46, 1983, 5–25, esp. 13.

Figure 2.2   The railway line between Amsterdam and Haarlem, opened 1839
(the line ran parallel with the barge canal between the cities)

Source: Dutch Railway Museum, Utrecht.

capital would be undermined. Hence, they undertook no initiatives to stimulate construction during the first decades of the railway. They reacted by issuing regulations and influencing the direction and location of the railway routes. When railways were first introduced, many people were sceptical about their benefits. The existing road and canal routes as well as the other waterways between Amsterdam and Haarlem could easily handle the movement of people and goods between the two cities. It was feared that railways would lead to job losses. Property owners were afraid that the land through which the railway passed would be devalued. The skippers of the barges, united in skippers' guilds, mounted protests to protect their jobs. This kind of opposition can be compared with the obstructionist efforts of coaching firms in other countries. But the direct involvement of city councils in barge canal operation seemed to make it more effective.

The barge operators fought back by lowering their fares. A few months after the opening of the Amsterdam-Haarlem route in 1839, the remaining skippers cut their fares by 25 per cent. Soon after the opening of the railway line between Amsterdam and Utrecht in 1844, fares were lowered even further by almost forty per cent![9] But these substantial fare reductions did not succeed in attracting passengers, because the railway turned out to be an enormous time-saver by comparison. The rail traveller from Amsterdam to Utrecht reached his destination in one hour and ten minutes instead of the seven hours needed by barge. The competition anticipated from the barge did not materialise. The vast majority of travellers switched to the railway as soon as it was introduced. The first to be confronted with the new competition was the Amsterdam-Haarlem canal. The hourly schedule of barge departures that had plied this route for over two centuries suddenly lost its rationale when the first railway was opened. To serve local needs, two barges were kept running on this route. A few years later, when the railway was extended from Haarlem to Leiden, the skippers' guilds responsible for this route promptly disbanded. In 1841 more than 30,000 passengers used the route between Haarlem and Leiden. Two years later, the first full year of railway competition, the number of barge passengers shrank to less than 2,000. This experience in the first years of the railway gave the directors of the HSM sufficient confidence in the superiority of their mode of transport to raise the third class fare by 12 per cent in 1844.[10]

The same tragic story can be told for the inter-city coach traffic. The declining toll receipts show that wherever the train appeared, the amount of road traffic seriously decreased. The toll receipts on most of the comparatively new highways fell by seventy per cent. In contrast, the toll receipts on the roads nearer the cities did not fall as dramatically as the receipts on the tolls that were located at some distance from them.[11] The railway clearly concentrated traffic around the cities. It gradually superseded paved roads for the conveyance of passengers except for short distances and local convenience. Faced with the decline in traffic, road expenditure was reduced. In a few cases the width of the roads was even reduced from 4.5 to 3.5 metres.

Barge competition proved to be no more threatening than coach competition was in other countries. But the competitive measures were different from those that destroyed the coach, because the barges operated at lower costs. Fortunately however, all of the obstacles that the canal network threw in the way of railway construction were only temporary ones. They may have delayed the first railways but they did not affect subsequent projects. The train proved so superior that the barge and the coach were almost immediately forced to retreat into a position where they provided only local services. Within a few years the heart of the Dutch barge canal network had almost vanished. By the mid-nineteenth century inter-city passenger transport in the provinces of Holland and Utrecht had been almost completely taken over by the train. Throughout the rest of the century the barge

---

[9]   See J. de Vries, *Barges and Capitalism; passenger transportation in the Dutch economy, 1632–1839* (Utrecht 1981), 201–7.

[10]   See J. H. Jonckers Nieboer, *Geschiedenis der Nederlandse spoorwegen, 1832–1938* (Rotterdam 1938), 27.

[11]   See Henk Schmal, ''s Rijks groote wegen in de 19e eeuw', in A. P. de Klerk et al., eds., *Historische geografie in meervoud* (Utrecht 1984), 78–94, esp. 86.

and the coach only played a role locally, or in those areas without railways. The barge era was effectively at an end.

The struggle of the barge to survive partly explains the slowness of railway construction in The Netherlands. Other explanations can be found in the nature of the terrain which railways had to cross. For example, the marshy land between Amsterdam and Haarlem required that virtually the entire length of the track had to be built on a specially raised bed. Elsewhere, the line was beset by continual problems of subsidence. The fact that the country was criss-crossed by drainage canals and to a lesser extent, navigable waterways, necessitated the construction of numerous bridges. Between Amsterdam and Rotterdam, for example, there were no fewer than 98 bridges, twelve of which were swing bridges, all helping to push up construction costs.[12] An even more important contributing factor to the rising costs was the way in which the sale and expropriation of the necessary land was arranged. The implications of the imprecise legislation resulted in high costs and time-wasting. This affected the size of dividends and the price of shares. The poor performance of Dutch railway shares deterred foreign investors from placing more capital in similar ventures in the country.[13] Finally, in the 1860s, the government started to promote and build railways. This resulted in the creation of a national network of widely scattered lines opened in the 1860s and 1870s.

During the early days of the railways in Holland and elsewhere, there was a heavy dependence on passenger travel. This continued for an even longer time on the Dutch railways. Around 1850, when the Belgian railway from the port of Antwerp to Germany, the so-called 'Iron Rhine', was fiercely competing for the Dutch transit trade, railways in Holland were still used almost exclusively for passenger transport. The HSM, which operated the line from Amsterdam to Rotterdam via Haarlem, Leiden and The Hague, continued to derive over 76 per cent of its total revenue from passenger service until the late 1870s.[14] The remaining revenue was largely derived from the transport of personal luggage and parcels rather than heavy freight. The situation of the NRS was more or less the same. As late as 1878 passengers accounted for sixty per cent of the revenues.[15]

The geography of the railway lines and the location of the stations

Whereas the railway companies in Great Britain owned enough capital to create stations well within the existing towns, the United States with their grid-like-

---

[12] See Anonymous, *Hollandsche IJzeren Spoorweg-Maatschappij 1839–1889* (Amsterdam 1889), 34–5.

[13] See R. T. Griffiths, *Industrial retardation in The Netherlands, 1830–1850* (Den Haag 1979), 66–74.

[14] See H. P. H. Nusteling, *De Rijnvaart in het tijdperk van stoom en steenkool, 1830–1914* (Amsterdam 1974), 495.

[15] See J. de Vries, *Barges and Capitalism; passenger transportation in the Dutch economy, 1632–1839* (Utrecht 1981), 202.

patterned towns owned enough space to let the railway in. Neither capital nor space could be found in the Dutch cities. The cities in The Netherlands were characterised by an infrastructure of small streets and densely-packed buildings surrounded by fortifications and canals. Building within the city walls would be rather expensive and would take a long time because of the many parcels of land that had to be expropriated. As in most cities on the continent, the railways in The Netherlands ended near the city wall or passed cities on their fringes. Most of the stations were situated near one of the city gates.

In the debate on the railway during the 1830s and 1840s the national and local governments, and the Chambers of Commerce always focused on the significance of the railway for the transport of goods. The HSM, however, concentrated on passenger traffic from the start. These intentions are reflected in the route, the location of the railway stations and their equipment. The route of the HSM neglected harbours, rivers and canals that could be used for the transport of goods. Contemporaries even spoke of a company with 'hydrophobia'. But the primary reason for this state of affairs was, quite simply, costs. The high capital investments and maintenance costs pushed the price of rail freight far above the rates charged by the waterways. Having resigned themselves to this fact, the directors of the HSM did not provide any of the necessities, such as storage facilities or branch lines, which might have stimulated the development of freight traffic.

Time played a major role only for the transport of people. It was less important for the transport of goods. As a result, the stations were not equipped for storage and were situated at locations that, in most cases, were hard to reach by ship. The HSM did not even intend to fight for a strong position in this market. This was somewhat surprising, given that early discussions on the introduction of a railway always underlined the possibilities of rail transport competing with water transport.

But the NRS line was initially run as a passenger line as well. The Weesperpoort terminal in Amsterdam had no connection with the port, and the same applied to the temporary terminal at Arnhem. Even more importantly, the line had no connection with the German network. So there were no conditions in place for the international transport of goods. The need to create such conditions was made clear by the results. Between Utrecht and Arnhem the railway line passed an area with low population density. The number of passengers that used the train and could be expected to use it was rather small. Between Amsterdam and Utrecht the situation was somewhat different. The railway physically paralleled the formerly busy barge line between these large population centres, and led to the expectation of large numbers of travellers. But altogether the results of the NRS line were disappointing. In almost none of the years between 1845 and 1860 did the shareholders receive the original price for their shares, and dividends were very low. Extensions proved to be necessary, focusing primarily on upgrading the already existing system for the transport of goods. In 1847 the connection between

Weesperpoort Station and the port of Amsterdam was completed.[16] The city had greatly influenced this development in the following way. In the original plans the line passed many private parcels of land that would have to be expropriated. This would have proved to be a difficult and expensive operation so the plans were changed and the connection was projected mainly over properties that belonged to the municipality. The city of Amsterdam offered these parcels to the NRS under reasonable terms.

Figure 2.3 The railway station *Willemspoort* in Amsterdam, opened 1843
           (in the middle the city gate *Willemspoort*)

Source: The Amsterdam Municipal Archive.

It took a long time to realise a railway station on the NRS connection between Utrecht and Rotterdam. The railway company preferred a Rotterdam terminus near the harbour. Others opted for a direct link with the station of the HSM, possibly with a side connection to the port. In the end it was decided to develop a terminus at the port, and after the usual discussion between governments and private property owners, the station could be opened in 1855. The next year the connection with Germany was also completed and so from 1856 on, it was possible to transport goods directly by rail from the ports of Amsterdam and Rotterdam to the Rhineland. The railway lines of the HSM and the NRS connected a number of important cities within The Netherlands. Both companies had terminals in Amsterdam and Rotterdam.

Most terminals had buildings on both sides of the railway lines and were sometimes connected by a front. The station was then intended as a definitive

---

[16]   See J. C. Westerman and G. M. Greup, *Gedenkboek samengesteld ter gelegenheid van het 125 jarig bestaan van de Kamer van Koophandel en Fabrieken voor Amsterdam* (Amsterdam 1936), 265.

terminal, as in the case of Amsterdam *Willemspoort*. The station was built just across the newly erected city gate that served as a toll bar. This was the starting point of the road and the barge canal to Haarlem. The railway was constructed parallel to this infrastructure. The Amsterdam terminal station was constructed just to the North of the canal. When a traveller left the city for the trip to Haarlem, he could choose his mode of transport at the very last moment.

Figure 2.4 The railway station *Delftsche Poort* in Rotterdam, opened 1847

Source: The Rotterdam Municipal Archive.

In Rotterdam the HSM station missed a front. The company left open the possibility of being connected with the projected NRS line that would enter the city from the other side. The architecture of most of the early stations was based on Classicism. The HSM station at Rotterdam, built in the English Gothic style, was an exception.

The station at Haarlem was the only station located within the city walls. Haarlem had a lot of empty parcels of land. In 1850 the population of Haarlem had fallen by about thirty per cent compared with two centuries earlier.[17] Initially, the city council rejected the plans of the railway company to locate the station inside

---

[17] See Henk Schmal, 'Patterns of de-urbanization in The Netherlands between 1650 and 1850', in H. van der Wee, ed., *The Rise and Decline of Urban Industries in Italy and in the Low Countries* (Leuven 1988), 287–307, esp. 291.

the city walls. During this period much of the income of the cities came from local taxes on incoming goods. Haarlem feared it would lose this income if a railway line opened the city. The council finally agreed when measures were introduced to ensure the payment of local taxes by the travellers. Secondly, it anticipated that the railway line would stimulate building activities in less densely populated areas.

In The Hague the railway ran at some distance from the canals that surrounded the city. The council pleaded for a route closer to the city, but ran into opposition from the railway company because of the dense concentration of buildings outside the city. The distance to the edge of the city was over 500 metres and the railway station was initially situated outside the local boundaries of The Hague. The station was situated in the meadows of the village of Rijswijk and was opened in 1843. A year later, The Hague acquired ownership of this area. The station was located on the city side of the railway. Horse-drawn carriages could make use of a new road stretching from the station entrance to the nearest arterial road, from which they could enter the city and pass the excise office. A path for pedestrians gave direct access to the city.

In Delft, Leiden and Schiedam the railway line passed the old fortifications. The railway company and the city councils preferred a location as nearby as possible. The local council in Delft also strongly supported this idea and offered the former fortifications for its construction. Consequently, in this case, the railway line touched the edge of the city. The station was built on one of the bastions and a bridge offered direct access to the city. In Schiedam and Rotterdam the stations also arose outside the city. The same applied to the cities on the Amsterdam-Arnhem line via Utrecht. In most of the cities the stations are still at the same location. While Amsterdam was alone in getting a central station, Rotterdam's station was moved slightly to the West. However, these developments took place later on. Some people pointed out that having the two stations located on either side of the town would advantageously stimulate the local economy by passengers crossing the city.[18]

Concentration of traffic

The introduction of the railway triggered a dramatic rise in the number of passengers travelling. Experience in other countries showed that the number of passengers travelling between cities could even double or triple. The accuracy of this assumption is borne out by the results of the first railway lines that easily can be compared with those of the barges. As most of the railway tracks and even the terminals more or less followed the barge canals, the traffic was concentrated at the same places as before although now at a far greater volume. This occurred not only because of the growth of the traffic as such, but also as a result of the far greater conveyance capacity of the train compared with a single barge. Moreover, the

---

[18]   See P. Saal and F. Spangenberg, *Kijk op stations* (Amsterdam 1983), 13–23.

railway stations were exclusive concentration points, while a barge could stop at several places to take on passengers. The railway connected cities stopping only near key population centres. This resulted in the new means of transportation neglecting the smaller towns and the countryside, thus concentrating railway passengers at specific places.

As we have seen, most long-distance barge and coach carriers suffered from competition by the railways. On the other hand, the short-distance operator, who served only a limited area, such as a town and its surrounding rural districts, managed to keep going throughout the nineteenth century, sometimes in co-operation with the railways. Because the railways brought more people to and from the towns, these carriers often found in many instances that their volume of business had increased considerably.[19]

No single function attracted and focused more traffic than the railway stations. They were the embarkation points of a great deal of the cab traffic, and their names figured on the destination boards of many of the new horse-drawn omnibuses. Omnibus companies planned their routes on the basis of the railway stations. Passengers arriving by rail were obliged to dismount from their train and continue their journey on foot, by horse-drawn carriage, or any other means of transport that was available. The arrival of passengers, with their luggage, caused a dispropor-tionate amount of confusion and congestion on the approach roads to the stations. Most of the railway arrivals dispersed throughout the town. In Amsterdam and Rotterdam there was a certain amount of traffic between the terminal stations. The numbers of cabstands increased within the town, but especially around the stations. As early as 1839 a private company in Amsterdam started a network of omnibuses with ten lines, all beginning at the railway station. Until that year people who did not own a private carriage had to rent a cab or a so-called *toeslede*, a little carriage with wooden gliders instead of wheels. In most of the other cities omnibuses started from the station and brought the travellers to a central location in the city. The area at the front of the stations was paved. Carriages could park there and wait for customers. The Amsterdam Omnibus Company even obtained exclusive rights to park at the front of the stations.

Though the growth of traffic was heavy, the resulting geographical patterns were rather stable compared with those of the old days of the barge. Following in the same footsteps of the barges, the starting points of the railways were also located at the edges of the cities. The flow of traffic from the stations was concentrated on the city centres. Even the station square can be compared with the old wagon squares near the city gates.

---

[19]   See J. H. Fuchs, *Beurt- en wagenveren* ('s-Gravenhage 1946), 379–82.

The railway and the geography of the cities

What was the impact of the railway on the urban topography of the cities? In the early days of the railway the train did not penetrate the city. The flow of traffic from the stations to the city centres could easily be absorbed by the existing infrastructure. In some cases, new bridges were erected to link the station with the city. For instance, a year after the opening of the station in 1844, the *Catharijnepoort* in Utrecht was demolished and a new opening to the inner city with more capacity was realised. In Utrecht, and in some of the other cities in which the train passed on the periphery, the railway line was not laid within the existing geographical structure. In these cases, the station was built at some distance from the original entrance to the city.

The utilisation of space in the area surrounding the stations was inextricably tied in with the railway, attracting all kinds of land users. Refreshment and entertainment facilities, eating and lodging houses, and retailers gathered conveniently around the stations. The squares and streets where the stations were situated automatically led to a confluence of people and traffic, which pushed up the demand for sites of all descriptions in the immediate vicinity. The larger stations acted as magnets for hotels. Sometimes the traditional inns and lodging houses were enlarged to meet the rising demand for accommodation. Around 1860 initiatives were launched to create a neighbourhood for the well-to-do in close proximity to the railway stations. In Amsterdam (*Weesperpoort*), The Hague and Haarlem these initiatives were successful. The railway station in these years was seen as an exclusive preserve of the rich. However, within a few decades, most of the railway stations had lost their attraction for the upper classes when cities extended beyond their official boundaries and non-residential activities found a place nearby.

The literature expresses serious doubts on the significance of the railway in relation to land-use patterns in central districts. In Boston, the seven railway terminals (1835–1855) 'apparently exerted only limited influence on the emerging central land-use pattern'.[20] John R. Kellett concludes that 'their perceptible effect, even in the long term, upon the location of central business district functions was smaller than has sometimes been suggested'.[21] The building of stations can be viewed more as a response to existing trends rather than as an instigator. This seems likewise to be the case in The Netherlands, at least during the early days of the railway. In Amsterdam, by far the largest economic and population centre of The Netherlands, the existing functional order of the city was not affected. Growth could take place within the city. Even the filling in of some of the canals around 1860 cannot be related to the increasing traffic intensity, but was rather more a question of hygiene. The railways were significant elements in themselves but apparently not pre-eminent among the factors causing change. It seems that the

---

[20] H. Carter, *An Introduction to Urban Historical Geography* (London 1983), 168.
[21] John R. Kellett, *Railways and Victorian Cities* (London and Henley 1979), 269.

most significant role of the railway was not in the internal reorganisation of city functions as such, but rather in hastening the process of suburban extension and segregation. The train and omnibus ended the notion of the pedestrian city, at least for a rich selective group. For a large section of the population, walking to work and to shops remained characteristic into the twentieth century. In short, the changes operated differentially according to one's ability to pay, thus becoming a powerful tool in segregating the rich from the poor.

The introduction of the railway stimulated sub-urbanisation. Although it was not exactly a revolution, the railway routes and the long time it took them to grow, deeply influenced the trend of sub-urbanisation. Rich Amsterdam families were already going to their country estates during the seventeenth and eighteenth century. In most cases the presence of beautiful, water-enriched scenery dictated where these estates would be built. During the first decades of the nineteenth century the sites most favoured were determined by the new network of paved roads. Many aristocrats and wealthy merchants built their summer residences around Amsterdam, in sandy areas stretching from the dunes in the west to the *Gooi* in the East, about twenty kilometres from the town. There were also many estates around The Hague. The introduction of the railway created new possibilities for living outside the town.[22] For instance, in the 1850s, many affluent people from Amsterdam spent the summer in Arnhem, about a hundred kilometres from their house in the city. Meanwhile, the well-to-do from Rotterdam suddenly found that the region of The Hague with its beautiful dune landscape was within reach. Some of them later settled permanently at their suburban location. But despite these developments, sub-urbanisation remained a somewhat rare phenomenon during the second half of the nineteenth century as only very few citizens could afford a second house elsewhere. In addition, local councils were seriously perturbed by the departure of this elite class. It was seen as a bad development that so many of the well-to-do had left within such a short space of time, depriving the city of considerable tax revenue. The emerging suburbs were the domains of the rich. The main bulk of the working class stayed in the city. This introduced a trend towards segregation between town and countryside, a phenomenon that is still in evidence today.

Conclusion

The relationship between the railway and the city is a phenomenon that cannot be easily isolated. In this chapter we have studied the two main railway lines in The Netherlands during the early period between 1839 and 1860. We could conclude that initially the cities showed very little interest in this new means of conveyance, although during the 1830s, the railway did become an issue for the city of

---

[22] See Henk Schmal, 'Stedelingen in het Gooi; vestiging van de zeventiende tot de twintigste eeuw', *Amstelodamum*, 84, no. 4, 1997, 99–108, esp. 99–102.

Amsterdam for the transportation of goods. But most cities took scarcely any notice of the railway as a means for transporting goods or passengers. They were convinced that the existing infrastructure could easily meet the actual demand. The city councils would not invest in a mode of transport that would ruin the already existing system of barges and coaches. Some private entrepreneurs however, realised more importantly that, in addition to current demand, an enormous latent desire to travel was also growing. The first railway line proved the truth of this assumption, and in a short period, 255 kilometres of track were realised.

Between 1839 and 1860 the railways were almost exclusively used for passenger traffic. The railway line between Amsterdam and Rotterdam connected the key cities of Holland and ran parallel to the main line of the barge network in the western part of The Netherlands. Within a few years the old system had faded away.

The cities that were connected tried to influence the route of the railway line in that they wanted it to be built as nearby as possible. The location and design of most railway stations reflect the orientation towards passenger traffic. The NRS continued to promote the traffic of goods in their location policy, trying to establish a connection to the German network and the ports of Amsterdam and Rotterdam. It was Amsterdam in particular, that supported these initiatives. The immediate consequence of the introduction of the railway was the incredible growth of traffic in towns. The omnibus entered the city to meet this concentrated demand. At the same time, other private initiatives were undertaken to satisfy the basic needs of travellers. Shops, inns, lodges and hotels were erected or enlarged around the stations. In some cities the connection between the station and the inner city did not fit in with the existing infrastructure. In these cases the local council took action to meet the new needs.

During this period the railway scarcely influenced the existing functional order of the city, but it did have some effects on the social order. The train was a means of conveyance for the well-to-do. In some cities the immediate surroundings of the station were filled with big houses for the rich. In the nineteenth century most of these initiatives had already diminished as the environment of the stations became less attractive. On the other hand, the first tentative steps towards sub-urbanisation and the subsequent segregation become visible around 1860. But it took a century before this development would reach full strength.

CHAPTER THREE

Railways, towns and villages in Transylvania (Romania): Impact of the railways on urban and rural morphology

Michel Tanase

From a traditional question to a new type of problem

The history of the railways is first and foremost the history of rail networks, followed by that of track technologies, engineering structures and fixed installations that bring them to life. Countless books, studies and articles have been devoted to this history and the case of France was recently analysed in a general overview.[1] Technical parameters are very similar from one European country to another. However, these approaches all tend to neglect the 'human component', namely the relations that develop, when a new track is built, between the railway and the people living along its path. These relations are shaped by the positive and negative impacts affecting these people, impacts which transform the patterns of land use in the areas concerned. The existence of such situations and relations as structuring elements of the landscape, the basis of all population settlements, were taken into account for roads.[2] But although, in many respects, the railways are indebted to the road-building culture, these new relations have rarely been analysed by railway historians. How did the direct or indirect impacts of new railway lines affect urban or rural morphology and what were their consequences over time? This is the key question, the question that raises a whole new type of problem. Several theoretical aspects, taken from a previous case study on Transylvania, are also worth examining in relation to this new type of problem[3]:

---

[1] See François Caron, *Histoire des chemins de fer en France*, 2 vols. (Paris 1997).

[2] A seminar on *Man and Roads in Western Europe during the Middle Ages and in Modern Times*, was held on this question at the *Deuxièmes Journées internationales de l'Abbaye de Flaran*, September 20–22, 1980.

[3] In a limited historical sense, 'Transylvania' is defined as a territory located between the eastern and western Carpathians (Intercarpathian arc). After the First World War, the term took on a broader administrative definition, encompassing the extra-Carpathian provinces of Maramureş, Crişana and Banat, all attached to Romania. This is the definition used for my study.

- General geomorphology of the site.
- General and local economic development objectives/trends.
- The composition/structure of the land crossed by the railway.
- The structuring role of the railway and the topology of rail connections.

Two case studies of railway impacts in Transylvania

The term 'impact', now widely used in environmental studies, was initially used in ballistics to define the collision of a projectile with another object and the traces left behind. Later, the notion was also applied to the effects of any sudden, brutal action. More recently, in around 1950, the notion of impact was defined in many scientific fields – notably in urban planning – as the influence of one or more factors on the evolution or transformation of a landscape, site, etc. Though the term is recent, the process it describes is as ancient as humanity itself. With regard to the railways, I would define two types of impact, either 'aggressive' or 'beneficial'. For example, the presence of unsightly electric pylons in the landscape can be seen as an aggressive impact while successful engineering structures – from the *Pont du Gard* Roman aqueduct to the viaducts of Gustave Eiffel, Garabit and Rouzat – enjoy a more positive image and are considered to enhance the landscape. Certain impacts, railway stations for example, may have both positive and negative consequences – with structuring or destructuring effects on the economy of a town or region – which may be difficult to foresee as they are not immediately visible.

At a seminar devoted to different forms of transport, my paper highlighted various aspects of the impact of roads on rural and urban morphology in Transylvania during the nineteenth century, at a time when the 'modern' road network was being newly constructed.[4] Two typical examples concerned the roads along the Târnava-Mare river and those of the Olt valley – more precisely the Făgăraş depression. This time, my study of the railways in these same two valleys starts with two preliminary questions:

- To what extent did the railways benefit from the proximity of existing roads?
- Was the choice of railway route dictated by purely technical imperatives or were other local or central political factors involved?

But before examining the impacts of the railways, we should refer back to certain key theoretical and geo-historical components of the initial study, namely those which explain how the old Mediaeval paths and roadways were successively

---

[4] See Michel Tanase, 'Contribuţie la studiul evoluţiei drumurilor în Transilvania. Continuitateşi substituiri în partea meridională (Contribution to the study of road development in Transylvania. Continuity and replacements in its southern regions)', *Historia Urbana*, 3, no. 1, 1995, 79–104, and Anonymous, *Voies et villes. Les transports routiers, ferroviaires et navals dans le développement des villes, from October 7–8, 1994* (Bistriţa 1994).

replaced by nineteenth-century roads. This analysis is based on a principle generally applied in studies of urban and/or parcel morphology whereby space is dynamic, generating movement through natural fluidity and through the pressure of economic and political forces.[5] All these factors contribute to the development of major road infrastructures, followed by rail networks. On the basis of these principles, I analysed numerous examples of impacts, selecting just two for this

Table 3.1   Names of rivers and places

Romanian	Hungarian	German
Alba-Iulia	Gyulafehérvar	Weissenburg
Arpaşul de Jos	Also-Arpas	Unter-Arpasch
Avrig	Felek	Freck
Beşimbac	Besimbak	Beschenbach
Beclean	Betlen	Betlen
Blaj	Balazsfalva	Blasendorf
Cluj	Kolozsvar	Klausenburg
Cârţa	Kercz	Kerz
Copşa-Mică	Kis-Kapus	Klein-Kopisch
Daneş	Danos	Dunesdorf
Dridrif	Dridrif	Dreidrich
Dumbrăveni	Erzsebetvaros	Elisabethstadt
Făgăraş	Fogaras	Fogarasch
Hârtibaciu	Hortobagy	Harrbach
Hoghilag	Holdvilag	Halwelagen
Lunca	Lunka	Langendorf
Mediaş	Medgyes	Mediasch
Micăsasa	Mikeszasza	Feigendorf
Olt	Olt	Alt
Oradea	Nagyvarad	Grosswardein
Porumbacul de Jos	Also-Porumbak	Unter-Porumbach
Satu-Mare	Szatmar	-
Sâmbăta de Jos	Also-Szombatfalva	Unter-Sombath
Scorei	Skorei	Skore
Sibiu	Nagy Szeben	Hermannstadt
Sighişoara	Segeswar	Schäsburg
Târnava-Mare	Nagy-Küküllö	Kokel
Ucea de Jos	Also-Utsa	Unter-Utscha
Viştea de Jos	Also-Vist	Unter-Wischt
Voilà	Voilà	-

---

5   See Pierre Merlin, ed., *Morphologie urbaine et parcellaire* (Saint-Denis 1988).

article. Though based in the same valleys, they are set in very different geomorphological and political contexts so as to validate my ideas on the nature and consequences of these impacts. The first example, on the Târnava-Mare river, concerns a process of railway development which 'engulfed' the urban landscape of Mediaş (Medgyes/Mediasch) and which disrupted the logical pattern of development in Daneş village.[6] Both cases are examples of 'aggressive impacts'. The second example concerns the Făgăraş depression, where the railway route was clearly chosen to avoid aggressive impacts on the villages served – or simply bypassed – by the line. But before presenting the results of this analysis, it is important to understand the historical context because the causes are deep-rooted.

Though for many westerners, Transylvania conjures up the mythical character of Dracula, few people are familiar with the history of this country.[7] A brief geo-historical overview is in order. The existence of Dacia as a state dates back to the first century BC. It was covered by a dense communications network comprising short- and long-distance pathways and dirt roads. Dacia was attached to the Roman Empire in 106 and for 200 years benefited from a 'new' network of Roman roads. Three of its main arteries appear on the 'Peutinger Table'.[8] After the military and administrative withdrawal from Dacia in 271, the new Daco-Romans suffered successive invasions by so-called 'barbarian' peoples (Gepidae, Avars, Visigoths, etc.) between the third and tenth centuries. These invasions transformed the landscape and modified land use. The road networks also suffered through lack of maintenance and the destruction of civil engineering structures. The old Roman road network, built primarily for strategic purposes, fell into severe disrepair despite the fact that, like everywhere else, the Romans had chosen the driest routes, following contour lines on the top of south-facing *thalwegs*, avoiding the extensive marshy areas formed by meanders.[9] The pathways and tracks linking the villages of native Roumano-Slav people continued to exist, though the old Roman roads were never fully repaired.

After the Magyar conquest of this territory on the 'other side of the forest' – hence the name *Transsilva* – between the tenth and twelfth centuries, Germanic settlers (Saxons) were installed in the country by the kings of Hungary. The Magyar occupation, the arrival of the Szeklers, in the northern Olt valley and the Saxon colonisation transformed the country's ethnic makeup, its landscape and its communications.[10]

---

[6]   In Transylvania, most towns, rivers and mountains have names in Romanian, Hungarian and German (see table 1.1). From this point on, I have chosen to use the official Romanian name, though the Austrian geological survey maps give the Hungarian name first.

[7]   Thanks more to the novel by Bram Stoker and to the cinema than to any historical facts...

[8]   See Karl Miller, *Die Peutingersche Tafel des Weltkartes des Castorius* (Stuttgart 1929), Segments VII–VIII.

[9]   See Raymond Chevallier, *Les Voies romaines* (Paris 1997).

[10] Szeklers were people akin to the Magyars who finally settled in the south-east of the Carpathian arc.

From the sources to the approach: roads and railways in Transylvania

More than a simple method, my approach involves a detailed cartographic analysis, backed up with general or local geo-historical data, to formulate hypotheses on the formation of transport routes. It is a well-known fact that the Middle Ages was not a time of major road building. Works were limited to the refurbishment of existing Roman roadways. These routes – even those which have since disappeared – are generally visible on maps or by observation in the field, though the surfacing materials disappeared long ago. Given the similarity between the routes of the ancient roads and those of the railways, these maps remain valid.

Several remarkable maps produced by the topographers of the Austrian army are useful for this type of analysis. These maps were regularly updated by the process called *Reambulierung*, a term which has long disappeared from the language of the profession. This neologism was created from the Latin word *ambulare* meaning 'to walk around', since the maps were revised on the basis of data collected by Austrian topographers during excursions in the field. As the only English word in the same semantic field is 'deambulation', i.e. 'the act of walking abroad or about' the word 'reambulation' is probably a good translation. Unfortunately, primary sources linked to the birth of the railways are hard to obtain in Romania and bibliographies are difficult to establish.[11]

Following the Treaty of Carlowitz (1699) between Austria and Turkey, and the Satu-Mare peace treaty (1711) between Austria and the Hungarian insurgents, Transylvania (under Turkish suzerainty since 1526) became part of the Habsburg Empire. A long period of national reconstruction began. The first stage began with the creation of a 'Military Edifices and Forts Division' at Alba-Iulia, where the first military and city maps were produced. But it was not until after the 1848 revolution that major road building programmes, new roads and refurbishment of old ones, were initiated throughout the Empire. A second and more important stage began in 1890. The model adopted for the new road system was that applied on a major scale for Austrian regional development. Hence 'in accordance with the military and economic interests of the Empire, major roads known as *Reichstrassen*

---

[11] Maps and charts used in this article: *Neue Kriegs Charte von Siebenbürgen* (de J. C. Schreiber, Leipzig 1720); *Nova et accurata Geometrica Mappa DACIAE MEDITERRANEAE seu Moderni Principatus TRANSILVANIAE* (…), (Carte géométrique, nouvelle et soignée, de la Dacie méditerranée ou de l'actuelle principauté de Transylvanie), 1:180.000, established in 1735 by J. C. von Weiss, drawn by L. von Luchsenstein; *Kriegs-Charte des Grossfürstenthums Siebenbürgen* (Carte de guerre de la grande principauté de Transylvanie), scale 1:28.800, firstmap to be drawn by the Austrian (1769–1773); *Spezialkarte von Österreich-Ungarn, Reambulierung 1889–1915*, 1:75.000, Second edition (1873–1887), and *Plan de cadastre de la ville de Mediaş* (1895), échelle 1:1.440. The author wishes to thank all those who helped him with his bibliographic research: Österreichische National Bibliothek, Vienna; Valer Ciobanu, Regional Railways Division, Braşov; Judith Pal, History and Archeology Institute, Cluj.

were built in predefined directions and a second period of modernisation began in Transylvania in 1890'.[12]

Though Austria was soon included in the leading 'peloton' of European railway builders, priority was granted to railway construction in the central part of the Empire, with the more remote provinces remaining somewhat neglected.[13] The reason for this was essentially political. The attachment of several provinces to Austria was marked by frequent protests on the part of certain minorities and was a source of conflict between Hungarian national reform movements and the Austrian

Figure 3.1 Layout of the railways in Transylvania at the end of the nineteenth century

Source: Based on data from D. Iordănescu and C. Georgescu, *Construcţii pentru transporturi în România* (Constructions for the transport system in Romania) (Bucarest 1986), 58, and Radu Bellu, *Mică monografie a căilor ferate din România*, vol. 1: Regionala Braşov (Short monograph on the railways in Romania, vol. 1: Braşov region) (Bucarest 1995).

---

12 Béla Köpeczi, ed., *Histoire de la Transylvanie* (Budapest 1992), 537.
13 See Clive Lamming, *Les Grands Trains de 1830 à nos jours* (Paris 1989).

authorities. So for the construction of railways in Transylvania, the state preferred to adopt a wait-and-see attitude. Transylvania too had become a melting pot of populations – native Romanians, Hungarians and Saxons – that were difficult to control. Austrian regional development policy had to take account not only of these ethnic components, but also of the economic interests of Saxon towns with the status of 'Free Royal Cities', sometimes in competition with each other.

In 1832, the Budapest Parliament examined a proposal to build thirteen new railway lines in Hungary, including two in Transylvania (Figure 3.1): I. Budapest – Oradea – Cluj (with an alternative route to Sibiu or Braşov) and II. Budapest – Arad – Alba-Iulia – Sibiu. But it was not until 1854 that the Oradea – Braşov route, with connections to Alba-Iulia, Târgu-Mureş and Sibiu was finally chosen. From then on, the question prompted lively debate, fuelled by the protestations of the towns that were left by the wayside. While the two main players – the central Austrian power and the Hungarian administration – proceeded by way of laws and provisions, the representatives of the Saxon towns expressed their claims by way of *ad hoc* expert assessments, reports and documents.[14] Hence, between 1858 and 1865, several works were published, both in Vienna and Transylvania, 'concerning the question of the Transylvanian railway', to support either the town of Sibiu or of Braşov by arguing the importance of railways in the development of foreign trade.[15] The publication of reports by companies with vested interests and of biased expert assessments further clouded the issue. Karl von Ghega, builder of the famous Semmering line, consulted by the town of Sibiu in 1858, came out – predictably – in favour of a route passing through the town, in preference to the route backed by the town of Braşov.[16] In fact, it was not until the Austro-Hungarian 'Compromise' in 1867 that railway construction began in Transylvania. This compromise transformed the Habsburg Empire into a constitutional monarchy with two centres – Austria and Hungary – and limited the autonomy of the 'free royal' Saxon cities.[17]

It was a law of 1868 which triggered the construction of the first line, from Arad to Alba-Iulia. Completed in 1868, it was financed by the Austrian

---

[14] See Hilde Mureşan, 'Proiecte privind construirea primelor căi ferate în Transilvania (Projects concerning the construction of the first railways in Transylvania)', *Anuarul Institutului de Istorie şi Arheologie* 17, 1974, 268–79.

[15] See Carl-Franz von Becke, *Die Siebenbürger Eisenbahnfrage aus dem Gesichspunckte des österreichischen auswärtige Handels* (The question of the Transylvanian railways with regard to Austrian foreign trade) (Kronstadt, today Braşov 1864), and Anonymous, *Die Wahrheit in der siebenbürgischen Eisenbahnfrage. Eine Denkschrift an den Reichsrath.* (The truth on the question of the Transylvanian railway. Report to the Imperial Council) (Wien 1865).

[16] See Otto-Bernharde Friedmann, *Der gegenwärtige Stand der Eisenbahnfrage in Oesterreich* (The current situation on the question of railways in Austria) (Wien 1865), and Radu Bellu, *Mică monografie a căilor ferate din România*, vol. 1: *Regionala Braşov* (Short monograph on the railways in Romania, vol. 1: Braşov region) (Bucarest 1995), 23.

[17] Béla Köpeczi, ed., *Histoire de la Transylvanie* (Budapest 1992), 654.

Rothschilds.[18] The route of the second line, Oradea – Cluj – Războieni – Mediaş – Sighişoara – Braşov, was modified (with respect to the discussions of 1832) to serve the last three towns but not Sibiu. However, several branch lines to Sibiu were built in 1872 and to the town of Târgu-Mureş in Hungary, in 1871. This new line, financed by the 'Eastern Hungarian Joint Stock Railway Company' with Anglo-Austrian support, was completed in 1873.[19]

Though from the very outset of discussions in 1858, and right up to 1871, there were plans to build junctions with Romania via Sibiu or Braşov at the south-eastern ends of lines I and II, they were not a priority for the Romanian government.[20] Indeed, on the other side of the Carpathian mountains, the initial preference was for a median railway route, linking the two provinces of Moldavia and Walachia which formed the Romanian kingdom from 1859. Though an agreement between Romania and Hungary, ratified in 1891, provided for the construction of rail junctions at Ghimeş-Palanca and Turnu-Roşu, these external links from Romania to the Austrian empire were not completed until 1879, six years after the opening of the Teiuş-Braşov line in Transylvania.[21]

'Aggressive' impacts in the Târnava-Mare valley: historical and geomorphological context

The railway sector concerned, stretching eighty kilometres from Blaj to Sighişoara and built between 1870 and 1873, separates two distinct zones of the Târnava valley: The right bank zone was made up of Hungarian 'comitats', governed by the kingdom of Hungary. It was scattered with Hungarian, Romanian and Saxon villages belonging to two morphological categories: street villages along the ancient Roman road and valley villages along the Târnava-Mare river. The left bank zone, comprising two 'seats' around the Saxon towns of Mediaş and Sighişoara, was also made up of villages inhabited by these three ethnic groups, most of them situated well back from the Târnava-Mare river to avoid marshy meanders.[22]

The railway route in this sector has a number of specific features. Along the right bank from Blaj to Lunca, the route follows runs parallel to the local road and follows a series of large-radius curves. After Micăsasa, the railway crosses the

---

[18] See Radu Bellu, *Mică monografie a căilor ferate din România*, vol. 1: *Regionala Braşov* (Bucarest 1995), 29.

[19] A company bought up by the Hungarian state in 1876 and attached to the 'Hungarian Railways' (*Magyar Államvasutak*, MAV). See Béla Köpeczi, ed., *Histoire de la Transylvanie* (Budapest 1992), 537.

[20] See Anonymous, *Joncţiunea Căilor Ferate ale României cu Ungariaşi Transilvanie* (Bcureşti-Braşov 1871), and Radu Bellu, *Mică monografie a căilor ferate din România*, vol. 1: *Regionala Braşov* (Bucarest 1995), 31–3.

[21] Bellu, ibid., 114.

[22] In Transylvania, the Mediaeval *comitatus* was a county. 'Seats' were a sort of autonomous *comitati* of the Saxon settlers.

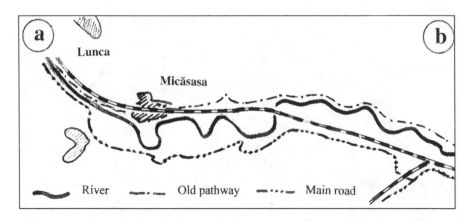

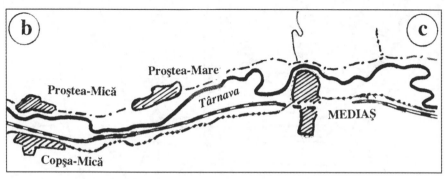

Figure 3.2   The railway route between Lunca and Mediaş

Source: *Plan de cadastre de la ville de Mediaş* (1895), échelle 1:1 440, section 5572.

river. At Mediaş, it has a direct impact on urban morphology. At Daneş, it creates a brutal impact by cutting diagonally across the town. Yet the best way to avoid technical constraints – bends, infrastructures, etc. – would have been to stay on the right bank of the Târnava-Mare. On this side of the river, practically no straight length transitions were required, since large-radius curves were well-adapted to the local morphological structure – dry zones, southern exposure and low gradients – and practically no excavations or retaining walls were necessary. It was constraints of a different kind that dictated the railway route, one political, the other technical: Firstly, in accordance with a government decision, a branch had to be constructed towards Sibiu, a town forty kilometres away, and this could only be done by crossing the river before Copşa-Mică. Secondly, there was strong local pressure from the town of Mediaş, which wanted a station close to the town centre. So the river was crossed by a bridge around five kilometres beyond Micăsasa and the station at Copşa-Mică, connecting the main line with the spur to Sibiu, was built 5.5 kilometres further along. It would certainly have been cheaper to cross back over the river some four kilometres from Copşa-Mică, after establishing the branch

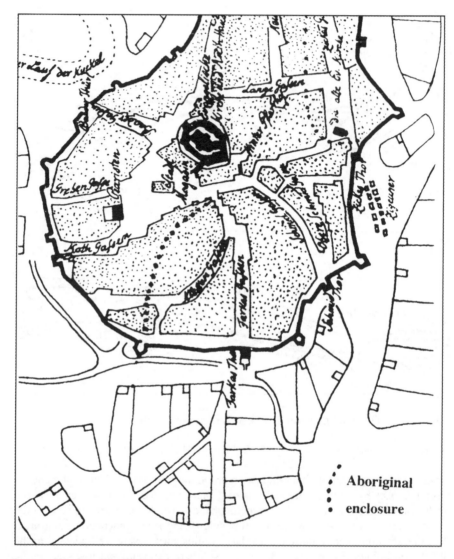

Figure 3.3 The divisions of 1498

Source: From Captain Theumern map, 1750.

line to Sibiu. Moreover, this solution would have provided a more direct line to the
town of Dumbrăveni, 18 kilometres beyond Mediaş.

Figure 3.4 The railway route in 1871

Source: *Plan de cadastre de la ville de Mediaş* (1895), échelle 1:1.440.

Mediaş: Old divisions and new crosscuts

For a better understanding of the consequences of these impacts on urban morphology, it is worth making a brief historical flashback, since the first divisions cutting through the town date back to 1498. The site was originally occupied by the enclosed fields and pastures of the native peoples, by the street villages of the Saxon settlers and other scattered ethnic groups. To gain the status of a town, the construction of an enclosing wall was necessary, though the Romanians opposed the idea. In response to complaints from the Saxons and opposition from the Romanians, the king of Hungary, Vladislas II, ordered the Romanians to be expelled from the town if they refused to co-operate. Finally, the enclosed land was

divided up and its inhabitants forced to move outside the town walls. The route of the
new railway line passing one-hundred metres south of the enclosing wall also cut
through Romanian residential districts outside the town walls. This had two main
consequences over time: The dispossession of certain inhabitants, the division of one
of their streets and the isolation of certain districts.[23] But the choice of this route also
offered immediate access to the station and to sidings that served new industrial
activities in the area. These advantages have benefited the town ever since.

   This choice of route involved major excavation work for the railway builder. A
trench measuring 400 metres in length, thirty metres in width and twelve metres in
height was dug and retaining walls were built.[24] An overpass was constructed to link
the southern part of the town and a connecting channel was built under the track to
extend the canal that drained wastewater from the town. The large volume of
extracted earth was used to dry a marshy plot of land set aside for station
construction and a second plot in the town centre intended for residential
development.

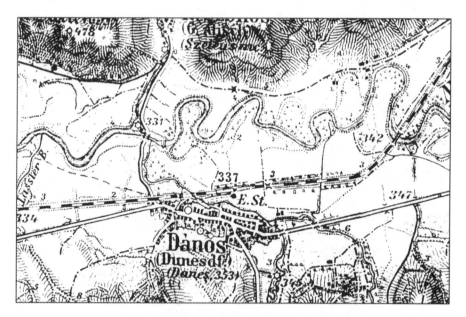

Figure 3.5 The diagonal crosscut in Daneş

Source: *Plan de cadastre de la ville de Mediaş* (1895), échelle 1:1.440.

---

[23]   This is not shown in Figure 3.3.
[24]   Still today, the Romanians of Mediaş called the overpass *Podul Telenilor*, the Italians'
       Bridge. This is perhaps a reference to the workers who built it.

The diagonal crosscut in Daneş

The village of Daneş, dating back several centuries, is a street village built along a former roadway linking settlements to the south of the river with those to the north. The general orientation of the village, hence of the ancient roadway, is slightly oblique with respect to the new road built at the end of the nineteenth century and which crosses the village in a series of 'zigzags'.[25] The passage of the new railway close to the village boundaries blocked any further development towards the north-east.

Positive regional impact in the Fagaras Depression: contrasting geo-historical features of a Transylvanian valley

The Olt valley divides southern Transylvania into two zones: The Hârtibaciu plateau in the north, comprising villages of different morphological types and inhabited by the three different ethnic groups. The area is surrounded by two more economically advanced regions (Sibiu and Braşov), with a road link crossing through the middle, the former Roman road on the right bank of the Olt having been abandoned long ago. The Făgăraş basin (depression) in the south, on the left bank of the Olt, a less economically developed zone, populated by a majority of Romanians (*Districtus Fagaras*). Here, the native people inhabited 'valley villages' built from south to north, following the direction of annual migrations between mountain and plain. This explains the absence of roads linking the villages in an east-west direction. When Transylvania fell under Austrian domination, the authorities decided to build a new road along the left bank of the Olt as part of an overall regional development policy. We still do not know exactly when this road was built. It is not marked on the general map of 1735. We can assume that it was completed some time after 1890, during the second period of modernisation.

To counterbalance the powers of the central authorities, 'Special Commissions' were set up – in Sibiu in 1866 and in Făgăraş in 1889 – to organise the joint construction of a rail link between these two towns using funds obtained through local taxation. The Budapest government reacted swiftly, granting a concession in March 1889 to connect the Sibiu-Făgăraş line not at Braşov, as intended by the two Commissions, but at Homorod, around sixty kilometres before Braşov on line II. This choice was clearly prejudicial to the Romanian populations in the Făgăraş district. For this reason, the scope of debate extended well beyond mere financial considerations, involving the region's different ethnic groups via Romanian and Saxon newspapers produced in Sibiu. In the end, the 'Făgăraş-Avrig Joint Stock Local Railway Company' was set up on September 15, 1891 and the 'Sibiu-Turnu-

---

[25] See *Plan de cadastre de la ville de Mediaş* (1895), échelle 1:1.440, section 5573.

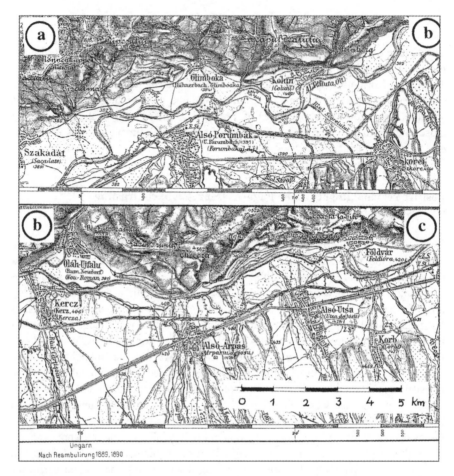

Figure 3.6　Typical railway route in the Olt valley

Source:　　*Plan de cadastre de la ville de Mediaş* (1895), échelle 1:1.440.

Roşu Joint Stock Local Railway Company' was founded on February 22, 1892 to manage the construction of this line (III), together with a connection to Avrig.

The 'zigzag' railway route

Without making an in-depth contextual analysis, a comparison of population trends on either side of the valley shows that after 1890, the former line of force which crossed the Hârtibaciu plateau was progressively replaced. The interior road was abandoned in favour of the new railway and the new road (*Reichstrasse*). This became the new line of force, between Sibiu and Braşov, to the south of the Olt river.

The choice of route along a distance of 51 kilometres between the village of Avrig and the town of Făgăraş (terminus) is rather surprising. Indeed, though the Făgăraş regions is generally flat, the builders chose a zigzag route with 'sudden' transitions, sometimes with a curve radius of less than one-hundred metres, though the site topography did not justify this layout.[26] The main objective was apparently to provide immediate railway access to most of the twelve villages along the track. Indeed, the track appears to literally hug the villages in its embrace! But this route was not chosen simply to please the local inhabitants, few of whom travelled long distances. The true motives were economic, as the railway was a major goods transport route. In order to provide shipment ramps, the stations had to be close to the villages and roads leading to the Carpathian valleys.

The sub-Carpathian zone crossed by this section of railway included many rivers and numerous industrial zones that used water as a source of power: five roller mills, three glassworks, three distilleries and three sawmills. In its issue of August 7, 1889, a Romanian newspaper, *Gazeta de Trasilvania*, lamented that these industries were experiencing major difficulties due to a massive rural exodus and pointed out that the distilleries had closed down completely.[27]

The choice of site for Făgăraş station was based on similar reasoning, its purpose being to serve the region's growing industrial infrastructures. Unlike the situation in Mediaş, where a central station was preferred, Făgăraş station (a terminus at that time) was located not close to the town centre where conditions were ideal, but one kilometre to the south, near a large paper mill.[28] Proof that economic pressures weighed upon the decision-making process?

In conclusion

This article is not a detailed study of Transylvanian railway history. It aims simply to present a few ideas and hypotheses on little-known factors brought to light by studying maps of the regions crossed by the railways. This article produces more questions than answers. One of its main objectives is to draw the attention of researchers in Romania or elsewhere to aspects of railway development which may appear insignificant at first sight, namely its impacts. These realities may shed light on whole new areas of railway development in Transylvania. Because a more in-depth study – taking account of unexplored archives and of cadastral maps – would give a clearer picture of the decision-making process involved in the choice of railway routes and its impacts on rural and urban morphology.

---

[26] Contrary to western standards: wide-radius curves did not exceed 800 metres.
[27] See Radu Bellu, *Mică monografie a căilor ferate din România*, vol. 1: *Regionala Braşov* (Bucarest 1995), 114.
[28] In 1880, the two towns were of similar size: 5307 inhabitants in Făgăraş, 6489 in Mediaş.

CHAPTER FOUR

The advent of transport and aspects of urban modernisation in the Levant during the nineteenth century

Vilma Hastaoglou-Martinidis

During the second half of the nineteenth century a surge of intense activity in railway construction took place in the Levant – a region including today parts of Greece, Turkey, Lebanon, Israel and Egypt. The incorporation of this region to the Western economy resulted in a tremendous increase in trade, which in turn triggered various processes of modernisation. With the advent of the railway came developments in harbour and road building, and other infrastructure facilities. Regions and towns now acquired a modern transport system, which would eventually lead to a radical transformation of the traditional regional and urban context thus reshaping the physiognomy of the Levantine city.

The traditional context: regions and cities before the age of railways

The state of the development of the railway system in 1850 in the Levant stands in stark contrast to the major railway nations. Britain by then had already constructed 9,800 kilometres of track. Likewise, Austria and Hungary had maintained 1,357 kilometres and Italy, another 620 kilometres. By comparison, not a single piece of track had yet been laid down anywhere in the Levant where transportation was still based on the caravans of pack animals traversing the vast interior plains, or on the sailing ships that carried out the coastal trade.[1]

Due to changes in the conditions of agricultural produce, there was a gradual shift of economic activity from the countryside to the port after the mid-eighteenth century. This brought the once entrenched supremacy of the inland cities into direct question and transformed all the important coastal towns into economic centres thus making them *entrepôts* of their vast hinterland. Because of the growing demand for agricultural and raw materials of European industries, port-cities became the focus of the trading activity. Steamers came to the Levant around

---

[1] See Donald Quataert, 'The age of Reforms, 1812–1914', in H. Inalcik and D. Quataert, eds., *An Economic and Social History of the Ottoman Empire, 1300–1914* (Cambridge 1994), 759–823, esp. 804.

1830, and in the next twenty years it became increasingly apparent that the Levantine cities did not possess the transport facilities that they required, thus further emphasising the glaring inadequacy of the existing infrastructure. The shabby piers on the waterfronts of the once great port-cities and the poor condition of heavily used land roads could in no way meet the increasing demands of trade. Ships had to anchor at sea and passengers and goods were conveyed to land by lighters. Frequent accidents occurred due to tides or storms, as for example in Smyrna in 1867 when its wooden piers and shabbily-built warehouses were destroyed, or as in the case of Beirut in 1863 where they caused steamers to run ashore. Long strings of caravans were taking many days to cross the heavily used and unsafe routes in the interior, and, as British consuls stated, in 1863 the bulk of the produce in the vicinity of large cities, such as Salonica, Smyrna or Trabzon, was transported by horses, mules, and donkeys.[2]

In the early nineteenth century, Alexandria was a settlement of 12,000 inhabitants. Located in a unique natural setting, on the fluvial route of the Nile, it occupied the small peninsula of Agami, flanking a double port shaped in two crescents and yet in spite of this ideal location its shores were deserted, and served as a refuge to only a few boats.[3] Smyrna's prominence as a Mediterranean port-city grew from the eighteenth century onwards. However, even by 1854 the city had still not yet developed an adequate infrastructure for transit trade. Its ancient port had long been landfilled and was gradually being taken over by the busy market. The city served more as a relay point in Europe's trade with Asia, and caravans were carrying the produce of the region overland.[4] Constantinople (Istanbul), the leading city of the Mediterranean transit-trade during the Byzantine era, retained its position as the main trade hub for the Black Sea and the Anatolia region during the following Ottoman centuries. However, after the Crimean War the lack of proper transport infrastructure was gravely felt. The city was confined within its walls, and its natural harbour, the *Golden Horn*, was far from satisfying the needs of maritime trade. Enclosed in its walls, on the rocky shore of Saint George bay, Beirut was an insular and inward-looking town with oriental attributes. When the city suddenly witnessed a growth of commerce in the mid-nineteenth century, the port found itself in possession of only a small pier, lighthouse, and a shabby customs house.[5] Salonica (Thessaloniki), was 'suffocating' within its medieval walls until 1869. Even when the growth of trade in Macedonia raised the city to the level of *entrepôt* of the southern Balkans at the beginning of the nineteenth

---

[2] See Smyrna 1863, Consular Commercial Reports, Public Record Office, London. In the following quoted as 'FO, CCR'.

[3] See C. Birault, 'Le port d'Alexandrie. Historique et travaux en cours d'exécution', *Le Génie Civil*, 46, no. 6, 1904, 81–5, esp. 82–3.

[4] According to Italian engineer Storari, charged with the cadastral plan of the city, in Luigi Storari, *Guida di Smirne* (Torino 1857), 28–9; see also Emin Canpolat, *Izmir, kurulusundan bugüne kadar* (Istanbul 1953), 82, and Resat Kasaba, 'Izmir', *Review*, 16, no. 4, 1993, 387–410, esp. 392.

[5] See May Davie, *Beyrouth et ses faubourgs, 1840–1940* (Beyrouth 1996), 19–23.

century, transit trade was still carried out by caravan routes overland and through the small wooden pier outside the sea gate.[6] Until its nomination as the nation's new capital in 1833, Athens was an insignificant fortress, crammed with monuments, and Piraeus, with its ancient Emporium, had long disappeared.[7]

Railways: The new dimensions of geographical mobility

It was these port-cities that led the Levant nations to develop railways. In 1851, the opening of the first section of the railway from Alexandria to Cairo marked the advent of railways in the Levant. In the following year, construction of the Smyrna-Aydin line began signalling the emergence of this novel means of transport in Anatolia. Three years later, a small stretch of railway linking Piraeus to Athens was concrete evidence that this concept had spread in the southern end of the Balkan peninsula.

International geopolitical considerations exerted a most powerful influence. Following the development of their own national railway networks, European countries turned to the expansion of railways eastwards thus making the road to India their next major objective. With the opening of the Suez Canal, the broader Levant area became an arena for two great projects, which were inherently antagonistic to one another. One being a west European railway to Marseilles or Brindisi which would then continue by steamship to the Suez, and the other, a central European one through the Balkans to Istanbul and Baghdad with the provision for an 'exit' to Salonica. However unpredictable the outcome of these antagonisms might have been in the 1870s, the future geopolitical significance of those arteries was all too obvious for the countries in the Levant to ignore.

The concept of technological progress in general and of the railway in particular, was transplanted in the Orient by the Saint-Simonists. In 1832, M. Chevalier, a leading figure of the movement, published his *Système de la Méditerranée*, an ambitious plan for uniting the western and eastern worlds in the Parisian *Globe*. The 'means' for this was to be the railway and he proposed a dense network of railways connecting the West with the most important port-cities and commercial centres of the Mediterranean. The amelioration of maritime transport and the building of large technical works, such as the opening of the Suez Canal, were part of the same scheme. In Egypt and in Greece, members of the group were employed in various projects or staffed state departments.[8]

---

[6] Nikos Svoronos, *The commerce of Salonica in the eighteenth century* (Athens 1996), 384.

[7] Liza Micheli, *Piraeus: From Porto-Leone to Manchester of the Orient* (Athens 1988), 28–58.

[8] For instance, Ferdinand de Lesseps in Suez and Linant de Bellefonds as Minister of Public Works, in the 1860s in Egypt, or G. D'Eichthal and A. Roujoux, in 1835 in Greece. See Gustave D'Eichthal, *Economic and Social Situation in Greece after the*

Egypt is noted for the early development of its railways. The opening of the Suez Canal, that placed the country on the road to India, triggered the construction of an extended rail system. The plan had been under consideration from 1834, but the negotiations were concluded in 1849 and in 1851 Robert Stephenson, son of the inventor of steam-drive, was granted a concession for the line from Alexandria to Suez via Cairo. While the track linking Alexandria to Cairo was completed in 1856, the railway to Suez via Zagazig and Ismaïlia was being made ready for the inauguration of the Canal in 1869. These two developments made up a part of the broader Delta Railways which had been developed by Viceroy Ismaïl and had brought the total distance of track laid to 1,338 kilometres. The Alexandria-Cairo junction was followed by the construction of Upper-Egypt railways. In 1890 this line reached Aswan, in order that it would later be extended to the Sudanese border. By 1905, the whole network comprised some 3,000 kilometres of track. [9]

Figure 4.1　Map of the Levant, by Kiepert, showing the development of the railways and the steamboat routes in 1876

Source:　Private collection.

Revolution (Athens 1974). For the activity of Saint-Simonists in the Orient see Magaly Morsy, *Les Saint-Simoniens et l'Orient* (Aix-en-Provence 1989).

[9] For the Egyptian railways see Robert Ilbert, *Alexandrie, 1830–1930* (Le Caire 1996), 35; Alexandria, 1872–73, Consular Reports, Public Record Office, London. In the following quoted as 'FO, CR'. See also Henri Lorin, *L'Egypte aujourd'hui. Le pays et les hommes* (Cairo 1926), 170–1.

The rail-building period in the Anatolian and European provinces of the Ottoman Empire started just after the Crimean War. Already in 1854, the Council of Tanzimat, expressing the political will for reforms, was favourably impressed by the economic future promised by railways.[10] From 1857 onwards, Smyrna became the railhead of the first two rail tracks in western Anatolia. The works of the Smyrna-Aydin 129 kilometres line began in 1857 financed by French capital and by 1890 it was further extended 248 kilometres to Dinar and Çivril.[11] The Smyrna-Kasaba 93 kilometres line began in 1863 and completed in 1866 by British capital, was extended to Alasehir in 1875, now totalling 168 kilometres, with a branch to Bournabat.[12]

The *Société des Chemins de fer d'Anatolie*, established with German capital in 1888, submitted a project for the extension of the Haydar Pasha-Izmid Railway via Ankara to Baghdad. By 1893, the line to Ankara, with a total length of 575 kilometres, was completed, and was soon extended to Konya and later to Bulgurlu. In 1908, the entire Anatolian network encompassed 2,359 kilometres.[13] The rail connection linking the Bosphorus to the Persian Gulf was one of the most ambitious projects of the Sublime Porte, attracting the interest of statesmen and entrepreneurs for its commercial, political, and strategic importance. However, the implementation of the project was to be delayed due to British and French diplomatic manoeuvres and the route did not reach Baghdad until the Balkan Wars.[14]

The construction of the first railway line in the European provinces of the Empire was granted in 1869, to the *Société des Chemins de fer Orientaux*, the company of the Belgian banker, Baron Maurice de Hirsch, with Austrian, British, French and Belgian capital. From 1871 a 355 kilometres line connected Istanbul to Adrianople (Edirne) and to the border, while in 1872 another 148 kilometres track assured the exit of Adrianople to the Aegean shore, at Dedeagatch (Alexandroupolis). In 1874 the line was extended from Adrianople to Sofia, with a branch to Yamboli. It was the greatest of the Balkan lines and part of the wider plan covering the European provinces of the Empire, to ensure the link with the

---

[10] Donald Quataert, 'The age of Reforms, 1812–1914', in H. Inalcik and D. Quataert, eds., *An Economic and Social History of the Ottoman Empire, 1300–1914* (Cambridge 1994), 759–823, esp. 805.

[11] Smyrna 1864, FO, CR, and Smyrna 1889, FO, CCR.

[12] Smyrna 1874, FO, CR.

[13] Between 1871 and 1873 the Haydar Pasha-Izmid 91 kilometres line was opened. It was incorporated after 1888 into the project for the Baghdad railway. See Ar. Mouratoglous, 'The railways in Asia Minor', *Archimides*, no. 9, 1908, 56–8, esp. 58, and Louis Godard, 'Les chemins de fer en Turquie', *Le Génie Civil*, 55, no. 12–14, July 3, 1909, 189–93, esp. 190.

[14] Since the first manifestation of international interest for this line by a British company in 1851, various projects have been successively submitted for the routing of the artery such as the plans by the German engineer Wilhelm von Pressel, by the Briton Chesney, or the Russian Kapnist. See Ar. Mouratoglous, 'The railways in Asia Minor', *Archimides*, no. 10, 1908, 105–9, esp. 108.

central European network. In 1869, the project was granted to the company of the Belgian banker, Baron Maurice de Hirsch, with Austrian, British, French and Belgian capital. Forming part of the same project, between 1871 and 1874 a second track of 362 kilometres linked the major seaport of Salonica to Mitrovitsa and the Balkan hinterland. In 1888 the line was connected to the Serbian network thus providing Salonica with direct access to Europe.[15] By 1892 another 218 kilometres line was built from Salonica to Monastir (Bitola) with German capital. Lastly, French capital financed the construction from 1893 to 1896 of the 512 kilometres *Jonction Salonique-Constantinople* via Dedeagatch and by 1909 the European Turkey network totalled 1,682 kilometres, with Salonica as the railhead of three lines.[16]

In the Syrian provinces, the construction of land roads preceded the advent of railways. In 1863 the *Compagnie impériale ottomane des diligences* had completed the only carriageway in Syria, known as the new Beirut-Damas road. This company was owned by Count de Perthuis, a prominent French entrepreneur of Beirut.[17]

In 1878, the arrival of Midhat Pasha as Governor-General of Syria nourished the hopes for a railway project. Well known for his commitment to the reform of the Empire, Midhat favoured a rail plan connecting Beirut to Damas and from there to Tripoli and Aleppo as well as to the Euphrates railway.[18] Yet, due to the insurmountable obstacle of the range of Mount Lebanon, the plan had to be postponed until 1891. That year the concession to build the Damas railway, 147 kilometres in length with Beirut as the railhead, was eventually granted to another of Perthuis's companies. Construction was finally completed in 1895. The Damas-Hawran section of 101 kilometres had opened in 1894, and two years later a regional service of the *Tramway Libanais* began operating over the 19 kilometres between Beirut and Jbail. By 1908, the railway network was extended to 847 kilometres, connecting the port-cities of Jaffa, Haiffa, Beirut and Tripoli to the inland towns of Jerusalem, Dera, Damas, Rayaq, Homs, Hama, and Aleppo. Another 1,320 kilometres line of the Hejaz railways connected Damas to Medina in the Arabian Peninsula.[19]

---

[15] The detailed account of the enterprise is given by Vahdettin Engin, *Rumeli demiryollari* (Istanbul 1993), and Dimitrios Papadimitriou and Christos Kalemkeris, *The trains in Northern Greece* (Thessaloniki 2000).

[16] Louis Godard, 'Les chemins de fer en Turquie', *Le Génie Civil*, 55, no. 12–14, July 3, 1909, 189–93, esp. 190.

[17] Beirut, 1880, FO, CR.

[18] Beirut, 1878, FO, CR.

[19] For the Syrian railways see Jens Hansen, 'Ottomanizing Beirut under Sultan Abdülhamid II, 1876–1909', in P. Rowe and H. Sarkis, eds., *Projecting Beirut* (New York 1998), 41–67, esp. 48, and Beyrouth, vol. 12, 1896, Correspondence Consulaire Commerciale, Archives du Ministère des Affaires Etrangères, France. In the following quoted as 'CCC'. See also Louis Godard, 'Les chemins de fer en Turquie', *Le Génie Civil*, 55, no. 12–14, July 3, 1909, 189–93, esp. 190.

The concept of railways had been introduced into the Greek state by the Frenchman Feraldi in 1835, only a few years after the proclamation of national independence. Yet, it would not be until 1869 that the new capital would be connected to its seaport, Piraeus, by a mere 8.5 kilometres stretch of rail. The activity restarted in 1882, when contracts for the construction of 700 kilometres were signed. By 1890 three lines were opened, one was a line of 417 kilometres connecting Athens with the north shore of the Peloponnese, while another 67 kilometres line connected the capital with the mining town of Lavrion. The third line of 202 kilometres constituted the local network of the grain-producing region of Thessaly with the small seaport of Volos as the railhead. In 1907 the railway plan was completed and a new 441 kilometres track from Athens to the north border made the nation's capital the central junction of the system. Thus, in 1910 the Greek railway network was a total of 1,600 kilometres in length.[20]

Despite their modest proportions compared to those of major railway countries of the West, these railway systems had a tremendous impact on the development of the regions and cities they served. It was not accidental that some of the major technical projects such as road construction, bridges, irrigation plans etc., were undertaken and even implemented during that period.[21]

On a regional level, railways reshaped the commercial map of the area. They channelled all import and export trade, as well as passenger traffic, to their railhead towns, which were mainly major ports. The shifting of the balance from the interior to the coastline resulted in the increasing concentration of population and activities in the littoral, which in turn greatly stimulated the economic and demographic growth of coastal cities, attracting people of various ethnic, religious and regional origins.

The building of the Balkan and Anatolian railways established Istanbul as the central point of the most strategic artery of the Empire, connecting central Anatolia to Europe. The *Orient Express*, operating since 1883, linked Istanbul to the Western world. The concentration of factories, banks, and trade firms in the city after 1870 was hardly coincidental. Of the 282 manufacturing establishments counted in the 1913 census, 155 were in Istanbul.[22] The rail link between Alexandria and Cairo brought about a radical change in the significance of this port, and rendered it as the focal point on the route to India. The traffic in its harbour increased enormously and soon works were undertaken for its modernisation. Both the new harbour and the railway gave Alexandria an edge over the rivalling port-cities of Damietta and Rosetta in capturing the trade of the hinterland, a hegemony the city maintained until well into the twentieth century.

---

[20] AFR, *The Greek Railways* (Athens without date), 176–230.

[21] By the end of the nineteenth century important irrigation works had been undertaken in the plains of Maritza (Evros), Meander and Ermos (Gediz) around Smyrna, and Adana, or the drainage of El-Amouk plain near Antioch, and the landfill of swamps in Alexandretta. See Louis Godard, 'L'irrigation en Turquie', *Le Génie Civil*, 56, no. 15, February 12, 1910, 282–5, esp. 282.

[22] See Resat Kasaba, 'Izmir', *Review*, 16, no. 4, 1993, 387–410, esp. 405.

Salonica soon evolved into being the major outlet in the southern Balkans for the entire Macedonian region. The railhead of three lines, it soon drained the economic activity of other provincial centres in its vicinity, such as Serres or Adrianople. The city experienced a remarkable burst of factory building covering practically the whole range of manufacturing sectors.[23] Smyrna's predominance in the Euro-Asian trade dated from the mid-nineteenth century. It was a leading port for exports in the Ottoman Empire, second only to Istanbul in imports, as well as in industrial activity. Its population grew with people of various ethnic and religious origins, among which the members of the Greek community held a considerable part of trade and manufacturing.[24] The construction of the Beirut-Damas road established the mid-nineteenth century Beirut as the unrivalled port-city and the major *entrepôt* of the Syrian coast. The city soon became the diplomatic capital of Syria, attracting a strong body of consular establishments.[25] After the opening of the Corinth Canal

Table 4.1   The evolution of population in Levantine cities

	1821	1838	1848	1865	1882	1897	1907
Alexandria	13,000	60,000	104,000	180,000	232,000	319,800	403,000
Cairo	263,000	n.a.	256,700	n.a.	374,800	570,000	791,000
Beirut	8,000	15,000	27,500	60,000	80,000	120,000	150,000
Istanbul	359,000	n.a.	390,000	n.a.	546,000	1,100,000	1,203,000
Smyrna	120,000	130,000	130,000	156,500	187,000	230,000	275,000
Salonica	40,000	40,000	50,000	80,000	120,000	150,000	160,000
Piraeus	-	1,011	5,300	8,500	21,000	50,200	73,000
Athens	9,000	16,600	26,300	43,000	84,900	123,000	167,500

n.a.: not available

Source: The figures of the table are drawn from the following sources: For Alexandria, see Robert Ilbert, *Alexandrie, 1830–1930* (Le Caire 1996), 758. For Cairo, see Jean-Luc Arnaud, *Le Caire; mise en place d'une ville moderne* (Arles 1998), 20. For Beirut, see May Davie, *Beyrouth et ses faubourgs, 1840–1940* (Beyrouth 1996), 141. For Istanbul, see Tekeli Ilhan, *The Development of the Istanbul Metropolitan Area: Urban Administration and Planning* (Istanbul 1994), 1–47, passim. For Smyrna, see Charles Issawi, *The Economic History of Turkey, 1800–1914* (Chicago 1980), 34, and Resat Kasaba, 'Izmir', *Review*, 16, no. 4, 1993, 387–410, esp. 387. For Salonica, see Basil Gounaris, 'Salonica', *Review*, 16, no. 4, 1993, 499–518, esp. 500–1. For Piraeus and Athens, see Lila Leontidou, *Cities of Silence. Working-class colonization of urban space, Athens and Piraeus 1909–1940* (Athens 1989), 48.

---

[23] See Basil Gounaris, 'Salonica', *Review*, 16, no. 4, 1993, 499–518, esp. 507–8.
[24] See Ilhan Tekeli, 'The transformation in the settlement pattern of the Aegean region in the nineteenth century', in *Three Ages of Izmir* (Istanbul 1993), 125–41, esp. 130.
[25] See Eyüp Y. Özveren, 'Beirut', *Review*, 16, no. 4, 1993, 467–97, esp. 475.

had altered the shipping routes in 1893, Piraeus would, seven years later in 1900, become the major port of Greece, and a truly industrial city with a total of 114 factories. After its rail connection to the mainland, it drained much of the manufacturing activity from the provincial centres of Patras and Volos.[26]

As a direct result of the development of the railway, small settlements gained new importance and experienced demographic and economic growth. In Greece, the rail network forced a new regional hierarchy of economic activities, which in turn resulted in the decline of some traditional local centres, such as Tripoli in the central Peloponnese, and the rise of newer ones, such as Patras and Volos. On the Syrian littoral, Tripoli regained its economic strength, and Haiffa emerged as the port of Palestine.[27] The small network of the Smyrna railways cutting across the most fertile parts of the region developed the productive sources of the Vilayet of Aydin, and brought serious changes in the settlement pattern.[28] Newly-emerging towns such as Ismaïlia, Suez, and Port-Saïd owed their creation to the opening of the Suez Canal. Another clear example of this is the new town of Dedeagatch in Thrace which was founded in 1872 by the railway company as the maritime port of Adrianople and was populated by the merchants of the surrounding area.

Railways and harbours, a joint enterprise

As major coastal cities, échelles or entrepôts, became the heads of the railway network linking inland regions to the coast, the modernisation of their ports became imperative. For those cities whose economic prospects were connected to sea trade, harbour works flourished afterwards, and soon matched, the development of railway building. The 'ground' had been prepared as a result of certain prerequisite infrastructural improvements. According to the contract signed with the Hirsh Company, in order to ensure the efficient operation of the Balkan rail network which would in turn lead to the development of agriculture and trade, the Ottoman government was obliged to develop connecting roads, as well as to build harbour facilities in the ports of Salonica, Dedeagatch, and Varna.[29]

Pressing the governments for improvements, the consuls of European powers intervened in favour of navigation companies, trading firms, banks, and contractors, for which railway building and harbour works represented a source of considerable profits. Local merchants frequently played a decisive role, undertaking initiatives for the improvement of docks and roads for transit trade. In Beirut, when the issue of a railway to Damas was initially raised in 1878, the inhabitants were presented with the offer to participate in the construction cost for

---

[26] See Marianthi Kotea, 'The industrial zone of Piraeus, 1860–1900', in Chr. Loukos, ed., *The city in the modern era* (Athens 2000), 115–123, esp. 118–19.

[27] See Eyüp Y. Özveren, 'Beirut', *Review*, 16, no. 4, 1993, 467–97, esp. 481.

[28] See Smyrna 1889, FO, CCR, and Tekeli, 'The transformation', 138–41.

[29] Anonymous, *Actes de la concession des chemins de fer de la Turquie d'Europe* (Constantinople 1874).

the opening of an eight kilometres tunnel under *Mount Lebanon*.[30] In 1869 the merchants of Alexandria decided on paying a voluntary tax on export goods so as to generate revenue for paving the streets in the quarters where their warehouses were situated.[31] In some cases, the newly-established municipal authorities in Alexandria, Salonica, Beirut, Piraeus etc. tried to obtain the management of such projects.

The competition for the construction of transport infrastructure ignited antagonisms between the west European countries and their contracting firms. While British and German companies fought for the concession of railways, harbour works were virtually monopolised by French contractors. All of these had secured long-term concessions and special follow-up privileges, particularly in the Ottoman Empire.

The building of modern harbour facilities was the constant concern of the princes in Alexandria. Supported by the local elite, their goal was finally achieved only after the 'cotton boom'. The work was granted in 1869 to the London firm *William Bruce Greenfield & Co* and by 1880 the new harbour encompassing 2.7 kilometres of docks was ready. The harbour of Smyrna was the first and most successful in the Ottoman Empire. It was built between 1869 and 1875 by *Joseph et Élie Dussaud Frères*, a French contracting company with extensive experience in France and abroad. Their work included the construction of a quay 3.5 kilometres in length along the old sea front and two well-protected wharves. In Beirut, a concession was issued in 1888 to the society set up by the French shareholders of the Beirut-Damas Road Company. Their construction of modern docks was completed in 1895 with a 1,000 metres long sea front. In Istanbul, harbour works were begun in 1891 and completed by 1900 by the French company of Marius Michel Pasha, the Empire's General Administrator of Lighthouses. The new docks were distributed along 1,160 metres on either side of the *Golden Horn*. In 1900, a German company subsidiary of the railways was granted the concession for the harbour works at Haydar Pasha (in Skutari) which was the railhead of the Anatolian railways. The project was implemented by 1903 and the new railway station was built between 1905 and 1909. In Salonica, harbour works started in 1869, with the construction of a linear quay along the old sea front. However, this quay rapidly proved inadequate and the construction of a proper harbour was granted in 1896 to Edmond Bartissol, a public work contractor and former Member of Parliament from Paris. The new seaport of Piraeus was laid out in 1834 with no provision for adequate harbour facilities. The development of its harbour was undertaken by the port Fund and the municipality and by 1907 it had encompassed docks of 4,000 metres in length, moles and a navy yard. It was connected by rail to Athens in 1869 and to the rest of the country after 1880.[32]

---

[30]   Beirut 1878, FO, CR.

[31]   Alexandria 1878, FO, CR.

[32]   A detailed account of harbour works in the Levantine cities is given in my two articles, Vilma Hastaoglou-Martinidis, 'Les villes-ports du bassin oriental de la Méditerranée à la fin du XIXe siècle: travaux portuaires et transformations urbaines', in C. Vallat, ed.,

Minor cities soon followed suit in the building of harbours. According to the agreement between the Oriental Railway Company and the Sublime Porte, projects for the harbours of Dedeagatch and Varna were immediately put forward. From 1873 onwards in Dedeagatch, projects were drawn for the harbour by L. Dussaud, the contractor of the Smyrna quay, by Aslan, in 1890, and eventually by Conrad Schokke in 1910. For the port of Varna, the main outlet of the Principality of Bulgaria in the Black Sea region, successive projects were produced by Hilarion Pascal, in 1873, by Sir Charles Hartley in 1890, and by Auguste Guérard, in 1894. The works started after 1895.

In 1873, the project for the harbour of Patras was assigned to H. Pascal. The works were started in 1881 and delivered in 1894 after the laying down of the Peloponnese rail network was implemented. The projects for the harbours of Samsoun and Trabzon were granted between 1908 and 1909, while in Jaffa, the task was undertaken consecutively by A. Guérard, E. Fancy, and Amat.[33]

However, these initiatives did not evolve smoothly. The new railways and quays eliminated traditional jobs and work sites, and entailed an increase in transportation costs. When railways and trams were installed on the quays in Smyrna, Salonica, and in Beirut, hundreds of porters lost their jobs, and their guilds repeatedly halted commerce.[34] The *guerre des tarifs* launched by lightermen, navigation companies and merchants in Smyrna and Istanbul soon after the new quays were opened, has been repeatedly quoted.[35] The opposition to expropriations by individual landowners often caused significant delays to construction works as well as alterations to the original plans such as in Istanbul and Smyrna.[36] In Istanbul, the routing of the railway along the shore of Marmara, occasioned the conflict of interests between the tramway and railway companies.[37] Nevertheless, the advantages of new transport means soon prevailed, and commercial movement increased so much that in the beginning of the twentieth century, new extensions of railway lines and harbour facilities were required.

On the other hand, the new infrastructures were hailed by the political and commercial milieu of the cities. Solemn ceremonies, open to the public, were organised for their inauguration and were attended by state officials, contractors, press representatives, diplomats and members of the financial world. These events became an important vehicle for the authorities to convincingly and effectively demonstrate their image of a modern city as well as strengthening the bonds

---

Petites et grandes villes du bassin méditerranéen (Roma 1999), 507–25, and Vilma Hastaoglou-Martinidis, 'The harbour of Thessaloniki, 1896–1920', in A. Jarvis and K. Smith, eds., *Albert Dock: Trade and Technology* (Liverpool 1999), 133–41.

[33] Data drawn from my on-going research on the Levantine ports, under preparation.

[34] See Donald Quataert, 'Workers, peasants and economic change in the Ottoman Empire, 1730–1914', in H. Batu and J. L. Bacqué-Grammont, eds., *L'Empire Ottoman, la République de Turquie et la France* (Istanbul 1986), 159–73.

[35] Smyrna, 1871, FO, CR, and Smyrna, 1877–1881, FO, CR.

[36] See Charles Issawi, *The Economic History of Turkey, 1800–1914* (Chicago 1980), 167, and Smyrne, vol. 51, CCC.

[37] *La Turquie*, February 3, 1871.

between the state and local elite and easing public opinion into accepting European innovations and interests.[38]

Urban transformations

Coastal cities now well equipped with modern harbour facilities coupled with being heads of an expanding railway network made them the centre of economic activity in their provinces. By the end of the nineteenth century, they changed from serving as a commercial *entrepôt* of their hinterland and became in many ways what Braudel called 'dominant cities', imposing themselves economically, politically, socially, and culturally on the region.

Under the double impact of the changes in transport, these urban centres soon altered their status from being merely railway relays or ports to being proper cities in their own right with their own rhythms and demands for modern amenities. The sustenance and renewal of the urban space gradually became a driving force of economic development. The cities witnessed a systematic and pervasive implementation of urban management, including the enforcement of laws and regulations, and the establishment of municipal, commercial and health councils. This emergence of a consciousness and a will for modernising the parochial city, was much reflected in the initiatives and projects undertaken by local authorities in the following years.

The positioning of modern transport infrastructures in the traditional fabric of the Levantine cities followed more or less uniform patterns. Railway terminals were all placed on the old access-points of land roads, in the vicinity of the port. These points were usually located on the perimeter of the old nucleus where land was available, or within the urban fabric so as to be in direct contact with the business centre, the market and the burgeoning industrial quarters.

In Alexandria, the first railway terminus was located in 1856, in the very heart of the business quarter of Gabari and mainly served the harbour's needs while in 1876, a passenger station was erected in Bab al-Jadid, serving the expanding eastern residential districts. In Stamboul, the railway terminal was conveniently placed by the docks of Sirkeci and the busy traditional markets of Eminonü. In Piraeus, the central location of the terminal caused the city to be divided into two parts: one being the industrial quarter in the north and the other, the residential quarters along with commercial and shipping facilities in the south. In Salonica, Adrianople and Smyrna, terminals were located on the outskirts. Smyrna had two terminals, one for the Aydin and another for the Kasaba Railways. They were both

---

[38]   Detailed records of events held for the opening of railways lines, stations or the foundation of modern quays were abundant in the press of the time. See for instance *The Levant Times and Shipping Gazette*, June 11, 1870, *The Levant Herland*, issues of June 7, 1874, and January 18, 1875, and *Neologos*, October 23, 1890.

In order to accommodate modern transportation systems and to facilitate communication, the demolition of medieval walls became imperative. In Salonica, the installation of railways on the western side of the city and the construction of the quay required the demolition of the sea wall in 1869 and later in 1890, large sections of the side walls. The Genoese walls of Galata were pulled down in 1863 while in Stamboul the Byzantine walls were pierced in many spots to allow the passing through of the railway in the early 1870s.[39] In Beirut, the demolition of the walls began in the 1850s when the Ottoman barracks and military hospital were erected. The old castle and seaside fortification eventually gave way to the demands of the new harbour and by the 1880s the city walls no longer existed.[40] In Alexandria, demolition of the Arab enclosure on its north side began in 1855 and continued with the pulling down of the west side by 1868 to assure the connection

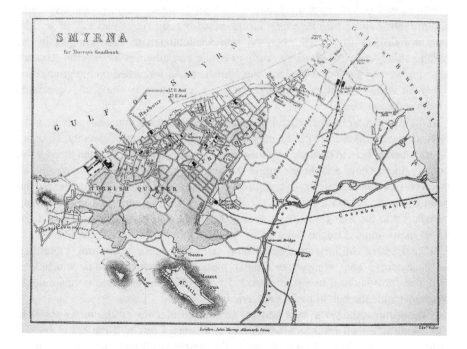

Figure 4.2 The city of Smyrna in 1878
(the new quay and the building of the railways are delimiting the area for the future expansion of urban space)

Source: Murray's Handbook for travellers in Turkey in Asia, 1878.

---

[39] See Zeynep Çelik, *The Remaking of Istanbul: Portrait of an Ottoman City in the Nineteenth Century* (Berkeley 1993), 70, and *La Turquie*, February 3, 1871.
[40] May Davie, *Beyrouth et ses faubourgs, 1840–1940* (Beyrouth 1996), 35–7.

with the port and Gabari district. In 1876, the south wall was pierced for the installation of the new passenger terminal and would later be entirely demolished by 1902.[41]

Thus, after long centuries of enclosure, the Levantine cities burst forth from the limits prescribed by their walls to widen and spread out of their traditional nuclei. Railway terminals acted as focal points defining the guidelines for the expansion of the city. They restructured the inherited urban patterns and reordered urban functions. Manufacturing workshops and factories were attracted to the vicinity of railway terminals and new docks. Examples of this are Alexandria where the railway terminal and the new docks transformed the area of Gabari into an industrial quarter, Salonica where the western extension near the railway station and the harbour was developed into an industrial zone and Piraeus where the area North of the railway station was turned into a workers' residential district.

The areas gained from the demolition of walls were used for widening roads and providing space for modern buildings, housing projects, or parks. This was the case in Salonica after 1890 when the new residential zone was arranged in the eastern side for wealthy families from all ethnic communities of the city. Another example are the parks and gardens (the Nouzha park) fashioned on the grounds of the south walls that helped create Alexandria's reputation as one of the 'greenest' Mediterranean cities.

Old quarters were re-arranged in regular street patterns and new arteries were opened to connect them with the major communication points of the city. Housing developments were in demand by those new inhabitants attracted to the area by the railway, the harbour and the growth of trade at large. New civic places were being created. In Alexandria, the remodelling of the famous Consuls' Square by the Saint-Simonist Joseph Cordier in 1860 gradually led the centre of gravity being transferred to the triangle between the square, the Cairo passenger station and the 4,000 metre long corniche built along the east port by the municipality between 1901 and 1907.[42] In Smyrna, the new land gained along the waterfront (more than forty hectares) was arranged in regular plots. Its northern section, which was excluded form harbour use, soon attracted fashionable residences, theatres, hotels, etc., to become the hub of social and civic life.[43]

These transformations were boosted by the introduction of the tramways as a new mode of urban transport, which had a distinctly modernising effect on the urban landscape. Pulled by horses in the beginning, and electrified by the early twentieth century, they contributed to the regularisation of the tortuous street pattern as well as to the continuity and densification of the urban fabric. They also connected distant suburbs to the city centre and brought about the creation of new

---

[41] Robert Ilbert, *Alexandrie, 1830–1930* (Le Caire 1996), 325.

[42] See M. F. Awad, 'Le modèle européen: l'évolution urbaine de 1807 à 1958', *Revue de l'Occident Musulman et de la Méditerranée*, 46, 1987, 93–109, esp. 96–8.

[43] An extended account of the building of the Smyrna quay is given by Mübahat Kütükoglu, 'Izmir rihtimi insaati ve isletme imtiyazi', *Tarih Dergisi*, 32, no. 3, 1979, 495–558.

residential districts, associated mainly with the thriving new urban strata. For the passing of tramways through the narrow lanes of the densely built fabric, radical measures were applied and streets were widened and aligned. In Istanbul, all the streets through which the tramway passed were greatly improved and the cost of expropriating housing property and of paving the streets fell entirely on the Tramway Company.[44] By the time Beirut's electric tramway had opened in 1909 many streets had already been aligned, paved, and widened alongside the rails.

By the beginning of the twentieth century, tramways were operated in all major cities, passing along wide avenues and covering almost the entire urban space. In Istanbul, from 1872, two lines traversed the narrow lanes, one in Stamboul and another in Galata and by 1912 there were five tramway lines, three in Stamboul and two in Galata. In Alexandria a narrow gauge train line was operating from 1865 for the emerging resort suburb of Ramleh and by 1902 the tramway system served the entire urban area. In Cairo, tramways started to operate in the 1890s. By 1905 the total length of the network covered 43 kilometres entailing a spectacular expansion of the residential areas. In 1909, the city of Smyrna introduced electro-motion in the existing two horse-drawn tramway lines. In Beirut, an electrified tramway system of five lines was built between 1898 and 1909. In Salonica, the inauguration of a ten kilometres tramway system took place in 1893. In 1882, an extended animal-tracked tramway network connected the centre of Athens to Piraeus and the distant residential quarters and suburbs. Between 1906 and 1909, electrification was introduced for the 21 lines.[45]

All those changes propelled an unprecedented expansion of urban space. Between 1850 and 1880 the surface area of Alexandria was almost quintupled from 120 to 500 hectares, and its population, a unique cosmopolitan mixture from every Mediterranean region, rose to 230,000 inhabitants. In Salonica, the extramural extensions of urban space had, by the 1890s, added an area of 150 hectares to the old nucleus (320 hectares). In the late nineteenth century Beirut, the new town with its modern houses, carriage roads, and gardens, colleges, schools and hotels was scattered within a radius of a mile and a half around the medieval nucleus. In Smyrna, the unbuilt areas between the railway lines and the mid-century urban perimeter were completely covered by modern residential extensions by the 1910s and the surface area of the city had grown from 190 to circa 400 hectares.[46]

These spectacular transformations were doubled by further initiatives for the improvement of urban living, such as street paving and lighting, sewage and water lines that were undertaken by the municipal services. Prestigious railway stations

---

[44] Constantinople, 1881–82, FO, CR.

[45] See for Istanbul Joanne Guide, *De Paris à Constantinople. Hongrie-Balkans-Asie Mineure* (Paris 1912), 192; for Alexandria see Robert Ilbert, *Alexandrie, 1830–1930* (Le Caire 1996), 345–6; for Cairo Jean-Luc Arnaud, *Le Caire; mise en place d'une ville moderne* (Arles 1998), 283; for Smyrna see Smyrne, 1909, CCC; for Beirut see Hansen, 'Ottomanizing', 51; for Salonica see Salonica 1891–92, FO, CR, and for Athens see AFR, *The Greek Railways* (Athens without date), 50–74.

[46] See Ilbert, ibid., 172–3, and Beirut, 1871, FO, CR.

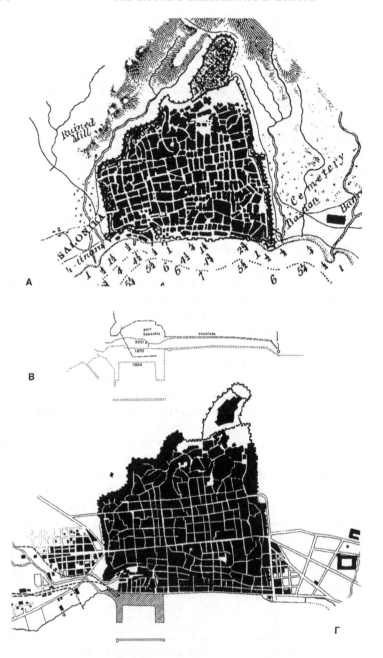

Figure 4.3 The transformation of Salonica between 1850 and 1900

Source: Established by the author after various sources.

and massive custom houses were erected such as the Sirkeci Station designed by the German architect Jachmund in 1890, and that of Haydar Pasha by Helmut Cuno and Otto Ritter in 1910. The construction of the Gabari station in Alexandria in 1856 was the work of the British architect Edward Baines and in Salonica the railway station was built in 1894 according to the plan of the Italian architect Pietro Arigoni. Its style was used for the terminal buildings in Adrianople and Skopje. These new types of buildings introduced and disseminated the use of concrete and iron structures in the building of the city. A fact worth noting is that by 1910 the *Bureau Technique* of François Hennebique, the concrete patent-holder from Paris, held regional agencies with associate concessionaires in Istanbul, Smyrna, Salonica, Athens, and Cairo.[47] The concept was soon taken over in the subsequent construction of new bank and office buildings, manufacturing premises, department stores, apartment buildings, modern hotels, etc., thus producing a renewed urban environment which matched the demands of international transactions. Although traditional trades persisted in the souks and bazaars in the old nuclei, because the urban landscape was radically transformed, they now served as the residence of the poorer classes. The centre of gravity shifted irrevocably to the renewed areas of the city, the new quays, civic and business places and residential quarters that had little or nothing of the oriental in their composition.

The advent of modern transport acted as a major catalyst in the nineteenth century Levantine cities, transforming them radically within just a few decades. Introvert cities that centred around their vital centre – the market – let their ancient quays and roads slip into decay. Their urban spaces evolved slowly over time due to their sluggishness in assimilating economic demands and changes caused by both nature and war disasters.

The building of railways and new harbours reversed this situation. It opened up cities to the world and new eras and endowed them with spaces for exchanges with the Occident. The modern railway facilities and quays, symbols of the Levantine cities' incorporation into the world of international trade, were the principal locus for the intermingling of 'self-contained' ethnic groups and the creation of new – economically determined – hierarchies. It was the first time in their recent history that the cities of the eastern Mediterranean expanded their space to such a great extent and this through a construction process that surpassed the individual initiatives taken by ethnic communities, to be raised to the level of public utility.

Instruments of change that brought to the fore new protagonists, the railway and the harbour became nodal points for the restructuring of the urban space. Their operation created new areas of concentration for industry, services and markets, and soon brought about new expansions in the city. As singular urban creations as well as 'devices' of development, the railway and the harbour introduced novel planning and architectural models: an early form of zoning with specialised functions and rational organisation of the site, contracting the surrounding

---

[47]   *Le Béton armé*, 150, no. 11, 1910.

traditional fabric; and a new architectural aesthetic and modern construction technology, both of which influenced the conception of the buildings within the city. In the beginning of the twentieth century the modern identity of the eastern Mediterranean city was solidly established.

CHAPTER FIVE

The impact of the Trans-Siberian Railway on the architecture and urban planning of Siberian cities

Ivan V. Nevzgodine

The oldest historical construction in Novosibirsk, the capital of Siberia, was demolished at the turn of the century. It was the railway bridge over the Ob' river. Only one truss of it was preserved and placed at the waterfront as a reminder of the year 1893, the date of the start of the bridge construction, which Novosibirsk celebrates as its official year of birth. Standing today in this contemporary city of one and a half million inhabitants, it is difficult to imagine that one hundred years ago, its main avenue, *Krasnii prospect*, was just a glade through a forest of ancient pines.

The first idea of constructing a railway through Siberia dates from the 1830s. By this time, the Moscow-Siberian Post Track, which came into existence in the middle of the eighteenth century, obviously lacked the capacity for the increasing flow of goods. As a result of this situation, numerous projects were proposed for different railway routes in Siberia. These plans were mostly based on economic reasons. Although the government refused them all, it was itself too slow to begin construction partly because of the lack of information about the region. On the other hand, the idea of constructing a railway in Siberia generated a spurt of topographical, geological and climatic investigation.[1] From 1887 to 1890 the Russian Imperial Technical Society was involved in investigation and discussions. This society formed a special 'Commission on the question about a railway through all Siberia'.

It was customary at that time to compare Siberia with Northern America. As regards to the railway construction itself, the conditions were undoubtedly comparable. Because of this similarity, Russian railway engineers had been sent on study trips to the USA and Canada in the 1880s. One of them, engineer Nikolai P. Mezheninov, directed the construction of the mid-Siberian section of the Trans-

---

[1] From 1857 till 1894 merely in Siberian periodicals about one thousand articles and correspondences about Trans-Siberian Railway were published. See the bibliography of 'The Railway Question of Siberia' drawn up by the librarian of the Museum of the Tobol'sk province S. N. Mameev, *Bibliografiia zheleznodorozhnogo voprosa Sibiri* (Tobol'sk 1895).

Siberian Railway (*Transsibirskaia Zheleznodorozhnaia Magistral'*, Transsib). The American method of light rails and the economical use of wood construction were just a few of the measures taken and implemented in the building of the *Transsib*.[2]

The final decision to construct the *Transsib* under the treasury of the government was made at the end of the nineteenth century. Two politicians, Sergey Yu. Witte and Petr A. Stolypin played leading roles in influencing this decision and effecting its realisation.[3] However, it did not arise from economic considerations, but was rather a consequence of the international policy and military strategy of the Russian Empire. Because of the political situation in the Far East, Russia needed facilities for the quick transportation of its army to the eastern border of the Empire. In addition to this, there were other considerations such as the ability to reach the wealth of Siberia and the establishment of an extensive market with China.[4] The military purpose was obvious even in the chosen route of the railway. The choice was made for the simplest and cheapest route and although this may seem incredible it was precisely for that reason the railway did not come to the old Siberian capital of Tomsk.

It is remarkable that the chronology of the industrial revolution in Russia was so different from that of Europe. In the latter, the revolution in the textile industry led to an explosion in the heavy industry sector that in turn necessitated changes in transportation and communications. In Central European Russia however, it was just the reverse. In the 1860s the construction of the railways stimulated both the establishment of heavy industry and the first stage of the industrial revolution in the 1870s. In one of his speeches Petr Stolypin, the Chief-Minister of the Russian government said: 'In other countries the construction of the railways started, when the elaborated networks of unpaved and high roads already existed; in our case we

---

[2] The railway engineer Nikolai Pavlovich Mezheninov (1838–1915) graduated from St. Petersburg Institute of Transport Engineers. About the application of the North-American experience in the *Transsib* construction see the well documented article of S. K. Kann, 'Opyt zheleznodorozhnogo stroitel'stva v Amerike i proektirovanie Transsiba (The experience of the railway construction in America and design of the Transsib)', in L. M. Goriushkin, ed., *Zarubezhnye ekonomicheskie i kulturnye sviazi Sibiri (XVIII–XXvv.)* (Novosibirsk 1995), 114–36.

[3] Sergey Yul'evich Witte (1849–1915) being a Minister of Roads and Transportation and later Minister of Finance of the Russian government proposed dramatic reforms which would accelerate the industrialisation of Russia. Then reforms were applied by Petr Arkad'evich Stolypin (1862–1911), the Chief-minister of the Russian government. About Witte's and Stolypin's influence on the construction of the *Transsib* see M. V. Nashchokina, 'Gradostroitel'naia politika Rossii kontsa XIX – nachala XX veka v deiatel'nosti S. Yu. Witte i P. A. Stolypina (Town-planning policy of Russia in S. Yu. Witte's and P. A. Stolypin's activity during the second part of the nineteenth and the beginning of the twentieth century)', in I. A. Bondarenko, ed., *Arhitektura v istorii russkoi kul'turi. Vypusk 4: Vlast' i tvorchestvo* (Moscow 1999),138–45.

[4] The Tsar Nicholas II confirmed this in his rescript about the twenty-fifth anniversary of the beginning of the construction of the 'Great Siberian Way'. See Anonymous, *Vysochajshii Reskript na immia ministra putei soobscheniia, po sluchayu 25-letiia pristupa k postroike Sibirskoi zheleznoi dorogi*, May 19, 1916 (St. Petersburg 1916).

began to lay the rails in territories with a great lack of roads. Even more, the railway construction killed the just started high road constructions in the bud.'[5]

Both of these 'Russian phenomena' became even more apparent in Siberia than in European Russia. Thus, on May 19, 1891, a new era had begun in the development of Asian Russia with the construction of the Great Siberian Railway. Work had started at both ends, Vladivostok and Cheliabinsk, simultaneously. In spite of the wild terrain, harsh climate and lack of detailed maps, the work was done with enormous speed.[6] In 1896 the Western-Siberian section from Cheliabinsk to the Ob' station Krivoschekovo, began to function as did the Mid-Siberian from Ob' to Irkutsk three years later in 1899. To cut distances the East-Siberian section from Irkutsk to Vladivostok, would pass through Manchuria over an important stretch, the so-called 'Chinese Eastern Railway' (*Kitaisko-Vostochnaia Zheleznaia Doroga*, KVZhD). The East-Siberian section was constructed in two stretches: from Vladivostok to Baykal Station in 1897 and Irkutsk to Baykal in 1900. Although the railway from Cheliabinsk to Vladivostok was pretty much finished in the first half of the year 1900, two-thirds of the KVZhD had been destroyed by the Boxer Rebellion (*I-ho ch'üan*, Righteous and Harmonious Fists). After the rebellion had been suppressed and rebuilding had begun, the rail construction of the KVZhD was finished on October 21, 1901. There were even stretches of it where traffic had already begun operating although many of the tunnels and bridges were still under construction. Thus the Chinese Eastern Railway was not to make its official start before July 1, 1903 when it would then provide a direct rail link from St. Petersburg to Vladivostok.[7] Although this was the official date for the end of the construction of the Trans-Siberian Railway, the entire network of railways within Russian territory, excluding the KVZhD, would not be up and running until October 5, 1916 when the bridge over the river Amur near Khabarovsk began to be used.[8]

The decree of March 11, 1893 allowed the 'expropriation and temporary occupation of the ground for the construction of the Siberian railway' by railway

---

[5]   P. A. Stolypin, *Nam nuzhna velkaia Rossiia: polnoe sobranie rechei v Gosudarstvennoi Dume i Gosudarstvennom Sovete. 1906–1911* (We need Great Russia: complete collection of the speeches in the Duma and the State Council, 1906–1911) (Moscow 1991), 234.

[6]   May 19 in 1891 was the official date, when the Grand Duke Tsesarevich Nicholas Alexandrovich, August President of the Committee of the Siberian Railway, started the first stretch near Vladivostok, and laid the first stone for the building of the railway station of Vladivostok. From 1891 until 1900 the speed of the construction was 600 kilometres of railway per year. Usual for that time in comparison with Northern America where the Canadian Pacific Railway was constructed with progress of 470 kilometre per year.

[7]   It had an interruption at Baykal Lake, where a ferry was used. At this stretch the Around-Baykal line was open for regular traffic only on October 16, 1905.

[8]   Best description of the history was given in S. V. Sabler and I. V. Sosnovskii, *Sibirskaia zheleznaia doroga v ee proshlom i nastoiaschem* (The Siberian railway in its history and today) (St. Petersburg 1903).

builders even against the will of the owners. In Siberia the 'Cabinet of the Emperor' owned part of the land.[9] When the *Transsib* was constructed its one and only customer, the Tsarist government, tried to avoid the chaotic location of the railway repair works, depots, storehouses and other facilities by devising a more rational distribution of services along the 6,500 kilometres long railway. This problem had previously been characteristic of railways in European Russia because of the different owners. The Siberian railway required special norms and standards, which were different from those in Central Russia. These were intended to make the *Transsib* construction easier, quicker and cheaper and were more strictly applied. Because of its route through the wilderness, the distances between stations, up to 53 kilometres, are exceptionally long compared with the 27 kilometres allowed in Central Russia.[10] The distances between main stations, with a depot and small repair workshops, could be up to 160 kilometres. This was in direct contrast to the maximum of 85 to 107 kilometres for Central Russia.[11]

The first concepts of urban planning in Siberia and the railway complexes

The importance of the railway for the urban development of Siberia was already recognised in 1895 by an architect from St. Petersburg, Dmitrii A. Lebedev.[12] In his report to the Ministry of Roads and Communication he presented an urban prognosis for the territories where railways should be constructed. He proposed collecting important socio-economic information about the most prospective settlements. He also suggested designing master plans for them with special zones in which harbours, storage and migration places as well as housing colonies would be concentrated near a railway station. The town should have three zones, for housing, industry and transport junction. To prevent the pollution of water to be used by the town's inhabitants, Lebedev suggested placing all railway structures and industry downstream, which was usually north of the housing districts. He established a set of standards by which the distances between the houses, the width

---

[9] The 'Cabinet of the Emperor' was a special institution to manage the Siberian territories of personal ownership of the emperor's family.

[10] The distance between the fifth and fourth classes station was limited by the maximal way, which an engine could ride between water supply places.

[11] See N. A. Sytenko, 'Obschiy vzgliad na sostoianie zheleznodorozhnoy seti v Rossiyskoy imperii, sovremennoe St.-Peterburgskoy sessii mezhdunarodnogo zheleznodorozhnogo kongressa (The general view on the state of the railway system of the Russian Empire)', in: *Ocherk seti russkih zheleznih dorog, ee ustroistva, soderzhaniia i deyatel'nosti po 1892 god*, 2 vols. (St. Petersburg 1896), vol. 2, 1.

[12] Between 1860 and 1863 the architect Dmitrii Afanas'evich (1833–1904) studied at the Academy of Arts. From 1863 on he lectured at the Building College of the St. Petersburg Institute of Civil Engineers and in 1875 additional at the Institute of Transport Engineers as well. See Anonymous, 'D. A. Lebedev', *Zodchij* (The Architect), 19, 1904, 225–6.

of streets and the supply of the necessary greenery would be regulated. Light-wells for instance would be prohibited. Although Lebedev's suggestions for the construction of the Siberian Railway were seriously considered by the Committee, it decided not to force the situation. Thus, instead of taking Lebedev's perspective, the committee erroneously concluded: 'In Siberia the appearance of the new settlements does not go with such speed, that we should care about the establishment of big settlements in the near future.'[13] It was a dramatic mistake that Lebedev's progressive zoning with respect to the direction of the stream of the rivers was ignored in Omsk as well as Krasnoyarsk, Irkutsk and Chita, and it was only by sheer accident that it was put into effect in Tumen', Novonikolaevsk and Barnaul.

The architecture of the Central Russian Railway buildings was characterised by using foreign prototypes as their point of reference. According to N. A. Sytenko, the railway expert and editor of *The Journal of the Ministry of the Roads and Transportation*: 'Although in time our stations underwent many changes, we can easily recognise that they were inspired by English, French, Austrian and Prussian prototypes.'[14] The shortcomings of the buildings in the Central Russian Railway appeared when they came into use and it soon became clear that all sorts of improvements and modifications would have to be made. Therefore, when the designing of the Siberian railway began, its buildings presented the next step in the evolution of the architecture of these building types. The 'Special Design Drawing Workshop' of the railway ministry in St. Petersburg elaborated a typology for industrial, passenger and civil buildings for each part of the Siberian railway.[15] The experiences of Central Russian and European railway constructions were used but

---

[13] Central state historical archive of St. Petersburg, f. 1273, op. 1, d. 329, and State archive of Krasnoyarsk region, f. 595, op. 59, d. 106, pp. 1–46. (Citations of Russian archival materials by *Fond/Opis'/Delo/List* are abbreviated: f. #, op. #, d. #, p. #.) See also V. I. Tsarev and Yu. I. Grinberg, *Achinsk: gradostroitel'naia istoriia* (Achinsk: an urban history) (Krasnoyarsk 1992), 31–4; Nikolai P. Zhurin, 'Gradostroitel'nye idei arkhitektora D. A. Lebedeva v sviazi so stroitel'stvom Transsibirskoi zheleznodorozhnoi magistrali (The architect D. A. Lebedev's urban ideas connected with the construction of the Trans-Siberian railway)', in *Problemy istorii, teorii i praktiki russkoi i sovetskoi arhitekturi* (Leningrad 1978), 123–6.

[14] N. A. Sytenko, 'Obschiy vzgliad na sostoianie zheleznodorozhnoy seti v Rossiyskoy imperii, sovremennoe St.-Peterburgskoy sessii mezhdunarodnogo zheleznodorozhnogo kongressa (The general view on the state of the railway system of the Russian Empire)', in: *Ocherk seti russkih zheleznih dorog, ee ustroistva, soderzhaniia i deyatel'nosti po 1892 god*, 2 vols. (St. Petersburg 1896), vol. 2, 2.

[15] In 1842 the 'Special Design Drawing Workshop' of the railways department in St. Petersburg was established for the designing and keeping of the drawings for the railways construction. In 1899 the drawing workshop was moved to the management of the railways construction. Designs for the Siberian railway elaborated there were published in the albums of the presentation and working drawings. See Anonymous, *Al'bom chertezhei Zapadno-Sibirskoi, Zlatoust-Cheliabinskoi i Ekaterinburg-Cheliabinskoi zheleznyh dorog. 1891–1896gg.* (St. Petersburg 1897), and Anonymous, *Al'bom tipovih i ispolnitel'nyh chertezhei Krugobaikal'skoi zheleznoi dorogi. 1900–1905gg.* (St. Petersburg 1907).

were adapted to Siberia's specific economic demands and climate, one such adaptation to the climate being the construction of the foundation in the permafrost territories. Other well-known measures to preserve the warmth were the construction of the lobby, the use of double-glass windows and extra insulation materials for the exterior walls.[16]

Figure 5.1   The third class station Ob' in Novonikolaevsk (Novosibirsk), opened 1896. Photo by I. R. Tomashkevich, 1899

Source: Photograph courtesy of Ivan V. Nevzgodine.

It was the passenger buildings that received most of the architectural attention. The Trans-Siberian Railway had up to five different classes of passenger stations. The second and third class stations were constructed near towns or large settlements whereas the fourth and fifth class ones were built in areas where very little development was expected. This resulted in no passenger buildings being built in the lower class stations. Passengers were allowed to wait in one of the employee houses, where a room of 55 square metres was set aside for them. The second class stations of Omsk, Krasnoyarsk, Irkutsk and Chita were built in brick with eclectic combinations of Russian and Western architectural motifs. Omsk and Krasnoyarsk were the largest of these and had the biggest main storage and main railway workshops. The third class stations were usually built in wood with the exceptions

---

[16]   Curiously the thickness of the walls was the same as for Central Russia.

of Petropavlovsk, Kurgan, Kainsk and Sliudianka, while the fourth and fifth class stations were all made of wood. The Neo-Russian style of these wooden passenger stations symbolised the connection with Central Russia. Their architecture, although strictly typical, was spared from presenting an overall impression of boring predictability because their builders were permitted to change the decoration details. This meant that there was a greater variety of modified versions to be seen. These wooden buildings were the closest to the traditional native architecture and were constructed in the same manner as the houses in villages or towns.

Because the size of the rooms used for passengers and service in the Siberian passenger stations was much smaller than for those in Central Russia there was overcrowding when they were first being used. It happened in Novonikolaevsk, where the engineer Vladimir K. Zhandr erected the first station Ob' in 1896 following the standard design for a third class station.[17] It was a wooden, one-storey building in Neo-Russian style. Later, Konstantin K. Lygin built additions to both sides in several stages. In 1912 he constructed a two-storey brick structure and a single-storey wooden one which, two years later in 1914, would have a single-storey brick extension added onto it.[18] Standardised plans for the location of stations, rails and buildings were developed for the different classes of stations. The plans were reworked to adapt them to local conditions. The most important condition was the possibility of making extensions to the railway buildings. Another condition was the most optimal location of a passenger building, a water tower and depots on the side of the existing settlement to make room for the possible future extension of the rail line at the other side.[19]

The railway complexes consisted of a passenger and goods station with a square, utility buildings for car or engine depots, workshops, storage, water supply, migration stations with refreshment and medical services.[20] The town structure included residential areas for railway employees, hospitals, colleges, churches, and schools. An excellent example of this can be found at the station at Omsk. In

---

[17] From 1893 on, the engineer Vladimir Konstantinovich Zhandr (born in 1863) was the director of the Mid-Siberian section of the Trans-Siberian railway.

[18] The architect Konstantin Konstantinovich Lygin (1854–1932) graduated from the St. Petersburg Academy of Arts in 1879. From 1900 on, he gave lectures at the Tomsk Technological Institute, where he became a professor in 1924.

[19] This condition, with the aim to systematising the railway arrangement, was in some cases in direct contradiction to others, as for example in the Mid-Siberian section, where the recommended location of the station should be on the left side of the railway's direction Ob'-Irkutsk. See Anonymous, *Sooruzhenie Sredne-Sibirskoi zheleznoi dorogi 1893–1898.: Sbornik technicheskih uslovii, instruktsii i poiasnitel'nih zapisok* (The construction of the Mid-Siberian railway 1893–1898: collection of the technical conditions, instructions and descriptions of the designs) (St. Petersburg 1901), appendix, 36.

[20] About the Siberian railway complexes see E. A. Smirnova, 'Iz opita formirovaniya prizheleznodorozhnih kompleksov transsibirskoy magistrali (From the experience of the construction of the complexes near the Trans-Siberian railway)', *Izvestiya visschih uchebnih zavedeniy: Stroitel'stvo i arhitektura*, 6, 1984, 60–64.

addition to the passenger station, it had to construct over seventy more buildings to meet the requirements of the railway. 'Here are the chief workshops and stores for railway materials, an extensive engine house and a hospital. Fifty-one houses afford accommodation for the railway employees.'[21]

The main workshops in Omsk were constructed as pavilions, which could be enlarged twice their original size. This additional area would soon be utilised. There were usually five to seven houses with gardens designed for the railway stations' employees per station. Furthermore, there were special norms for the amount of dwellings per kilometre of the railway line. They were different for each stretch of the *Transsib*.[22] At the Sixteenth Congress of Transport Engineers in 1898, the construction of 'railways colonies' was proposed for the lodging of the railway employees in areas with low population density.[23] These 'colonies' could be built either on the territories of the railway property where station construction was not intended or on land purchased from the municipalities by the railway. The railway employees could rent the lots for the construction of their houses. The railway gave them a lease for twenty years. The railway colony for the main workshops at the Chita railway station consisted in only seventy houses with around 1,000 people living in them. The layout consisted of six blocks, four in a square of 128 metres each and two blocks with a length of 128 metres by 64 metres each. The width of the roads was 21.5 metres. Whereas the housing was constructed on the perimeter of the blocks, 9,216 square metres were set aside for a garden in the centre.

In conclusion, it can be said that the whole of the complexes, buildings and structures of the *Transsib* formed a huge architectural entity, a sort of ensemble. The use of the same design, materials, details and decoration along the entire track created an architectural unity and integrity which was further strengthened by the application of identical colours. Wooden buildings were painted in green and light brown while others were in red and white, using brick and plaster for decorative details. After the construction of these railway complexes, the terrain adjoining them began to develop and grow spontaneously. Housing settlements appeared in a rectangular block system parallel to the railway on both sides of the rails. Eventually the inevitable proliferation of different kinds of railway buildings, spreading outward on hitherto undeveloped land without a systematic plan, complicated the structure of railway complexes and destroyed their original functional zoning system.

---

[21] A. I. Dmitriev-Mamonov and A. F. Zdziarski, *Guide to the Great Siberian Railway, 1900* (New York 1972), 200.

[22] With 107 square metres per kilometre the highest density of houses was planned for the After-Baykal line. The lowest one was 28.36 square metres for the Western-Siberian and the Mid-Siberian railway. The number of different types of houses had also increased from five types in the After-Baykal section to 50 for the Mid-Siberian railway.

[23] Anonymous, *XVI Soveschatel'nii s'ezd inzhenerov sluzhby puti russkih zheleznih dorog: protokoly zasedanii, trydi* (The sixteenth Consultative Congress of the engineers of the Russian railways: the protocols of meetings, reports) (St. Petersburg 1898), 195–209.

The pure architectural style of engineering constructions of the railway bridges brought particular features of the urban image to the railway complexes. Russians had already had experience in building railway bridges before the construction on the *Transsib* began.[24] However, the construction of bridges for the *Transsib* was on an even more grandiose scale. From Cheliabinsk to Irkutsk 635 one-span bridges and 23 multi-span bridges were built. The total length of metal bridges in the Trans-Siberian Railway measured around ten kilometres. While performing this task the Russian engineering schools developed their own bridge construction and methods of calculation.[25] Their engineering achievements were shown in the pavilion of 'The Construction of the Great Siberian Railway' at the Nizhnii Novgorod Exhibition of 1896. Further substantiation of this came the next year in 1897 when the British journal, *The Engineer*, reported the following concerning the general growth of engineering knowledge in Russia: 'The Russian engineer is rapidly rising to a place amongst the better engineers of Europe.'[26] In Siberia, wide span railway bridges using pioneering constructions transformed the city's image. The necessity of quick construction of a great number of bridges in what was technically regarded as 'undeveloped areas', resulted in an economy of materials and in using standardised procedures and constructive innovations. Eleven different types of trusses were used in combination with specially designed ones that resulted from the variations in the land surface and landscape. Examples of this were the special six fathom (12.8 metre) deck trusses that were designed for the riverside spans of the mid-Siberian railway.

At first, small one span bridges were constructed in wood but later these would be replaced by metal ones. The leader of a school for bridge construction, Nikolai A. Belelubsky (1845–1922) developed a system of replacing the wooden bridges by steel ones without interruption of the train traffic. In 1894–1899 the famous Russian engineer and founder of the other engineering school for bridge constructions, Lavr D. Proskuriakov (1858–1926), designed the longest bridge, measuring 850 metres, in Siberia over the Yenisei River in Krasnoyarsk.[27] The

---

[24] The engineer Dmitrii Ivanovich Zhuravskii (1821–1891) made an important contribution to this field. He elaborated a theoretical method for the calculation of strain in the Howe truss. He also suggested a solution for the calculation of the dynamic stresses.

[25] See Belelubsky, 'Zum Brückenbau in Rußland: Neuere Brückenbelastungen, Brückenmaterial, freie Querträger', *Zentralblatt der Bauverwaltung*, 28, no. 51, 1908, 349–50, and E. O. Patton, 'Neuere bemerkenswerte Brückenbauten in Rußland', *Zentralblatt der Bauverwaltung*, 28, no. 99, 1908, 657–9.

[26] 'The Nijni Novgorod exhibition', *The Engineer*, January 22, 1897, 80.

[27] For superb illustrations of Siberian bridges from the Archive of the Russian Academy of Science see Rosemarie Wagner, 'Der Brückenbau', in Rainer Graefe, Murat Gappoev, and Ottmar Pertschi, eds., *Vladimir G. Šuchov 1853–1939: die Kunst der sparsamen Konstruktion* (Stuttgart 1990), 136–49. For the historic photos of the construction of the bridge over the Yenisei and for the other Siberian bridges see ibid. 142–7, 280–9, and 290–6. Contrary to Wagner's claim only a few of the bridges illustrated in her article were built by Shukhov and none of the Siberian examples. Shukhov merely supervised the reconstruction of the bridges that had been damaged during the Civil War.

engineer Evgenii K. Knorre (1848–1917), carried out the construction. This bridge has six main spans of 144 metres, with strut-framed trusses of a polygonal type. It was awarded a gold medal at the *Exposition Universelle* in Paris in 1900.

Figure 5.2   The bridge over the Ob' in Novonikolaevsk (Novosibirsk), built by engineer Nikolai A. Belelubsky between 1894 and 1897. Photo by I. R. Tomashkevich, 1899

Source: Photograph courtesy of Ivan V. Nevzgodine.

Between 1894 and 1897 Nikolai A. Belelubsky used the system of Heinrich Gerber for the bridge over the Ob'. It was the third cantilever bridge in Russia.[28] Belelubsky had also designed, with a total length of 640 metres, the bridge over the river Irtish in Omsk and over the river Kitoy.[29] Belelubsky invented his own

---

[28]   In 1866 the German engineer Johann Gottfried Heinrich Gerber (1832–1912) patented 'Balkenträger mit freiliegenden Stützpunkten' and in 1867, following this principle, he constructed the first bridge over the Main near Hassfurt. The engineer of the bridge over River Ob' wrote a book with the calculation of its costs. See N. A. Belelubsky and N. B. Boguslavskiy, *Most cherez reku Ob otverstiem 327, 50 sazh. Konsol'noi sistemi* (The bridge over the Ob' of the cantilever system) (St. Petersburg 1895).

[29]   The bridge over the river Kitoy was built in 1898. See Rosemarie Wagner, 'Der Brückenbau', in Rainer Graefe, Murat Gappoev, and Ottmar Pertschi, eds., *Vladimir G.*

system of freely supported transversal beams with horizontal struts, which became famous abroad as the *Russkiy metod*. The bridges became symbols of progress, while changing the scale, image and landscape of the Siberian town. The economy of steel and cheap labour allowed differentiation of the thickness of the girder's profiles, which followed their load. This resulted in expression of the forces (compression/tension) in construction and brought lightness in its appearance. It is particularly interesting that in spite of this, the engineering beauty of metallic bridges had no aesthetic influence on the work of architects at that time. Later Selim O. Chan-Magomedov points out that even in the 1920s one cannot see any serious influence of modern bridge tectonics on the work of the Union of Contemporary Architects (*Ob'edinenie Sovremennykh Arkhitektorov*, OSA), later called 'OSA-Constructivists'.[30] Ironically, this was the group that had declared the importance of using new constructions in their architecture. However, I believe that the Russian metallic railway bridges together with the Eiffel Tower in Paris must have surely had an influence on the monument of the Third International by Vladimir E. Tatlin and on the famous architectural fantasies by Iakov G. Chernikhov.[31] Although it seems that the Constructivist journal *Sovremennaia arkhitektura* (Contemporary Architecture) was not interested in the Russian bridges, the less propagandistic but more practical periodical *Stroitel'naia promyshlennost'* (The Building Industry) did generate discussion and even publication.

The impact on the regional planning system and architecture

The *Transsib* construction led to unforeseen migrations in the region and intensified the urbanisation of Siberia. Between 1897 and 1917, twenty-three settlements were officially declared as 'towns' while the urban population increased by 2.3 times its original size.[32] Cities that were located along the new railway line, like Omsk, Chita, Krasnoyarsk and Irkutsk, developed rapidly. The population of Tomsk, Krasnoyarsk and Irkutsk more than doubled in the period

---

Šuchov 1853–1939: die Kunst der sparsamen Konstruktion (Stuttgart 1990), 136–49, esp. 146.

[30] Selim O. Chan-Magomedov 'Die Konstruktivisten und die Stilbildung der sowjetischen Architektur-Avantgarde', in Rainer Graefe, Murat Gappoev, and Ottmar Pertschi, eds., *Vladimir G. Šuchov 1853–1939: die Kunst der sparsamen Konstruktion* (Stuttgart 1990), 168–72.

[31] The famous Russian artist, architect and designer, Vladimir Evgrafovich Tatlin (1885–1953) graduated from the Moscow College of Painting, Sculpture and Architecture in 1910. Tatlin is considered the founder of Constructivism movement in art. The architect and graphic artist, Iakov Georgievich Chernikhov (1889–1951) graduated from the Leningrad branch of the Higher State Artistic Technical Institute in 1925.

[32] The population increased from 327,860 to 767,273 inhabitants. See the official census in M. K. Azadovskii, A. A. Anson, and M. M. Basov, eds., *Sibirskaia sovetskaia entsiklopedia* (Siberian Soviet encyclopaedia), 4 vols. (Novosibirsk 1929), vol. 1, 705–6.

between 1897 and 1911. Omsk grew by more than three times and Chita by even more than six.[33] The growth of these towns was much quicker than in Central Russia. Other towns, like Tomsk, Tobol'sk, Berezov, Kolyvan' and Kuznetsk, consequently developed much slower and eventually lost their importance.[34]

The *Transsib* exercised 'such a mighty influence on the growth of economic life in Siberia that its commercial success far exceeds the most extravagant expectations (...). The unexpected commercial success of the Siberian Railway' brought annual revenue to the government.[35] But the railway needed improvements: higher speed, replacement of the light rails by heavy ones, and the improvement of the roadway. When it became obvious that one track with a total length of 6,500 kilometres was not enough, a second track of 3,620 kilometres was laid from Omsk to the Karymskaia Station from 1907 to 1915. But the *Transsib* only made a great economical impact on a narrow strip of about 200 kilometres along the railway. In order to spread its influence more widely, from the 1910s onwards, private companies constructed branch lines that extended to agricultural areas and mineral resource sites further away.

The *Transsib* construction contributed to the development of the self-government in Siberian towns. The growing bourgeoisie formed the policy of the municipalities, and tried to be involved in the policy-making for the further development of the railway. Therefore, representatives of Western Siberia and the Steppe region organised a congress in St. Petersburg 'about the question of the railway construction' in the years 1909 and 1910.[36]

In 1903, the journey from Moscow to Vladivostok or Port Arthur, comprising a distance of about 8,534 kilometres, took ten days. The conveyance by the Siberian Railway from London to Shanghai required 16 days, and was 'over twice as quick as, and 2.5 times cheaper than that now existing'.[37] The Russian government expected that this connection would encourage international trade, post and tourism. The Trans-Siberian Railway even had its 'Guide to the Great Siberian Railway' translated and published in English in 1900 in order to stimulate

---

[33] Between 1897 and 1911 the population of Tomsk grew 2.1 times, Krasnoyarsk 2.9, Irkutsk 2.5, Omsk 3.4, and Chita 6.5. See G. V. Glinka, ed., *Aziatskaia Rossiia, Luidi i poriadki za Uralom*, (Asian Russia), 2 vols. (St. Petersburg 1914), vol. 1, 293.

[34] In Eastern Siberia the railway went the route of the Moscow-Siberian post track. In Western Siberia it went south of the track and therefore did not pass Tobol'sk, Kolyvan' and other cities. Between 1897 and 1917 the population of Kolyvan' decreased from 11,711 to 9,953 inhabitants, and Kuznetzk grew only from 3,117 to 3,154 inhabitants. See M. K. Azadovskii, A. A. Anson, and M. M. Basov, eds., *Sibirskaia sovetskaia entsiklopedia* (Siberian Soviet encyclopaedia), 4 vols. (Novosibirsk 1929), vol. 1, columns 705–6.

[35] A. I. Dmitriev-Mamonov and A. F. Zdziarski, *Guide to the Great Siberian Railway, 1900* (New York 1972), 76, and 79.

[36] Anonymous, *Sibirskiy Torgovo-Promyshlennii Kalendar' na 1911g.* (Siberian Calendar of Trade and Industry for the year 1911) (St. Petersburg 1911), 65.

[37] A journey via the Suez Canal by steamship takes from 34 to 36 days. See A. I. Dmitriev-Mamonov and A. F. Zdziarski, *Guide to the Great Siberian Railway, 1900* (New York 1972), 78.

American and British tourists and businessmen. But far more than for rich foreigners, the *Transsib* was a welcome means for the poor immigrants of European Russia to reach the Asian plains.[38] The necessity to solve the problem of the deficit of the agricultural land in Central Russia brought forward the migration law of 1889. From 1892 on, migration to Siberia and the Far East was planned and regulated by the Russian government. In 1896 a special management department was established in the Ministry of Internal Affairs to co-ordinate migration and colonisation of the new territories. Peasants in Central Russia were motivated by both: the Tsarist government and in the years between 1907 and 1911, by the 'Stolypin Reform' for the emancipation of peasants to move to Siberia. It was a task never attempted before on such a grand scale. The government used the North-American experience of colonisation as their model in order to accomplish this. Settler stations for the immigrants were constructed. These lodged 150 families and were equipped with a doctor and a medical assistant. Larger migration stations were established in Omsk, Tomsk, Novonikolaevsk and Krasnoyarsk. These had a medical office, canteen, barracks, storehouses, administrative buildings, schools, and churches. Also migration from Siberian villages to towns was taking place. Because of the diminishing commercial acitivity in rural regions peasants left their fields for the first settlements, where they got work and soon adapted themselves to city life. Many people from Berdsk, Suzun, Kainsk, and Kolyvan' migrated for example, to Novonikolaevsk. From 1896 until 1902, three thousand people came from Kolyvan' to Novonikolaevsk alone, thus causing serious housing shortage problems. These were temporarily solved by putting up the cheapest possible timber construction, which were erected at high speed. In many places there were plenty of forests, but some towns grew so quickly that complete wooden houses were being shipped to them. The greater part of timber houses was built by construction teams from European Russia, arriving by rail for 'seasonal construction work'.[39] They brought their specific detailing abilities from their native regions and incorporated them into the Siberian architecture.

Another aspect of mobility was the phenomenon of the mobile church. Because of the shortage in churches along the Siberian railway, a church car was constructed in 1896 at the St. Petersburg Putilov plant. It was large enough to hold up to seventy believers and travelled along the Trans-Siberian line. This was the forerunner of the famous post-revolution propaganda trains, the so-called *Agit* (Agitation) trains, which operated during the years between 1918 and 1920. These trains travelled all over Russia and were equipped with printing presses and movie projectors.

---

[38]   After the *Transsib* construction, we see an increase in migration from agricultural regions. In the 1860s and 1870s only 110,000 migrants arrived in Siberia. In the 1880s the stream increased to 440,000, and rose to 971, 000 in the 1890s. See Donald Warren Threadgold, *The great Siberian migration: government and peasant resettlement from emancipation to the First World War* (Princeton 1957).

[39]   'Seasonal Work' means working in the period from May thru September.

Figure 5.3   The portable church constructed for the Trans-Siberian Railway was built in the St. Petersburg Putilov plant in 1896.
Photo by I. R. Tomashkevich, 1899

Source: Photograph courtesy of Ivan V. Nevzgodine.

The railway made travelling so quick and convenient, that one architect could build anywhere in Siberia. It could also take architects abroad more easily. In 1907, the Civil-Engineering Department of the Tomsk Institute of Technology sent two young teachers, Andrei D. Kriachkov and Vikentii F. Orzheshko, on an educational trip throughout Germany, France and Italy. They became the most productive architects in Siberia.[40]

The railway brought new approaches, styles and typologies in building and eliminated the more traditional remnants of Siberian architecture. It is certainly not surprising that some of these approaches, styles and typologies were partially or entirely based on historical models. This is particularly true in the case of the railway churches, employee's houses, stations and water towers, whereas other structures such as the business buildings were more progressive in their design. From 1894 onwards, the 'Fund in Honour of the Emperor Alexander III'

---

[40]   The Siberian architect Andrei Dmitrievich Kriachkov (1876–1950) graduated from the St. Petersburg Institute of Civil Engineers in 1902. The Siberian architect, Vikentii Florentinovich Orzheshko graduated from Petersburg Academy of Arts in 1902.

Figure 5.4   The interior of the portable church designed by artist E. E. von Baumgarten. Photo by I. R. Tomashkevich, 1899

Source: Photograph courtesy of Ivan V. Nevzgodine.

constructed Russian Orthodox churches along the railway as a manifestation of Russian power. It also built schools 'to meet the requirements of a numerous population.'[41] Churches were built in official Neo-Russian or Neo-Byzantine styles. By January 1, 1903 the Fund had already erected 166 churches with 24 still under construction. There were also 168 parish schools finished and now opened, with a further 16 in the process of being completed.[42] The architects took the Prussian experience as their model for the organisation of these settler schools and churches.[43] In 1895, the Tomsk-based management of the Mid-Siberian Railway invited Konstantin Lygin from St. Petersburg to fill the position of an architect. During the years from 1896 to 1899 he constructed a church for 1,000 believers near Ob' station. This church was named in honour of the patron of the founder of the Siberian Railway, Emperor Alexander III, St. Alexander Nevsky. Later, the place would be called Novonikolaevsk and after 1926, Novosibirsk. It was the largest church building on the Trans-Siberian Railway, a monument between the Western Siberian and the Mid-Siberian parts of the railway.[44] Lygin also designed the churches for Petropavlovsk, Chita, and Taiga. The most interesting example of his work is the church for the Taiga station, which he built in 1899 in the style of seventeenth century Russian architecture.

In the larger towns where there had mostly been single-storey constructions, multi-storey buildings began to appear for the railway management's offices as well as for technical schools and trade and joint-stock companies. The architects designed them using modern materials and construction techniques. This was also true for the construction of business buildings in which concrete and steel constructions made the covering of large areas and the foundations of big shop windows now possible.

In 1912, a competition was organised for the management building of Omsk Railway. The well-known architect Fjodor I. Lidvall from St. Petersburg won this competition with his classical interpretation of *Art Nouveau*.[45] The building was

---

[41]　A. I. Dmitriev-Mamonov and A. F. Zdziarski, *Guide to the Great Siberian Railway, 1900* (New York 1972), 75.

[42]　See Anonymous, *Sibirskie tserkvi i shkoli fonda imeni imperatora Aleksandra III k 1 ianvaria 1903g.* (The Siberian churches and schools of the Fund in Honour of the Emperor Alexander III on January 1st, 1903) (St. Petersburg 1903). For further information see Anonymous, *Sibirskie tserkvi i shkoli: K desiatiletiyu fonda imeni imperatora Aleksandra III (1884–1904).* (The Siberian churches and schools: for the tenth anniversary of the Fund in Honour of the Emperor Alexander III, 1884–1904) (St. Petersburg 1904).

[43]　See the memoirs of Alexander N. Kulomzin, manager of the Committee of Siberian Railway in Collections of manuscripts, Russian State Library, f. 178, op. 9803, d. 7, 1–2, and 16–17.

[44]　This church in Neo-Byzantine style was similar to St. Petersburg's Exult Gods' Mother Cathedral, which was built by the architects Vasilii A. Kosiakov (1862–1921), and Dmitrii K. Prussak (born in 1859) on the *Bol'shoi prospect* on *Vasilievskii Ostrov* in the years between 1889 and 1898.

[45]　Architect Fjodor (Frederick) Ivanovich Lidvall (1870–1945) graduated from the Academy of Arts in 1896, and became an academician of architecture in 1909. Lidvall

Figure 5.5   The water tower at the Oiash railway station, built in 1896. Photo by I. R. Tomashkevich, 1899

Source: Photograph courtesy of Ivan V. Nevzgodine.

lived in Stockholm from 1918 on. See. H. O. Andersson and F. Bedoire, 'Fjodor Ivanovitj Lidvall – ett rysk-svenskt arkitektöde', in *Arkitekturmuseet. Årsbok*, 1980, 6–19.

constructed in the period between 1914 and 1917. Its façade in Ionic style had four sculptures of allegoric female figures symbolising 'a Way', 'a Traction', 'a Moving' and 'an Administration'. In the same competition, a project with the slogan 'Moscow-Irkutsk' by the architect Andrei Kriachkov from Tomsk, received the third prize. The Neo-Russian decorative elements of Kriachkov's station with its towers and spires imitating the forms of Moscow's Kremlin, symbolised a direct rail-connection with the capital of the Empire. The first railway technical schools, built in Khabarovsk and Krasnoyarsk, were modelled after the 'brick style' projects which had combined the Old Russian, Gothic and Classical decoration. These frequent architectural competitions played an extremely important role in furthering progressive ideas in construction and design. An excellent example of this is the 1913 competition for a building for the Commercial College in Omsk. The importance of hygiene as well as the creation of a simple means to extend the building had been stressed in the programme. Because none of the thirty projects presented had fulfilled all the above requirements, the jury was not satisfied. The local architect F. A. Chernomorchenko ended up creating a building that combined together the best elements from all the competition's designs proposed.

The railway made importing materials and equipment from Europe possible. For example, a local architect, A. P. Artyushkov, had the great stained glass window for the shop of L. B. Meretzkiy in Irkutsk made in Paris after drawings. Architects from St. Petersburg and Moscow built in Siberia for European firms, branch offices and shops. In 1915 an architect from St. Petersburg, Nikolai N. Verevkin, built commercial buildings for the *Salamander Insurance* and the *Treugol'nik* (Triangle) companies in Omsk. Both of these structures employed the Central Russian architectural devices of Neo-classical decorations compact composition with such a high density that eighty per cent of the surface was covered using light-wells.[46]

In the first two years of World War I Andrei Kriachkov constructed the trade filial of the Bogorodsko-Gluhovskaya Company in Novonikolaevsk for the Morozovs, a famous business family from Moscow. The two-storey Neo-classical building had a concrete frame using the famous *Hennebique* system and huge horizontal windows between Ionic columns. He also built Novonikolaevsk's trade building and the Town Management Department in the *Jugendstil* design in the new market square. The building was comprised of shops on the ground floor and the municipal offices and a city hall on the first floor. The shops had underground stores covered by cast iron grids filled in with glass.

The business buildings transformed the face of the city centre. The erection of structures of a different character and on a bigger scale dominated the edges of the city centre. The Ministries of War and Railways quickly constructed settlements

---

[46] Nikolai Nikolaevich Verevkin (1877–1920) graduated from the St. Petersburg Institute of Civil Engineers in 1901 and Petersburg Academy of Arts in 1906. He was the architect of the Salamander Insurance Company, for which he built the headquarters and apartment buildings in St. Petersburg. Verevkin also erected one building for Salamander in Kharkov.

for soldiers and railway workers there. These were complexes of dwellings with the newest and most progressive basic facilities. Between 1910 and 1913, thirty-seven brick buildings for an infantry regiment and an artillery division were constructed by the engineers I. P. Sokolov and A. P. Golubov at the *Voennyi Gorodok* (military barracks) on 33 hectares outside the city limits of Novonikolaevsk. It was a complex made up of *Zeilenbau*-barracks, residential housing, stores, a hospital, a bakery and a church. For the new town of Novonikolaevsk, this complex was exemplary in the quality of its brick construction. The model of the Ministry of War Building was used for the construction. Construction of the military barracks near the Novonikolaevsk railway station began in 1912 with a clear zoning system: barracks, the commandant's office, stores and services. The military town of the barracks of the Twenty-eighth Siberian Infantry Regiment in Irkutsk was also built on a grand urban scale and in a functional setting. However, the other reason the railway and the army had urgently began to stimulate industrial development was because of their own needs. Examples of this are the plant for the construction of carriages in Krasnoyarsk, factories for the impregnation of railway sleepers with creosote in Omsk and Krasnoyarsk and sawmills in Omsk and Novonikolaevsk. These were all located near the railway and rivers. The army's food supply was also placed near the railways, as in the case of Meal Grind and the Cracker Factory in Novonikolaevsk. It is apparent, therefore, that the land around the railways attracted more and more warehouses and industrial buildings.

Garden cities

The Society of the Moscow-Kazan' Railway realised 'the first garden city in Russia'. On the basis of a plan designed by Vladimir N. Semionov and Aleksandr I. Tamanov, the settlement at the *Prozorovskaia* Station was erected in 1912. It was situated forty kilometres east of Moscow.[47] This successful experiment made the garden-city idea so popular in Russia that in 1916 the Ministry of Transport decided to build similar garden-settlements for railway employees of the Omsk and Tomsk Railways in Siberia.[48] At the same time, the stock company of Kuznetsk

---

[47] The architect and city-planner Vladimir Nikolaevich Semionov (Semënov) (1874–1960) graduated from the St. Petersburg Institute of Civil Engineers in 1898. Semionov is the most influential practitioner and theoretician of Russian-Soviet town planning. The architect Aleksandr Ivanovich (Ovanesovich) Tamanov (Tamanian) (1878–1936) graduated from the Petersburg Academy of Arts in 1904. In 1914 he became an academician of architecture. See layout of the *Prozorovskaia* settlement in E. A. Borisova and T. P. Kazdan, *Russkaia arkhitektura kontsa XIX – nachala XX veka* (Moscow 1971), 73–4.

[48] See *Zodchij* (The Architect), 21, 1916, 203, and *Zodchij* (The Architect), 48, 1916, 434. For the general account of the Garden City movement in Central Russia see: Catherine Cooke, 'Activities of the Garden City movement in Russia', in *Transactions of the Martin Centre For Architectural and Urban Studies*, 2 vols. (Cambridge 1976), vol. 1,

Metallurgy Mines began the construction of a garden city at Kuznetsk Station, a *cul-de-sac* station of the privately constructed Kolchuginskaia Railway which was a branch line of the Trans-Siberian Railway.[49] Andrei Kriachkov was the architect who had designed the master plan for this station. There were nine different types of one-storey houses for railway employees, two-storey dwellings for bachelors, a brick factory and a four-storey building for the railway management.[50] He used a Neo-classical solution for the layout of the town with the three radial streets starting from the Station Square. The same style was used in the decorative details as well. To create a sort of environmental buffer between the housing and the noise and pollution, Kriachkov placed a sanitary green belt between the blocks and the railway.[51]

In Barnaul, the capital of the rich Altay region south of the *Transsib,* 'a group of local intelligent people, who were familiar with the idea of Howard, founded the All-Russian Garden Cities Society'.[52] This group was headed by the manager of the Altay Railway, A. V. Larionov. The secretary of the Duma of Barnaul, A. I. Petrov played an important role in the promotion of the garden city. After a big fair in 1917, the municipality approved a plan by the Barnaulian city-architect Ivan F. Nosovich for the northern part of the town as a garden city. In contrast to the usual rectangular block system, the city layout had radial and circular streets as well as a lot of greenery integrated within its structure.[53] Petrov reported the following in the English journal *Garden Cities and Town Planning*:

> The third garden city was founded near the biggest town in Siberia – Omsk. Here, as well the housing problem has gone through its crisis, and in 1918 they rapidly brought into being a co-operative building society, which bought the property of Kulomzino, situated near Omsk at the railway station, on the bank of the river Irtysh, and divided it among its 900 members.[54] Then several people joined the society who shared the ideas of Howard, and they succeeded in convincing all the members of the advantages of building a garden city instead of an ordinary town. They worked out the plan, bought a brick factory and worked energetically.[55]

225–49, and Catherine Cooke, 'Russian responses to the Garden City idea', *Architectural Review*, 6, 1978, 353–63. See also S. Frederick Starr, 'The revival and schism of urban planning in twentieth-century Russia', in Michael F. Hamm, ed., *The city in Russian history* (Lexington 1976), 222–42.

[49] State archive of the Tomsk region, f. R-26, op. 1, d. 16.
[50] Central State Historical Archive of St. Petersburg, f. 350, op. 20, d. 307.
[51] Ibid. f. 350, op. 2, d. 304, razdel IV.
[52] A. I. Petrov, 'Mr. Howard's Ideals in Siberia', *Garden cities and town-planning*, 15, no. 4, 1925, 94. The article was first published in the Esperanto Journal *Teristo*.
[53] The architect Ivan Kilist-Feodosievich Nosovich (born in 1862) graduated from the St. Petersburg Institute of Civil Engineers in 1889. He was a city architect of Barnaul from 1914 to 1919. In the beginning of the 1920s Nosovich immigrated to Poland.
[54] Later Kulomzino became the town Novo-Omsk. In 1926 more than 11,000 inhabitants were living there.
[55] A. I. Petrov, 'Mr. Howard's Ideals in Siberia', *Garden cities and town-planning*, 15, no. 4, 1925, 94.

Howard's ideals had a profound impact on later developments in Siberian town planning. One can see their influence in the urban designs for Novosibirsk, Scheglovsk (Kemerovo), and Kuznetsk, – later known as Stalinsk and present-day Novokuznetzk.

Urban development and its problems

When the railway was designed and constructed, the possibility of new towns such as Novonikolaevsk and the later development of towns currently in existence was not well prognosticated. The railways possessed huge amount of land, 1.6 to 3.7 kilometres wide, at the periphery of these cities. This was because of the low prices of the lots there and the necessity of reserves of territories for future development. This situation would later lead to problems for the already-existing town centres because new ones were developing closer to the railway station. Their connection with the old centre became difficult. In Omsk, they constructed a railway branch line of 3,734 metres that connected the station with the town and the river Irtysh.[56] Most cities developed a complicated urban structure in which the railway, with its annexes, became a continuous obstruction between the city-districts themselves as well as between the town and the river. This is still the case in Novosibirsk.

Because from the beginning the railway was ignored as a city-forming factor, railway complexes could occupy as much as 300 hectares in each city. The rapid development of railways required more and more territory. Therefore, the new railway facilities were placed outside the city's boundaries. Later they even became a barrier for the growth of housing areas. The sought after territory for dwellings was already occupied by railway facilities. The connection with the wharf cut the access of the housing districts to the rivers. This happened in Omsk, Barnaul, Blagoveshensk, Tumen, and Novonikolaevsk. In Krasnoyarsk, Chita, Omsk and Novonikolaevsk, thanks to the railway bridges, new dwelling districts appeared on the opposite bank of the river. More and more cities were losing their historically compact structure.

There is no doubt that the most striking example of the impact of the railway construction is the history of the contemporary capital of Siberia. Because Novonikolaevsk is strategically located where the river Ob' and the Trans-Siberian Railway cross, it developed from a settlement into a city almost overnight. From only 764 inhabitants in 1893 it shot up to 1,093 in 1894. It continued its rapid growth from 7,832 in 1897 to 26,028 inhabitants in 1905 and in 1910 to 63,552 and finally in 1917 to the amazing figure of 107,129.[57] Because of this phenomenal rate of increase of the population the town understandably received

---

[56] A. I. Dmitriev-Mamonov and A. F. Zdziarski, *Guide to the Great Siberian Railway, 1900* (New York 1972), 200.

[57] See Anonymous, *Ves' Novonikolaevsk. Adresno-spravochnaia kniga na 1924–1925 gody* (All Novonikolaevsk. The address and reference book for the years 1924–1925) (Novonikolaevsk 1924), 30.

the nickname *American City*. Based on the 'American' rectangular block system, the first plan of the town was primarily designed for easier tax collection. Its layout is similar to that of any quickly constructed colonial towns found anywhere in the world at that time and thus, the urban structure of the town developed spontaneously.

The military and railway workers settlements, railway services and factories were erected without any planning. Their positioning was defined solely by the location of the railway and the wharf. In 1907, the railway services in Novonikolaevsk occupied 327 hectares, 32 per cent of which was that of the town's territory. Twenty-two town blocks, making up one fourth of the town (800 houses), were lost during the big fire of 1909. The fire could not be stopped because of the lack of water and it was the railway that blocked the way to the river. This sad event provided the municipality with a governmental subsidy which was also used for the construction of twelve primary schools. These *Jugendstil* two-storey brick buildings were placed at corners of the city blocks, at distances from 1,000 to 1,600 metres, according to the density of the population.

The October Revolution started a new period in the history of the *Transsib*. During the Revolution and the civil war many railway bridges and buildings had been damaged. This led to the erection of newer and bigger structures for the depots and the stations. The famous Russian engineer, Vladimir G. Shukhov, supervised the repair of some Siberian Railway bridges. Because of the lack of steel, old trusses and their elements were recycled wherever possible.[58] After the revolution the railway became the basis for the industrialisation of Siberia. The level of industrial development in the region was still very low. In 1926 it was only 0.9 per cent of the entire industry of the Union of Socialist Soviet Republics (USSR). It ought to have increased with the implementation of the first five-year plan. At that time the idea of the *Sverhmagistralizatsia* (Super main line) of the *Transsib* for the increased transportation of the goods and raw materials was discussed.[59] The *Ural-Kuznetsk kombinat* was planned. The Stalinsk (Novokuznetsk) plant would use iron ore brought by trains from the Urals, while Magnitogorsk used coke brought back on the return journey by rail from the Kuznetsk coal basin (*Kuznetskij ugol'nii bassein*, Kuzbass). The railway stations clearly needed to be modernised during this period. For instance, by the end of the 1920s the Novosibirsk railway station, which had survived the civil war and the revolution, had become too small. Therefore, in 1929, the Moscow Architectural

---

[58] Big railway bridges over the rivers Tobol, Ishim, Irtysh and Ob' were destroyed. About the engineer Vladimir Grigor'evich Shukhov (1853–1939) see G. M. Kovel'man, *Tvorchestvo pochetnogo akademika inzhenera Vladimira Grigor'evicha Shukhova* (The work of the honourable academician engineer Vladimir Grigor'evich Shukhov) (Moscow 1961), 215–25.

[59] The improvement of existing lines and the electrification, the construction of the second track, the enlargement of the rail network, increase in the velocity and a more intensive time schedule were suggested to improve the freight transportation between Siberia and Ural.

Society (*Moskovskoe Arkhitekturnoe Obshchestvo*, MAO) organised a national open competition for the project for a new railway station in Novosibirsk.

The Leningrad architect Igor' G. Yavein delivered the most interesting design. His avant-garde building was based on a finely developed functional scheme. Influenced by Kazimir S. Malevich, Yavein gave the station a simple cubic volume and a virtuous interior layout.[60] The architecture is comparable with the later works of Ludwig Mies van der Rohe. Its modern appearance however did not satisfy all the members of the jury in Moscow. This is why the design only received the second prize. The architect Nikolai G. Voloshinov won the first prize instead. His project was favoured because of the rational connection of its buildings with the railway. Voloshinov wanted to build the first railway station in the Union of Socialist Soviet Republics (USSR) with a layout of an elongated railway station with a transverse upper portion. This design scheme, taken from a station of the American railways in Cincinnati, foresaw different levels for the platforms and the building, which would be partially built over the tracks. This had the convenience that passengers could descend to the platforms directly from the level of the entrance hall. This meant that passengers would avoid having to go up and down, or respectively down and up, to reach the platforms.[61] However, in July 1930 his design was subject to harsh criticism at an exhibition in Novosibirsk. The Novosibirsk Planning Commission was not satisfied by the 'architectonic appearance of the building' and they claimed that it 'looked more like the box for an industrial building than a passenger station'.[62] The final result was a façade with an enormous arch. The arch was a traditional element in architecture and would be used here to symbolise the railway station as the gate to the city. A monumental decoration with semi-columns in exaggerated Tuscan style and an arched window would make up the motif in this façade.

At the same time as new industrial towns were being constructed the problem of articulation of the railway passenger station in the city structure arose. The architect of the State Institute for the Projecting of New Metal Works (*Gosudarstvennyi Institut po Proektirovaniiu Novykh Metallurgicheskikh Zavodov*, GIProMeZ), Vladimir N. Taleporovskii designed the first plan for the town of Kuznetzk, together with the New Metallurgical Plant in the years of 1928 and 1929.[63] The town had three radial streets starting from the plant's management building. The central street was to connect the railway station with the management building. Later, in 1931, the German city-planner Ernst May did not

---

[60] The architect Igor' Georgievich Yavein (1903–1980) graduated from the Leningrad Institute of Civil Engineers in 1930. The Russian artist Kazimir Severinovich Malevich (1878–1935) founded Suprematism.

[61] Alfred Fellheimer and Steward Wagner, architects from New York, designed the building in 1929. This building was known in Russia because of its technological scheme and beautiful mosaics in the interior. Both caused an intense debate.

[62] State Archive of the Novosibirsk Region, f. 920, op. 1, d. 26, p. 92.

[63] Vladimir Nikolaevich Taleporovskii (1884–1958) was an architect, graphic artist and architectural historian who mostly worked in St. Petersburg (Leningrad).

pay much attention to the urban clarification of the station in the city structure.[64] This of course, ran contrary to the traditional Russian understanding of the importance of the railway. Interestingly enough, the three radial streets originally designed to start from the railway station reappeared in the master plan of 1948 and they were eventually realised. We find a similar situation in Novosibirsk. Although it had originally been planned in the 1920s, the connection of the railway station with the central square of the city centre was only realised in the late 1960s.

At the time of Stalin's compulsory industrialisation and later, during World War II, when many factories were evacuated to Siberia from European Russia, the centres of industry were determined by railways and by the location of natural resources. Many new local lines were constructed and as a result, the rail-networks became more complicated. As a result of that Novosibirsk currently has a serious problem that is characteristic of other Siberian cities such as Omsk, Irkutsk, Krasnoyarsk. Because of economic and geographical reasons the railway was built parallel to the river Ob'. As a consequence, they separated the city from the river. Although this line was originally built as a temporary measure, it has lasted, meanwhile, for a hundred years. Today plans are being drawn up to create a highway parallel to the existing railway line and to develop the land for high-rise towers to create public and business centres. Housing is obviously out of the question because of the noise and the acoustic restrictions of the zoning ordinances. The urban planners also intend to create a pedestrian link either above or below the railway from the city centre to the river quay. The river Ob' is planned to play an important role in urban development and so a solution has to be found for the railway line. Because of the important role of railways for the heroic beginnings of the city, remains of the old railway bridge should be set aside and used for a monument on a prominent place in Novosibirsk.

In conclusion, it should be stressed that the state construction of the Trans-Siberian Railway provided the foundation for industrial as well as all other developments in Siberia. Before the introduction of the railway, Siberia was primarily a place for prisoners to serve out their sentences in penal colonies in exile. The two construction principles of the *Transsib* were economy and building long stretches more quickly. Passenger stations, dwellings, hospitals, and churches were all designed using foreign expertise and standardised regulations. New town planning ideas shaped the physical organisation of town networks on the level and brought the construction of garden cities. A set of state regulations also evolved from the building construction in these towns. The Trans-Siberian Railway made possible the construction of building complexes by the Ministries of Defence, Transport and Education on a major urban scale. Two extremely important factors in this scenario were the state's role in urban development as well as the state's

---

[64] German city-planner Ernst May (1886–1970) headed the team of foreign city-planners and architects, which worked in the USSR in the 1930s, although his Russian designs were mostly criticised for their aesthetic components. I consider the ignorance of the railway importance in urban plans for Siberian cities like Scheglovsk, Leninsk, Prokopevsk, and Stalinsk as his most essential mistake.

ownership of the land. These factors were unique in the case of Siberia from the end of the nineteenth century into the beginning of the 1920s and continuing into the Soviet era. The buildings and constructions of the *Transsib* which still remain today obviously have a great historic, cultural and architectural value. They should be documented and selected for restoration, preservation and re-use.

CHAPTER SIX

Portuguese cities and railways in the nineteenth and twentieth Century

Magda Pinheiro

The creation of the rail networks (1853–1890) and their importance for the urban hierarchy

One of the most remarkable features of Portugal's human geography, inherited from its old political and social system – the *Ancien Régime* – is the location of its two main cities on the estuaries of the country's two largest navigable rivers. Consequently, most goods traded in Lisbon and Porto were shipped along the coast or carried by river. Alongside these two main cities, Portugal's other seaports included Viana de Castelo in the North, Aveiro in the centre, Setúbal and Faro in the South. Figueira da Foz, a port on the mouth of the Mondego river, acquired city status in 1882.[1] However, this coastal development did little to offset the lack of adequate overland communications with the interior of the country. Indeed, the poor state of the roads reflected the low level of trade on the domestic market.

Owing to the predominance of Lisbon and a lack of medium-sized towns, the Portuguese urban system was often qualified as immature. However, this imbalance – by comparison with the standard model of urban development – must be seen in the context of the Portuguese colonial empire and its market, which also benefited mainland Portugal. In Lisbon and, to a lesser extent, in Porto, craftsmen, industry and trade depended not only on the urban and rural mainland markets, but also on Brazil. After losing the trading monopoly with Brazil, whose ports were opened to British traders in 1810, Portugal entered a phase of structural readjustment. Lisbon's population levelled off, following a downward trend until well beyond 1850. Porto, with its limited industrial fabric, completed the restructuring process more quickly and its population began to rise. This explains why Lisbon, one of Europe's major cities in the early eighteenth century, had a

---

[1] The privileges enjoyed by cities were abolished in 1834, though the corresponding honorary status is still granted today. A law dating from 1982 defines the conditions of entitlement. See Teresa Barata Salgueiro, *A Cidade em Portugal* (Oporto 1994), 420, and François Guichard, *Porto, la ville dans sa région*, 2 vols. (Paris 1992), vol. 1, 492.

population slightly below that of Marseilles in 1864.[2] Excluding Porto, with its population of 86,800, no other town in Portugal counted more than 20,000 inhabitants. Braga, in the North, with 16,900 people, Funchal on the island of Madeira with 14,700, Ponta Delgada, in the Azores with 14,100, Coimbra in the centre with 11,500, Angra do Heroísmo in the Azores with 11,200 and Setúbal, south of the Tagus, with 10,700, complete the list of towns with city status counting more than 10,000 inhabitants.

Against this background, the construction of a rail network, started in 1853 but completed essentially between 1860 and 1890, can be seen as an attempt to make up for the country's development lag. The rail network was built at a time of severe financial difficulties, with the help of foreign capital obtained at very high interest rates. The engineers who designed it always sought to follow existing communication lines and to choose the least expensive routes. The logical result was a branched rail network centred on Lisbon and, to a lesser extent, Porto. This structure led to busy traffic between these two cities and the provincial towns though did little to link these provincial towns with each other.

The network was designed with the idea of restoring the port of Lisbon to its former splendour. The international lines serving the capital, whose high-ranking status was a matter of pride, were always built with this priority in mind. The Saint Simonian utopia that inspired many of the design engineers emphasised the importance of major international links. The renewal of Lisbon as a 'port from Europe to the Americas' could be seen as an illustration of this ideal. Moreover, for the small group of individuals who saw the railway as an instrument of Iberian unification, Lisbon was destined to become not only the port of Madrid but also the capital of the peninsula. The international lines between Lisbon and the border, following the most direct available routes, were designed to tie in with the rail links between Lisbon and the district capitals. These towns had important administrative functions. For example, right up to the 1970s, they held a monopoly over secondary public education.

Towns not linked to the rail network in the nineteenth century do not appear to have suffered any adverse economic effects before 1890. This was the case for Viseu, which was not connected to the Beira-Alta line because of its hilly topography. The industrial town of Covilhã, a centre for woollen textiles in the Beira Interior region, also developed before the arrival of the railways, thanks to the abundant availability of water power, raw materials and qualified manpower.

The first international line, completed in 1864, linked Lisbon to Madrid via Elvas. The line between Lisbon and Porto was also built during this period, and work began on the line serving the towns of Évora and Beja with a terminus on the left bank of the Tagus, south of Lisbon. The prominence of Lisbon as a terminus for international lines was contested by the inhabitants of Porto, who demanded

---

[2] When studying Lisbon from a European viewpoint, geographers tend to forget its imperial dimension. See Magda Pinheiro, 'Crescimento e modernização das cidades no Portugal oitocentista', *Ler História*, 20, 1990, 79–107.

CITIES AND RAILWAYS
1926

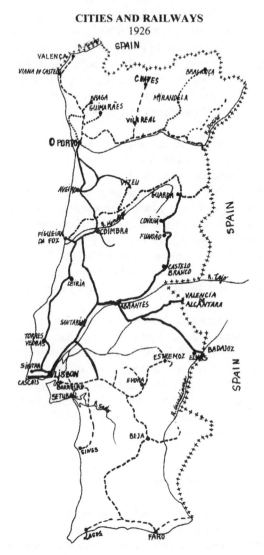

Portuguese Railways Company _____
Beira Alta Company _·_·_·_··
State Company-----------
Other companies...............

Figure 6.1 Cities and railways in Portugal, 1926

Source: Magda Pinheiro, *Chemins de fer, structure financière de l'État et dépendance
            extérieure au Portugal 1850–1890*, 3 vols., University Paris I Ph. D. thesis,
            1986, vol. 3, 7, and Gaspar Correia Fino, *Legislação sobre Caminhos de
            Ferro*, 4 vols. (Lisbon 1884–1904), vol. 3, and vol. 4.

that rail links be built to Vigo and Salamanca. The pressure they exerted was sufficient to obtain government approval for the construction of these lines in 1867, amid a severe economic crisis. In the 1880s, after completion of a new line between Madrid and Lisbon via the Caceres branch, the Porto lobbies applied renewed pressure. When it became clear that the Spanish government had little intention of linking the railways of the Douro to those of Salamanca, they succeeded in persuading the Portuguese government to subsidise construction on Spanish soil.

For the Beira-Alta railway, whose ultimate purpose was to provide a link between Lisbon and the French border, the plan was to build a terminus in the port of Figueira da Foz. The western line from Lisbon to Figueira da Foz and the Beira-Baixa line, completed just before and during the crisis of the 1890s, had no precise international objective, though their routes were sometimes the subject of heated debate. In these early days of railway construction, though the hierarchy of small towns remained largely unchanged, Lisbon and Porto grew at a rapid pace. In 1890, Lisbon had 301,200 inhabitants and Porto 138,900. This period was marked by an ever widening gap between the smaller towns and the two main cities, Lisbon in particular. In 1890, Braga was the only town with a population of more than 20,000.

It is impossible to obtain precise statistics on urban population growth in nineteenth century Portugal since all figures relate to parishes (*freguesias*) which do not necessarily correspond to urbanised areas. A parish with more than 2,000 inhabitants did not always have an identifiable urban centre. However, in 1890, only one parish of more than 10,000 inhabitants did not belong to a city in the legal sense of the term.[3] If we take all cities, in the legal sense, of more than 10,000 inhabitants, the average growth rate was 1.41 per cent between 1864 and 1878, and 2.2 per cent between 1878 and 1890.[4]

Urban markets and rail transport demand

As a large population generates high levels of economic activity, Portugal's two main cities were its two biggest markets. Lisbon and Porto imported a large share of the foreign products entering the country and it was their customs houses which collected most of the country's import duties – which represented almost half of all state tax revenue. During the *Ancien Régime*, Portugal suffered a chronic grain shortage and Lisbon was supplied mainly by foreign food imports. After 1820, the situation reversed and until the 1880s, the city consumed a majority of home-produced agricultural products.

---

[3] On the urban hierarchy, see also Ana Tomás, 'As cidades', in Nuno Valério, ed., *Estatísticas Históricas Portuguesas*, 2 vols. (Lisbon 2001), vol. 1, 127–48.

[4] Data from Anonymous, *Censo da Populaçao 1911*, 2 vols. (Lisbon 1917), vol. 1, 343.

According to Miriam Halpern Pereira, Lisbon and Porto played a vital role in the development of Portuguese domestic trade. She notes that between 1874 and 1890, practically half of all the meat sold in Portugal was destined for these two cities.[5] She affirms, however, that population growth after 1890 did not give rise to increased consumption. In 1878, 21,117 head of livestock were taken by rail to Lisbon for slaughter, rising to 25,190 in 1882. At the end of the 1880s, the expansion of public works in the capital attracted a population of impoverished migrants and per capita meat consumption decreased, though demand for potatoes rose spectacularly. Consumption of wine in Lisbon also increased rapidly in the second half of the nineteenth century, slowing down from 1876.[6]

These trends had inevitable repercussions on rail traffic. Most grain destined for Lisbon travelled on the southern line, while wine, a major export commodity, accounted for a large share of freight traffic on the other lines. On the southern line, food products represented slightly less than forty per cent of the tonnage transported in 1877. This percentage fell in 1884 as the share of fuels and industrial products increased. On the northern and eastern lines, run by *Companhia Real*, food products accounted for forty per cent of shipments in 1877 and fifty per cent in 1884, falling back to forty per cent in 1889. In the same year, wine represented twenty per cent of goods carried on the Companhia Real network and 25 per cent of traffic on the western line, owned by the same company. By 1888, the figure had increased to 41.5 per cent. In the North, on the state-owned Douro line, wine accounted for 21.3 per cent of goods traffic in 1886 and food products in general represented 54.3 per cent. In the 1890s, the wine crisis had a major impact on the income of railway companies. On the Douro and Minho lines, both state-owned, large numbers of cattle were shipped to Porto, from where they were exported to England to supply British butchers, until the arrival of frozen meat from America.

A sign of the low level of industrialisation in Portugal, industrial products and raw materials represented a smaller share of freight traffic, though volumes gradually increased. Growing quantities of charcoal, used by urban dwellers as a heating fuel, and cork for new factories around Lisbon, were transported on the southern and south-eastern lines. But despite the growth in rail transport, the small volumes carried – 2.3 million tonnes in 1890 – were a sign of Portugal's economic underdevelopment. In his study of Portuguese domestic market growth between 1810 and 1913, David Justino suggests that rail network development strengthened the advantages enjoyed by Lisbon and Porto while doing little to offset the handicaps of less privileged provincial areas. He highlights the delays in linking the town of Covilhã to the rail network. But he remains prudent about the positive effects that a different route might have generated. The railways needed to safeguard their profitability by responding to demand in areas where existing

---

[5] Note also that the city limits have been extended to include the poor outlying districts. This data does not necessarily reflect a drop in living standards among existing inhabitants, but rather the arrival of new, impoverished social categories.

[6] See Miriam Halpern Pereira, 'Niveis de Consumo e Niveis de Vida em Portugal, 1874–1922', in *Das Revoluçoes Liberais ao Estado Novo* (Lisbon 1994), 162–203.

traffic was already dense. The low level of traffic between northern and southern Portugal, a problem pinpointed by David Justino for the year 1850, was not remedied for many years, due largely to the fact that the rail network south of Lisbon was state-owned, while all lines in the centre of the country were in private hands. The two networks were not linked until after 1890.[7]

Table 6.1   Passengers departing from cities in the south of Portugal

Year	Lisbon[1]	Santarém	Portalegre	Elvas	Total[2]
1868	148,582	21,724	5,445	9,151	-
1869	1,541,155	22,392	5,581	12,440	-
1870	143,414	20,461	5,620	12,540	-
1871	141,972	20,916	5,633	14,347	-
1872	145,879	22,639	5,743	14,106	-
1873	161,976	25,961	6,970	16,463	-
1874	172,723	26,991	7,045	15,986	-
1875	188,244	27,308	7,190	16,667	-
1876	189,311	30,309	4,658	15,880	-
1877	19,340	30,050	6,206	15,736	1,893,098
1878	194,998	30,897	7,212	17,914	1,966,535
1879	187,323	24,419	7,980	17,845	2,063,522
1880	191,040	26,376	6,290	17,799	2,129,570
1881	1,866,664	30,963	6,434	17,929	2,187,835
1882	205,569	31,362	5,914	17,926	23,399,774
1883	194,588	35,973	5,226	24,863	2,449,966
1884	195,490	31,954	4,604	18,857	2,581,004
1885	206,810	36,928	5,388	14,681	2,617,405
1886	230,105	40,461	5,678	17,018	2,919,727
1887	214,594	39,991	6,505	15,279	3,531,272
1888	286,661	41,323	6,129	17,230	4,256,900
1889	331,257	39,820	5,679	17,275	4,860,891

[1] To northern and eastern lines only.
[2] Total travellers in the country.

Source: Frederico Pimentel, *Apontamentos para a História dos Caminhos de Ferro Portugueses* (Lisbon 1892), 250.

---

[7]   See David Justino, *A Formação do Espaço Económico Nacional, Portugal 1810–1913*, 2 vols. (Lisbon 1988), vol. 1, 176–90. See also, Magda Pinheiro, *Chemins de fer, structure financière de L'État et dépendance extérieure au Portugal, 1852–1890*, 3 vols., University Paris I Ph.D. thesis, 1986, vol. 1, 532.

Passenger rail transport developed more quickly than freight. In Portugal, passenger transport revenues were always relatively high. In 1889, passengers heading East or North by train from Lisbon represented six per cent of all travellers in the country. By 1892, this proportion had risen to 11.6 per cent. The profile of passenger traffic from Porto was very similar on lines north of the Douro river: twenty per cent of passengers on the Minho line and a quarter of those on the Douro line departed from Porto station.

Table 6.2   Passengers departing[1] from cities in the centre and north of Portugal

Year	Oporto[2]	Coimbra[3]	Aveiro	Braga	Penafiel
1868	6,698	43,065	20,284	-	-
1869	6,384	41,862	21,752	-	-
1870	82,956	40,362	23,522	-	-
1871	87,420	39,732	22,615	-	-
1872	98,073	47,106	23,746	-	-
1873	104,407	47,684	25,823	-	-
1874	119,116	47,773	27,885	-	-
1875	127,623	55,196	31,238	-	-
1876	120,978	52,004	29,887	-	-
1877	130,370	52,500	32,708	-	-
1878	133,350	52,897	32,364	-	-
1879	122,581	55,635	32,366	-	-
1880	130,551	58,489	30,526	-	-
1881	137,060	59,036	32,242	-	-
1882	317,633	59,179	32,844	53,683	20,225
1883	312,983	60,537	35,806	50,999	19,862
1884	301,743	55,312	30,591	53,393	17,915
1885	303,450	48,015	31,677	57,259	18,017
1886	323,939	20,584	38,520	59,726	16,934
1887	363,552	16,051	38,056	61,481	15,968
1888	428,179	16,387	46,082	67,162	16,243
1889	449,744	20,647	51,572	68,867	16,334

[1]   For the total see table 6.1.
[2]   All travellers from Gaia and Porto heading to all destinations.
[3]   To northern and eastern lines only.

Source : Ibid.

The country's new transport capacities provided growing numbers of people with access to new leisure and cultural activities, often talked about in the press. While the elite headed to spa resorts or to the beach, the working classes preferred to travel in groups. Escorted by the local band, they visited community associations in other towns. As pointed out by Maria Fernanda Alegria, goods and passenger rail traffic became progressively concentrated along the Lisbon-Porto line as the network increased in size.[8]

Railways and urban modernisation

As population growth was slow in most Portuguese towns, urban modernisation was a gradual process, though its objectives were similar to those of other European cities. Though the question has not been studied in detail, the role of railway station construction deserves to be highlighted. As land was expensive, new railway stations were generally built outside the historic town centres. Sometimes, their distant and inconvenient location was blamed for the slow growth in goods traffic. The arrival of the station often prompted the development of new residential districts or tree-lined avenues, in accordance with hygienist precepts. In Sintra, a traditional summer resort for the aristocracy, a whole new residential district was built in the 1850s around the plot set aside for the railway station. This new district, called *Estefânia*, was peopled by members of the new business bourgeoisie and by railway engineers. The actual railway line did not arrive until the 1880s, when the municipality transferred the Town Hall to a new, more prestigious urban location, symbolically more distant from the royal palace. In Aveiro, a town whose most influential politician is famous for bringing the station closer to the town, the avenue linking the station to the historic centre was planted with trees. Its construction prompted new inward urban development. The avenue is now a central thoroughfare lined with some of the town's most stylish boutiques.

In Lisbon, the first two railway stations were located in areas earmarked for modernisation. The choice of location for the first station caused little controversy. An initial proposal to build it in the north-eastern part of the city centre, in the Intendente district, was rejected despite its low cost. There was an obvious need to bring the railway closer to the port. In 1853, when the decision was taken, the port of Lisbon had still not been built. Ships unloaded their cargoes in the middle of the Tagus, opposite the customs house. The rail terminus was deliberately sited in close proximity, along the *Cais dos Soldados*. When the permanent building was erected in 1866, Santa Apolónia station was equipped with a special pontoon for goods loading and unloading. The wharf of the navy arsenal was the only other installation to possess such a pontoon. The area in front of the station was also made into a square. Despite early proposals for a railway bridge across the Tagus, Lisbon was not linked to the southern rail network. A station was built South of the

---

[8]   See Maria Fernanda Alegria, 'O tráfego de passageiros e mercadorias', in Maria Filomena Mónica, Magda Pinheiro, Fernanda Alegria, and José Barreto, eds., *Para a História do caminho de Ferro em Portugal* (Lisbon 1999), 62–87.

Tagus in the small town of Barreiro. As many outlying districts were connected to the capital by branches built successively along a track shared by several lines, no new railway construction took place in Lisbon until the 1880s. Plans for simultaneous construction of new lines and major harbour works were put forward at a time when many other projects, planned over previous years, were getting off the ground. It was during this period that the circular line was built, linking the new port of Lisbon to the northern and eastern rail networks.

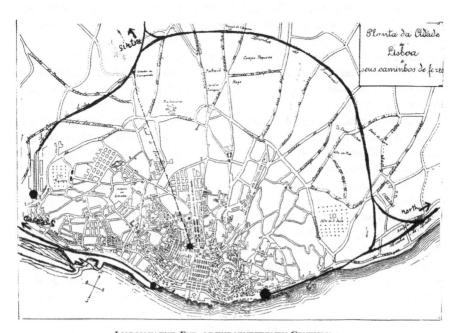

LISBON IN THE END OF THE NINETEENTH CENTURY
THE RAILWAY STATIONS

SANTA APOLÓNIA ●
ROSSIO ✳
ALCÂNTARA ●
CAIS DO SODRÉ ■

Figure 6.2   Map of Lisbon, 1892

Source: Anonymous, *Atlas Escolar Portugês* (Lüddecke 1897), plate 1, and *O Século, no. 3299, April 12, 1891.*

For strategic reasons, the western line terminus, with a branch towards Sintra, was located in the Alcantara district, close to the new port. However, a tunnel link was built to the central Rossio station. The new station, of neo-Manuelian design, was built in grand architectural style, unlike Santa Apolónia, which was deprived of such a privilege. Sited almost directly above the Mediaeval fortifications demolished in the eighteenth century, it marked the starting point of the new

Avenida da Liberdade which was to replace the Pombaline Passeio Público garden. To highlight its cosmopolitan ambitions, it was incorporated in an architectural ensemble that included the new Avenida Palace Terminus Hotel.

Trains departing from Rossio station took Lisbon's city dwellers to the resort town of Sintra. A line was also built to take the growing numbers of summer holidaymakers to the beach at Cascais. This new line was inaugurated in 1897 with a temporary terminus at *Cais do Sodré*. Built without public funding as a branch of the northern and eastern line, the aim was to bring the line all the way to Santa Apolónia station. But this would have meant building a viaduct opposite the majestic Terreiro do Paço square. Luckily for the beauty of Lisbon, the crisis at *Companhia Real* and the empty public purse prevented construction from going ahead. The tram network, electrified in 1901, was the main driving force behind urban expansion, growing in size as the legal city limits were extended to make way for new development.

In Porto, construction of the northern line stopped in 1864 at Vila Nova de Gaia, on the left bank of the Douro. It was not until the end of the crisis, in 1877, that the Eiffel-Seyrig bridge was built to take the railway to Campanhã. The location of Campanhã station, on the eastern edge of the city, ran counter to previous projects, which had not planned for such a high bridge and which had sited the station in the city's lower district. The station site was decided in 1872, in line with the position of the bridge. Though the building is of little architectural interest, the arrival of the railway played a key role in the urbanisation of Campanhã's neighbouring districts.

Meanwhile, engineers working for the Minho and Douro railways looked for ways to bring the railway to the city centre. The branch line from the customs landing pier, which was to link up the Mira Gaia district on the banks of the river, was intended to handle goods traffic to and from the port. It was built progressively from 1881 and completed in 1888. According to the engineers, the Mira Gaia station would help to clean up a district reputed for its insalubrity.[9] In 1886, when the branch line was on the point of completion, the traders of Porto contested the siting of the new station next to the customs house, a location which, in their view, was lacking in prestige.

In 1887, the new São Bento central station project was presented to the municipality. The new station was built on a diagonal with respect to Don Pedro square, like Lisbon's station in relation to Rossio square. Inaugurated in 1916, it also gave rise to a new avenue, now called Avenida dos Aliados. Though its architecture is heavy compared to that of Lisbon's central station, the *azulejos* tile mosaics that cover its walls give the building a certain majesty. As was the case in Lisbon, the station shifted the city centre away from the river banks. In Porto, the tram network, electrified in 1905, also played a key role in urban expansion.

---

[9] See the descriptions given by contemporary engineers, such as that of Luciano Carvalho, 'Caminhos de ferro de Minho e Douro. A linha urbana do Porto', *Revista de Obras Públicas e Minas*, 27, 1897, 128–52.

Urban growth, industrialisation and railways in the twentieth century

Anabela Nunes studied Portuguese urban development between 1890 and 1990. She found that growth rates were very slow, remaining below one per cent until the 1950s. But the pace of urban growth increased in the 1970s, especially in towns of more than 20,000 inhabitants. In 1991, forty per cent of the Portuguese population lived in towns of more than 5,000 inhabitants, 34 per cent in towns of more than 10,000 inhabitants and 25 per cent in towns of more than 20,000 inhabitants. In 1991, 187 municipalities had more than 5,000 inhabitants, hundred had more than 10,000 and 39 had more than 20,000.[10]

Though the strongest trend marking the twentieth century was the extension of suburban areas and the subsequent development of Lisbon and Porto as metropolitan centres, this movement has slowed down since 1991, in the Lisbon region at least. As a result, the weight of small towns is increasing and new urban centres are emerging. In the wake of these changing demographic realities, the number of towns with city status has increased substantially since the 1970s.[11]

When it comes to company towns, the only Portuguese example is that of Entrocamento, on the junction between the northern and eastern lines, a town which owes its development to the railways. Entrocamento acquired city status in 1991, despite a population of only 13,900 inhabitants. In Barreiro, where the southern and south-eastern lines have their terminus and which had a large railway workshop, the population rose above 10,000 in 1920, though the town did not obtain city status until 1984. However, it was the arrival of chemicals plants and cork treatment factories in 1911, due probably to the presence of the railway, that fuelled Barreiro's growth in the twentieth century. Cork was transported by rail from Alentejo. The railway was also used by the chemical industry to bring in raw materials and ship out fertilisers. But Barreiro is located in the metropolitan zone of Lisbon so its growth is also linked to the process of suburban extension.

Railway construction slowed down in the twentieth century. The network reached its maximum size in 1952 with 3,597 kilometres of track. In 1966, the number of lines in service began to decline, falling to a minimum of 3,054 kilometres in 1992.[12] Since then, the trend has been reversed, thanks to the construction of new track sections in the metropolitan areas of Lisbon and Porto. During the twentieth century, the main rail construction projects were the new

---

[10] See Anabela Nunes, 'Portuguese Urban System: 1890–1991', in Pedro Telhado Pereira and Maria Eugénia Mata, eds., *Urban Dominance and Labour Market Differentiation of a European Capital City, Lisbon 1890–1910* (Boston et al. 1996), 7–47.

[11] Ibid.

[12] Though there are just three doctoral theses on the history of Portuguese railways in the nineteenth century, there is not a single university study of their development in the twentieth century. The only information source is a set of statistics published in Magda Pinheiro, 'Transportes e Vias de Comunicação', in Nuno Valério, ed., *Estatísticas Históricas Portuguesas*, 2 vols. (Lisbon 2001), vol. 1, 357–96, and some pages in Antonio de Oliveira Marques, 'Meios de Comunicaçao', in *Historia da Primeira Republica* (Lisbon 1978), 245–89.

Sado valley line in the South of Portugal, built as part of a programme to improve the port infrastructures at Setúbal; the Tomar branch in the centre of the country, connecting the town of Tomar – newly linked to the rail network – to Entrocamento; the Vouga valley line from Aveiro to Santa Combadão in the centre-North; and lastly, tracks linking the Douro line to Vila Real and Bragança north of Porto.

The First World War was disastrous for the Portuguese Railways Company (*Companhia dos caminhos de Ferro Portugueses*, CP) and, contrary to the trend in other countries, the crisis led to the privatisation of state-owned lines. The transport co-ordination bill of September 7, 1945 unified the network into a single private company. It was not nationalised until 1975. From 1934, competition from the roads was seen as the main factor behind the railway crisis.[13] Rail freight reached an all-time high in 1930, with 8,084 million tonnes transported, though by 1935 this figure had dropped to 4,076 million tonnes. The average annual rate of decline between 1930 and 1966 was 2.6 per cent, compared with a growth rate of 3.7 per cent on average between 1900 and 1930.[14] And the record levels of 1930 remained unbeaten until 1995! In 1955, cereals accounted for 17.8 per cent of the tonnage transported at low speed; only fertilisers and mining products were carried in similar quantities, with 20.4 per cent and 17.8 per cent respectively.[15] Fuel represented no more than six per cent of low-speed tonnage. The annual report by the board of the CP also mentions, for that same year, a decline in oil transport on the rail network. Wine, included in the drinks category which represented 3.3 per cent of tonnage transported, no longer occupied the leading position it had held in the previous century. These statistics reflect the limited role of the railways in Portuguese industrialisation after the Second World War. The reasons for this are by no means obvious. Portugal had no oil, its roads were poor and its economy was, to a large extent, co-ordinated by engineers who were strong advocates of rail transport. Indeed, the law of 1945 was interpreted at the time as a measure to protect the railways. Notwithstanding, the financial position of the railway company got steadily worse.[16] Note that Portugal's industry was concentrated around its ports and that domestic consumption capacity was limited.

The pattern of growth in passenger transport was totally different. Between 1900 and 1930, the average annual growth in passenger traffic was 3.1 per cent.

---

[13] This is reflected in documents written by engineers of the CP who, from 1934, took this new reality into account.

[14] See Magda Pinheiro, 'Transportes e Vias de Comunicação', in Nuno Valério, ed., *Estatísticas Históricas Portuguesas*, 2 vols. (Lisbon 2001), vol. 1, 357–96.

[15] Companhia dos caminhos de Ferro Portugueses, *Relatório do Conselho de administração parecer do Conselho fisca- Exercício de 1955* (Lisbon 1956), 15–21.

[16] This decline is rendered even more inexplicable by the fact that company management was in the hands of well-known economists, some of whom had been transport ministers, such as João Maria de Oliveira Martins who, in his book entitled *A Questão ferroviária*, blames a lack of investment. The colonial war certainly had a part to play. See João Maria de Oliveira Martins, *Estudos Ferroviários – A Questão Ferroviária* (Lisbon 1996), 210.

The crisis of the 1930s was followed by a period of renewed growth from 1937 with a slight dip in 1940 and 1941. The mean annual growth rate between 1930 and 1960 was 3.7 per cent.[17] The railways played a key role in the development of Lisbon and Porto as metropolitan centres, and the growth in passenger transport after 1952 reflects this reality. In just thirty years, between 1947 and 1977, the number of passengers tripled, despite the absence of any significant infrastructure developments, with the exception of suburban line electrification. In 1957, the report by the company board attributes this increase to urban deconcentration and to the electrification of the Sintra line completed the previous year.[18] In 1970, passenger transport on commuter lines represented 47 per cent of total passenger traffic, with the cities of Lisbon and Porto accounting for ninety per cent of this volume. By 1990, commuter lines represented 62 per cent of total passenger traffic. From 1980 however, there was a definite trend away from this form of public transport which, at the time, offered little in terms of service quality. This trend accelerated after Portugal joined the *European Economic Community* (EEC) and living standards improved. It was not until 1987 that two working groups, based in Lisbon and Porto, were set up with the aim of reversing this trend.

Two lines built in the 1890s to carry passengers on leisure outings contributed to Lisbon's suburban development, though they served the western suburbs only. The northern and eastern lines served new districts built along the Tagus, though the areas North-east of Lisbon and South of the Tagus had no rail link to the city centre, relying mainly on bus services. From the nineteenth century, it was boats that contributed to the city's southward development, followed by buses from the 1950s. The railway did not cross the Tagus until 1999. It forms part of an urban infrastructure designed around the car and is unlikely to have an impact on private vehicle use.

Porto is a major regional centre attracting people from the whole of northern Portugal. Urban development along the south bank of the Douro was facilitated by the Dona Maria bridge, and has extended as far as Espinho thanks to the presence of the railway line. The narrow-gauge railway from Porto also played a major role in the development of Povoa. Trofa and Valongo, thirty minutes from Porto's central station, developed before the 1940s. Here too, urban expansion began in the 1960s, with strong reliance on buses and private cars.

Conclusion

The railways have played a limited role in the evolution of Portuguese urban hierarchies, contributing above all to the supremacy of Lisbon and, to a lesser

---

[17] See Magda Pinheiro, 'Transportes e Vias de Comunicação', in Nuno Valério, ed., *Estatísticas Históricas Portuguesas*, 2 vols. (Lisbon 2001), vol. 1, 357–96.

[18] See Companhia dos caminhos de Ferro Portugueses, *Relatório do Conselho de administração parecer do Conselho fisca- Exercício de 1955* (Lisbon 1956), 54.

extent, Porto. Rail network development has been concentrated along the route between these two cities. Industrialisation after the Second World War coincided with a steady decline in goods transport by rail due to strong competition from the roads and the concentration of industry around the country's port cities.

The railways appear to have played a positive role in urban modernisation and expansion during the nineteenth century. The nineteenth century rail infrastructures built in the two main cities had a positive impact on twentieth century suburban development, though their effects were limited by their absence in many areas. With high urban pollution levels and severe traffic congestion, the people of Lisbon and Porto are now paying dearly for the absence of a modernised commuter network.

CHAPTER SEVEN

Downtown by the train: the impact of railways on Italian cities in the nineteenth century – case studies

Andrea Giuntini

Railways and cities in Italy: a particular story

If a country exists where the impact generated by the coming of railways to cities, and the building of railway stations in the urban fabric has influenced more than anywhere else the city planning development, that country is surely Italy.[1]

The particular configuration of most municipalities in the peninsula – with a medieval urban plan – brings us to this conclusion both for the nineteenth century, when the railway novelty made its initial impact; and for the twentieth, when city planning became more important. Even today the impact of railways in cities can be felt, on the one hand by the construction of High Speed Lines, the well-known *Direttissime*, and on the other hand by the second wave of railway station constructions. These called for greater architectural efforts than in the past compared with the previous nineteenth century examples: the new stations became part of towns which were rapidly growing, this time in the perspective characterised by the appearance of the automobile. Finally, the Italian case is so peculiar that one has to exert special care due to the artistic and urban uniqueness of the country.

Railway history has its start in the major cities of Italy at the middle of the nineteenth century and represents a crucial stage in the formation of modern city centres. Thus, we have to start from this assumption in order to deal with each case. Although each requires its own inquiry, the cities have, at the same time, certain characteristics in common with many other examples of lesser importance: at any rate, they fully belong to Italian history, be it urban, regional or related to transportation.

The three cases analysed here have in common the way in which their stations were constructed. During the mid-nineteenth century, the three stations of Milan, Florence, and Rome were built, introducing the general problem of urban railway

---

[1] Editor's note: All literature and sources mentioned in the following text are included in the bibliography of the article.

planning. In addition it must be considered that all three stations that today make up the urban rail hubs in these cities were all built during the Fascist era.

In this respect, Milan, Florence and Rome are cities that are particularly significant, though they do not exhaust the large and differentiated range of cases present in Italy. Selected on the basis of their geographical position, so as to represent the various geographical areas of Italy, the three cases also differ in their evolution. This divergence occurs from the nineteenth century, since the cities under analysis belong to different states. In all three cases the arrival of the first trains brought about similar problems for city planners at a time when the first series of nineteenth-century stations were installed, which were then renovated on a grand scale in the following century. And again, all the three examples are, today, the focus of heated debate and interest due to overall restructuring of each of these hubs.

Despite the fact that the subject lies outside the author's area of expertise, it is nevertheless necessary to make some rapid comments concerning the problem of the architectural styles which are progressively marking the realisation of the railway stations. The main goal of this paper is the analysis of the impact of railways on cities; so it would be out of place to focus unduly on architectural language. Still, the stylistic choices are strictly linked to the complexity of urban and related economic issues which make the impact of railways and the construction of railway stations one of the significant moments in the formation of modern cities.

The impact of railways on urban and economic development: some substantial problems concerning the Italian case

After having reaffirmed the important character of this theme in order to understand Italian urban development in the nineteenth century, it is necessary briefly to point out several topics involved. First, however, a few words on semantics are in order. The word 'impact' calls to mind one or more breaks in the pre-existing equilibrium, whose consequences are overwhelming. That means, further, that there arises something to defend against and something to control. The word also gives the idea of unexpected and often unwanted consequences. Impact, understood in this way, provokes change in particular of the form of the city as a result of the push felt upon the arrival of railway transport. We are not here dealing with a series of marginal transformations, rather with changes that influenced the overall urban economic structure. The influence of railways on the urban environment, from the traumatic unhinging of urban equilibria that had been unchanged for centuries, to the consideration of railway stations as the primary architectonic urban object, surely constitutes research material for the railway historian, suggesting that a broad range of paths be followed. The morphology of most Italian cities changed radically with the advent of the railway, also regarding the ensuing social impact. Therefore railways should be considered, above all, as the engine powering enormous urban transformations. So strong is the impact, that the mildness of the architectural styles of the stations was conceived as a mitigating element and, in the last analysis, to guarantee a wider compatibility with urban life. Historically the façade of the building that faces outward toward the city acts as a go-between while the inside part remains more strictly related to the functions it serves. The clean façade acts to convince city-dwellers of the goodness of this new invention, the railway, while the 'dirty' side faces inwards.

The panorama of cases analysed is immense and demonstrates an extremely interesting series of reactions to the breach produced by the arrival of the train: from the breaking down of the city walls to the necessity of rethinking the urban design. The city plan, as many studies demonstrate, appears everywhere to be closely tied to the coming of the railways. The history of the birth of the railway and then of the consequences of its impact in a certain place is, in the last analysis, fundamental to the understanding of city dynamics: this encompasses industrial development and building construction, movement of the functional centre of gravity, growth in the infrastructure, separation of the various urban zones accentuating social divisions, valuing some areas to the detriment of others. All these elements have a major role in the history of the Italian city in the nineteenth century.

In spite of these unequivocal signs, one of the issues of urban history that until now has been of little interest to historians regards city railway set-up, including not only railway stations, but also the rail lines, the depots, and everything related to railways inside the city, such as the maintenance shops, the railway crossings and all aspects relating to the operation of railways.

Actually, that was the main issue with which all the major cities and a good number of minor ones had to confront at the turn of the century. One begins to understand, in this era, that the determination of the ports of call, but even the location of the stations themselves within the selected sites represent primary elements for the planning of the entire metropolitan transportation system. Around the 1880s this debate was launched almost everywhere in Italy: it was deeply felt and included the participation of a many professional groups, as well as political and administrative groups, of the cities involved. Far-sighted engineers, town planners still in the bud, administrators and technicians understood that the railway articulations were in a position to reorient the economic functions within the city and urban development itself. From this point, marked attention was paid to the interdependence between the railways and the new economic equilibria that between the nineteenth and twentieth centuries underwent a complete metamorphosis. A typical pathway emerged: the first phase was the realisation of an urban railway system that was still unavoidably inadequate. This was then followed by a total rethinking of the railway services, that however, did not always translate into a radically innovative plan when compared to the previous one.

All this occurred in contexts that were often highly conflictual. In other words, the city was transformed into a battlefield where opposing sides confronted each other harshly. On the one side there were several private railway companies and then, from 1905 the public administration, which obeyed a logic of caring about their own interest, often unrelated to general urban interests. On the opposite side were the city administrations ready to defend the main interests of the cities, from a position of greater attention to the possible interrelations, to which every development of the railways must be submitted.

In the end it is not possible to define a single model, a common framework recognised for the development of town planning as a result of the coming of the railways to Italian cities. The terms under which the impact of the introduction of railways in the first phase was felt are highly variable, although the longer term impact cannot be denied.

The railway station as a gateway to the city

The introduction of railways is central to the urban transformations that changed the face of the country during the second half of the nineteenth century. What describes the industrial city are the buildings or the large city services, more than the factories, often located on the outskirts of the city limits. First and foremost among these buildings are the railway stations, still located in heart of the city throughout the nineteenth century. It is possible to single out a continuous thread in the Italian experience relative to the first phase of the nineteenth-century railway history. It is not difficult to find a kind of standard adopted as a consequence of the arrival of the railways be it related either to new constructions or even to the general city layout. For the most part, the stations were situated at the edges of the historic centres of the cities, delimiting the separation between the city and the countryside. Behind these first, often rudimentary buildings, one could see not infrequently the gardens and fields criss-crossed by the railway tracks merging with the distant horizon, marking an open and distant space before it. The station is the frontier and its positioning is not determined on the basis of an accurate forecast of possible future city developments. The industrial peripheries will be accommodated beyond the stations, often after the arrival of the first tracks to the Italian cities in the nineteenth century. For the first time a space is clearly designated for the specific purpose of public transportation, something that was previously unheard of. The railway station is emphatically defined as the monumental door to the city. At this point, the desire is to bring the station as close to the centre of the city as possible, allowing to offer a better service for the city and, at the same time, to take advantage of the economic potentialities connected to the traffic of the passengers and goods near the station. The station emerges at one end of the square and faces the city, blocking the view of the tracks and the equipment needed for train operations. The flow of the horse-drawn carriages attracted by the coming and going of passengers and goods cause the first traffic problems in nineteenth-century cities. In the *piazza* two types of traffic meet: that of the railway and that of the city. This becomes, therefore, a point of intersection of these two trajectories, the mediation between the station and the city.

Throughout the nineteenth century, the Station Square is still a part of the city. With the passage of time it is transformed into a mere place of exchange, depriving it of its original significance. The increasing concentration of means of transportation in the train station square accelerates this process; a particular role is played by the tramways, whose tracks encroach upon public space that was originally destined to be freely traversed, also for leisure. An outline of this sort characterised in particular the terminal stations.

Most of the stations built during this time period were architectonically indistinct. Only certain buildings were decorated with a symbolism that went beyond what mere function of a station would warrant. For the most part, stations were adapted to what was already present. The efforts of the architects were concentrated on the façade, whose task was to ease the impact created by the new building. In order to make the upset caused by the introduction of the railway less traumatic, classic styles were used, since they would blend in well with the already existing architecture of Italian cities. In truth such a solution represented a necessary go-between given the absolute novelty of the railway, that leads to architectonic references to industrial, educational and public buildings. Remaining hidden, instead, was the technological structure made up of an iron and glass vault. This was a way to stress the separation between the functional and technological image on the one hand, and the decorative on the other. These two functions are seen everywhere and bring about a decided decomposition of the building into two clearly distinct parts even from a formal point of view, as represented by the gallery for trains and the hall for travellers.

Timid results of an architecture still too young and inexpert in Italy visibly denounce the conflict between the academia and industry in the nineteenth century. Italian engineers had designed these stations on the wave of more famous examples in Europe, trying to leave some mark of originality. However, this effort did not always succeed, though the range of results is somewhat varied and is a witness to the vivacity of Italian engineering in the pre-unification era: it shows, however, an obvious backwardness with respect to the more developed models of European railway architecture.

One of the recurrent formulas, in particular for medium-sized cities, consisted in making the railway arrive near the walls or the early boulevards circling the city that had come in the meantime to replace the ancient walls. At that point the station was erected, connected to the centre by a wide avenue that brought together welcoming services such as cafes, restaurants, and hotels, and was surrounded by residential areas. Everywhere the areas located between the station and the centre increased in value and took on a new identity, one which will prevail from this point on. The avenue leading to the station in the nineteenth century became the backbone along which new residential and business areas were built. Around the stations specialised areas for the reception of passengers and the provision of services for them were born, while their position determined the accessibility and location of public buildings. The process of social differentiation, that the Italian cities experienced intensely during the second half of the nineteenth century, underwent a considerable acceleration with the arrival of the railways. From that moment on, the issue of rent values made an indelible mark on Italian urban history. Until then the urban centre had been a place of local exchange, well-defined thanks to a stable rural environment; with the station it became just a link in an increasingly decentralised production structure characterised by a system of exchanges without boundaries.

Asking builders and administrators of this era to show an urban sensibility was an exaggerated expectation. In the first railway phase the location of the infrastructure hubs was decided on the basis of construction costs and it never proceeded on the basis of a wider calculation of its overall impact. At this stage, urban planning was an unknown discipline, that was to be born and to develop only many decades later. The impact such a presence could make on the city still did not represent a particularly difficult hurdle to jump. Above all it is not based on the new plan that came to be created, that is the platform for future city development. More insistent worries concerned possible damage to pre-existing situations, against which rose the typical urban protest: tearing down the walls deprived citizens of places to walk, the interruption of roadways by the tracks imposes unbearable detours, the crossing over of waterways leads to flooding. These conflicts were caused by the loss of centuries-long habits that the advent of railways interrupted without warning. The arrival of the railway solidified varied and often competing interests, as they found common ground in the refusal to accept the railway which was seen as a development that seriously damaged their interests. Documents of the time hardly ever report wider considerations on the future outcomes of the new *forma urbis* that the railway imposed. Nevertheless the positioning of the train stations and the resulting overall urban rail arrangements already constituted one of the more useful keys for the understanding of successive urban developments. Errors, underestimations, naivety, mistakes, all common milestones in the railway experience of nineteenth-century Italy, would deeply condition a later phase in the history of cities in this country.

Milan: the role of industry

The first rail line reached Milan in 1840, but the central station, with transit tracks, was not completed until more than twenty years later, in 1864. It was situated right outside the walls of the city and was the work of the French engineer Buchot. Begun in 1857, it unified the terminals of the lines for Como and Venice. The pace of growth of the Lombard city very quickly brought into plain view the inadequacy of the station and demonstrated from the very beginning that its location was an obstacle to urban expansion. The building constituted a kind of bastion that squeezed the city into an iron belt that acted as an artificial obstacle to growth. Next to the main station were soon placed the freight station of *Porta Garibaldi* and, in the space of just a few more years, other secondary stations, rendering the

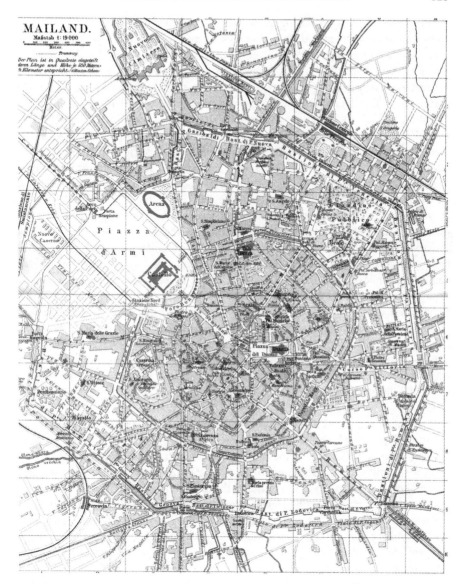

Figure 7.1 Map of Milan, 1890

Source: *Meyers Konversations-Lexikon. Eine Enzyklopädie des allgemeinen Wissens*,
            vol. 11 (Leipzig and Wien 1890), 108–9.

railway construction an insurmountable barrier. Every station acted as a magnet for
productive activities, attracting in its own vicinity a high concentration of factories.

In effect, this was a strategic error common to other nineteenth-century Italian cities and spurred intense debate. The system of the railway belt, that began to encircle the city during the 1880s, coinciding with the opening of the Gottardo railway line, marked the definitive encaging of the urban layout; tracks and stations surrounded every part of the city, choking rather than liberating space for the peripheries of the city. During this time, someone began to realise that the industrial takeoff of the city could not cohabit with a station that attracted the industrial plants to the city centre, when their natural location would be in the outskirts of town. Extended fissures in the region and crossing difficulties weighed intolerably on the city layout. The issue of redesigning the urban railways became, starting with the last twenty years of the century, one of the absolute priorities for all the administrations that came to guide the city.

Armies of technicians participated in the debate on the reorganisation of the railways, each with his own idea of the overall arrangement and never with an idea of partial adjustment to patch up a situation that had become increasingly obvious and embarrassing. Numerous commissions both at the central and local administration levels worked non-stop to find a solution to the problem. On the one hand, we find those who backed the need for a series of interconnected terminal stations like a belt as could be found in Paris. On the other hand, were those who pushed for the construction of a grand station for national and international lines, leaving freight handling to those stations located in the northern part of the city. The most heated moment in the debate came at the end of the century, at a time when the nationalisation of the railways was imminent. Put into effect in 1905, it evidently influenced opinions concerning the reorganisation of the railways in Milan.

Nationalisation acted as a catalyst for the consolidation of the positions that had already emerged which called for a general modernisation of the existing infrastructure, the abolition of the railway belt, with the exception of the southern section of rails, the construction of a new station for low speed freight, the strengthening of Porta Vittoria station, the creation of a secondary passenger station and one grand shunting station near Lambrate and finally the realisation of a new central terminal station. The plan contained in the town planning scheme of the first years of the century had to its merit to take to heart the great issue of the reorganisation of the railway system, without forgetting the remarkable increase in the volume of traffic that had obliged the city to keep in mind the dimension of infrastructure in all its modernity. The plan was the expression of the relationship between the ideas of the city's engineers expressed in the infrastructure layout and the vision of the city held by the Milanese ruling class. Contrasts and conflicts were not lacking, even between the municipal administration of Milan and the administration of the railways resulting from the need to divide the costs between the two entities. The same clash arose between private and public interests, with the former strongly leaning toward a solution where the city centre would consist of office buildings thus freeing it from industrial plants that would be progressively located in an increasingly rundown periphery.

Another of the more debated points concerned the nature of the station: although many advocated a terminal station solution, which was later adopted, the question remained uncertain for a long time. Indeed at a certain point a solution of two transit stations was adopted, one on the line for Turin and another on the line for Venice, to be connected underground. Supporters of this alternative solution had understood one of the great problems of the city, that is, that an exclusively monocentric development based on a prospective growth by concentric circles, would be in contrast with having a single fixed station. Even if it could be situated in a new location with respect to the previous one, it too would risk to be once again an obstacle to urban growth. Unlike the way it had been for Rome, the idea of the reorganisation of the railway in Milan foresaw that the railway belt could not place a limit on urban expansion, but rather should be seen as yet another ring of growth which could be crossed towards the industrial periphery to the North and West of the city. The choice of the terminal station emerged as the most suitable one, offering the advantage of being able to be spread out in the city along various radii and thus not interrupting the main roads leading from the centre to the periphery, but instead involving only the secondary arteries. It was in this way that the error came in practice to be repeated, in spite of the lessons of forty years of impetuous development that the city had experienced between the construction of the first station and the official urban plan at the start of the century. A decision of this kind made a great impact on the destinies of cities in Italy. In the case of Milan, the choices concerning the railway system were central to the progressive creation of the city configuration during the course of the twentieth century.

More recent events pertaining to railways in Milan have demonstrated how the choices of the past make themselves felt in the functioning of the city. Today the railway can once again carry out an essential role in the restructuring of the city based on the renewed integration among connecting spaces, open spaces and built-up spaces brought together as an organic unit, playing a decisive role in the present complex relations in the urban development model. This long path, undertaken since the end of the Second World War, leads to the awareness that the Milan railway system belongs to a wider regional context, into which it must be inserted and made to function. Such a process reached its goal in 1997, with the inauguration of the first section of that underground rail link which is considered an essential element of the refurbishing plan of the railway system in Milan. The idea is to keep separate the local passenger traffic from that of long distance travellers, starting a regional railway service that allows for the better distribution of traffic creating more stations in semicentral areas and peripheral zones subject to urban transformation. The restructuring of Garibaldi Station is crucial in this vision of a new system of regional railway service, since it encompasses a system of peripheral transit stations aiming to take away some of the congestion at the main station, and it is the main gateway to the underground rail link.

Florence: the city in a cast

If Florence is commonly accused of following a do-nothing policy, of being unable to carry out renewal, and of not knowing how to adapt its infrastructure to the changing times, a good part of the guilt should probably go to the way in which the railway question has evolved.

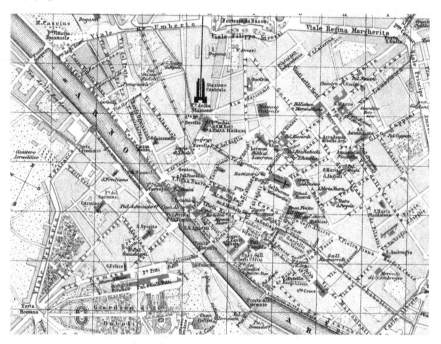

Figure 7.2   Map of Florence, 1890

Source: *Meyers Konversations-Lexikon. Eine Enzyklopädie des allgemeinen Wissens*,
            vol. 6 (Leipzig and Wien 1890), 381.

The history of the railway in nineteenth-century Florence is characterised by a peculiarity: it had, in fact, two stations, each opened in 1848 within the distance of only a few months from each other, in coincidence with the arrival of the first two lines that reached the city. And, setting it apart from other examples of the same time, one of the two stations was permitted within the walls of the city while the other was built right in front of the city walls. It was the smaller of the two at the time that eventually would win out and relegate the other to the rank of train depot.

Leopolda Station, according to observers of the time, had considerable dimensions and probably represented, in the panorama of the early Italian railway architecture, an example of remarkable interest. From a social and urban point of view, it represented the first step in a process of channelling the interests of the bourgeoisie towards that part of the city. In fact, right after the station began to function, two new quarters of the city emerged, one zoned for expensive homes, the other zoned for middle class and low-cost homes. This marked the onset of an intervention plan for residential areas. The first of the two quarters, at the edge of the main park in the city, represents the first organic and planned development of the city outside the walls. From a city that had been socially uniform, Florence became, simultaneous to the construction of the two stations, a city with very socially and economically defined quarters.

The other station was the smaller of the two, and was named after the reigning Grand Duchess Maria Antonia. This was the site where, some decades later, the current station of Santa Maria Novella was constructed. By the date of construction, this was the first station of Florence. In a rare case in the entire peninsula, this station was allowed to occupy a space within the city walls. Its construction marked the beginning of a series of urban demolitions which generated a system of concentration that later had no alternatives, setting in motion, in a certain sense, the beginning of the modern urban planning history of Florence.

The Florentine railway establishment feels deeply its original character even today. What was achieved, and what for other reasons was not, has imposed lasting constraints on the urban development of Florence. The evolution of this situation over time can be synthesised in the statement that the railway structure has remained stationary whereas, in the meantime, the concentration of traffic on Santa Maria Novella Station has led to the realisation of a web of connections. These form an inextricable tangle towards the north-west, with systems of underpasses forming an obstacle to an easy connection toward the sections of the city that developed later in the direction of the industrial district. Thus, one of the many reasons little has been done in this city from an urban planning point of view in the last few decades, can be singled out in the railway layout, which has remained unchanged since 1927. In nearly a century and a half, the city has endured passively, and without managing to adapt itself, to the vicissitudes of the railway, irrefutably showing its inability to take positive action to resolve problems connected to the growth of the city.

Before the unification of Italy, urban planning issues posed by the presence of the two stations were not thoroughly understood in what concerned the future development of the city. Today it may seem foolish to erect two buildings with identical purposes only a few metres from one another; it would have been better to make the two lines come together into a single station, as the most prescient had proposed. But the fact that two different companies constructed the lines was decisive; indeed a third station was constructed some years after servicing the south-west. The problems with the railway were seen with a new vision when, in 1865, Florence became the capital of Italy. At that point, a famous urban plan foresaw a concentration of the railways in a single grand station that would be able to foster the expansion of the city, now in need of an adequate social profile and a rigorous rationalisation of its functions: this definitively marked the bourgeois transformation of the city.

However, the idea of a single station was short lived because of the high estimated costs. The transfer of the capital completely blocked the project. Thus, the railway scheme of the city was postponed indefinitely, and for some 15 years the issue was set aside to be revived by the Board of Architects and Engineers which showed its interest for the issue. The debate over the city's railway predicament, in fact, remained restricted to technical experts assigned to the jobs. At the end of the century, then, Florence had three stations, but still the railway system cut it in two.

The Florentine railway story outlined here long neglected the zone to the north-west of the city in order to concentrate on the south-eastern side. Indeed, the entire affair can be read like a long debate on how the railway coming from the South should have been moved, presenting local administrators with a difficult question, at a time when the natural tendency of the city's industrial development was mainly to the north and north-west. Thus, the railway did not contribute enough to favour this development.

The events connected to the construction of the new Santa Maria Novella Station during the 1930s, with the Fascist regime at its height, are well known and represent one of the most famous episodes of 'rationalist' architecture in Italy. The re-arrangement of the station had been decided upon since the beginning of the century, in 1909, and was part of a wider picture of urban railway reorganisation. It was at this time that the competition for the construction of the new passenger station was launched.

Rome: the capital of classical antiquity

Of the three cities considered in this study, the one in which the railway history had the least impact is, paradoxically, the largest one – Rome. Subject to papal rule until 1870, Rome took on the question of railways with some delay. Linked up with Frascati from 1856, it lagged behind all the other big cities in Italy. When other lines were planned and underway, some people had the idea to build a single terminal which could reunite them. The debate that developed in those years regarding the location of the station, was steered by some high prelates close to the Pope for speculation purposes. This led to the singling out of a peripheral zone on the site of the ruins of the Terme of Diocleziano. The plan to build a new residential area around what is today *via Nazionale* represents one of the stronger reasons behind the decision of where to situate the station. In general it is possible to state that the decision about where the station in Rome should be built is motivated by speculative real estate motives and the desire to create a hotel district for travellers in the immediate vicinity.

Termini therefore were soon born; starting in 1862 the area was circumscribed, but not without inciting critics who pointed out its peripheral position with respect

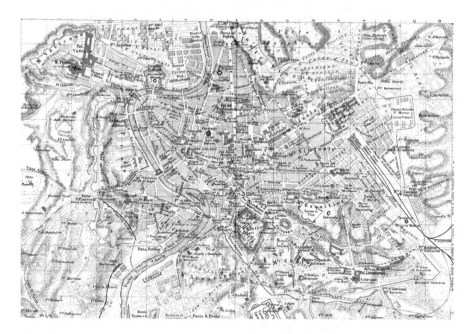

Figure 7.3 Map of Rome, 1890

Source: *Meyers Konversations-Lexikon. Eine Enzyklopädie des allgemeinen Wissens,*
            vol. 13 (Leipzig and Wien 1890), 904–5.

to the heart of city life. This was, all together, a rather anomalous case in the
overall panorama, which clearly favoured the positioning of the stations and the
access to the railway as close to the centre as possible. The station was completed
in 1874 by Salvatore Bianchi, who did not leave a particularly original mark on the
architecture of the building. Apart from the criticism due to the remarkable
sacrifices imposed on the surrounding zone by the restructuring, the first Termini
Station opened an infinite series of court cases. In fact, after but a few years, critics
were asking that the station be moved, starting a heated debate on the overall railway
system in the city in Rome, as it was happening in Milan and Florence. In a short
while, the location, believed to be too far from the centre, became, on the contrary, an
obstacle to urban expansion since it was now thought to be too centrally located
given the progressive growth of the city. Unquestionably the localisation of the
station promoted the drafting of a development plan that the city would not have
been able to implement had the station been placed closer to the city centre.

The debate that emerged towards the end of the century led to an important
decentralisation of the railway functions, mostly concentrated in Termini at first, in
favour of other stations that had slowly grown up in the city. What remained in the

great square built in front of the station, was mainly the terminus of the tramways, first run by steam and then electricity, servicing the city and the outskirts.

Starting immediately after the Second World War, those in favour of moving the station were again heard, and even though its location did not change much it ended up being reconstructed according to the architectural style deeply influenced by the classical antiquity of the city's past.

Towards a redefinition of the relationship between railways and the city

This brief overview makes clear that in the overall Italian experience railways have not been used as a conscious instrument capable of giving direction to broader regional planning choices, but rather have provoked consequences demanding ex post remedies. This claim can easily be verified examining evidence dating from the nineteenth century. In some cases the negative effects on urban development were endured by the city and in other cases city planners have taken these projects as given and non-negotiable. In both cases, even when strangely intertwined, the net result has been to have contributed more problems to the city than were solved.

One moves from the initial developments where the station was the centre of attention to cases in which the establishment of the railway network translated into physical barriers, an obstacle that was hard to overcome in the process of urban expansion. More recently development has been more heterogeneous and discontinuous and has been characterised by a great mixture of diverse activities. From this point of view, most of the interventions that follow the initial establishment of the network can be seen as being aimed at reconciling the difficult relationship between the railway network and the urban social fabric, and at understanding the slow process of reclaiming a regional balance consisting of a technical network built around the station as a hub.

The three cases briefly analysed above possess obvious elements in common and, at the same time, show their own peculiarities. In the first place an element that is easy to isolate is the pivotal role played by the railways which in the three cities heavily conditions their respective urban layouts. On the whole, then, it is possible to assert that they reflect the overall Italian experience since they are characterised by the lack of ability to carry out long-term urban planning. Briefly stated, and at the risk of being excessively reductive, the fact of having given more confidence to the architects than to urban planners has bequeathed a large quantity of unresolved issues upon these three cities. The result is that, with respect to urban railway planning, these Italian cities were left far behind other similar European cities. In Milan, as in Florence and Rome, decisions are always made in emergency conditions, after previous planning proved disastrous because of unforeseen evolution of urban needs. In truth, it was difficult to forecast the trends in urban development ensuing from the rapid and disorderly economic growth in Italy in that period. But it is also true that the episodes analysed above confirm the assumption that the Italian case shows the lack of a connection between city planning needs and needs related to the railways and to infrastructure in general. The two systems have ignored each other for too long or, however, they have not taken their mutual interdependence enough into account, though not so much at the moment of the realisation of the first railway systems as in the successive phases of city expansion. This has led to situations of significant prejudice that have prevented appropriate city development: this is also due to real estate speculation against which railways have had better ways of defending themselves, though never emerging unscathed. The total elimination of railway hubs from city centres cannot be seen as a correction for past errors, as is often claimed.

From the nineteenth century to today: a continuous history

In the course of the last twenty years important changes have taken place. The increase in energy consumption provoked by traffic congestion in urban areas and the halting of the phenomenon of internal migration, starting in the 1980s, led to a tendency to improve and strengthen the mid-range regional and metropolitan areas rail networks. This is based on the idea that the overall transportation system hinges on the integration of the means of transportation and no longer on their mutual interchangeability. The result is a new strategy favouring the regional rail networks which has on the one hand found concrete applications in the organisation of routes and timetables and on the other has led to the definition of some projects that are extremely ambitious for their size and complexity. In the 1980s a long series of big projects were started, which often were political feathers in the cap of municipal administrations, in the area of infrastructure. The conviction that the modernisation of cities must pass through the elaboration of exaggeratedly overgrown infrastructure plans leads administrators and town planners down the path of big, often privately financed, projects that are incapable of fully responding to public needs. The example of the big projects connected to the development of the World Football Championship in 1990 is a good example of this. Tangentopoli has brought to an abrupt end this season of grandeur, provoking a sudden retreat in the area of infrastructure.

In the last twenty years the great railway systems inserted into the urban fabric have evolved, increasingly becoming centres of exchange between the various means of transportation. With the passing of time the division between the railway system and ground transportation system has eroded. The remarkable increase of mobility tied to the exponential increase of the phenomenon of commuting and the new economy based on services has determined a strong technological evolution of the systems of rail transportation, due also to the strong competition with other non-rail means of transportation. In the past, the strengthening of the systems was obtained by means of the parcelling out of services that could be transferred elsewhere without compromising passenger service. The solutions envisaged were therefore the transfer of the locomotives, of the freight services, of the maintenance and cleaning services, and of the assembly of trains. Today all this presents many difficulties and the systems tend to be concentrated once again in the station, like in the first railway phase. This is done with the aim of favouring passenger services, whose importance with respect to freight is overwhelming. The main objective turns out to be the increase of the operating potential of the main station. Therefore the decentralisation of industrial factories makes the localisation of freight traffic in the centre of the city useless, thus the aim is to establish new decentralised freight services to replace the current ones and to eliminate the circulation of freight trains inside the hub by using, strengthening, or designing suitable peripheral routes or lines whose purpose is to diffuse the circulation of freight away from the main lines. Driven by new requirements and types of use the traditional station model has taken on an important new form: the commuter station. Briefly, this refers to a traffic switching hub conceived of as a transit space for the person with little time, but who knows his own route. What this entails is that train passengers of this type are motivated by needs that are the complete opposite of those which have traditionally conditioned the habitual parameters of train use. The need arises to find workable solutions that allow for the reconciliation of the operation of a station in which the travel formalities are reduced to a minimum as they are for a subway station, with that of a station in which the potential user needs various services, from information to hospitality during layover times. It is for this reason that a stronger need is felt for underground stations that are more similar to subway stations. The prevailing tendency today is to go beyond the needs presented by long distance transportation in order to accommodate the possibility of carrying out regional services. The winning solution seems to be one in which advantage is taken of the railway lines already absorbed into nearly central positions in the urban fabric so as to provide short distance local services. This would be done with the aim of adding them to the circulation of long distance trains upgrading the middle distance lines with modern technologies of signalling and automatic traffic management. The objective is to design networks of metropolitan transportation services running on the railways leading to suitable suburban stations in which the exchange is made with long distance trains. Thus, the stations can gain efficiency and functionality only by respecting their history and by connecting them within a general transportation system that is integrated with the urban environment. This solution would entail a redefinition of the station's role from an exclusively enclosed space to make it become an urban space as crossroads where other activities can be brought in and accommodated.

In conclusion, today's railway stations introduce reasons for change that go in several directions, but that have not pushed towards a redefinition of the meaning of having a pivotal point of this importance inside the city. The restructuring that has occurred has been implemented without resorting to a specific logic: the original function was abandoned and the spaces have been filled. The building has lost all identity and, as a consequence, an indiscriminate and disorderly use of every surface has ensued. The railway station appears more and more to be a mere container. Pure functionalism, the denial of historical references, simplification pushed to exaggeration and the cancellation of every specific sign that can serve to identify unequivocally the vocation of the railway building increasingly characterises the current period. The progressive loss of identity and specificity of the railway space from the rest has paralleled the loss of efficiency in this same service. A rampant architectonic conformism has imposed a figurative and communicative language on the station on loan from other dominant archetypes, from the airport to the shopping centre. In particular the airport has transmitted a sense of inferiority to the train relative to the airplane. Today stations no longer stand out in the urban context, having, in practice, lost their memory.

Therefore, they no longer count as buildings closed unto themselves and able to act as symbols, but as hubs of interconnection between the network and the region. That which they have lost in image, they have regained in terms of city planning, which defines functions, layouts and strategies that value the potentialities of the network according to a logic that does not disregard its technical aspects or the physical context of reference. The relationship between infrastructure and the creation of new attraction points cannot be seen only as a relationship between a transportation project and the ensuing effects, in that the action to change infrastructures often carries also a localisation plan that should be the natural consequence of the quality of the network and of the hubs. What seems at the origins of the current evolutionary process of the station is the introduction of a third dimension in the city, an underground development allowing levels of transportation that guarantee the customers a switch from one network to another.

As a concluding remark, let us refer to the two main topics in the present context: the first one is related to the High Speed Trains, or to be more precise, to the crossing of the city by these High Speed Trains. The issue may reproduce the same explosive problems posed by the impact of the railway in cities at the origins in the nineteenth century. There are numerous striking similarities. Another issue is that of urban connecting lines (*passanti ferroviari*), that is, of the underground crossing of the city: it is a subject which is receiving increasing attention on the part of the main municipal administrations in Italy, in terms both of the many problems that it poses, and of a rediscovery of railways as a means of transportation. This rediscovery is made necessary in a country increasingly suffocated by a strong presence of motor vehicles. These issues characterise many opposing political programmes in the major cities and electoral competitions are likely to be played around them. More than a century and a half from its advent in the cities, the railway has conquered a space and a role that it had not previously succeeded in obtaining.

PART II

The Metropolis and the Railway

Wonderful trains ! From morn till night,
Clattering though tunnels without daylight.
Hither and thither they run, up and down,
Beneath the streets of London Town.

Many prefer these trains instead
Of the cabs and 'busses' overhead,
For they run much faster than horses can,
Miss Dot's papa is a busy man,
And goes to the City every day
By the underground – the quickest way.

(Children's book, *London Town*, 1883)

CHAPTER EIGHT

Railway development in the capital city: the case of Paris

François Caron

The history of Paris and its railways can be viewed from two separate angles: that of the capital's integration into the national rail network and that of the Parisian rail network's integration into the regional transport system.[1] This history is paradoxical. Up until the 1960s, while the national network was characterised by a dense network of railway lines converging on Paris, the regional network was underdeveloped and suffered from a total absence of co-ordination between the lines inside Paris, managed by the metropolitan companies, and those serving the Paris region, managed by the railway companies. The development of high-speed rail lines (*Train à Grande Vitesse*, TGV) since the 1980s and of the rapid transit system (*Réseau Express Régional*, RER) since the 1970s has profoundly modified the relations between Paris and the rest of France and transformed the structure of regional railway services. This article begins by describing the system which dominated French national and regional geography up to the 1960s, then goes on to examine the dual revolution brought about by the TGV and the RER.

Paris in the national network: From early days up to the 1960s

French geographers unanimously deplored the so-called 'hypertrophy' of the Parisian region in the nineteenth century, attributing this trend to the radial structure of the railway networks. The debate can be summed up in three key questions:

- What were the initial choices?
- Were inter-suburban lines given adequate priority?
- What was the impact of these choices on French urban geography?

---

[1] This text was pronounced at the inaugural session of the Second International Railway History Colloquium organised in Aranjuez by the *Fundación de los ferrocarriles españoles* from February 7 to 9, 2001. The author wishes to thank professor Gabriel Tortella Casares (*Universidad de Alcalà*), Chairman of the Organising Committee, professor Javier Vidal Olivares (*Universidad de Alicante*), committee member, and Miguel Muñoz Rubio, head of the Foundation's Archives and History department, for allowing him to publish the English translation in the present collection.

A bill passed in 1842 defined the main railway lines to be franchised by the State. The proposed network, comprising a series of radial lines linking Paris to the main provincial towns, was based on proposals made in 1838 by Alexis Legrand, Transport Director at the Ministry of Public Works. It was called the *Étoile Legrand* (Legrand Star). Between 1842 and 1859, the national network was divided into six major networks of which five – *Nord, Est, Paris-Lyons-Mediterranea, Paris-Orléans* and *Ouest* – were composed of lines converging towards the main lines of the Legrand Star. There are few subjects which have given rise to so many fanciful notions. Let me put the record straight on just two of them.

Number one. Certain geographers claim that the Legrand Star was designed exclusively to defend Paris from attack and that, for this reason, the lines were drawn as straight as possible. In reality, the aim of building lines to the French borders was, according to the law of 1842, as much 'to develop relations with neighbouring countries, thereby furthering the cause of peace' as to 'facilitate troop concentration'. As for the choice of route, the lines rarely followed a 'direct' path, to employ the expression used at the time. Admittedly, there was disagreement in most cases regarding the choice of option – direct or indirect route – though the indirect route generally won the day. *Number two.* It is true, on the other hand, that under the very terms of the 1842 Act, the trunk lines were to start from Paris, 'the centre of the country's administrative, commercial and industrial life'. The aim, said Armand Dufaure in 1837, was to strengthen 'the action of central power, too frequently dissipated in an excessive preoccupation with local interests'.[2]

But the political argument was not the only justification for a radial system centred on Paris. Profitability assessments made by the authorities and banks showed that the only lines capable of ensuring an adequate return on investment were those serving the capital city. For the history of Paris as the centre of French economic life largely predated the arrival of the railways. Its prosperity was due not only to the size of its population and the wealth of its inhabitants, but also to the power of the business networks centred on the capital and symbolised by its prestigious merchant banks. In 1823, the *Conseil de Salubrité de la Seine* (Seine Sanitation Authority) rightly noted that the city of Paris 'has always been the centre of trade and can today be considered as the centre of industry'.[3]

Regional lines were first seen as a necessary complement to the lines converging on Paris. They were perceived as a means for France to play an active role in international transit and to facilitate direct international trade. Several such lines were built in the 1860s and 1870s on the initiative of local community leaders

---

[2]   For 1842 Railway Act see Rapport de la commission de la Chambre des députés. *Moniteur Universel*, 17 April 1842. Quoted in A. Picard, *Les Chemins de fer français*, 2 vols. (Paris 1883), vol. 1, 249. For the quotation of Armand Dufaure see Discussion du projet de loi pour la contruction d'un chemin de fer de Lyon à Marseille, *Moniteur Officiel*, June 8, 1837. Quoted in A. Picard, ibid. 56.

[3]   Rapport du Conseil de salubrité de la Seine for 1823. Quoted in Guillaume de Bertier de Sauvigny, *Nouvelle histoire de Paris: La Restauration* (Paris 1977), 289.

wishing to counterbalance the dominance of Paris. But regional lines were largely neglected in the organisation of the French railway system. Most of them were formed by the 'juxtaposition of sections constructed at different times and for different reasons'.[4] They were always difficult to run and service quality in terms of punctuality and speed was never able to match the standards of the radial lines. According to the Atlantic port authorities, the low density of shipping traffic could be attributed to the poor quality of the rail transport services.

The maps of goods and passenger railway traffic drawn up by the French railways (*Société Nationale des Chemins de fer Français*, SNCF) in 1972 show that most traffic still converged on Paris, though major regional lines had developed in north-eastern France over the years. Etienne Auphan concludes his 1985 analysis of rail services by stating that 'regional trunk lines are practically non-existent'.[5] Jean Varlet studied SNCF timetables to analyse the accessibility of various French towns in the early 1980s. He concludes that Paris is 'clearly ahead of all other cities (...) with services covering ninety per cent of the country by means of good, very good and excellent rail links'.[6] Lyons, which comes second, covers only fifty per cent of the country. Moreover, initial network centralism was reinforced by a centralised mode of operation. This centralisation is both the cause and the consequence of the capacity of Paris and its region to attract new inhabitants and new economic activity.

The growth of Paris and the French urban geography

The figures show that the growth of Paris accelerated from the 1840s with the start of rail network construction. In 1820, Parisians represented 2.8 per cent of the total French population, compared with 16.2 per cent in 1936. Since then, the population of the Paris region has grown at the same rate as elsewhere in France. But the capital's zone of influence has spread far beyond the agglomeration itself. It now covers not only the entire metropolitan area (*Île-de-France*), which in 1944 represented 19 per cent of the French population, but also the whole of the Parisian basin. For many years, the two rings of suburban towns surrounding Paris suffered from their proximity to the city, largely because the railways were designed above all for long-distance transport. But since 1950, this trend has been reversed and the capital exerts its attraction over an ever wider area, covering the entire Parisian basin.

---

[4] Maurice Wolkowitsch, *L'Économie régionale des transports dans le Centre et le Centre ouest de la France* (Paris 1960), 83.

[5] Etienne Auphan, 'L'espace et les systèmes à grande vitesse', in 'Les impacts du TGV sur l'organisation de l'espace en France et en Corée', *Cahiers du Centre de recherches et d'études sur Paris et l'Ile-de-France (CREPIF)*, no. 61, special issue, 1997, 9–38, esp. 20.

[6] Jean Varlet, *Géographie des relations ferroviaires en France*, Université de Clermont II Ph.D. thesis, 1987, 120.

This demographic and spatial hypertrophy reflects the growing economic weight of the capital. In the nineteenth century, thanks to the convergence of the various transport networks, Parisian traders gained control over an increasing number of product markets. The Paris region, central focus of the various communication channels, was well placed to attract the industries of both the first and second industrial revolutions. Indeed, Paris provided manufacturers with the infrastructures they needed to ship raw materials in and finished products out, thanks largely to the rail network. The development of commercial activities was stimulated by the exceptional quality of the passenger rail links with the rest of France, already in place by 1850.

Analysing developments in French urban structure between 1836 and 1911, the geographer Denise Pumain observes that 'the railway network is generally an indicator rather than a factor of urban discrimination' and that 'it has maintained or aggravated long-standing disparities of size and demographic vitality, without necessarily being their cause'.[7] Indeed, the network was designed according to the size hierarchy of existing towns and cities. The earlier the arrival of the railway and the larger the junction, the more profound its effects on the town. So large towns grew faster than smaller ones. It was as if the radial network layout favoured the towns and cities possessing the best rail connections with Paris, the main network junctions being located along these radial lines. Moreover, the railways enabled the major provincial towns to affirm their prominence, thereby accentuating, in line with promoters' wishes, the influence of the capital. The current problem is to determine whether the development of the high-speed train network is liable to accentuate this process of attraction or, on the contrary, to attenuate it.

Is the TGV reinforcing Parisian centralism?

The decision to build the *TGV Sud-Est* was taken in 1974. The line was inaugurated in 1981. In 1998, the TGV network totalled 1,286 kilometres of lines. But the regions served extend well beyond the stations on the dedicated high-speed line, since TGV trains are capable of running on ordinary track. The TGV network appears to be reproducing the centralised, radial network model first created in the nineteenth century. Some say that is has even amplified its effects since the TGV lines tend to follow the most 'direct' routes. The TGV lines were designed 'solely to provide high-speed, long-distance links between the capital and the regions, to the exclusion of all other traffic flows'.[8] Towns served by the old lines have been by-passed. The TGV stations built in the countryside or close to small villages

---

7   Denise Pumain, 'Chemins de fer et croissance urbaine en France au XIXe siècle', *Annales de géographie*, 507 (Septembre–Octobre), 1982, 529–48, esp. 536.

8   Etienne Auphan, 'L'espace et les systèmes à grande vitesse', in 'Les impacts du TGV sur l'organisation de l'espace en France et en Corée', *Cahiers du Centre de recherches et d'études sur Paris et l'Ile-de-France (CREPIF)*, no. 61, special issue, 1997, 9–38.

symbolise this strategic choice which reproduces the air travel model and would appear to exacerbate the effects of centralism.

In practice, this highly radial network structure has been offset by a number of factors. Firstly, speed alters the relations between the railway network and the national geography. It favours not only Paris, but also other provincial towns and cities. As noted by Jean Ollivro, high speed 'brings the French provincial cities closer to the Parisian heart'. This gives rise to 'the development of a rail periphery around the core of the country'.[9] Moreover, line interconnection in the Paris region has made it possible to develop a denser network of links between provincial regions. The first commercial TGV link between Lille and Lyons, using the TGV line and an ordinary line, was opened in 1984. In 1990, the project for 'TGV interconnection in the *Île-de-France* region' was adopted. The eastern part of this link was opened in 1994, the western part in 1996. The Paris region has thus become a hub crossed by the major axis of the network: a continuous high-speed line from Calais to Marseilles via Lille, Roissy and Lyons Airport. Inter-regional traffic is increasing at a rapid pace and new links are developing which avoid the Paris hub altogether. Lastly, the TGV network is extending across Europe. Lille is no longer a terminus but an exchange platform linked in with the different national networks, a crossroads midway between London and Brussels. In south-eastern France, Lyons is gaining independence from Paris as a transport hub towards Switzerland and Italy. The future Lyons-Turin line and the Languedoc-Roussilon TGV will accelerate this process. The TGV has thus revolutionised the relation between the railways and the national geography, benefiting provincial cities just as much as Paris.

Railways in the Paris region: from the earliest days to the 1960s

The relation between the railways and the Paris region can be viewed from two successive angles – that of the brutal intrusion of the railways into Paris between 1837 and 1859 as the major rail networks started to take form, and that of the progressive formation of a Parisian rail system, shaped by the demands of a growing population, increasing urban spread and the role of Paris as a transit hub. This system underwent radical transformation in the 1960s. The arrival of the railways in the city of Paris raised three problems:

- How many stations are needed?
- Where should they be built?
- Where can the rights of way, other than stations, be located?

---

[9]   Jean Ollivro, 'Le réseau des lignes à grande vitesse: prégnance centralisatrice ou redéfinition de l'espace français?', *Revue d'histoire des chemins de fer*, 12–13, special issue: 'les très grandes vitesses ferroviaires en France', 1995, 196–219.

Following protracted controversy and numerous conflicts of interest, the Parisians decided to build several terminal stations, each corresponding to the endpoint of a network. The Pereire brothers, promoters of the first Parisian railway, the Paris-Saint-Germain, made a first unsuccessful attempt to attract all traffic coming in from the north and west. Later, when a site was needed for the Paris-Melun terminus, later to become the *Gare de Lyon*, the solution of a common section shared with the Paris-Orleans line was rejected. To justify this decision, the Paris city council declared that the income generated by two main lines arriving in Paris was sufficient to cover the cost of station construction and that the operation of the same station by two separate companies would have 'disadvantages which cannot be predicted'. So the choice was rational and not, as some have claimed,

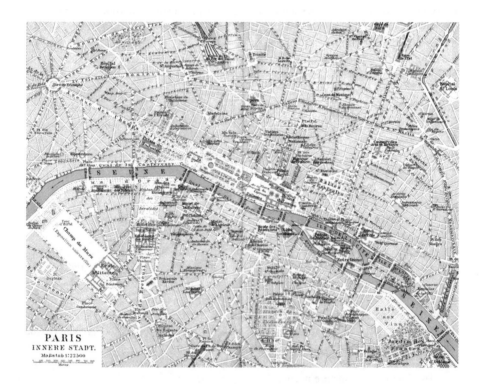

Figure 8.1 Map of Paris, 1890

Source: Meyers Konversations-Lexikon. Eine Enzyklopädie des allgemeinen Wissens, vol. 12 (Leipzig and Wien 1890), 718.

'grotesque'.[10] The terminal stations of the network were located on the edges ofParis, thus preserving the capital from the environmental nuisance of steam. The sites were chosen on the basis of available land and the routes of existing incoming lines. As aptly expressed by Clozier, the lines and the stations were 'slotted into the empty spaces'. Moreover, the chosen sites had to be served by 'wide streets and convenient, simple modes of communication' to avoid additional traffic congestion, already a severe problem.[11] But some stations were better placed than others. *Gare d'Austerlitz* and *Gare de Lyon*, for example, were far from the business centre, which was tending to migrate towards *Gare St Lazare*. For this reason, an extension of the Paris-Orléans line was built between *Gare d'Austerlitz* and *Gare d'Orsay* and opened in 1900. Lastly, vast railway installations – goods stations, marshalling yards, workshops, depots, housing developments for railway workers – were built around the edge of the city and in the suburbs, mainly in the north and south-east. They played a significant role in the creation of new districts and in the structuring of the urban fabric.

Urban growth and commercial and industrial development in the region brought a rapid increase in railway traffic to which the Parisian railway system was obliged to adapt. For more than a century, up until the 1960s, there was no co-ordination of any sort between railway policy and urban policy. Developments focused in three main areas:

- transformation of the main passenger stations
- a poorly managed regional network, marked by the failure of centralism, a lack of circular lines and the growth of a commuter network based on a radial structure
- a growing need for coherence among regional rail network companies

Alongside the Parisian mainline stations, a number of new stations serving suburban lines were opened. In the East, *Gare de Bastille* opened in 1860 to serve the Vincennes line. In the South, two stations were opened on the Sceaux line, Denfert-Rochereau in 1846 and Luxembourg in 1905. In the West, the *Gare de Paris-Invalides* was opened in 1902 to serve a new line towards Versailles.

Long-distance travellers with their voluminous luggage used the same buildings as swarms of commuters. As passenger numbers grew, the companies were obliged to innovate and station interiors were constantly modified to raise capacity. *Gare du Nord* and *Gare du PLM* underwent major transformations in the 1880s and 1890s. *Gare St Lazare* was rebuilt in the 1880s and *Gare d'Orsay* was erected between 1896 and 1900. *Gare de l'Est* was renovated in the 1930s. Railway stations were often the testing grounds of technological and architectural

---

[10] Archives nationales, F14 9003: Letter of the Président du Conseil municipal de Paris attached to the transmission of a Délibération du Conseil municipal, dated 3 March 1845.

[11] See René Clozier, *La Gare du Nord* (Paris 1940).

innovations and the arrival of electricity, providing lighting and motor power, was one of the main instruments of their modernisation.

The construction of railway stations in Paris made it necessary to revise the urban programmes already in progress. They thus signalled the completion of ongoing urban development projects. But they also modified the nature and scope of these projects, as illustrated by the *Quartier de l'Europe*, where the intrusion of the *Gare St Lazare* totally disrupted the programme under way. With the arrival of railway stations, much wider streets were needed. In 1853, the *Commission pour l'Embellissement de Paris* (Committee for the Improvement of Paris) stated that one of its priorities was 'for all main streets to lead to a railway station'.[12] In fact, changes to the street layout mainly affected the immediate neighbourhoods of the stations, rather than urban layout as a whole. *Boulevard de Strasbourg*, which served *Gare de l'Est*, was planned before the arrival of the railways. *Rue de Rennes*, built between 1860 and 1867, ended up as a *cul de sac*. Despite an extension of *Rue Lafayette*, access to *Gare St Lazare* and *Gare du Nord* was not easy. And even the street construction projects realised after 1870 did not give priority to railway station access.

Several studies based on notarial archives are now under way to analyse the property speculation which accompanied and followed the construction of the Parisian railway stations. One of these studies, headed by Karen Bowie, concerns *Gare du Nord*.[13] Immense property transactions were orchestrated by the banker James de Rothschild, who controlled the *Compagnie du Chemin de Fer du Nord*, and by other businessmen operating at a more modest level. Large areas of land were bought up by the Rothschilds to construct leased property which included shops, bourgeois rented apartments and goods depots. Their architecture was very mundane and indeed, there is little sign of architectural harmony in any of the railway station districts. A wide variety of activities grew up in these districts and each one has its own distinct character. The most active was the district around *Gare St Lazare*, which became the business centre of Paris. Business activity inside the stations was generally limited to buffets and bookshops. When *Gare St Lazare* was rebuilt in the 1880s, a hotel complex including a shopping arcade was included in the programme. An inspired example of foresight. The dissociation of railway projects and urban development projects thus remained the rule.

From the outset, the Parisian transport system suffered a severe handicap, namely the absence of a central node linking the lines of the different railway companies. When the idea of building an underground railway was put forward in the 1870s, several major companies suggested building a network to take the regional trunk lines beyond their existing terminuses to a central station at *Palais*

---

[12] Commission des embellissements de Paris, 'Rapport à l'empereur Napoléon III', in Pierre Casselle, ed., *Cahiers de la Rotonde*, vol. 23 (Paris 2000), 1–205.esp. 11.

[13] See Karen Bowie, ed., *Polarisation du territoire et développement urbain: les gares du Nord et de l'Est et la transformation de Paris au XIXe siècle. Une étude sur l'instauration et l'évolution des rapports entre les acteurs des grands aménagements ferroviaires urbains, première étape (1830–1870)*, 2 vols. (Paris 1999).

Royal. This idea was rejected by the municipal authorities, who decided to build a metropolitan network for strictly local use, with no links to the mainline network or to the suburban municipalities. The five mainline networks were linked via two circular lines – the *Petite Ceinture* and the *Grande Ceinture*, managed by a 'syndicate' grouping the five companies. These two lines enjoyed contrasting fortunes. The various sections of the *Petite Ceinture* were opened between 1852 and 1867. It was the first Parisian mass transit line, with thirty million passengers in 1899. But, unable to compete with the metropolitan railway, the *Petite Ceinture* was closed to passengers in 1934. This decision was a serious mistake. The *Petite Ceinture* was used extensively to transport goods between the networks. It provided rail links with several major commercial and industrial establishments, such as the *Gare de Paris-Bestiaux*, though traffic progressively declined from the 1930s. But the *Petite Ceinture* failed to inspire any large-scale urban development projects. It simply crossed through the industrial zones and towns it served. From 1864, however, it was used by the train carrying the English mail between the various Parisian railway stations and, from 1880, by trains travelling from London to Switzerland, central Europe and the French Rivi-era.[14] Passengers thus avoided an uncomfortable transfer from one Parisian station to another, though the trains must have been painfully slow. The *Petite Ceinture*, a precursor of today's TGV interconnection, was progressively dismantled after the war. Line C of the RER now follows a part of its route.

The fate of *Grande Ceinture* was very different. Opened between 1875 and 1882, measuring 120 kilometres in length and forming a ring ten to twenty kilometres from the capital, it is linked to the main radial lines serving the Parisian railway stations. It never carried much passenger traffic, a fact that the towns along its route attributed to 'the inadequate number of trains and the inconvenient timetables'.[15] On the other hand, the *Grande Ceinture* was an immediate success for goods transport between the networks, to the point of creating constant traffic jams at the junctions with the main radial lines. The line was progressively electrified and modernised after the Second World War. In 1992, an internal SNCF document stated that traffic on the eastern *Grande Ceinture* now totalled thirty million tonnes of freight per year, the equivalent of 1,500,000 loaded trucks. Passenger traffic, previously seasonal in nature, was also increasing. The circular lines thus fulfilled two distinct functions: local passenger traffic before the arrival of the metropolitan railway and goods transport, with the *Grande Ceinture* forming a key component of the national freight network. However, these lines were never the vectors of a new urban development policy.

The mainline networks and later the SNCF found themselves in charge of an increasing volume of commuter traffic, always viewed by operators as unprofitable and not entirely 'respectable'. The development of railway services led to growing

---

[14] We wish to thank Bruno Carrière for this information.

[15] Conseil Général de Seine et Oise in 1909. Quoted by Bruno Carrière, *L'Aventure de la Grande Ceinture* (Paris 1991), 88.

suburban urbanisation and industrialisation, a trend which accelerated from the 1890s. To begin with, most passengers on these lines were Parisians on weekend outings. But they were soon outnumbered by commuters travelling from their homes in the suburbs to their workplace in Paris. Indeed, traffic increased at an

Figure 8.2   The trunk French railway network in 1860

Source: Lartilleux, *Géographie des chemins de fer français*, 2 vols. (Paris 1962), vol. 1.

unexpectedly rapid pace from the 1880s, with passenger numbers totalling 193 million by 1913. The busiest station was *Gare St Lazare*, with more than 58 million passengers, 82 per cent of whom were commuters. In 1970, 63 million long-distance travellers and 387 million commuters used the Parisian railway stations. The busiest station was still *Gare St Lazare*, with 148 million passengers, 95 per cent commuters. The percentages were 89, 84 and 70 per cent at *Gare de l'Est*, *Gare du Nord* and *Gare de Lyon* respectively.

The growth in commuter traffic forced the operators to rethink the system of access to the Parisian railway stations and to reorganise the platforms on a regular basis. Following several serious accidents in the 1870s, it became necessary to achieve 'complete independence and simultaneous movement' of long-distance

Figure 8.3 The interconnected French railway main network, 1910–1930

Source: Ibid.

and commuter trains by laying new tracks parallel to existing ones and building specialised lines. It was at the *Gare St Lazare* that the situation was most critical. In fact, the real solution to the problem of track congestion was electrification.

Electrification of the Parisian commuter lines began in 1900. The Paris-Orleans main line extension from *Gare d'Austerlitz* to the new *Gare d'Orsay* was built underground along a distance of 3.1 kilometres. Electric power was used to 'pull smoke-free trains', thus creating the very first electrified section of the French network.[16] The line was electrified up to Juvisy station, in the suburbs, in 1904. Similar equipment was installed by the *Compagnie de l'Ouest* on the new Paris-Invalides-Versailles line. Electricity soon proved itself to be the best power source for suburban trains. After the First World War, the suburban line electrification committee set up in March 1920 adopted an ambitious plan which was only partly realised. Between 1924 and 1936, 120 kilometres of lines were electrified on the suburban lines serving St Lazare, though the suburban network as a whole counted only 204 kilometres of electrified lines.

In the 1950s, electrification was limited to links that followed certain trunk lines which were themselves already electrified, such as Paris-Lyons and Paris-Lille. The dedicated suburban lines were not electrified until the 1960s. Indeed, it was not until the end of the decade that steam trains finally disappeared from *Gare St Lazare*, *Gare du Nord*, and *Gare de l'Est*. And yet commuter traffic increased by sixty per cent between 1953 and 1980. In 1982, the railways transported 15.6 per cent of travellers using public transport in the Paris region, though accounted for 39 per cent of passenger-kilometres. The mean journey length on the railways was 17 kilometres compared with seven kilometres for journeys in general. The railways were the number one choice for long-distance regional public transport.

The system of railway installations grew up around the sites of the earliest stations and depots. The goods stations were broken up into a set of specialised sub-units, such as *Gare de Paris-Bestiaux* (for livestock). From the 1870s, each network was obliged to build one or more marshalling yards – Noisy-le-Sec and Pantin in the east, Villeneuve-Saint-Georges and Trappes on the PLM, Le Bourget in the North, Achères in the West – located close the junctions between the *Grande Ceinture* and major radial lines. Works to improve access to the major Parisian stations launched in the 1880s included a rationalisation of railhead zones. For example, on the PLM line, the workshops were moved from Paris to the Villeneuve-Saint-Georges marshalling yard in the south and the goods stations were reorganised. Between the two World Wars, a new site was built at Châtillon, to the South of Paris, and the Vaugirard depot, first opened in 1852, was transferred to this new location. It is now used as a TGV train depot. The Parisian system of railway installations has thus been regularly reorganised and rationalised to take account of developments in the regional network.

Railways in the region since the 1960s: the RER

In the inter-war years, local authorities finally realised that railway policy is a key component of urban development and sought to integrate the railway programme into a more global regional development project. The first project for a regional

---

16   Anonymous, 'La traction électrique sur le prolongement du chemin de fer d'Orléans à Paris', *Revue générale des chemins de fer*, 21–2, no. 5 (November) 1998, 384–7, esp. 380.

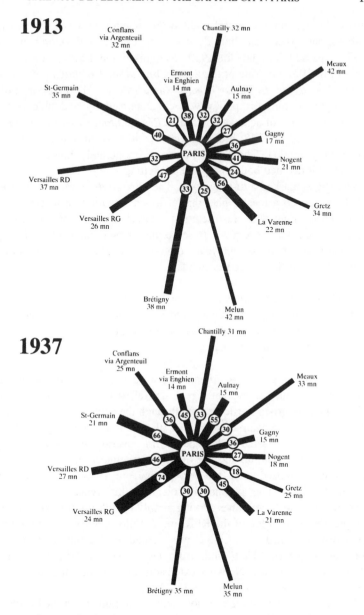

Figure 8.4 Directions, traffic flows and travel time for local trains from Paris, 1913 and 1937

Source: Bruno Carrière, *Les Trains de banlieue*, vol. 1: *1837–1938* (Paris 1998), 162.

network built around a central node at the junction between the two main north-south and east-west radial lines dates back to 1927. The development plan, adopted in 1934, passed into law in 1939, recognised the need to develop a regional network. In 1932, the sale of the Sceaux line to the *Compagnie du Métro Parisien* by the *Compagnie du Paris-Orléans* was a step in this direction. From 1945 to 1960, regional transport policy was characterised by a double lack: a lack of projects and a lack of achievements. The *Régie Autonome des Transports Parisiens* (RATP), created in 1948, bringing together all Parisian bus and metro lines, was inadequately funded. The SNCF was only moderately interested in a transport system that it deemed both costly and unexciting.

The 1960s marked a turning point. The *District de la Région Parisienne* set up in 1961 proposed a master plan that affirmed an ambition to create 'new towns' outside Paris along with 'restructuring centres' of more modest dimensions. The role of the transport system was to serve these new urban centres. This master plan was greatly modified over the years, though it remained a reference document. The options chosen reflect three key trends:

- the birth of true centralism
- the creation, both in the centre and in the outer suburbs, of business hubs and of exchange nodes around points of railway access
- the failure of transversality

In the 1965 master plan, new urban zones were to be served primarily by a network of motorways. But the idea of a regional rail network organised from a central node with all suburban traffic passing through the centre, originally proposed in the 1950s, was taken up again in the master plan. This was the origin of the RER rapid transit system. But for the RER to take form, several miracles were necessary. The most unexpected was the success of the interconnection between the SNCF and RATP lines, imposed upon the two partners in 1968. It met with only minor teething troubles. The second miracle was the reuse of numerous existing infrastructures, with new lines serving simply to link up pre-existing sections. For example, the eastern leg of the RER line A follows a section of the Paris-Bastille line at Boissy-Saint-Léger. Line C was created, on the initiative of the SNCF, by interconnecting two SNCF lines from *Gare des Invalides* to the underground station at *Gare d'Orsay*. Network extension towards the suburbs was achieved by reusing parts of the old *Grande Ceinture* line.

A new conception of the railway station as a multi-functional centre of activity integrated into the life of the town, first emerged in the 1950s. The reconstruction of *Gare de Montparnasse*, launched in 1958, provided an opportunity to design a new station complex constructed around a 'commercial business hub'. This hub grew in importance when *Gare de Montparnasse* became the terminus for the *TGV Atlantique*. Numerous property developments of this kind were built in the 1970s and 1980s. On the RER line A, for example, the La Défense, Les Halles and *Gare de Lyon* districts are not only intermodal transport hubs but also centres of administrative, commercial, cultural and university activity. The new towns, on the other hand, have suffered from a long history of poor railway services. Marne-la-Vallée is the only area to have benefited from a transport service that has kept pace with urban development. The eastern branch of the RER A line has been defined as the 'spinal cord of the new conurbation'.[17] Other railway nodes have formed along the RER regional lines, the TGV lines and even at airports. The construction of the TGV interconnection provided an opportunity to design highly modernistic stations linked to the RER: Roissy-Charles-de-Gaulle, Marne-la-Vallée-Chessy to the East, which serves Disneyland Paris and Massy in the south, linking up to the *TGV Nord*, *Sud-Est* and *Sud-Ouest* with the RER network and with one of the traditional inter-suburban lines forming part of the RER line C, from Versailles to Massy.

A permanent feature of transport policy in the Paris region has been the non-implementation of projects for construction of inter-suburban lines included in the various programmes. A study in 1984 showed that two-thirds of car journeys were from one suburb to another and that the railways held only a 13 per cent market share in this segment. In 1994, the *Île-de-France* regional master plan gave priority to 'tangential' lines – inter-suburban lines far from Paris – because, according to the plan, 'they are less heavily used than radial lines but necessary for long-term development of peripheral centres'.[18] But these projects have been sacrificed in favour of programmes, such as *Météor* and *Éole*, aiming to resolve the problems of severe congestion along the central sections of the radial lines. In fact, passengers travelling from one suburb to another are obliged to use the radial lines. It is as if the choice of a radial system for inter-suburban or inter-regional transport was the only available option for the RER and for the TGV alike.

Conclusion

The history of railway transport in the Paris region highlights a number of general factors affecting the relations between the railways and the world's major cities. The railway networks were designed to fit into an urban structure inherited from a previous era, and whose general layout and hierarchies were accentuated rather than modified as a result. In the case of France, the effect of Paris' position as a capital city was amplified by network centralisation. But with the development of the TGV, we are witnessing a more general trend which, by favouring inter-regional relations as much as relations between Paris and the provinces, appears to be benefiting the regional cities to the same extent as Paris itself.

The pattern of urban development and population growth in Paris and its region has been closely linked to the routes of its main railway lines. In the early days,

---

[17] Service de documentation de la SNCF, SNCF, *Contribution à l'élaboration d'un nouveau schéma directeur de l'Île de France* (Paris 1992).

[18] Claude Bordas and Marc Gayda, *De Saint-Germain-en-Laye à Marne-la-Vallée* (Valignat 1992), 87.

railway stations were the focus of spontaneous and largely unstructured development. Since the 1960s however, they have become major business hubs including wide-ranging activities, competing with or providing a complement to the major road systems. Recent network centralisation has reinforced the unity of an increasingly tentacular region, aggravating the problems of central congestion despite the development of new suburban centres of activity. The most urgent task, already identified some forty years ago, is to promote the development of direct relations between these peripheral centres by means of inter-suburban links.

CHAPTER NINE

Railway stations and planning projects in Prague, 1845–1945

Alena Kubova

The very first train arrived in Prague central station on August 20, 1845. The opening of the new line between Vienna and Prague was a major spectacle, as well as a society event widely reported in the press.[1] Could it be that the birth of Prague as a modern city was due to the railways? To understand why this first train caused such a sensation, it is important to grasp the significance of the new railway line. At the time, Prague, former capital of the kingdom of Bohemia and of the Habsburg empire, was a provincial city. Dominated by the political centralism of Vienna, it had lost much of its earlier prestige. Its affirmation as a cultural centre was held back by its lack of political status. Until the proclamation of the Czechoslovak Republic in 1918, the Czech Lands formed part of the Austrian Empire. The arrival of the first train was doubly symbolic: it showed that Prague was both a modern city and a European capital.

The role of the station in modern Prague

Dreams began to overtake reality. The new image of Prague was based on a vision of a railway network criss-crossing the whole of Europe. For a while, there was even a blurring of the boundaries between the urban development projects for the city itself and the political project to make Prague into the capital of an independent nation. Beyond the construction of a railway network, countless new possibilities for communication and trade were mooted. Indeed, it is striking to see the shift in intellectual attitudes that took place. In place of the initial political project, new demands for cultural modernity and for affirmation of the Czech identity within Europe started to take shape. But only a project of national scope would be capable of taking such ideological ambitions on board.[2]

Soon it was the turn of the artistic world, caught up in the general movement, to express its profound desire for national emancipation as part of an overall vision of modernity. In Prague, the aim was to re-conquer Europe. So the almost mythical

---

[1] Jiri Kohout and Jiri Vancura, *Praha 19. a 20. stoleti: Technicke promeny* (Prague 1986), 71–2.

[2] See T. G. Masaryk, *Ceska otazka* (The Czech Question) (Prague 1936).

image of a train arriving in the city was presented to the public much like an artist's painting. But why so little interest in the design of the railway station itself? Was it a deliberate desire to show reticence with respect to Vienna? Or just an oversight? If the latter is true, why did the comments on its architecture remain so laconic, even many years later? In *Praha narodniho probuzeni* (Prague at the time of the national outburst), the authors of this important work skim over the station's architecture, describing the façade and style in a bare few lines.[3] There is no reference to the station as a modern component of the city's urban infrastructure, to

**Figure 9.1   Map of Prague. A: Prague central station, 1845,
B: Prague main station, 1906**

Source: Map made by Alena Kubova.

---

3   Emanuel Poche, Dobroslav Libal, Eva Reinhartova, and Petr Wittlich, eds., *Praha narodniho probuzeni* (Prague 1980), 101.

the relationship between the station and the city. Descriptions of the passenger building architecture – rarely eloquent – must be seen in the context of the period. Caught between political reality and the dream of new links with Europe, the station, like many other contemporary administrative buildings, embodies the power of Vienna. And yet its opening radically transformed the city.

From Vienna to Prague: the reasons for the City-to-City link

The first station was inaugurated in 1845, at a time of political gloom. Prague was a fortified city, an important strategic site from the military viewpoint. At the time, it had 120,000 inhabitants and was by far the largest city in Bohemia. Liberec, the second Czech city, had a mere 16,000.[4] With 600 kilometres of high-quality roads forming a star-shaped network around the city, Prague was already a major economic centre at the time of the Prague-Vienna railway line opening. As the city developed along the banks of the Vltava river, river traffic provided another equally important mode of transport.

The first development plan for Prague was presented in 1816.[5] Broadly, it provided that polluting industries, such as abattoirs, were to be sited outside the city limits, while traditional activities, such as textiles, were allowed to remain inside the old city walls. With the rapid growth of industrial activity around the periphery of Prague, new entry points into the city became necessary and Emperor Ferdinand I granted permission to breach the city's fortifications. New suburbs soon developed as a consequence. But the Emperor was a distrustful ruler, hostile to all ideas of technical progress. His attitude had a direct and negative impact on the pace of industrialisation, and the railway line between Prague and Vienna was not begun until after his death.

It was the company founded by the Rothschild brothers which financed the construction of the first track section between Brno and Vienna. As early as 1835 the project received the support of Chancellor Metternich, a powerful politician, and in 1839 the first section of the line between Vienna and Brno was opened to traffic. In 1841, the line was extended from Brno to Olomouc and then to Kolin, a small town around fifty kilometres from Prague. Construction work was supervised by two engineers, the Swiss Alois Negrelli and the Czech Jan Perner. From 1842, the central station in Prague became operational and the passenger building was completed within a short few months in 1845.[6]

The station site, covering 13 hectares and located on the edge of the city, quite close to the historical centre, belonged to the army. Station construction made it necessary to breach the city walls and the station was always closed during the

---

[4]   Jiri Kohout and Jiri Vancura, *Praha 19. a 20. stoleti: Technicke promeny* (Prague 1986), 31.

[5]   Ibid. 32.

[6]   Ibid. 71.

night. Indeed, it was perhaps the military status of Prague which represented the key political obstacle to the laying of a railway line. The programme provided for a terminal station with five tracks for goods trains and a further five tracks for passenger traffic.

The strong political links with Vienna can best be illustrated by the decision to construct a building for passengers. This building symbolised the difference in administrative status between Prague and other Czech cities served by the railway. Though Prague was a provincial city, it was nevertheless a strategic point in state organisation. Could it be that the birth of Prague as a modern city was due to the railways?

The Ssation as an urban facility

The railway station was an urban paradox. Though the passenger building was intended to represent the authority of the state, its architecture was simple in the extreme, resembling a mundane administrative building or military barracks. And this architectural simplicity raised the question of its relation with the city.

The architect and engineer Antoine Jüngling designed the passenger building in the form of two perpendicular volumes at the junction between two streets, fitting in with existing urban structures and scale. But the symmetrical façade, flanked by two towers, offered little to attract the eye and gave few clues as to the layout of the central concourse. For obvious economic reasons, the façade was plain and lacking in architectural ornamentation, resembling in all respects a functional public building. Its main highlight, the façade with its two towers, was the only feature to convey the new image of a railway station.

That the station blended so discreetly into the city testifies to its status as a purely utilitarian building. The station was certainly not a monument; its design was quite unexceptional and the habitual trappings of monumental architecture were absent. It was a piece of urban infrastructure, important for its function and not for its looks, a simple addition to the existing fabric. It was soon decided to build another line, heading north of the city. But before it could be constructed, a difficult and costly problem had to be solved. Differences of relative altitude of up to 15 metres existed along the proposed route, raising major technical difficulties for line construction. Negrelli dealt with the problem by building a viaduct, still in service today. This viaduct was a considerable technical feat, though it also served as a factor of exclusion for the Holesovice district close to the station. Over the years, and even prior to the development of many new districts, the 1,100 metre Negrelli viaduct formed a physical boundary – even more imposing than the ancient fortifications – between the edge of the city and its historical centre.[7]

---

[7]   Ibid. 68.

Figure 9.2 Prague central station opened in 1845. Built by architect and engineer Antoine Jüngling

Source: Photo: Alena Hanzlova

At a time when Prague was expanding beyond its historical centre, but when urban development plans did not yet encompass the city as a whole, the presence of a station close to the city centre attracted the attention of investors. Other new types of building, such as the post and telegraph office and the customs building were erected during the same period. Commercial activity boosted construction in the district. Several banks moved into the area and numerous hotels and restaurants were opened, some of which exist today. This new relationship between station and city was illustrated even more clearly by the construction of new districts outside the fortifications. Residential buildings were built in a square grid pattern, though their architecture was predictably uninspired. The juxtaposition of new suburban districts with the railway station gave a foretaste of Prague as a 'great city'. Opened to the public in 1845, the first station was still the only one inside the city. Others were constructed in neighbouring municipalities, such as Smichov.[8]

The Station as a Paradoxical Entity in the Urban Scheme

The notion of functionality provides the key to understanding this new relation between the station and the city. Located at the boundary between the old city and the industrial suburbs, the station transformed the very notion of the city centre. The station was a truly paradoxical urban structure. In 1866, the end of the war between Austria and Prussia initiated a period of major change in Prague. The fortifications, which no longer served any purpose, were demolished and the emperor offered new land to the city. In the Czech bourgeois community, the idea of national emancipation was taking hold. By opening up to the modern industrial world, the Czech bourgeoisie soon became a powerful economic force, despite the troubled political situation. From then on, it would be difficult to prevent Prague from playing its role as Czech capital. The very functioning of the station district confirmed the confidence felt by advocates of national emancipation that Prague could be a truly modern city.

In 1881 the Jubilee Exhibition took place. The central pavilion was built in striking architectural style, with two side towers setting off the transparency of the glass-walled central hall and with electric lighting that highlighted the slender metallic framework. It was reminiscent of the modern new stations built in the major cities of Europe. The fact that most of the Empire's industrial infrastructure was based in the Czech Lands strengthened the economic power of the emerging bourgeoisie. The political project for national emancipation appeared to tie in with technical progress. The plans to build a second major railway station in Prague were a logical next step forward. However, this second station, built by

---

[8]   Ibid. 72.

V. Barvitius inside Prague and whose architecture resembled a 'Renaissance Italian villa' soon proved inadequate and was quickly demolished.[9]

The station as a monument of the modern city

In 1899, a competition was launched to build the Franz-Josef I railway station, now the main station, on the site of the demolished fortifications, at the edge of the old city, not far from the first station. The winner was Josef Fanta, a famous Prague architect. He was a protagonist of the 'Czech Renaissance', and his style illustrated the link between architecture and the project for the capital.[10] In complete opposition to Jüngling's approach, Fanta gave full prominence to station architecture. Fanta integrated empty space into the very design of the building, a prerequisite for all monumental structures – as if the construction of a new station involved a clear link with the history of the city. It is this link with history, in the broadest sense of the term, that was reflected in the new station architecture. The difference between Fanta's station and a historical monument no longer lay in the intrinsic design, as was the case for the first station, but in the originality of the programme.

The design of the passenger building was determined by this relation with the existing city. The first priority was to include the station, more exactly the large passenger building, in a field of vision that obeys the geometrical rules of perspective. The lessons learnt from Renaissance architecture were immediately apparent. The modern station was designed to stand out. The most ornamental façade was, of course, the one which faced the old city. The massive main façade, decorated with numerous sculptures, was intended to impress and the central hall, built using new techniques, was visible from afar. In his way, the Czech architect interpreted the image of other stations built in other major European cities. In Prague, this was no ordinary building. However, the two large metal-framed halls designed by the engineers J. Marjanko and Kornfield are rarely mentioned in the literature.[11] The construction of Prague's main station, which occupies a large area of the city centre, is based on a traditional distribution of roles between the architect and the engineer. Fanta's architecture makes a clear distinction between the different functions of the station. However, the architect also introduced a technical innovation, with access to trains by underground corridor.

The idea of a modern monument was taken up again in the proposal for an urban boulevard linking the station to the city centre, more precisely with the National Museum, built a short time before by Josef Fanta's elder, Josef Schulz.

---

[9] Emanuel Poche, Dobroslav Libal, Eva Reinhartova, and Petr Wittlich, eds., *Praha narodniho probuzeni* (Prague 1980), 143.

[10] See Alena Kubova, 'Les fondements de ma modernité tchèque', in Alena Kubova, ed., *L'Avant-garde architecturale en Tchécoslovaquie 1918–1939* (Liège 1992), 11–34.

[11] Jiri Kohout and Jiri Vancura, *Praha 19. a 20. stoleti: Technicke promeny* (Prague 1986), 75.

Figure 9.3   Prague main station opened in 1906. Built by architect Josef Fanta

Source: Photo: Alena Hanzlova

It would appear that Fanta, who was close to Schulz, wished to reflect the monumental architecture of the National Museum in the layout of his boulevard, which followed the path of the old fortifications.[12]

The two architects embraced the fundamental themes of 'Czech art' – a new architecture reflecting a universal history of styles, monumental public buildings, relations with the existing urban fabric. Significantly, the urban development plan for Prague as a whole was given only secondary importance. From the viewpoint of Vienna, Prague was a provincial city. The vision of Prague as a capital was nevertheless discreetly alluded to in the architecture of a new type of public building, typified by the railway station. The relation thus created with Czech society was just one aspect of a more general conception of Prague and its role as capital city. The proposals for extending the city onto land previously occupied by the fortifications ignored the question of urban development in the station district. A new residential quarter grew up on the other side of the station. The challenge facing new projects was to find a means to restructure the relations between the different parts of the city. The new station could have played this role.[13]

Political centralism very slowly gave way to the demands of the Czech people. In 1900, at the Universal Exposition in Paris, the Czechs were represented as a nation for the first time. The main station was inaugurated in 1906. The first modern art exhibitions were held in Prague and the new, unadorned architecture, claiming rationality through modernity, contrasted with the massive proportions of the railway station. In 1911, at the height of the Czech cubism period, its supporters proclaimed 'There is no reason why what is happening in Paris, London or Rome should not also happen in Prague'.[14] Prague station was out of touch with modernity. Fanta's monumental architecture was a thing of the past. According to the latest statistics, Prague totalled 617,000 inhabitants, while Vienna counted 1,700,000.[15]

Was the birth of Prague as a modern city due to the railways?

The Republic of Czechoslovakia was proclaimed on October 28, 1918, with Prague as its capital, many centuries after its former glory. The vision of modern Prague inspired new architectural trends. It was at this time that a young architect, Max

---

[12]   Josef Schulz constructed the National Museum between 1885 and 1890. The Museum looks down upon the place Ventzeslav Piazza, in the very heart of the city.

[13]   See the town planning project presented by Josip Plecnik, an architect, in the 1920s. The Vinohrady district takes a new shape by the completion of the church of the Sacred Heart.

[14]   Stanislav Kostka Neumann, quoted by J. Pecirka, *Alois Wachsman*, (Prague 1963), 5. See also Anonymous, 'Le cubisme tchèque', in Alena Kubova, ed., *L'Avant-garde architecturale en Tchécoslovaquie 1918–1939* (Liège 1992), 37–50.

[15]   Jiri Kohout and Jiri Vancura, *Praha 19. a 20. stoleti: Technicke promeny* (Prague 1986), 109.

Urban, drew up his project for 'Grand Prague' which sparked vigorous public debate.[16] Urban saw the capital as an administrative and cultural centre not only for the country, but for Europe as a whole. This change in the city's function was to be brought about primarily by a reorganisation of the transport system. Max Urban was a student of Otto Wagner, who believed that 'the skeleton of a "major city" is created by its transport lines'.[17] This is the very core of its modernity. In his book 'Modern Architecture', Otto Wagner presents a new type of railway station: 'existing railway lines must, in the future, be rebuilt as elevated or underground tracks. '[18] The conception of the station as a monument visible from afar appears to be forgotten. It seems clear, since several types of transport are involved, that this new station will serve as a central transport hub. 'Transport must be rapid and traffic on the radial lines must travel in both directions so that any point in the city can be reached with just one change' writes Otto Wagner. He adds: 'passengers will use lifts to transfer between elevated railway, tram and underground railway. This solution also solves the problem of level differences.'[19] Indeed, this is a key problem in Prague, a city of highly complex morphology. As construction of a monumental railway station in Stuttgart neared completion, the young Czech architect saw the station as a locus for exchanges. It is the incessant movement and flow of travellers that determines his vision of the urban station. Wagner also says that all means of transport should be managed by the public authorities.[20]

Does this mean the end of railways stations as a monument of the modern city? This is where the controversy begins. Is it sufficient to organise passenger flows and to offer a means of transport, as certain proposals would suggest? In 1920, a State Commission was set up to draw up the 'Grand Prague' development plan. It was chaired by Max Urban.

When ideas for new urban amenities were put forward, the railway station as an architectural model was rarely mentioned. Attention focused on universities, schools and hospitals, not to mention the controversial National Gallery project. The former approach to urban railway development was no longer compatible with the idea of a modern city. Architectural reviews occasionally referred to the shortcomings of the station built by Fanta.[21] It was said to be dirty and difficult to maintain. Some even suggested that it be demolished. Was this the price to be paid for its status as a monument to the city's glory? Its resemblance to the *Gare du Nord* in Paris, for which it was criticised, sheds light upon Fanta's vision of the modern city of Prague as a true metropolis.[22]

---

[16] Karel Capek, 'Idealni Velka Praha', in Karel Capek, ed., *Spisy o umeni a kulture*, 2 vols. (Prague 1985), vol. 2, 46–50.

[17] Otto Wagner, *Architecture moderne et autres écrits* (Liège 1980), 87.

[18] Ibid. 90.

[19] Ibid.

[20] Ibid.

[21] *Styl*, 6, 1925–1926, 86, *Stavba*, 10–11, 1927, 170–7.

[22] See Oldrich Stary, ed., *Ceskoslovenska architektura od nejstarsi doby po soucasnost* (Prague 1985), 395.

Will the station no longer be a monumental presence in the modern cities?

In 1926, a competition was held for a 'General plan for development of a traffic system in Prague'.[23] The relation between the various modes of transport appeared to be a key issue. On several occasions, the word 'competition' appears in the comments to the entries received. Without consulting the city authorities, the railway administrators decided to build several goods stations in the suburbs of Prague, an initiative which ran contrary to the projects for city expansion. The architects objected to their plans and criticised the attitude of the Czechoslovak railway company, generally rejecting its commercial strategy. In any case, cars and not trains were now seen as the symbol of modernity, not to mention the difficulties involved in building new railway infrastructures in existing urban areas. This was especially true for goods stations. The architects paid little attention to the problem of integrating rail transport into their proposals for a transport network in Prague. The railway station as an exchange hub between different modes and types of transport was far from becoming a reality. When the Brno station was built, the review *Styl* highlighted the important link between city development plans and station design based on Max Urban's concept.[24] And yet few such stations are actually built.

In general, the architects taking part in the competition for a 'General plan for development of a traffic system in Prague' argued that it was impossible to maintain railway transport in the city. Some even suggested demolishing the stations located in the city or at least radically reducing the area that they occupied. They claimed that the space was needed to develop the surrounding districts. The first station, the central station built in 1845, was naturally the prime candidate for destruction. But could it really be razed to the ground? Was its mode of operation really so outdated? The construction of a transport hub outside the city centre was not a simple option. Demolition of the station posed a complex problem since its existence formed a focus of activity for the entire surrounding district. And indeed, the station is still in service today.

The station has become an underground transport hub

In the final analysis, the fact that protagonists of modernity showed little interest in a fundamental reorganisation of the railway networks owed less to the economic difficulties involved than to their vision of the modern city as the domain of the motor car. It could even be argued that in the projects for the city, the car held pride of place.

The economic situation in Czechoslovakia was favourable. Indeed, it would be interesting to establish a link between forecasts for rapid growth in automobile

---

[23]   *Stavba*, 10–11, 1927, 170–7.
[24]   *Styl*, 6, 1925–1926, 143.

traffic and the activity of the motor industry. Not forgetting that the cars produced by *Skoda* enjoyed considerable prestige. According to manufacturers, the number of cars would soon rise from 30,000 to 150,000.[25] So at the time of the competition in 1926, a mere upgrading of the existing transport system was not seen as a viable long-term solution. Some also objected that it was a problem of control and that the railway monopoly had become too restrictive.

In the avant-garde review *Stavba*, architects suggested that the trams be replaced by buses, thereby banishing all forms of rail transport from the city. Most suggestions conveyed one central idea: that all rail traffic should be moved underground. The railway line, transferred to the outskirts of the city, would be linked to the centre by high-speed underground trains. This solution would circumvent the conflict between the city and the railways, a problem with no immediate answer. With the emergence of air travel, there were even proposals to create an exchange hub between rail and air transport networks. On paper, these ideas were convincing. Air transport was developing fast. But in reality, there were no plans to build a new station in Prague. It was the project for an airport which captured the imagination of architects and the public at large. A close reading of

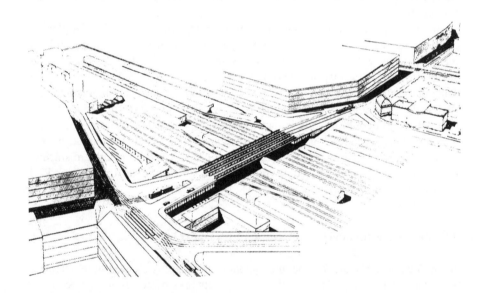

Figure 9.4   Iron bridge beneath the Wilson Station, Prague 1938

Source: Alexandre Piernitz, ed., 'Czechoslovakia. Documents of contemporary architecture, *L'Architecture d'aujourd'hui* (Architecture of today), 9, no. 10, October 1938.

---

[25] *Stavba*, 10–11, 1927.

the competition comments reveals that its key objective was in fact to organise a new road network. And the radial system proposed by Otto Wagner remained a major reference for projects drawn up in the late 1930s.

Yet in 1926, the idea of a motorway network was not a simple alternative to that of a network of railways. Architects were now looking at the relation between the city and its surrounding territory. Until then, the model of the railway station had never been a subject of debate. The railway station as an architectural type was of little interest to avant-garde architects, with the significant exception of the new types of suburban station which, they explained, represented the links between the three fundamental activities of modern man: home, work and leisure. From the 1930s, their vision of the 'functional city' was based on an efficient system of transport networks. As regards the station itself, the key objective was to organise traffic flows in a clearly perceptible manner. The new station had to be functional. In 1938, among other examples of modern architecture in Prague, *Architecture d'Aujourd'hui* presented the project for transformation of the station built by J. Fanta.

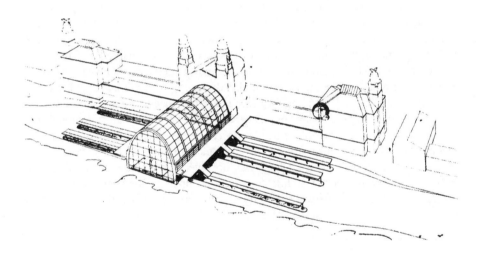

Figure 9.5   Railway Network: draft for converting the approaches to the Wilson Station, Prague 1938

Source: Ibid.

Alexandre Piernitz commented this picture with the following words in 1938: 'Draft of a temporary iron bridge beneath the Wilson Station, which would allow a motorway to be established during the period necessary for the railway to free the place. Fifteen years are estimated as the necessary time to get the land back.' One of the main problems is the city land surface occupied by the railway. The solution to allow road traffic is to build a bridge, which is however thought as 'temporary'.

The commentary of Piernitz in this case was: 'Draft for converting the approaches to the Wilson Station. A large hall above the piazza in front of the station gives access to platforms for motorcars, buses, tramways, serving the station. Arrivals and departures are separated. The project was accepted by the Ministry of Railways.' The main objective of this project was to link the different transport modes. The author of the project was not named, but the fact that the Czechoslovakian State Railways have approved it is stressed.

In 1944, in a political context hostile to architectural modernity, the review *Architekt SIA*, shared by architects and engineers, pursued the debate on the question of railway stations.[26] As regards the transformation of existing structures, the monumental main station underwent major transformation in the 1970s. Most of its functional areas are now located underground.[27] Moving on from its previous role as an inter-city link and a grand urban monument, the station has become an underground transport hub.

The difference to the conception of the very first rail station of Prague is striking. It impels us to rethink the relationship between the city of Prague, noted for its fragile status as a capital and the railway urbanisation. This poses the question what is a 'modern city'. If the decision to build the first station had been dominated by the necessity to connect Prague to Vienna, the capital of the Habsburg Empire, then the realisation of the second station marked a change, not in the choice of its location but in that the Czech architect, J. Fanta stayed an architectural object in the city. Despite already having 617,000 inhabitants, it was still a provincial capital, standing far behind in importance to Vienna, the capital of a multi-national Empire. It is when, in 1918, Prague became a national capital that the previous conception of urban railway developments is judged to be incompatible with the idea one has of the 'modern' city. When a network of motorways was proposed in 1926, it was however not a simple alternative to a railway network which the architects had stood up for. They integrate in their project the relationship between the city and its territory, when the location of a station was not, till then, a matter of debate.

---

[26] *Architekt SIA*, 43, no. 7, 137–160.
[27] See Josef Pechar, *Ceskoslovenska architektura 1945–1977* (Prague 1979). This project was planned by the following architects: Josef Danda, Jan Bocan, Alena Sramkova, and Jan Sramek, and realised in the years between 1971 and 1977.

CHAPTER TEN

Urban form, social patterns and economic impact arising from the development of public transport in London, 1840–1940

Neil McAlpine and Austin Smyth

The sudden and massive boom in railway building in Britain in the mid-nineteenth century through to the early twentieth century transformed the urban form and more significantly the public's perception of their place within city space. This trend continued through the early twentieth century with the emergence of the London Underground further expanding the concept of intra-city travel which was affordable to all. These new affordable forms of public transport affected travel behaviour and everyday life within cities. One of the pioneering communicators of the time, the solicitor of London, Charles Pearson argued that the railways were going to change the face of the city permanently.[1] However, other forms of transit were also available throughout London which helped to redefine urban form, travel and social patterns; the importance of the trams often being underestimated in evaluating the patterns of growth of London.

Much has been written about the railways since the mid-nineteenth century. The subject has spawned many theories and many more articles and books in history, economics and the social sciences as well as extensive literature in the engineering discipline. Within economics the literature on railways can be classified as encompassing economic and land use effects, social impacts, ownership, parliamentary business and the financial returns of the railway companies. Since transport history and in particular railway history, has become a subject in its own right, the methods for studying and analysing the subject have remained relatively static when compared to the progress made in the wider field of transport. The commentators have remained steeped in the way of traditional history and have been slow to move forward. According to Jürgen Habermas, until the mid-nineteenth century the 'discourse of history belonged to the field of what

---

[1] Charles Pearson, Letters to London Metropolitan Board of Works 1861, London Metropolitan Archives MBW 2683-2685.

today we would call literature'.[2] This quotation would appear to dovetail with the approach which has largely, but not completely, been taken to the History of Transport. Unfortunately, Habermas was describing the ways of the 1850s rather than modern day techniques. There are a plethora of books which criticise other work, have long liturgies of historical facts and plenty of railway statistics. Is this a comprehensive study of history? History has to contain the facts, but there should also be a qualitative or quantitative method to lift the discussion further than a simple account of the events.

Reinhart Koselleck would argue that any historical paper should clearly have an identity which is based on what happens and can be seen to be putting forward a new argument, thus creating a new identity or backing up an existing identity. An identity should be individualistic from the other modes of thought and should be backed up by highlighting the anomalies in the different points of view.[3] Charles V. Langlois states that 'facts do not have an absolute value by themselves' and that they gain their value when you 'reflect on the differences which arise from interpretations'.[4] These interpretations will change as different techniques are used by different authors and that is what keeps history fresh and stops the same argument from being regurgitated time after time. Such expectations of what an historical paper should contain are merely views put forward by eminent authors, but in the past the transport historian has diverged and not necessarily followed the convention of views, evidence and literature.

However, there does appear to be one of which virtually all the authors agree; the most vigorous period of historical expansion of the railway system took place between 1840–1860 and in particular 1844–1848.

The following table shows how important these years were to the newly emerging form of transport. This illustrates the growth for the whole of the United Kingdom but a similar pattern emerged in London, although due to space restrictions the growth came more in sudden spurts whenever land became available to the railway companies. The increase in growth can partly be attributed to entrepreneurs realising the potential in the railways. Once the original problems had been solved by the early pioneers costs began to reduce and the possibility of running a profitable railway company was now more feasible. However, not all railways were profitable and railway returns for the decades following the sudden expansion show a dramatic downturn in the number of companies as rationalisation happened either through mergers of companies or closures of unprofitable routes. The railway network had reached its peak by the early twentieth century and in terms of transport other technologies such as the underground and the car would dominate the first half of the century, and from the 1950s onwards the car was the

---

[2] Jürgen Habermas, *An ambitious connection with the past: modernity* (Frankfurt am Main 2001).

[3] Reinhart Koselleck, *Futuro Pasado. Para una semantica de los tiempos historicos* (Barcelona 1993), 6.

[4] Charles V. Langlois, *Introduction to the study of History* (Buenos Aires 1972), 5.

pre-eminent force in the changing of the social habits of the public and the ensuing changes that brought on the urban form of the capital.

Table 10.1 demonstrates that in terms of new lines and stations being built the middle years of the 1840s were of paramount importance to the emergence and eventual supremacy of the railways as the main form of transit.

Table 10.1 Growth of Railways in the United Kingdom

Year	No. of Companies	Mileage Sanctioned	Capital Authorised (£ millions)	Railway Share Index (June 1840 =100)
1841	1.0	14.0	3.4	83.8
1842	5.0	55.0	5.3	89.4
1843	3.0	90.0	3.9	98.2
1844	50.0	805.0	20.5	121.3
1845	120.0	2896.0	59.5	149.0
1846	272.0	4540.0	132.6	139.4
1847	184.0	1295.0	39.5	117.1
1848	82.0	373.0	15.3	95.5
1849	35.0	16.5	3.9	77.1
1850	3.0	6.8	4.1	70.4

Source: Railway Returns Figures for 1841–1850, National Railway Museum, York.

According to Philip Bagwell these figures only show a small part of the story as these were only the bills which gained the approval of Parliament with 'as many as 600 other bills which did not get as far as the first reading.'[5] Theo C. Barker and Michael Robbins argue that for London it was in fact the late 1850s and early 1860s that were the most important times in the emergence of the trains for the city as it was only in 1857 that train journeys outnumbered omnibus journeys for the first time.[6] The usurping of the omnibus as the predominant form of travel in London, after walking, was the first indication that the mechanical age was starting to predominate in travel behaviour. This modal shift had many significant effects on London, as people and industries were no longer forced to congregate in the Central Business District (CBD) as they had the opportunity to live on the outskirts and commute.

This leads to the question, how important were the railways to the development of the urban form in London. Although the railways were an important catalyst to change they were only one of many developments which were taking place at the time. Many of the changes happening in London had already commenced or were

---

[5] Philip Bagwell, *The Transport Revolution from 1770* (Oxford 1974), 84.

[6] Theo C. Barker and Michael Robbins, *A History of London Transport. Passenger Travel and the Development of the Metropolis*, 2 vols, (London 1963–1975), vol. 2, 159.

already in existence before railways became a mass user system, e.g. the omnibuses had already started to open up the possibilities for commuting short distances throughout the city. In addition the London tramways allowed for the development of large scale intra city movement for all. Maps of that period show London developing in line with the tram and train routes and the urban sprawl following the classical linear development along transport routes.

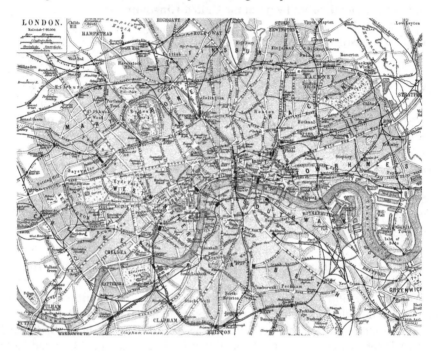

Figure 10.1   Map of London, 1890

Source: *Meyers Konversations-Lexikon. Eine Enzyklopädie des allgemeinen Wissens*, vol. 10 (Leipzig and Wien 1890), 896–7.

The first tram travelled from Porchester Terrace to Edgeware Road and opened on the 23rd March 1861, in response to over 25,000 passengers passing daily in or around this route on streets crowded with horse omnibuses. According to Paul Collins 'one vehicle with two horses will carry sixty passengers, instead of 21, and the fares may be reduced 33 per cent'. If this happened it would bring mass user transit into the availability of the general public for the first time.[7] Although these lines closed shortly afterwards, mainly after complaints form the *London General Omnibus Co.*, they ran for 800 days, covered 180,000 miles, took £20,000 in fares and most importantly carried in excess of 2 million people, showing that there was

---

[7]   Paul Collins, *London Trams. A View from the Past* (Hersham 2001).

a market for an affordable mass user transit system. By the early nineteenth century trams were actually carrying more passengers on the inner London routes than railways as they were a cheap alternative to private omnibuses and possessed a well developed network covering the majority of inner city London. The tram routes stretched throughout London in all directions of the compass but importantly also had a series of routes around the city centre giving access to the traditional work areas as well as CBD access from the outskirts. As the trams were developing the London Railway network was emerging providing the scope for an even larger mass movement of people and consequently changing the public's travel patterns as they no longer had to be within walking distance of their social and work life.

John R. Kellett argued that 'the railway network was the largest catalyst for social change in the Victorian era' as they brought about a fundamental change in the landscape and future developments of any cities which the railways came to.[8] This argument is based on figures produced by Charles Pearson, the Solicitor to London, who claimed that over 4 million people had to move or had their housing directly affected by new railway building, be it either new lines or stations. This would seem an extremely high estimate with London County Council records estimating that the figure would be closer to 2.5 million while the official figure of 50,000 by 1867 is too low. In all according to H. J. Dyos 'there were in all sixty-nine separate schemes, involving the displacement of over 76,000 persons, between 1853 and 1901. Fifty-one of these schemes affecting over 56,000 persons, occurred in the period before 1885.'[9]

Commentators such as Ellis C. Hamilton argued that the railways had a positive benefit to the people of London as they helped to clear slum housing and clean up many of the polluted areas of London.[10] The problem arose in that the displaced population had to relocate and instead of modern housing being supplied they generally moved to other slum areas, close to their original location. The Royal Commission on Housing states that the railways often made conditions worse in the vicinity of stations and attracted 'undesirables' which H. Binford states were 'loan sharks, drunks and the homeless'.[11] The evidence would appear to point in the direction that the railways had a vast social effect on Victorian Cities which was brought about by the forced changes in the geography of many towns and the reluctance by the landed classes and the government to act on the terrible conditions which were created.

Therefore the social costs of the railway network establishing itself were large and immediate. The most immediate consequences were seen in the unconditional demolitions of many areas, i.e. householders were told that their dwellings were going to be demolished to make way for the provision of new tracks or stations and

---

[8] John R. Kellett, *Railways and Victorian Cities* (London 1979), 25.

[9] H. J. Dyos, *Railways and Housing in Victorian London* (London 1959), 67.

[10] Ellis C. Hamilton, *British Railway History*, 2 vols. (London 1957), vol. 2, 217.

[11] See Royal Commission on Housing, quoted by H. Binford, *The Profitability and Performance of British Railways* (Oxford 1978).

they had no means of appeal. In addition there were conditional demolitions where people were offered a fair price for their land and had the ability to refuse. These demolitions, while welcomed by some as a way of gentrifying previously under-developed areas but were often used as a cheap method to relocate the working class. Local authorities were not immune to this as they saw this as an opportunity to increase rateable values through a land use change and also to pass on a proportion of the burden of poor relief to the railway companies. Canning's Metropolitan Railway Commission argued that many areas were not 'sensibly improved' by railway clearances and had blocked improvements of slums which may have been cleared, e.g. London and Blackwall Railway which stopped the formation on a new street from London Road to Commercial Road helping to alleviate chronic overcrowding.[12]

The specific example of the 1859 Charing Cross Railway Act is shown in table 10.2. It can be clearly seen from the table that there has actually been an increase in the amount of persons per house after the Charing Cross Railway Act. This area was already a slum before the Act and arguments put forward in the Private Bill were that the advent of the railway would help to encourage growth and alleviate the overcrowding and suffering of many of the tenants by helping them to relocate. However, as in many cases the local residents did not want to leave an area many of them had been raised in and instead chose to move to surrounding neighbourhoods. A direct consequence of the decrease in the number of households caused by the development of the railway led to an increase in the size of households and also a worsening of the social conditions to be found in that ward.

The large number of evictions caused by the railways generally had a negative socio-economic cost to those involved in the form of higher rents and less room as the housing market could not adapt as quickly as the clearances were happening. In addition the railway connections helped to raise land and property values in line with the improved amenities, further alienating the working classes from specific regions in London which they had previously dominated. The remedies for the

Table 10.2 Crowding in 1851 and 1861 in the Charing Cross ward

	Area 1		Area 2		Total	
	1851	1861	1851	1861	1851	1861
Total Houses	132	107	137	103	269	210
Empty Houses	10	3	3	4	13	7
Occupied Houses	122	104	134	99	256	203
Total Population	811	802	1226	954	2037	1756
Persons Per House	6.7	7.7	9.2	9.6	8.0	8.7

Source: Census Returns 1851 and 1861, Office of Natinal Statistics.

---

[12] Canning's Metropolitan Railway Commission, quoted by H. Pollins, *Britain's Railways: An Industrial History* (Newton Abbot 1971), 35.

social consequences of housing demolitions could be described as laissez-faire and they failed to adjust the housing situation which had been caused in Central London.

In 1853 Lord Shaftesbury tried to raise the matter of displaced occupiers and wanted to compel promoters of bills to provide homes at a reasonable distance within three years to those people who had been displaced.[13] This Standing Order was dashed by the Lords as being impractical as it would mean that the notion of the rights of the property owner would be abolished, i.e. they did not want to see any form of tenant right or compel landlords to receive tenants they would not wish to have, which would be the working class who were the people most affected. As a result of these difficulties no further action was undertaken and reformers had to rely on the Lodging Houses and the Torrens and Cross Acts which were both ineffectual.[14] For over twenty years, most railway acts when entering demolition statements for the column marked action to re-house, wrote none or no inconvenience anticipated. It was not until 1874 that any real action towards compulsory re-housing was undertaken and even then the 1884–85 Royal Commission on the Housing of the Working Classes related that no re-housing scheme was carried out by any railway companies.[15] Even when re-housing schemes were strictly enforced after 1885 they were not effective.

The amount of material which is available to railway historians has led to difficulties in displaying and analysing the data. Where this research differs is that the data is being held in a Geographic Information System (Arc/Info) allowing simple access to large amounts of data in addition to giving it a spatial reference. By possessing the data in this format the possibilities to manipulate the data and to test more contemporary techniques are opened to the researcher. The principle has been to have a base layer of maps from the period being studied, upon which various layers can be added. The technique has allowed railway returns, census returns and London County Council records to be viewed in the geographical areas they were collected from. In addition by using the same layering technique we can view the data through time allowing the researcher to determine the changes which have taken place.

An Arc/Info layered map showing the Paddington ward in 1874 was produced. The base layer is a digitally recreated map from original copies available through the London Metropolitan Archives which has had census data layered on top using the Geographical Information System. The census data relates to those areas surrounding the station which have witnessed an increase in household size since the building of the station. The areas defined on the map are arbitrary, i.e. they have no legal definition, but what can be noted is that in the majority of the

---

[13] Lord Shaftesbury, quoted by D. Turnock, *Essays in Comparative History* (Aldershot 1998), 189.

[14] House of Parliament Record Office, Houses of Commons Acts chapter c\xvii 47& 48 Vict, 18.

[15] Houses of Parliament Record Office, Royal Commisions, *Royal Commission on the Housing of the Working Classes*, 4 vols. (London 1874), vol. 3.

surrounding area there has been an increase in the average number of people residing in each house. The perceived notion that the building of the station would help to alleviate overcrowding and associated problems proved to be incorrect with the diametrically opposite happening. In addition previous to the building of the station the census shows the area to have a predominance of people working in middle class occupations such as office clerks, solicitors clerks, tax collectors, post the building of the station the majority of the occupants are working class with main householders working as labourers, street cleaners, gas lamp lighters. Significantly the overcrowding has become much more pronounced with many households having more than seven people registered as living at that address.

Virtually the whole of the surrounding area had demonstrated increased household size but perhaps the most interesting point to be deduced from the map is that the areas closest to the station have not increased at the same rates as those closer to the tracks. This anomaly can partially be explained as follows; in 1831, before the temporary station at Paddington was erected in 1838, the area was

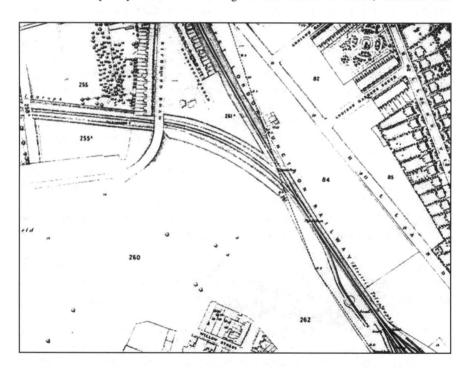

Figure 10.2   Ordnance Survey map, Holland Park and Shepherd's Bush, 1871

Source: 1871 Ordnance Survey Maps, London Metropolitan Archives.

almost exclusively residential while by 1841 although there was some evidence of more commercial properties it was still predominantly a residential area. The new station opened in 1854, and while changing the face of the whole of the surrounding area by increasing densities, it had the effect on adjacent properties of making them viable locations for business use thus reducing the residential population density. This pattern was repeated across London with the opening of more terminal and other major stations.

During the boom years of the railway age the builders and Parliament had a profound effect on the geography of the city. Dyos claims that 'railways had more radical consequences on the anatomy of the large mid-Victorian towns than any other single factor.'[16] He would argue that they increased both growth and prosperity and caused drastic changes in the layout of existing streets and communication. Moreover their effect did not stop at simply the physical change but brought about an irreversible change in daily lifestyle and social patterns.

While in the inner city railways were associated with clearances the opposite was true for the edge of the city; here the new technology was viewed as a way of expanding the city, opening up new areas of land which had previously been

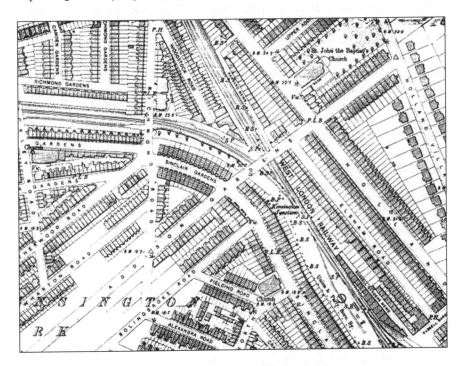

Figure 10.3 Ordnance Survey map, Holland Park and Shepherd's Bush, 1894

Source: 1894 Ordnance Survey Maps, London Metropolitan Archives.

---

[16] H. J. Dyos, 'Some Social Costs of Railway Building in London', *Journal of Transport History*, 11, 1955, 23–30.

largely inaccessible either for homes or businesses. This enhanced accessibility was restricted to higher income groups and the upper and middle classes until the provision of the workman's fares. This class based geography led to the outer edge of London becoming the high rent sector while the inner city areas suffered as many gentry who still remained took the opportunity to move to new build on the outskirts. London was developing in the classical star shaped formation, i.e. the main development of housing and enterprise was undertaken along the railway tracks and it was not until much later that any significant amount of infilling was undertaken.

Holland Park illustrates how the main line began to affect the property market and social conditions in London over a very short period of time. In 1871 Ordnance Survey Maps show an area free of residential development while equivalent maps just 23 years later show the improved accessibility brought about by the railway, resulting in almost complete coverage by new housing. The first signs of road transport are also in evidence with an increasing number of roads being built to residential areas. These maps provide evidence of a commuter lifestyle appearing in London.

The Census data shows this area to be predominantly middle class in 1901 compared to 1861 where the only listed residents in the vicinity are described as farmers and their labourers. The railways also opened up opportunities for industries which had previously been city centre based to relocate to the cheaper land on the edge of the city as for the first time there was an efficient and quick method of moving goods and personnel to and from their markets in the city centre and throughout the United Kingdom. However, it was not until the advent of cheap mass-produced cars and lorries that industry could take full advantage of these expanding areas as the need for a large workforce meant they also needed a completely mobile workforce.

In the beginning of the railway era most of the landed gentry were against the railways as they thought that it would lead to a degradation in their quality of life as peasants would now be able to move about much more freely. This meant, according to S. Ville, that the 'aristocracy forced the entrepreneurs to look for land on the edge of the towns'.[17] Very few aristocrats such as Lord Derby saw the potential financial reward in supporting the railway system. He happily publicised the fact that he was willing to sell his land to railway developers. This reluctance to welcome the railways with open arms meant that an interesting geography began to emerge in many towns and cities. This geography was reflected in circuitous routes and poorly located stations in a number of instances restricting realisation of the full potential of the new technology.

D. H. Aldcroft claimed that the negative effect of the railways on the working class was partially offset by their newfound freedom of movement and the

---

[17]   S. Ville, *Transport and the Industrial Revolution*, University College, London Ph.D. thesis, 1992.

affordability of the trains through the working man's fare.[18] Initially, however, the railways were almost exclusively the privilege of the upper and middle classes and used for freight due to their high expense. The *London Evening Standard* even went as far as publishing a set of rules to make rail transport more comfortable and this included the banning of those people who were wearing dirty clothes caused by them having to work in manual labour and stating that employees of a company should not be allowed in the same carriage as their boss.

It was not until government reforms and more importantly the wish for more profits that the working class fares were introduced, but with restrictions, in that they were only in force for certain hours during early morning and late evening peaks. P. J. Cain points out that these fares were only there on a trial period and it was only their success that persuaded railway companies, especially in London, to continue and extend their use outside of the normal journey-to-work hours.[19] With the arguments surrounding regulation of transport in today's society it is interesting to note that regulation abounded in the Victorian era and that positive effects came about apparently thanks to increased regulation and government intervention.

The railways in the latter part of the nineteenth century and the early years of the twentieth century began to take over from other modes of transport such as cycling, walking and horse drawn transport as the dominant way of moving around London by the working classes. Table 10.3 shows the number of passengers using the railways at peak hours at the main commuting stations in Central London.

Most importantly, the Railway had become the main method of travelling to and from work. This change in travel behaviour was brought about by the working man's fares and the continuing growth of London, allied to the decrease in the density of the middle class residential areas in the city centre and nearer to places of work. The railways had allowed people who could afford it, or who were forced to, to move to the outskirts of the cities either in the newly built working class estates, which had started to become a reality after the Royal Commission on Workman's Housing or in the more affluent private housing developments which had started to become the preferred living place of the middle class. The former did not fully offset losses in housing stock demolished as a result of new construction.

Table 10.4 shows the passengers at the various main line London Termini in 1920 and we can clearly see that compared to 1840 where railways had virtually no market share of the transport in London they now carried significant numbers in peak hours. This dominance of the railways as the main mass mover of the population into London during peak hours was relatively unchallenged until the emergence of the underground as a quicker and often more efficient way of travel. When we compare Table 10.3 to Table 10.4 we can see the huge difference in the

---

[18] D. H. Aldcroft, 'Urban Transport Problems in an Historical Perspective', in A. Slaven and D. H. Aldcroft, eds., *Buisness Banking and Urban History: Essays in Honour of S. G. Checkland* (Edinburgh 1982), 156–178, esp. 164.

[19] P. J. Cain, *Railways 1870–1914: The Maturity of the Private System* (Shepperton 1983), 56–58.

**Table 10.3   Passengers at London Termini – 1920 Weekday Averages
(Figures in thousands)**

Station	Arrivals			Departures			Total	Two peak hours
	24 hrs	7–10 a.m.	peak hour	24 hrs	4–8 p.m.	peak hour	24 hours	% of total
S. Region								
Cannon St	37	35	23	38	36	25	75	64%
Charing Cross	61	44	26	64	45	25	125	41%
Holborn[1]	37	33	19	30	26	17	67	54%
London Bridge	104	74	42	95	67	38	199	40%
Victoria[2]	81	55	33	82	59	33	163	40%
Waterloo[3]	99	72	45	97	70	38	196	42%
W. Region								
Paddington	32	7	6	32	NA	6	64	19%
L. M. Region								
Broad St	NA	6	4	NA	4	3	NA	–
Euston[4]	NA	5	4	NA	4	3	NA	–
St Pancras	16	6	4	17	6	3	33	21%
Marylebone	6	5	4	6	5	3	12	58%
E. Region								
Fenchurch St	21	18	12	21	18	13	42	60%
Kings Cross	15	6	3	15	6	3	30	20%
Liverpool St	90	61	44	91	67	42	181	48%
London Transport								
Baker Street	NA	15	8	NA	15	9	NA	–
Moorgate	NA	19	12	NA	15	11	NA	–

[1]   Including Blackfriars and Elephant and Castle
[2]   Excluding continental passengers
[3]   South Western Division station only
[4]   Suburban passengers only
NA: Not Available; Peak hour: the heaviest sixty minutes

Source: Railway Returns 1920 based on censuses carried out on selected days at each
station, National Railway Museum, York.

number of people travelling by tube even after you take into consideration
factorisation for peak hour travel. This rapid rise in the role of the underground can
be seen by the large increases of ticket sales in a seven year period.

Table 10.4 Growth of traffic at representative tube stations

	Millions of tickets issued, 1938	Percentage Increase, 1931–1938
Chancery Lane	2.7	18
Green Park	3.0	41
Holborn[1]	5.0	12
Hyde Park Corner[2]	1.6	33
Knightsbridge[3]	3.3	24
Leicester Square	6.8	13
Marble Arch	4.4	48
Warren Street	1.8	33
Totals	28.6	23

[1] Includes British Museum traffic in 1931
[2] Includes Down Street traffic in 1931
[3] Includes Brompton Road Traffic in 1931

Source: Covent Garden: London Transport Board Report, 1931, London Transport Museum.

Once again the emergence of a new form of technology had changed patterns of intra-London movement. This massive uptake in the market share of travellers was reinforced, as the only other feasible means of transport for working class were the buses and walking. The car was still not a mass user mode and would not be until the early 1960s. The growth of the underground in such a dramatic way can also be attributed to the affordable fare levels which meant that this mode of transportation was open to the majority of the population. The underground also had the attraction in the early years of the novelty value, i.e. when the Metropolitan line was opened there were 'people queuing to view the trains that travelled underground'.[20] According to A. Mee, this undoubtedly helped to create public enthusiasm for the new mode.[21] The speed of travel and the destinations of the underground also helped to change the property patterns and living styles of many people with places becoming accessible which previously had been the reserve of the middle class and the car owning fraternity. This helped the London sprawl as people moved further out into the suburbs and the working class started to move further away from their traditional homes in the centre of London.

It is evident from the literature that railways were an important factor in the growth and development of London. However, it must not be forgotten that other forces were also at work. The trams, omnibuses and underground railways all

[20] J. Glover, *Glory Days, Metropolitan Railway* (Hersham 1998), 10.
[21] A. Mee, *The King's England London North of The Thames except the City and Westminster* (London 1972), 174.

helped to develop the pattern of London both in terms of physical form and it's socio-economic conditions. London developed in a linear pattern along the main transport lines. The middle classes used the new transport technologies to relocate themselves from their original heartlands at the start of the industrial revolution but it took many more years and government legislation before a similar pattern began to emerge for the working class population. In conclusion it can be argued that while the railways were perhaps the major catalyst for change their impact was reinforced by the prevailing conditions brought about by other modes of transport and government intervention.

CHAPTER ELEVEN

Railways plans and urban politics in nineteenth-century Dublin

Hugh Campbell

Sweet Dublin! loveliest city of the day
Low have you fallen – to a mere highway
No traveller stops upon his journey through
But sighs and mutters 'Nothing here to view'
Your beauties sacrificed for public good
Your architecture's turned to railway food.[1]

The mutilation of Dublin

> The citizens of Dublin who take a natural pride in the traditional beauty of their capital, are just now united in a vigorous and determined effort to preserve it from invasion, and to save it, if possible, from the rude hands of the spoiler. It need scarcely be said that the Goths and Vandals who menace the Irish metropolis and threaten to destroy the fair vistas and stately avenues of stone that have delighted successive generations of its citizens, are the agents and representatives of that iron monster with the fiery breath that in our day wages such relentless war against architectural beauty in every shape.[2]

The threat of 'invasion,' which the *Daily News* reported in 1863, was contained in the *Dublin Metropolitan Railway Bill*. The bill, which was to become the subject of recurring debate and controversy over the course of the year, proposed to link all the existing railway lines into Dublin and to build a new central station at College Green, in the heart of the capital. At the time, the main rail routes into Dublin were from the south and west, terminating at Kingsbridge at the western end of the Liffey quays; from the north-west, terminating at Broadstone in the north-west of the city; from Belfast and Drogheda in the north, terminating at Amiens Street on

---

[1] Poem by William Scribble, published in *Dublin Builder*, April 1, 1863.
[2] *Dublin News*, February 24, 1863, MS Larcom 7644. Many of the newspaper reports quoted in this essay are collected in the scrapbooks of Sir Thomas Larcom (1801–1879) who, after serving as assistant to the Irish Ordnance Survey and as Commissioner of Public Works during the Famine, became Undersecretary for Ireland in 1853. Larcom kept extensive scrapbooks on many topics relating to improvement and development in Ireland. The scrapbooks are in the manuscript collection of the National Library of Ireland, and are referred to henceforth as 'MS Larcom…'.

the north side of the city centre; and the line from the ferry at Kingstown, south of
the city, which arrived into Westland Row in the southern city centre. These lines
were now to be linked by a railway beginning from Kingsbridge and running at a
height parallel to the river Liffey along much of its length, crossing all the north-
south streets en route on viaducts, then branching north across the river to link with
Amiens Street and south to reach Westland Row.

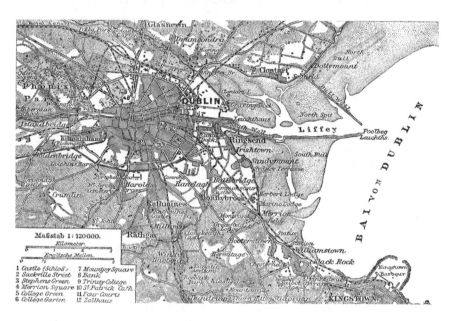

Figure 11.1   Map of Dublin, 1890

Source: *Meyers Konversations-Lexikon. Eine Enzyklopädie des allgemeinen
               Wissens*, vol. 5 (Leipzig and Wien 1890), 183.

The aim of the project was twofold: to allow direct rail access to the centre of
Dublin from all parts of Ireland – and from England – and to allow rail connections
between what had hitherto been completely separate, and separately owned lines. It
promised to make communication by rail for both freight and passengers far more
convenient. This was not, however, how it was being seen in the press – in a
strongly worded editorial, the *Express* had already voiced its opposition to what it
termed 'the sweeping Vandalism of this project':

> It is a bill for the mutilation of Dublin – for defacing its beauty and destroying every
> attractive feature of which it is justly proud – for obscuring by hideous screens the
> architectural grandeur of its public buildings, filling the noblest streets with
> unsightly deformities, disturbing its thoroughfares, impeding its traffic, impairing its
> business. A more reckless and at the same time a more uncalled for speculation has
> seldom been attempted. (...) It behoves the citizens of Dublin to take immediate and

active measures to protect themselves against a measure which, under the cloak of improvement, aims a deadly blow at this metropolis. There is no time to be lost. The invader has stolen a march upon them, and the civic officers, to whom they have entrusted their rights and interests, have made a poor show of resistance.[3]

Already, from this editorial – with its imputations of imperial motives to the railway and its accusations of municipal inaction – the complex political context

Figure 11.2   Kingsbridge Station in Dublin (Heuston Station), 2002

Source: Photo taken by Hugh Campbell.

within which the discussion of the bill took place begins to emerge. It was commonplace at the time to see the railway as an invasive, destructive force, both in the countryside and the city. In *Dombey and Son*, Charles Dickens describes the railway as 'the power that forced itself upon its iron way – its own – defiant of all paths and roads, piercing through the heart of every obstacle, and dragging living creatures of all classes, ages and degrees behind it.'[4]

But in the Irish colonial context, the railway could also be seen as a powerful instrument of empire. *The Daily News*, with its invading 'Goths and Vandals, (...) the agents (...) of that iron monster with the fiery breath' was obviously associating the rise of the steam engine with British rule in Ireland. Indeed, almost every aspect of the development of the Irish capital in the nineteenth century inevitably became enmeshed in issues of national identity and imperial domination. While

---

[3]   *Daily Express*, January 31, 1863. MS Larcom 7644.
[4]   Charles Dickens, *Dombey and Son* (Harmondsworth 1985), 354.

Dublin was certainly subject to many of the same forces which drove urban growth and civic improvement elsewhere, those forces were often stymied by local circumstance. Between the corporation's lack of power and purpose, Westminster's lack of interest and the merchant classes lack of cohesion, many opportunities to improve or develop the city were lost, many plans frustrated. The story of the *Metropolitan Railway Bill*, as it unfolded over the following year, encapsulates the tensions and difficulties that beset development in Victorian Dublin. But while Dublin, as the capital of Britain's closest colony, always had its unique circumstances, it nonetheless had a great deal in common with British cities. Thus, exploring what happened when the 'iron monster with the fiery breath' threatened the Irish capital should also contribute to a more general understanding of the impact of railways on the nineteenth-century city.

Changing Dublin

Dublin in the second half of the nineteenth century was a city coming to terms with a changed identity. During the eighteenth century the capital had been expanded and transformed on a grand scale by the wealthy Protestant Ascendancy.[5] The terraces and squares of elegant Georgian houses, the splendid public buildings, the new thoroughfares and improved streets all spoke of a capital sure of its own importance and its own autonomy. Dublin's coherent, classical face reflected perfectly the confident aspirations of its ruling elite. While the initial phase of eighteenth-century growth was characterised by the speculative development of large estates, later in the century the greatest influence on the city's shape and appearance was exerted by the Wide Streets Commissioners. Between 1756 and its eventual demise in 1839, this group was responsible for conferring a new unity on Dublin's streetscape and on its organisation. It widened and rebuilt existing streets and bound the city together with new streets through its centre and ring roads round its edge. The resulting unity was, however, somewhat misleading. As Roy Foster remarks, 'the Ascendancy built in order to convince themselves not only that they had arrived but that they would remain.'[6] They recognised, in other words, the inherent precariousness of their hold on power, understanding that the limited form of independence which they sought and the national identity which they promulgated were, by their nature, narrow and exclusive. *The Act of Union between Britain and Ireland* in 1800, and the removal of the Irish Parliament to London, signalled the beginning of their demise, and with it their vision of an enlightened, classically ordered city.

---

[5]   On the growth of Georgian Dublin see, for instance, Maurice Craig, *Dublin 1660–1860* (Harmondsworth 1992); Niall McCullough, *Dublin – an Urban History* (Dublin 1989); Hugh Campbell, *Contested Territory, Common Ground: Architecture and Politics in Nineteenth Century Dublin*, University College Dublin Ph.D. thesis, 1998. Much of the following originates from this thesis.

[6]   Roy Foster, *Modern Ireland 1600–1982* (London 1988), 194.

In its place emerged a much more fragmented, unstable urban culture. Overlaid on the homogenous scenography of eighteenth-century city was a new, more heterogeneous urban order that reflected the rise of new political and religious groups to power. Notable among these were the newly enfranchised Catholic Church and the expanding merchant class: 'Immediately (after the Union; Hugh Campbell) in Dublin, commerce rose into the vacated seats of rank; wealth rose into the place of birth. People who had never been heard of before, started into notice, pushed themselves forward.'[7] The city became a sort of stageset on which such people could display their competing identities and proclaim their newfound prestige. By mid-century Dublin's character had shifted decisively from patrician capital to bustling commercial centre. As the wealthy elite moved out – either back to their country estates or to the new suburbs – businesses moved in. The change was noticed in many contemporary guides:

> In Upper Sackville Street especially (formerly among the most prestigious residential addresses in the city; Hugh Campbell), the visitor will remark a number of buildings; – the greater proportion of them were originally intended to have been the town residences of the nobility; they are now without a single exception converted into hotels or places of meeting for public societies, shops, warehouses etc. (...) The proprietory is certainly very much changed but the picture has rather gained in interest by the transition; the solemn silence which generally reigns amid the palaces of the great, has been succeeded by the animation that accompanies a busy commercial scene.[8]

So the city had perhaps lost some of its grandeur, but in the process had gained a new liveliness and variety. And while the concern for a collective image had perhaps given way to a tendency towards individual aggrandisement, a shared ambition for Dublin's status and well-being nonetheless remained. But whereas in the Georgian era this ambition was focused on uniform image and civic authority, by the Victorian period it had become more concerned with, on the one hand, ideas of character and beauty – the city as a work of art – and, on the other hand, ideas of utility and efficiency – the city as a perfectly functioning system. This mixture of what the French architect Cesar Daly called 'science and sentiment' was by no means unique to Dublin. In fact it can be seen as the prevailing spirit of the age, with Haussmann's vast transformation of Paris in mid-century only the most ambitious of many attempts to reconcile utility and artistry on a grand urban scale, what Walter Benjamin diagnosed as 'the tendency which was noticeable again and

---

[7]   Sir James Brooke quoted by Maria Edgeworth, *The Absentee* (Oxford 1988), 83. The character Sir James Brooke, who makes these observations, explains how, after the Union, 'most of the nobility and many of the principal families among the Irish commoners, either hurried in high hopes to London, or retired disgusted and in despair to their houses in the country.' Ibid.

[8]   G. N. Wright, *An Historical Guide to the City of Dublin* (London 1821), 105.

again during the nineteenth century to ennoble technical exigencies with artistic aims.'[9]

Civic reform and civic improvement

In the decades of renewal which followed the Great Famine of 1845–9, Dublin became the focus of legislation and development aimed both at enhancing the city's beauty and at making it function better as a commercial and trading centre. An important factor in this renewed zeal for improvement was the *Municipal Corporation Ireland Act* of 1840. The Act's primary initiative was to replace the famously corrupt, self-perpetuating system for electing freemen and aldermen to the corporation with a simple property qualification.[10] The immediate effect of the Act was to encourage liberal Protestant and Catholic businessmen, previously excluded from, or disinterested in, municipal affairs, into the corporation: 'In 1851, in marked contrast to the unreformed corporation, fourteen members of *Dublin Corporation* were also bank or railway directors, or members of the Dublin Chamber of Commerce.'[11] This political reform was seen to have a fundamental effect on the fortunes of the city:

> The passage of the Municipal Reform Act in 1840 effected a wonderful change in the internal affairs of the Irish capital. (...) This new arrangement of municipal government seemed to infuse new life into the citizens, and (...) tended greatly to awaken public interest in the energetic and proper fulfillment of municipal duties (...). (It has) purified the management of the city's business, secured the more perfect accomplishment of public works and cleared the administration of the municipality from even the suspicion of apathy and jobbery.[12]

A reformed corporation, according to this argument, led to a renewed civic pride. However, the corporation's powers to instigate any changes were limited. As a body, it had nothing like the autonomy or authority that had been enjoyed by the *Wide Streets Commission*. Funds raised from the rates were not sufficient to contemplate any large-scale initiatives. Notwithstanding these limitations in its early stages, the corporation enjoyed the support of a broad spectrum of the city's interest groups. Initially at least, the reformed council proved a much more

---

[9] Walter Benjamin, *Paris – The Capital of the Nineteenth Century in Charles Baudelaire* (London 1997), 173.

[10] The old corporation was a completely Protestant organisation. Opposition to the reforms was often nakedly sectarian. See for instance Isaac Butt's extraordinary tirade against 'the bill for papalizing the Irish corporations', *A Speech delivered at the Mansion House, February 13, 1840* (Dublin 1840), 5 The Act required that future members be resident within seven miles of the city and either hold city property valued at £1,000 or pay rates of £25.

[11] Mary Daly, *Dublin, the Deposed Capital* (Cork 1985), 204.

[12] Anonymous, *Industries of Dublin* (Dublin 1890), 16. By the time this was written, there were in fact many allegations of 'apathy and jobbery' against the reformed corporation.

democratic, representative body, dedicated to power-sharing and dialogue; its passing of the *Dublin Improvement Bill* in 1849 held out the promise of decisive intervention in the city's problems.

Perhaps the most significant result of municipal reform was the fact that, for the first time, Dublin's merchant princes were enticed into the world of urban politics. This role of 'merchant prince' was filled most capably and enduringly by successive scions of the Guinness family. Throughout the nineteenth century the brewery, which the first Arthur Guinness (1725–1803) had begun in James's Gate in 1759, grew in size and strength so that by the 1850s it was firmly established as Dublin's principal industry. Arthur Guinness had one son, Arthur (1768–1855) who in turn was followed into the business by his two sons, Arthur Lee (1797–1863) and Benjamin Lee (1798–1868). It was Benjamin Lee in particular who was responsible for the expansion of the brewery in mid-century, and it was he who was first to step outside his appointed role of manufacturer and enter the political arena.

Benjamin Lee's predecessors had carefully avoided any substantial involvement in Dublin's politics. However, by the middle of the century, the Guinnesses began to feel more socially secure. With surprising rapidity, they had become members of the new elite.[13] Arthur Guinness had never felt at ease among the eighteenth-century Ascendancy. But now a different class was in the ascendant in Dublin, a class based on wealth rather than birth, among whom his grandsons could feel they were respected as equals, or even regarded as leaders. Nonetheless, Benjamin Lee was initially cautious about entering public life. It was not until 1851, when he was already 53, that he was persuaded by the corporation to become Lord Mayor of Dublin.[14] Guinness eventually overcame what seems like genuine reluctance and was inaugurated as Lord Mayor on January 2, 1851. The appointment captured the public imagination. Guinness was seen as a force for unity, someone capable of uniting the remaining aristocracy with the rising bourgeoisie and the working classes, and of reviving the city after the ravages of the Famine. *The Irish Times* saw the appointment as 'a public recognition of the liberation of the Irish capital from the servitude in which it was so long enthralled.'[15] Clearly, Guinness's appointment was considered a significant turning point. The involvement of leading merchants and businessmen in the administration of the city would set the seal on the widespread sense of renewal by upholding recognisable figureheads with whom the populace could identify.

In many British cities, the entrepreneurial spirit which had spurred their early growth began, around mid-century, to coalesce into more concentrated and

---

[13] As Frederic Mullaly puts it, 'Benjamin Lee personified the elevation of the brewery founders' kin from Dublin tradesmen into the seignural class'. Ibid. 22.

[14] See letter dated from November 26, 1850 urging Benjamin Lee to 'yield to the general feeling not merely of the Corporation, but of the city at large.' In Benjamin Lee, *Guinness Scrapbook, 1851–1868*, compiled by Benjamin L. Plunket, Plunket Papers National Library PL/1050.

[15] *Irish Times*, January 24, 1851.

sustained efforts at civic improvement. In the early years of Victoria's reign, the city often seemed like a machine which had spun out of control. Manchester, which was known as 'Shock City', 'was associated with size, with industry, with newness, with squalor, and above all else with unfamiliar and on occasion alarming social relationships.'[16] However by the 1850s, a new version of Manchester was beginning to emerge. Where the old image was one of economic wealth and social disorder, the newer vision was of a city that embodied both wealth and new and formative social values. These new values were promulgated primarily by the city's business elite. Manchester 'seemed to be creating a new order of businessmen, energetic, tough, proud, contemptuous of the old aristocracy and yet in some sense constituting an aristocracy themselves.'[17] No longer satisfied simply with amassing wealth, these businessmen now sought to translate wealth into political power, and into a social and civic gospel. The *Reform Bill* of 1835 ensured them a much wider electorate, more sympathetic to a Liberal, Free Trade message.

From mid-century onwards, cities which had seemed dangerous and beyond control began to appear confident, assertive, progressive. The new breed of merchants effected sweeping changes on the urban fabric in the name of social reform and civic improvement rather than straightforward self-aggrandisment. Although there were clear differences between, for example, Joseph Chamberlain's 'civic gospel' in Birmingham and the sponsors of Manchester's Free Trade Hall, there was a common belief that a city's architecture, shaped by a confident business community, could inspire pride in its citizens.[18] Guinness was a strong adherent of this distinctly Victorian creed, where labour would be rewarded, true worth recognised and where the city would unite culture and commerce in a new harmony. Sensing a mood for reconciliation, he stressed the need for a united approach to the capital's problems: 'Disunion is the base of our country and it is hard, almost impossible to start any project for the advancement of Ireland, and not find differences of opinion even among honest and well-meaning men, yet tending to mar that enterprise.'[19] Despite these high ideals however – or perhaps because of them – Guinness's dalliance with municipal politics proved short-lived. By 1853 he was anxious to retire from the council which he eventually did in 1855.[20] In fact, it is striking that Guinness's major contributions to the city's development and image came after his retirement from the council. By the end of the 1850s there was growing frustration at what was seen as the inaction of the corporation on pressing matters of urban improvement. Instead, more direct action through private bills or public philanthropy began to seem the best means of securing urban

---

[16] Asa Briggs, *Victorian Cities* (Harmondsworth 1990), 89.

[17] Ibid. 93.

[18] Throughout his work, Briggs is at pains to point out the specific nature of each Victorian city, despite their many shared characteristics.

[19] Guinness speaking in council, reported in *Daily Express*, August 22, 1851.

[20] A letter of July 30, 1853 explains that the business of Council takes up too much of his time. Plunket Papers, PL/255.

change, while Guinness's promised civic unity seemed as far away as ever. It was into this uncertain atmosphere that the *Metropolitan Railway Bill* arrived.

The railways in Dublin

As in most British cities, the first railways to arrive in Dublin were all private enterprises. The Dublin and Kingstown Railway Company opened the first line in Ireland between Dublin and the port of Kingstown in 1834. This was followed over the next twenty-five years by the opening of the Dublin and Drogheda, the Great Southern and Western, the Dublin and Belfast and the Midland Great Western lines. By 1860 there existed connections between the capital and most corners of the island. But each connection terminated at a separate station, each on the edge of the city. As Jack Simmons has shown, this was the common pattern among British cities, which generally lacked a single central station.[21] Increasingly, the need for a central terminus, or at least adequate connections between the disparate lines entering a city, was being recognised. In 1863, the same year in which the *Dublin Metropolitan Railway Bill* appeared, there were as many as thirty bills before Parliament dealing with connecting lines through London. A *Times* editorial vividly argued the case in their favour, by imagining a traveller arriving in London by train:

> At this point our train, which had passed so swiftly through a thousand natural obstacles, was suddenly brought to a standstill. The conductor opened the door and requested us to dismount, telling us that the tract of land before us had defied the ingenuity of the engineers and interposed an impassable gap in the railway communication. We alighted, and saw before us, under a dense canopy of smoke, as if shot up from innumerable volcanoes, vast rocky masses, intersected by rugged, slimy and tortuous paths.[22]

The inconvenience and loss of time resulting from the 'break in the railway system from north to south presented by the metropolis' – as the editorial explains: 'Even had we been fortunate to get through it in the promised time, it would have been equivalent, all things considered, to fifty or sixty miles of railway communication.

---

[21] Jack Simmons, 'The Power of the Railway', in H. J. Dyos and M. Wolff, eds., *The Victorian City: Images and Realities*, 2 vols. (London 1973), vol. 1, 277–310. 'Each main company built its own station; and though sometimes, as in Leeds and Manchester, two or more companies might share a station between them, this still left a multiplicity everywhere: two in Birmingham, Sheffield, Edinburgh, Bradford and Leeds; three in Leicester, Liverpool and Belfast; three or four in Manchester; four in Glasgow; five in Dublin.' Ibid. 280. It is worth noting that Dublin has more stations than any other city outside London.

[22] *Times*, January 30, 1863. Larcom MS 7644. The portrayal of the city as a dense, unnavigable territory was a commonplace of the time: 'A city, military people say, is a forest. it has precisely the same conditions and must be attacked, defended, penetrated and abandoned by the same rules as a forest.' Ibid.

As it was we lost a day, which is equivalent to five or six hundred miles.'[23] This led the *Times* to endorse enthusiastically the proposed links through the centre of London. Recognising the potential of the railway to damage the appearance of the city, it nonetheless argued that 'surely reform and convenience are not incompatible with appearance. (...) A little supervision, some forethought and, if not an absolute union of action, a moderate concurrence, would save us from some results which may prove long eyesores.'[24]

Opposition to the *Dublin Metropolitan Railway Bill* was expressed primarily on the grounds that it would indeed result in many such eyesores. What the *Express* had called 'a bill for the mutilation of the capital' was described in the *Dublin Builder* as 'a most wanton attempt to utterly destroy the symmetry of our metropolitan leading thoroughfares and general architectural character – admittedly beautiful – without any necessity whatever, and without any corresponding advantage.'[25] Not only was the project destructive and ugly, it was also unnecessary. The same argument was made by the *Irish Times*: 'We would gladly support any enterprise calculated to benefit Ireland, but not when that benefit would be purchased at the cost of irreparable injury to the appearance, trade and safety of Dublin with aid of the smallest advantage to the city.'[26]

It was not a question, in other words, of simply deciding between utility and beauty – the actual utility of the project was highly questionable. A petition against the bill was opened in the Commercial Buildings on Dame Street. The Chamber of Commerce, whose headquarters this was, was clearly opposed to the scheme, though it might be thought to be in the interests of improved trading in the city centre. Quickly, the *Express* could report that:

> a more comprehensive and influential expression of public feeling has seldom been encited by such a reckless scheme. The list of signatories includes those of leading merchants, bankers and traders and amongst them will be found the names of persons differing most widely upon other questions, but who are here cordially united to defend the city from adventurers from the London Stock Exchange who threaten it with a ruinous invasion.[27]

New themes emerge here in the discussion of the bill. Firstly there is the notion that disparate political voices could make common cause for the sake of the city. Secondly, there is the characterisation of the project as an invasion by outsiders, specifically by English venture capitalists. Both themes are obviously designed to strike a chord with readers, to recast the discussion from one about progress and improvement to one about 'us and them'. The show of unified opposition was evident at a packed public meeting held in the *Mansion House* – home of the Lord Mayor – on February 21. With the Lord Mayor presiding, powerful and influential

---

[23]   Ibid.
[24]   Ibid.
[25]   *Dublin Builder*, February 15, 1863.
[26]   *Irish Times*, February 10, 1863. Larcom MS 7644.
[27]   *Dublin Express*, February 16, 1863. Larcom MS 7644.

figures spoke out against the bill, notably the architect Sir Thomas Deane, the banker David LaTouche, and Benjamin Lee Guinness. Although such staunchly unionist businessmen could scarcely have endorsed the mayor's nationalistic fervour, who explicitly declared: 'Some of the splendid buildings which adorn our city are connected with the most glorious memories of Irish independence and progress. We look back to these splendid buildings and we gather from reviews and their historical recollections rigour to fight in the cause of our country.' The businessmen nonetheless could agree on a resolution opposing the bill.[28]

As the presence at the meeting of the Lord Mayor suggests, *Dublin Corporation* was also opposed to the scheme.[29] However it was finding it difficult to mount a successful campaign to defeat it. Following an unsuccessful attempt to have the bill thrown out on standing orders, their Law agent suggested in a report 'that active measures be taken out of doors, to pour in petitions against such an attempt by English capitalists not only to disfigure the best part of our city, but to annihilate some thousands a year of the rated property of the city.'[30] Effectively, the corporation was admitting its own lack of power and calling upon the private citizen to take the lead.[31] They did, however, take the step of erecting a full-scale mock up of the proposed railway bridge across Westmoreland Street to demonstrate its deleterious impact.[32] The debate about the proposed railway had now entered fully into the public domain:

---

[28]   *Dublin Express*, February 20, 1863. The *Resolution* read: 'That having heard with much surprise and regret that a bill had been introduced into the House of Lords intituled (sic) the Dublin Metropolitan Railway Bill, having for its object the completion of a central railway station in Dublin, with a view to connect the existing railways having their termini in this city; and it appearing from the plans that it is intended to erect upwards of fifty railway bridges, some of them crossing the most frequented and beautiful thoroughfares in the city, we are of the opinion that this contemplated undertaking is uncalled for by any public requirements and that the advantages, if any, to be derived from it would be more than counterbalanced by the disfigurement of the city, the injury to trade, the interruption to traffic, and other evils that it would create.' Reported in *Dublin Builder*, March 1, 1863.

[29]   A report by the City engineer, Parke Neville, prepared in December 1862, recommended that the corporation oppose the bill on the grounds that it disfigured many streets; that it was not necessary especially in light of a contemporary proposal to join some of the lines through the northern and western outskirts of the city; that it crossed over thirty streets and that it destroyed the Corporation's own stabling and stores on Winetavern Street. *Dublin Corporation Minutes* 1863.

[30]   Ibid.

[31]   'Under the circumstances the Corporation must be prepared to oppose the bill on merits and unless public opinion be brought to bear upon the matter, I apprehend that the efforts of the Council, divided as some of its members seem to be, will prove unavailing.' Ibid. The suggestion that the Corporation may not be unified in its opposition to the bill was prompted by many members' unwillingness to present memorials against it in Westminster.

[32]   'The City of Dublin Corporation are causing to be erected at Westmoreland-street, a full-size model of the bridge proposed to cross that fine thoroughfare by the promoters of the "metropolitan railway scheme", with the view to showing the citizens who may

The entire population of the city is divided into hostile factions, one of which, comprising a large majority of the citizens, condemns the project; while the other, very much less numerous but very noisy, shouts in its favour. Petitions, pro and con, are exposed for signature, and numerous placards calling for signatures (...) are hawked about the streets. Every one who you meet wishes to discuss the subject, and you are challenged at the corner of every street as to why you would disfigure our beautiful city, or why you would show yourself so old-fashioned as to prefer beauty, health, the little comfort and repose that may be obtained in a city, to what is called mercantile convenience.[33]

What seemed most galling about this proposed disfigurement of the city was the fact that it was seen as an English imposition, using largely English capital. The annoyance was exacerbated by the fact that, while in London every effort was being made to strictly control the planning and position of the railways, there seemed to be no similar concern for Dublin: 'If the citizens of Dublin are refused what they ask, they will say (...) that one rule is adopted with respect to London and another with respect to Dublin. They will consider themselves treated as the inhabitants of a small provincial town, and not of the second metropolis in the kingdom.'[34] As with other issues of civic improvement, such as the opening of public parks, Dublin's press was very sensitive to any slights to the capital's stature.[35] Across the political spectrum, there was a clear consensus that Dublin was not provincial.

From the nationalist viewpoint, there was also a perception that the linking of the railways was designed primarily to facilitate the Whig government's efforts at centralisation. By improving the connections from England through Dublin to all other parts of Ireland, the scheme allowed for the rapid deployment of troops throughout the country in the event of civil unrest – an increasing likelihood, given the activities of Fenian rebels. Thus, far fewer troops would need to be permanently stationed across Ireland. This made perfect military and economic sense, enough for the *Express* to predict that 'Mr. Gladstone will support the motion on the principle of economy, and a great stride will be taken towards reducing this metropolis to the condition of a mere provincial town.'[36] In this interpretation, the project might be seen as actually having little to do with Dublin, and more to do with the answering of what one of its promoters called a 'great

---

not understand perfectly from the drawings the position and character of this bridge. (...) This is a very practical mode of demonstrating a result. Unfortunately one of the great scaffolding poles employed (...) in the erection of the model bridge fell on a young lady (...) on Friday last, and nearly killed her.' *Dublin Builder*, March 15, 1863.

[33]

[34] *Evening Mail*, March 24, 1863. Larcom MS 7644.

[35] *Daily Express*, April 27, 1863.

In 1863, the first of a number of bills proposing to open St. Stephen's Green to the public was also before the Parliament. One of the grounds for the measure was the negligible amount of government spending on parks in Ireland compared to Britain. See Hugh Campbell, *Contested Territory, Common Ground: Architecture and Politics in Nineteenth Century Dublin*, University College Dublin Ph.D. thesis, 1998, 157.

[36] *Irish Times*, May 6, 1863.

imperial requirement.'[37] The Irish railway network was to become part of the machinery of empire. The *Nation*, a strongly nationalist newspaper, took a similar interpretation, but went even further:

> The connection of the existing lines was declared to be desirable for strategic reasons – that is to say, it would assist in making more sure England's gripe (sic) on the throat of the Irish nation. A native parliament would seek to beautify and improve the Irish capital; native governments in every country have a care not only for the prosperity, but for the elegance of their chief towns. Napoleon III has almost rebuilt Paris. It was said that his new streets were designed to have a great strategic value; but if so, they were, at the same time, vast improvements to the city, not only in an architectural, but also in a sanitary point of view. The foreigners who rule and rob Ireland act in a different spirit. Their wish is not only to hold, but also to despoil the captive; they are not satisfied unless the very chains that bind her be as hideous as they can possibly be made, so that they may shock her eyes as well as press upon her heart.[38]

But the example of Paris might also be invoked in support of the project. A letter in the *Irish Times* simply signed 'Civis' argued that the city 'must be like the heart through which the blood flows freely, entering in and going out for the sustenance of the general life, not like a fortified town menacing the peaceful land with her gates barred, her portcullis drawn up, and her ramparts manned by her Lord Mayor, aldermen and town councillors, to drive away the traveller and the merchant, they who would promote commerce and civilisation.'[39]

Here again is the city presented as a system, an organic body through which the sustaining life-blood of trade and commerce must be allowed to flow.[40] Arguments for and against were fully rehearsed during the third reading of the bill to the committee of the House of Lords in May. By this stage the proposal had already been weakened by having to abandon its link across the river to the Belfast line at Amiens Street.[41] Nonetheless, there was support for the bill from the influential merchants Thomas Bewley and Thomas Pim, both of whom spoke in favour of the plan. For both Pim and Bewley, with substantial businesses in the Dame Street area, the advantages of a central station at College Green were evident. Benjamin Lee Guinness, opposing the bill, suggested that Dublin was too small to sustain a

---

[37] Ibid.

[38] *The Nation*, June 13, 1863.

[39] *Irish Times*, March 16, 1863.

[40] Discussing Haussmann's work in Paris, Richard Sennett asserts that his streets were primarily channels for movement, 'a directional motion too rapid, too pressed, to attach itself to (local) eddies of life', and argues that such theories of urban development derive from William Harvey's discoveries about the circulation of blood through the body. Richard Sennett, *Flesh and Stone: The Body and the City in Western Civilization* (London and New York 1994), 329.

[41] This was as a result of a report from the Board of Trade on the 23 April, requiring that any bridge at this point on the river must be openable at high tide to allow uninterrupted boat traffic. In light of the report, the promoters quickly abandoned this portion of their scheme.

central rail system. Guinness's brewery, at the western edge of the city, would be equally well served by a loopline system, which he proposed as an alternative.[42] Indeed, there was a strong indication from the committee that they favoured a central station, but preferred to create a new line around the periphery of the city. This was no doubt due, at least in part, to the contemporary difficulties about the many proposed lines through London's centre.

Despite the concerted efforts of Guinness and others, and to the surprise and dismay of most commentators, the bill passed its third reading, albeit in a much reduced form.[43] The changes enforced by the committee now allowed the opposition to take a different tack:

> The proposed line is in the first place, but a fragment of the original plan, and if constructed in the intended way, will render it practically impossible to complete the connections between the excluded railways and the central station. The central station itself becomes, in fact, to a large extent unnecessary in the absence of the lines joining the Northern Railways and Dublin, Wicklow, Wexford. All the earlier pictures of a grand and perfect scheme fade away into the shrunken proportions of a London and Northwest and Cork junction. Whether we ought to spoil our city for such a miserable remnant of the original design, let the public judge. We shall not be wrong in holding that, as far as the Government is concerned, the chief motive for desiring this metropolitan monstrosity is the easy conveyance of troops through Ireland.[44]

The debate was then further complicated by the appearance of a second proposal, designed by a Dublin engineer, LeFanu. This scheme, in contrast to Barry's, managed, in the opinion of the *Freeman's Journal*, to 'preserve the beauty of our leading thoroughfares.'[45] It proposed a central station at ground level, but with the connecting lines travelling underground. The project was obviously influenced by the building of the Metropolitan Line in London. A new drainage system for the city was to run parallel to the track – similar to the sanitary improvements that accompanied Haussmann's transformations of Paris. 'In addition to all this, it will

---

42 *Evening Mail*, May 7, and May 8, 1863.

43 The reaction of the *Evening Post* was typical in its bemoaning of the lack of British understanding of Irish problems: 'We deeply regret this decision, pronounced by English and Scotch noblemen, who were activated by the best motives, but who, from their want of local knowledge of Dublin, were unable to form a correct judgement of the extent of injury which such a project was calculated to produce in the "Irish metropolis".' It went on to stress yet again the imperial motivations behind the scheme: 'In the case for the promoters of the Dublin Metropolitan Railway, one might imagine that the siege of Sebastopol was to be acted over again. There was Sir John Burgoyne and General Airey once more, with half a score of other engineers, seeking to establish the necessity of cutting up the principal thoroughfares of Dublin and throwing bridges across our leading streets, as a measure of imperial policy, absolutely required to stabilitate (sic) the union between Great Britain and Ireland.' *Evening Post*, May 12, 1863. Larcom MS 7644.

44 *Evening Mail*, May 20, 1863.

45 *Freeman's Journal*, June 6, 1863.

open a noble line of street in direct continuation with Dame-street, relieving the city traffic of the steep and awkward turn at Cork-hill, and at other points in its transit opening a way for improvements scarcely less desirable.'[46]

A rail tunnel ran under this new street with sidings into the breweries and distilleries of Thomas Street and High Street. This provision suggests that Guinness, Roe and the other powerful business interests in the west of the city may have had a hand in the conception of the scheme, or would at least be happier to support it.

However the main impetus for the project seems to have come from the corporation, who saw the introduction of this new scheme as the most effective means of opposing the original bill. And indeed Le Fanu's design was persuasive enough to mean that Thornton's bill was abruptly withdrawn in July.[47] 'We have the pleasing duty today of congratulating the citizens upon the decease of the great Metropolitan Railway scheme,' reported the *Evening Mail*.[48] In the wake of the bill's demise came a flood of alternative proposals, some the usual eccentric letters to newspapers, others more comprehensive and considered. McNeil and Hemans suggested a completely suburban network, similar to Guinness's proposed loopline.[49] The loopline solution was also favoured by Barnes, who envisaged a line running under the Grand Canal. Its chief advantage was seen as being 'the connecting of all the military barracks with one another by means of this circular railway for by it the quickest access is had from one to each, his line being proposed to pass the gates of the Richmond, Portobello and Beggars-bush Barracks, thereby forming a complete defence to the south side of the city should occasion ever occur for such.'[50]

Besides its obvious paranoia, its chief disadvantage was seen as being its failure to provide a central station. The exact location of the central station was also a matter of debate. While the block between Dame Street and the river proved the most popular, there were also suggestions for a station in Prince's Street off Sackville Street, and for a station spanning the Liffey between Abbey Street and Great

---

[46] *Evening Mail*, June 4, 1863. This new street had long been projected as a desirable improvement: 'The oldest inhabitant of Dublin does not recollect a time when the proposal was not before the citizens in some shape or other to cut a new street through Cork Hill. As far back at least as 1839 an effort on rather a large scale was made to effect this leading city improvement, but it came to nothing.' *Irish Times*, November 11, 1881. It soon became the subject of intense discussion itself.

[47] 'It is well known that the first bill was sponsored by Mr. Thornton an English railway contractor. When he saw the storms rage high, he said "There is no use in my advancing money to benefit the people of Dublin if they are not satisfied with my proposals. I can expend my money with an equal prospect of profit elsewhere, and with more thanks." Therefore, he ordered the bill to be withdrawn.' *Dublin Builder*, October 15, 1863.

[48] *Evening Mail*, July 11, 1863.

[49] Letter to *Irish Times*, August 14, 1863.

[50] *Dublin Builder*, October 15, 1863. Letter from Hederman. *The Builder* was itself opposed to Barnes' proposal. The scheme uses the railways to demarcate the limits of the city, reinforcing the edge which had been made by the canals and ringroads in the late eighteenth century.

Brunswick Street – later called Pearse Street.[51] Perhaps the most ambitious and unusual scheme was praised by the *Dublin Builder* for its 'boldness and daring':

> It consisted in arching over the Liffey the whole way from the Kings-bridge terminus to Carlisle-bridge, the span to consist of two arches. The Great Southern and Western was then to be carried down on arches over the centre pier, and on arriving at Carlisle-bridge it was to open into two branches to join the Amiens-street and Westland-row termini, spanning Sackville-street and Westmoreland-street with ornamental bridges. The arches underneath the railroad were to be converted into shops, the renting of which would in itself form a considerable source of emolument. A magnificent road would thus be formed the whole way to the Park, the sewer nuisance would be removed, and house property along the line immensely raised in value.[52]

Like many of the projects, this scheme used the opportunity of connecting the railways to upgrade the city's infrastructure, providing for a new sewer system, allowing the whole city to function more smoothly. By the end of the year, no fewer than seven bills had been tabled for the following Parliamentary session.[53] They fell into three categories: '1st. Those which propose to tunnel under the city. 2nd. Those which propose to cross through the streets. 3rd Those which propose to run round the city.'[54] The *Dublin Builder* selected the two which intersected the city as the most serious contenders: a proposal by Barton, engineer of the Dundalk and Enniskillen Railway and Barry's newly revised scheme, which owed much to LeFanu's ideas.[55] LeFanu himself was no longer involved, having taken up his appointment as *Commissioner of Public Works* in September 1863. The Barton proposal located the central station behind the commercial buildings on Dame Street, crossed the Liffey at Essex Quay to join the Great Western line at Broadstone and looped through Fishamble Street, Patrick Street and Kevin Street to join the Harcourt Street Line.[56] Barry was now committed to the underground solution. He retained the support of the Pims, along with other prominent merchants and traders. More importantly, he gained the endorsement of the corporation which, somewhat unenthusiastically, found his proposal 'the least objectionable'.[57]

---

[51] *Dublin Builder*, November 1, 1863.

[52] *Dublin Builder*, February 15, 1864. It may seem odd that the *Dublin Builder*, having bemoaned the disruption and disfigurement of the city proposed by the earlier bill, should now endorse the most elaborate, ambitious and arguably most intrusive project of all.

[53] 'Four metropolitan schemes, two for connecting Dublin with Rathgar and Rathfarnham, and one entitled the great Southern and Midland Junction Railway.' *Dublin Builder*, March 1, 1864.

[54] *Dublin Builder*, November 1, 1863.

[55] *Dublin Builder*, February 15, 1864.

[56] *Freeman's Journal*, December 31, 1863.

[57] *Irish Times*, February 24, 1864. The endorsement is unsurprising given how closely it was based on the LeFanu scheme which they originally supported.

However despite corporation support, Barry's project did not make it before the House of Lords committee. The two projects which they finally considered in May were Barton's overground, centralised scheme and Heman's loopline proposal. The discussion focused far more on the strategic advantages in military terms of each project than had been the case the previous year and it seems that in the end these were the deciding criteria. In early June, the committee decided that Dublin was too small to merit a central station, and approved instead the *Dublin Trunk Connecting Railway Bill*.[58] The bill was passed by the House of Lords on the 23rd of July 1864. Financial support for the plan soon collapsed however, and the connection to the docks from Amiens Street station was the only element of it to be carried out.[59] In 1867, the newly-founded *City of Dublin Tramways Company* began the construction of what became known as the Three Stations line, linking

Figure 11.3 Broadstone Station, Dublin, 2002

Source: Photo taken by Hugh Campbell.

---

[58] *Irish Times*, June 16, 1864.

[59] Although in 1873 the issue of a central station for Dublin briefly re-emerged. At a meeting in the Mansion House, Barry presented yet another version of his well-worn scheme, and again he was supported by the Pims and the Roes. In a new development, a line was proposed which ran close to the breweries and distilleries of the western city, suggesting their increased importance in Dublin's economy. See *Daily Express*, November 11, 1873.

the railway termini at Kingsbridge, Westland Row and Harcourt Street and effectively obviating the need for a passenger connection between the stations.[60]

So Dublin never did get its grand connecting railway, be it underground or overground, central or peripheral. From the outset, it had proved difficult to encourage private investment in Irish railways to anything like the same extent as in Britain.[61] The failure of the Dublin bill to be implemented made this difficulty freshly apparent. In the following years there were persistent calls for state intervention in the Irish railways. In a series of articles, the *Irish Builder*, which saw the provision of an efficient rail service as too important a matter to be left to the 'British Railway monopolists', depicted an inadequate rail system which was debilitating the mining industry and generally damaging Ireland's economic prospects: 'The point at issue may be really this – whether railway communication, being essential to the general interests of the nation, is not in itself of so imperial a character as to demand the care and supervision of the government, so as to secure that these interests shall not be sacrificed.'[62]

However, the government remained impervious to these demands, still preferring to rely solely on private enterprise to generate a rail network.[63] This may seem ironic, given their view of the railway as an essential instrument of imperial rule. In the long term, however, their laissez-faire attitude was enough to facilitate the growth of a comprehensive network. By 1900, 3,500 miles of track had been laid in Ireland, bringing a marked increase in economic activity and in internal migration.[64] The centre of Dublin, however, remained largely free of visible signs of the railway age. The Loop-line bridge, a vestige of the 1864 bill, finally connected Amiens Street and Westland Row stations across the Liffey in 1894. Its crude form still bears testament to what might have been if original plans for Dublin's rail links had been implemented in full.

---

[60] Michael Corcoran, *Through Streets Broad and Narrow: A history of Dublin Trams* (Athlone 2000), 9.

[61] 'By 1847 2,600 miles of railway had been opened for traffic in England and Scotland, while only 123 miles had been constructed in Ireland, which was one-fourth the size of the United Kingdom. This was the case, although Parliament, at great cost to the promoters, had passed acts authorising the construction of 1,523 miles of line for Ireland. There was very little home capital in Ireland, and English capital could hardly be expected to flow in when more promising investments both at home and in the United States of America could be found for it.' J. C. Conroy, *A History of Railways in Ireland* (London 1928), 18.

[62] *Irish Builder*, September 1, 1867. See also the issue from September 15, 1867. Although protestations about the inadequacies of Ireland's rail network are somewhat at odds with the statistical evidence: 'Ireland (...) had 65 miles of track in 1845, 1,000 in 1857, 2,000 in 1872 and with 3,500 by 1914 boasted one of the densest networks in the world.' Joseph Lee, *The Modernisation of Irish Society* (Dublin 1983), 13.

[63] In May 1867, the Devonshire Commission recommended against any state intervention.

[64] Roy Foster, *Modern Ireland 1600–1982* (London 1988), 385.

Conclusion

This partial implementation of a much more comprehensive urban plan is in fact typical of the pattern of development in late nineteenth-century Dublin. Grand ambition was almost inevitably frustrated by the complexities of the *realpolitik*. On the one hand there was the relatively toothless corporation, with its growing tendency to place national interests above municipal concerns. On the other hand there were the self-styled merchant princes, determined to shape the city to their own ends and resentful of municipal inaction. But while their private beneficence may have been sufficient to implement isolated projects like the restoration of the city's two cathedrals, the financing of more comprehensive projects would have to come from Britain.[65] And besides looking to Britain's venture capitalists for investment, any projects for the improvement of Dublin had, in the final analysis, to seek approval from Westminster. Here they met with a prevailing view which saw the Irish capital as at once provincial and colonial. Viewed as a provincial city, it was deemed unworthy of any special status. Viewed as a colonial outpost, it had to be drawn more completely into the imperial system. In neither case could Dublin's needs simply be considered on their own terms. At a time when rural Ireland was becoming the focus of nationalist agitation and of government action, Dublin's problems remained marginal to both. The nation's capital struggled to assert its own identity or to press its own case. So while Dublin retained its beauty and escaped 'mutilation' by the railways, it did so largely by default rather than by design.

---

[65] Benjamin Lee Guinness's restoration of St. Patrick's Cathedral was completed in 1865, while Henry Roe sponsored the restoration of Christ Church Cathedral between 1873 and 1878. Both projects were accompanied by broader ambitions to improve the surrounding urban fabric, but in neither case were these ambitions realised.

CHAPTER TWELVE

Following the tracks – railways in the city centre of Helsinki: bygone past or unwritten urban history?

Anja Kervanto Nevanlinna

Traces which disappear

For the post-industrial European city, railways are not important. At least so it would seem in the final volume of *Histoire de la France urbaine*, 'The city today' which focuses on the latter half of the twentieth century. It is interesting to note that the railways are hardly mentioned.[1] More precise, perhaps, is to observe that for the contemporary city, the railway no longer represents the dramatic leap which altered the concept of urbanism as it did for the industrial city a century earlier. Even though railways are an intrinsic part of the organisation of our major cities today they are at the same time gradually disappearing from city centres. Railway buildings are being converted or demolished, tracks transferred underground or dismantled and areas redeveloped. If the process continues, will there be any traces left of the industrial phase of our cities, or is it slowly becoming a relic from a bygone past?

Historically, railways were an essential element in the development of the European industrial city such as we know it today, not only as a concentration of capital and people, but also as urban fabric, forms and spaces. The introduction of the railway transformed many pre-industrial towns in the nineteenth century into rapidly growing conurbations. Railway stations and rail-yards changed the focuses and structure of the urban geography, particularly in the centre of the city. Yet in the histories written about cities and their built form, the significance of the railway has surprisingly been overlooked.

Urban historians have commonly placed the railway among means of transportation. They have regarded it as a technological innovation connecting places far apart, enabling the movement of masses of people, and instrumental in

---

[1] Marcel Roncayolo, ed., *Histoire de la France urbaine*, vol. 5: *La ville aujourd'hui* (Paris 1985).

accelerating the growth of cities.[2] Historians have emphasised its economic and social consequences particularly on the regional level, while analyses of its spatial or symbolic impact on the more immediate local surroundings have been few. Architectural historians have studied railway stations as a new kind of public edifice and example of a building type whereas other railway structures have offered them few objects seen to contain aesthetic value and so, are hardly worth the analysis.[3] Both urban and architectural histories seem to reflect a demarcation between prestigious national institutions and profane activities, with the railways being unequivocably associated with the latter. Much of the history of the railways in the city centre as an essential part of urban culture with its practices and spaces, still remains unwritten.[4]

In recent decades, the railways located in the centres of many European cities have been in the process of being fundamentally transformed. Some railway lines and stations have already been terminated. Extensive railway areas are being vacated at an increasing pace. For the business community with its growing demand for office buildings, the former railway areas are financially lucrative not only because they are centrally located but also because the exposed sites are sufficiently large and empty to be redeveloped without constraints imposed by existing buildings. For the organisations governing the railway, these areas provide a source of sound profits when they are sold site by site to prospective developers. Both parties perceive the various railway buildings, structures and tracks as obstacles to the improvement of the area. Although the occasional railway station or customs building may be included in the list of buildings to be preserved and therefore saved from demolition, all the others will be razed. Without the support of urban histories of railways, we may soon face the situation where an essential part of our urban culture and its history will be irrevocably lost and forgotten.

Railways in the heart of Helsinki

The histories of the centre of Helsinki illustrate how the railway disappears from the accounts of the city's past after the initial phase of construction. The 'Great Narrative' of Helsinki describes the establishment of the town in 1812 as the new

---

2   See, for example, Lewis Mumford, *The City in History* (New York 1961), 458–65; Asa Briggs, *Victorian Cities* (Harmondsworth 1990), 14–18, and Eric J. Hobsbawm, *The Age of Capital 1848–1875* (London 1977), 246–9.

3   See, for example, Spiro Kostof, *A History of Architecture* (Oxford 1985), 595–8; Nikolaus Pevsner, *A History of Building Types* (London 1976), chapter 14, and Alfred Fierro, *Histoire et dictionnaire de Paris* (Paris 1996), 765.

4   As an example of openings in this direction, see Wolfgang Schivelbusch, *Junamatkan historia* (The history of the train journey, orig.: Geschichte der Eisenbahnreise. Zur Industrialisierung von Raum und Zeit im 19. Jahrhundert) (Tampere 1996), 154–60. See also Jack Simmons, 'The Power of the Railway', in H. J. Dyos and Michael Wolff, eds., *The Victorian City: Images and Realities, 2 vols.* (London 1973), vol. 2, 277–310, esp. 301–2.

capital of Finland, Grand Duchy of Russia, won from Sweden during the Napoleonic wars in 1809. The administrative centre and particularly its neo-classical Senate Square became the political and symbolic heart of the country. It was designed by Carl Ludwig Engel, the *Berliner* whom the Czar had appointed as chief architect of the reconstruction of Helsinki. This interpretation has dominated in political and architectural histories of Helsinki. Noticeably absent from these histories have been references to the major port and rail-yard area established in the 1890s although it is immediately adjacent to the administrative core.

In the first half of the nineteenth century before the age of the railway and industrialisation, Helsinki grew because of its newly acquired position as capital. In 1810, it had been a small trade town with a population of some 3,600 inhabitants. A large part of it had been destroyed by fire immediately after the war. By 1830 it had grown to become the undisputed administrative, military and cultural focus of the country. Its population had increased to 12,000. The Czar's government supported the reconstruction of the capital with extensive funding for public works which included the construction of a large number of administrative and military buildings and the improvement of streets and port areas. When the work of the commission for the reconstruction of Helsinki came to an end in 1855, the city was seen as complete. Its population then was around 20,000.[5] During this phase, the development of towns, and in particular of Helsinki as the capital, strongly depended on the interests of the Czar.

The construction of the network of railways in Finland was also initiated by Czar Alexander II and his government. The railways were part of his programme to develop the economic foundation of the country and were connected to his policy to integrate Finland more fully into the Russian Empire.[6] The three factors which accelerated the process of industrialisation in the country were the railway, the liberalisation of trade in 1859–79, and the new legislation of 1875 which considerably increased the powers of the municipal government. The railway was introduced in Helsinki in 1862 to connect the city to inland areas and eventually, to the Empire. In 1870, the railway line brought Helsinki closer to St. Petersburg, a metropolis of grand dimensions with a multicultural population of nearly 670,000 and the capital of the Russian Empire.[7]

---

[5]   Population figures from Heikki Waris, 'Helsinkiläisyhteiskunta (The Helsinki society)', in *Helsingin kaupungin historia* (The history of the City of Helsinki), 5 vols. (Helsinki 1950–1967), vol. 3/2, 7–211, esp. 11.

[6]   See Martti Kovero, 'Helsinki liikennekeskuksena (Helsinki as a traffic centre)', in *Helsingin kaupungin historia* (The history of the City of Helsinki), 5 vols. (Helsinki 1950–1967), vol. 3/1, 255–365, esp. 328–9, and Markku Kuisma, 'Europe's Wood Basket Transformed. Finnish Economic History in a Long Perspective', in Tuomas M. S. Lehtonen, ed., *Europe's Northern Frontier. Perspectives on Finland's Western Identity* (Jyväskylä 1999), 50–85, esp. 68–9.

[7]   St. Petersburg was the fourth largest city in Europe after London, Paris and Constantinople. Some ten to twenty per cent of its inhabitants were non-Russian. See Solomon Volkov, *Pietari, eurooppalainen kaupunki* (St. Petersburg, a European city, orig. St. Petersburg – A Cultural History, 1996) (Helsinki 1999), 72–3.

Because of the railway and the beginning of industrialisation, the population of Helsinki soared to around 32,000 in 1870. This figure would double itself by 1890 when it rose to over 65,000 and yet again to 136,000 in 1910.[8] The new municipal legislation had made towns less dependent on the Czar's government. As a consequence of this, the emerging groups of entrepreneurs, industrialists and civil servants were not only being offered the instruments to influence the dramatic changes in the city but also, through the right to levy taxes, for example, the resources to turn ideas into reality. New opportunities for promoting local interests opened up to them.

The new city council of Helsinki perceived that in the long term, the future of the city could not be based on extensive government support, but rather on commerce and industry alone. Thus a modern port with good railway connections was essential. This also corresponded with the interests of the municipal economy, because the port brought a significant portion of its revenues.[9] Investments in the port would directly benefit the capital. During the latter part of the nineteenth century, the modernisation and extension of ports was common in many European cities due to several factors. The new opportunities offered by the steamship and the railway required modifications in the port arrangements. Increase in shipping was generated by the opening of shorter seaways such as the Suez Canal. In some ports, changes were also influenced by military interests.[10] In Helsinki, the establishment of a modern port was seen as an investment which would secure the economy of the city long into the future.

The location of the major port in Helsinki was of crucial importance. Modern shipping required that navigation routes to the port and docks were deep enough for ocean going ships. Quays were to be built so that they could sustain the weight of the transportation and hauling equipment such as locomotives and cranes. Space was needed for loading and unloading, and sufficient warehouse facilities for the storage and customs clearance of various kinds of goods were to be provided. Railway tracks were to extend to all the warehouses and quays. In the port area, the flow of traffic was to run smoothly. In Helsinki, Katajanokka peninsula which is

---

[8]   Population figures from Sven-Erik Åström, *Samhällsplanering och regionsbildning i kejsartidens Helsingfors* (Social planning and the formation of social areas in imperial Helsinki) (Helsinki 1957), 356–7.

[9]   In the 1870s, the largest municipal revenues in Finnish towns came from income taxes, with the port revenues second. See Jorma Kallenautio, 'Kunnallistalous, yhdyskuntatekniikka, liikelaitokset ja joukkoliikenne 1875–1917 (Municipal economy, infrastructure, public utilities, and mass transportation, 1875–1917)', in Päiviö Tommila, ed., *Suomen kaupunkilaitoksen historia* (The history of the town institution in Finland) (Helsinki 1983), vol. 2, 271–330.

[10] See Gordon Jackson, *The History and Archeology of Ports* (Kingswood 1983), 78–82. See also Roncayolo, Marcel, *Histoire du Commerce et de l'industrie de Marseille, XIXe – XXe siècles*, vol. 5: *L'Imaginaire de Marseille, Port, Ville, Pôle* (Marseille 1990), 86; Jean-Lucien Bonillo et al., *Marseille, Ville and Port* (Marseille 1991), 70–2, and Sigurd Jensen and Claus M. Smidt, *Rammerne spraenges*, vol. 4: *Köbenhavns historie, 1830–1900* (Copenhagen 1982), 245.

located south-west of the core was regarded as the ideal location for this kind of modern port.[11] In the 1860s, its western part had contained small wooden houses inhabited by fishermen's families. By 1870, however, these had been demolished to provide space for the planned extension of the urban structure. The cathedral for the Russian Orthodox parish and the National Treasury which produced the newly acquired national currency, the Finnish *markka*, paved the way for the new. In addition to the advantageous location of Katajanokka next to the centre of the city, there was also a natural deep-water channel flowing to it. Furthermore, it was possible to construct a railway connection to the main line from there. The major port was to be built right into the heart of the capital.

The development of the port and railway area in the centre of Helsinki was an event of grand proportions at that time. As a result of this process, what was originally only a small natural harbour for local boats was transformed into the country's leading port in passenger traffic and imported goods, a position it would retain for most of the twentieth century until the 1970s.[12] When completed in 1915, the new South Harbour comprised 2.3 kilometres of quays and had an average sea-depth of seven to eight metres which was suitable for ocean going vessels. Its operations were based on a new railway line built in the early 1890s in order to connect the port to the main line. In 1890, the estimated cost of the port railway line was three quarters of the annual budget of the city of Helsinki. The government covered 78 per cent of the expenses in exchange for gaining ownership of the land occupied by the railway line.[13] Seven kilometres long, the port railway line encircled most of the pre-existing developed urban area of Helsinki in the north and the seafront in the west and south and extended around the South Harbour.

Extending the railway line to the port transformed the seafront. Generous landfills at the seafront facilitated the construction of the railway line but caused the small islands to be swallowed up by the mainland and become part of the urban structure. Along the harbour, the exceptional combination of access by rail and sea made seaside sites more lucrative for wholesale and shipping services. The alignment multiplied the number of sites suitable for industries all along its length and on both sides of the tracks. While the seafront had earlier been used by the

---

[11] Anonymous, 'Frågan om ny stadsplan för Skatudden (The issue of the new urban plan for Katajanokka)', in *Tekniska Föreningens i Finland Förhandlingar* (Proceedings of the Technical Society of Finland) (Helsinki 1883), 1–15, esp. 9–11.

[12] See Martti Kovero, 'Helsinki liikennekeskuksena', in *Helsingin kaupungin historia* (The history of the City of Helsinki), 5 vols. (Helsingin kaupunki, Helsinki 1950–1967), vol. 4/1, 211–71, esp. 219–25, and Jukka Erävuori, *Helsingin sataman ja satamahallinnon historia* (The history of the port and port administration of Helsinki) (Helsinki 1981), *passim*.

[13] See Kovero, ibid., vol. 4/1, 219–25; Iisakki Laati, 'Kunnalliselämä (Municipal activities)', in *Helsingin kaupungin historia* (The history of the City of Helsinki), 5 vols. (Helsinki 1950–1967), vol. 4/2, 335–434, esp. 371–2.

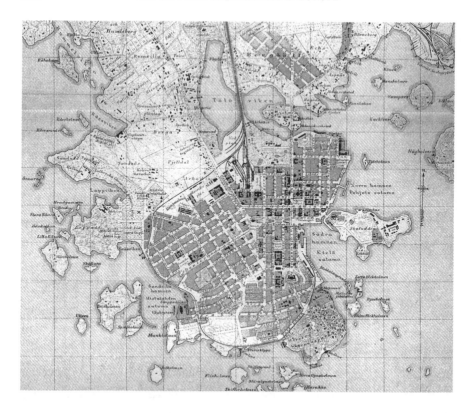

Figure 12.1   Map of Helsinki in 1894

Source: Author's collection.

inhabitants for washing clothes and for recreation, after its industrialisation it was
allocated for production and prohibited from public access.[14]

The new railway line to the port strongly influenced the development of
Helsinki. The railway station had been built at the same time as the opening of the
first railway line in 1862 and was situated north-west of the administrative centre.
It had already begun to attract both industries and commerce, causing the focus of
business to expand westwards of the old core. The new railway line strengthened
this process, increasing the development potential of the surrounding areas.
Agricultural or unused land was rapidly converted into residential sites, the more
prominent ones being those with five-storey buildings constructed of stone. The
city council sold sites on Katajanokka peninsula to developers. It was located
south-east of the core and next to the port. The small neighbourhood mushroomed

---

[14] See, for example, Väinö Tanner, *Näin Helsingin kasvavan* (I saw Helsinki grow)
(Helsinki 1947), 104, 109–10.

Figure 12.2   Freight train, Helsinki, 2000

Source: Photo taken by Anja Kervanto Nevanlinna.

within a single decade at the turn of the century and has only just recently been valued for the uniformity of its *art nouveau* architecture.[15] Another unplanned section of the city located north-west of the centre and later known as *Töölö*, had been projected as a residential area as early as 1883 but had remained untouched for nearly twenty years. It began to attract planners and developers only after the construction of the railway line and in 1899, it became the object of the first planning competition held in Helsinki.[16]

The planning of the alignment had been dominated by technical aspects without consideration of the effects of the railway line on the surrounding urban structure. With the rapid growth of the urban structure outside the new railway line, traffic across the tracks increased. Streets crossed the railway line on bridges only on the northern and north-western section where the alignment had been dynamited deep into the bedrock. At all other places, the train crossed the street on the same level.

---

[15]   See Sven-Erik Åström, *Samhällsplane-ring och regionsbildning i kejsartidens Helsingfors* (Helsinki 1957), 37–8.

[16]   See Riitta Nikula, *Yhtenäinen kaupunkikuva, 1900–1930. Suomalaisen kaupunkirakentamisen ihanteista ja päämääristä, esimerkkeinä Helsingin Etu-Töölö ja Uusi Vallila* (Harmonious townscape, 1900–1930. On the ideals and aims of urban construction in Finland, with Etu-Töölö and Uusi Vallila of Helsinki as examples) (Helsinki 1981), 170–3. After the Töölö area grew northward, the earlier, southern part was renamed Etu-Töölö.

For decades, this integration of the port railway line with the urban structure has bestowed a special *genius loci* on parts of central Helsinki. This can still be experienced where the railway line has not yet been dismantled.

Not even the historical core was left untouched. In the 1860s, it had been an area with administration, commerce, and residences of the elite, peaceful and restrained as was suitable for a provincial capital. Change began with the industrialisation and expansive growth of the capital from the 1880s. With the arrival of the railway line and the major port around the turn of the century, the character of the old core was transformed. Former activities were intermingled with small-scale industries, all kinds of services and accommodation for the full range of social groups. The *quartier* at the core became a mosaic of urban life where government and city officials and businessmen mixed with dockyard labourers, shopkeepers, housewives, and soldiers.

Reconstructing identity

In accounts of Helsinki, various aspects relating to the port have been discussed, each separately in its own field of history. These have included the social problems caused by the rapid growth of the industrial city, the economic role of the port in the national economy and the various phases of the planning and construction of the port and the railway line connecting it to the main rail-yard.[17] What remains to be written are integrative analyses of why a major port with an extensive rail-yard was established immediately adjacent to the historical core. The location of this area in the heart of the nation can be seen as more than a mere technical or economic solution, it also held symbolic meanings.

If the transformations of the centre of Helsinki are discussed in relation to national identity, the establishment of the port and its railway at the historical core at the turn of the century can be interpreted as an expression of a new way of thinking. During the latter part of the nineteenth century, industrial achievements became issues of pride and competition among European nations and their cities. Industrial development and the economic integration it entailed were seen as prerequisites in the process of constructing a national identity for these nations. This was also evident in the extent at which Finland participated in international exhibitions with increasing interest throughout the latter part of the nineteenth century, particularly considering it did not attain political independence from

---

[17]   See, for example, Sven-Erik Åström, *Samhällsplanering och regionsbildning i kejsartidens Helsingfors* (Helsinki 1957), 37–8; Martti Kovero, 'Helsinki liikennekeskuksena (Helsinki as a traffic centre)', in *Helsingin kaupungin historia*, 5 vols. (Helsinki 1950–1967), vol. 3/2, 328–9; ibid. vol. 4/1, 219–25, and Jukka Erävuori, *Helsingin sataman ja satamahallinnon historia* (The history of the port and port administration of Helsinki) (Helsinki 1981), *passim*.

Russia until 1917.[18] In this context, the modern port of Helsinki demonstrated the significance of technological progress and innovations for the country and its capital. Because of this, its location in the centre adjacent to the administrative core is self-evident.

By constructing the major port within the heart of the capital the citizens also constructed the identity of Helsinki. Until then, the national identity of Finland as an autonomous Grand Duchy of the Russian Empire had been created from above, through measures taken by the Emperor and government officials. At that time, the capital was regarded as the primary symbol of the nation's identity. With industrialisation, the identity of the city began to be seen to include the idea of a local identity. Helsinki was to be more than just an administrative projection of the government. The newly appointed city council together with the leading businessmen began to create an image of another kind of Helsinki. Through commerce and industry, they wanted to generate continuity for the urban community, locally founded and therefore free from the changing spheres of interest of the central government. During the latter part of the nineteenth century, the strengthening of local identity became common in European cities. The new objectives of Helsinki can be understood in the context of the general tendencies of the time. The modern identity of the capital began to take shape through more open and more international exchange such as the transfer of goods, knowledge, expertise, technology and practices.[19]

Constructing the port and its railway in the old heart of the city made the effects of industrialisation more visible. The Empire period of Helsinki was established through the main administrative institutions: the senate, the cathedral, the university, and the residence of the Governor General. Its architectural base of inspiration was the Neo-classicism of St. Petersburg. Although this style was realised in Helsinki on a smaller scale it was carried out with no less aesthetic fervour. The architecture of the core referred to the classical roots of European culture with its graceful columns, pale colours and symmetrical façades. The grand stone buildings dominated the skyline and promulgated the Emperor's power over his subjects. Around them spread a carpet of uniform regular blocks consisting of modest wooden buildings.

Industrialisation brought a change to this view. The scale of the existing city expanded. The senate and the university buildings which had dominated the townscape, began to be rivalled by the office blocks, apartment houses and industrial structures of the new bourgeoisie. Emerging from the new institutions based on technological and economic innovation were the industrial city's own

---

[18] See Kerstin Smeds, *Helsingfors – Paris. Finland på världsutställningarna 1851–1900* (Helsinki – Paris. Finland in world exhibitions, 1851–1900) (Helsinki 1996), passim.

[19] See, for example, Marjatta Hietala, *Innovaatioiden ja kansainvälistymisen vuosikymmenet* (Knowledge, know-how, professionalism. Helsinki as part of European development, 1875–1917), vol. 1 of Marjatta Hietala, ed., *Tietoa, taitoa, asiantunte-musta: Helsinki eurooppalaisessa kehityksessä 1875–1917*, 3 vols. (Helsinki 1992), 229–43.

**Figure 12.3   South Harbour with the Presidential Palace, Cathedral, and the
High Court, 1950s**

Source: Helsinki City Museum.

monuments: railway stations, banks, warehouses, and gas works. By the 1930s the solemn authority of the Neo-classical façades in the historical core of Helsinki had been juxtaposed with the practical dominance of the red brick landscape of the industrial city consisting of buildings such as the market hall, customs building, and bonded warehouses. In scale, some of them challenged but did not surpass even the largest of the older buildings. Around the South Harbour, the pattern of the pre-existing city was interspersed with moving engines, dancing cranes, busy trucks and railway wagons being loaded and unloaded, the air thick with steam, smoke, sounds and smells.

From 1910 to the 1970s, the identity of the heart of Helsinki was composed of two main elements, the neo-classical Old Town of administrative buildings and the port framing it with its railway structures and red brick buildings. Although intertwined in reality, in images taken of them they have been kept visually apart from one another. In photographs, the separation of the two was achieved through framing. This became more difficult when aerial photography gained popularity in the 1920s. In moving pictures such as the 1922 film *Finlandia* commissioned by the Ministry of Foreign Affairs to promote the newly independent nation and its industries with the ultimate goal of increasing exports, the proximity of the administrative part and the port area was nevertheless carefully hidden.[20] While pictures of the port and railway around the South Harbour showed a modern industrial nation, images of the Old Town served as a reminder of its past which was essential for a democratic society hoping to be accepted among European nations sharing a cultural heritage.

When independence came in 1917 it increased the significance of industrial development in forming a national identity. Industry was perceived as essential to the economy of the nation and therefore gained a prominent role in its pictorial depiction. In the presentation of the capital, images of the port and its railway were used to demonstrate the level of technological progress. Even after the Second World War, they were seen as manifestations of the capacity of a society to survive harsh natural conditions and unbearable historical crises. War indemnities forced the development of a modern metal industry, transforming, for example, the eastern parts of the Katajanokka area in the heart of the capital into a dockyard, the raw material transported to the site on the port railway around the centre and through the historical core. The visible prominence of the industries, railways and port equipment indicated their vital significance for the post-war society.

Today, however, the importance of industrial traces to the identity of the city has been reversed. The monuments of industrial development are increasingly being perceived as extinct dinosaurs, colossal relics of an ancient era. Many of these, including the railway structures, have become undesirable elements easy to

---

[20] The first aerial photographs of the core of Helsinki were published in Gustaf Strengell, *Kaupunki taideluomana* (The city as a work of art) (Helsinki 1923), and in Carolus Lindberg, *Helsingfors, Nordens vita stad* (Helsinki, white city of the North) (Helsinki 1931), the latter with texts in Swedish, English, German and French. Only fragments of the film *Finlandia* remain.

demolish even in city centres without any public protest. This has resulted in most of the traces of the railways being erased from the historical heart of Helsinki. We cannot follow the tracks, in a concrete sense, at least, on an unbroken path from the main rail-yard around the old Helsinki to the South Harbour because large sections have been dismantled. None of the 34 cranes which served as links between the ships, warehouses, and trains and which still dominated views of the port in 1970 have been preserved. Today, only the turning bridge and its railway tracks at the edge of the Market Place where all the trains passed to and from the eastern part of the port, still remain to remind us of the hundred years of industrial history of this place. Even this may soon change. An urban planner of the Department of City Planning has proposed its removal to restore the place to its 'original', that is, 'pre-industrial' planned form.[21] The contemporary identity of the centre seems to demand the erasure of its 'dishonourable' industrial past.

And yet something of the past still remains. The western parts of the port railway are still in use. Some ten freight trains pass daily to and from the main container port of the capital through the old goods yard, between the dense urban structure of the early decades of the century and past the new mixed housing and business area. The freight trains carrying containers may consist of over forty wagons which, while crossing at certain places at street level, can even interrupt both foot and vehicle traffic for periods of ten or more minutes each time. The less frequent transport of steel once or twice a week to the dockyard further southward has allowed grass to grow in between the tracks of the old port railway. Because the rail connection to the dockyard is its lifeline, dismantling the tracks would increase transportation expenses to the extent that the company would be forced to find a new location. Today, the dockyard is one of the few remaining traces of the industrial era in central Helsinki. Its buildings as well as the giant ships being constructed there for Caribbean cruises dominate the views towards the sea. The identity of this area is tied to the future of the dockyard.

Invisible railways

The beauty of the railways seems to be in the eye of the beholder. We see what we want to see. For those who have lived in Helsinki for a major part of their lives, the railway is essential to the spirit of the capital as we have grown to know it. There are, however, others who do not seem to be interested in its past. Responses to the future of the remaining buildings of the goods rail-yard opposite to the Parliament Building sharply reveal the polarisation. We 'natives' do not want to lose the last traces of industrial history in the centre of the city, but 'others' only see them as 'ugly, old-fashioned, and much too expensive to restore'. For 'us', the more effectively the destruction progresses, the more valuable the remaining fragments

---

[21]   Mikael Sundman, 'Kauppatori kunniaansa (The Market Place to its glory)', *Arkkitehti* (The Finnish Architectural Review), 91, no. 2–3, 1994, 78–9.

become, whereas for the 'others', the remaining shacks continue to spoil the image of the city.

The goods station constructed on the north-western side of the main railway station in the 1890s was established as part of the plans to develop a major port within the capital. Its construction was connected to that of the port railway, in both time and place. In this sense, the history of the goods station is an essential part of the industrial past of the capital. The history of the goods station and the port were intertwined to the end. After goods were increasingly being shipped in containers the goods port at the South Harbour was discontinued and the goods station was transferred elsewhere.[22] The site of the goods rail-yard to be vacated was seen as a piece of valuable real estate and immediately recognised as ideal for development. The congested commercial centre of the city could easily be

Figure 12.4   Aerial view of Töölönlahti area, central Helsinki 1998

Source: *Helsinki Music Center Architectural Competition: Architectural Competitions in Finland,* no. 1, 2001.

---

[22] On the move of the goods station, see Lasse Kajander, 'Rautatiet Pasilassa 1862–1997 (The railways in Pasila, 1862–1997)', in Harry Schulman and Mikael Sundman, eds., *Pasila, Helsingin uusi keskus* (Pasila, new centre of Helsinki) (Helsinki 1998), 83–8, esp. 85.

expanded into the area because of its proximity and by the fact that it was large enough for ambitious plans. Furthermore, it was unobstructed by buildings listed for preservation. The economic potential of the area was huge, in fact, among the highest in the country. Moreover, because it was surrounded by major national institutions and monuments such as the Parliament Building (1931) to the west, the Main Post Office (1939) to the south, the City Museum (1844), the National Museum (1910) and Finlandia Hall (1975) close by to the north it was also a prime site symbolically.

In 1985, the government and the city jointly organised a planning competition for ideas for the development of both the railway area as well as the bus station area just adjacent to it which was also available. In choosing the locations for the required spaces, the competitors were allowed to disregard the prevailing land ownership patterns, since most of the area was owned and controlled by the government or the city.[23] This was initially seen to facilitate the planning. Only later did the existence of a pact between the city and the government become publicly known. In the pact, the two land-owning parties agreed on the ratio of new floor area allotted for each, even before the planning process had begun.[24] This meant that only new buildings were seen as profitable and therefore acceptable. It also implied that preservation was unacceptable.

Political disagreements over how to develop the railways area have delayed its planning and realisation.[25] During the process, two new institutions have been built at the southern edge of the area, the Museum of Contemporary Art (1999) and the headquarters of the major media conglomerate *Sanoma Corporation* (1999). The pact narrowed the alternatives available from the very beginning. By 1999, the city's quota was nearly full, and the government, today replaced by the government property company, was to begin new public projects to keep the balance. In the years 1999 and 2000, the government, the city and the Finnish Broadcasting Company jointly organised a two-phase international architectural competition for the design of the Music Hall on the site of the goods station. All the entries that received prizes were based on the idea of an entirely new building. As the

---

[23]   Helsingin kaupunki, *Kamppi-Töölönlahti aatekilpailun ohjelma* (Kamppi-Töölönlahti idea competition programme) (Helsinki 1985), 37, and Helsingin kaupunki, *Kamppi-Töölönlahti* (Kamppi-Töölönlahti Ideas Competition Results) (Helsinki 1986).

[24]   The ratio was 38 per cent for the government and 62 per cent for the City of Helsinki. The different functions balanced with coefficients based on the estimated economic profitability of each function. The pact also defined the cost of deviating from the specified ratio. On a description of the pact and its realisation, see Rolf Martinsen, 'Maapoliittinen sopimus ja kaavoituksen pallomylly (The contract for land use and the ball game of urban planning)', in Rolf Martinsen, ed., *Uhattu Helsinki, Kirja Helsingin kaupunkisuunnittelun kriisistä* (Helsinki under threat. A book on the crisis of Helsinki urban planning) (Helsinki 2000), 81–105, esp. 84–7.

[25]   From 1991, the Department of Urban Planning has prepared several plans for the area, but they have not been enforced by the City Council. See, for example, Helsingin kaupunkisuunnitteluviraston kaavoitusosasto, *Töölönlahden asemakaavan muutoksen selostus* (Proposal for the Töölönlahti area plan), *January 4, 2001* (Helsinki 2001).

competition jury formulated, 'no proposals worthy of serious consideration were found among the small number of entries that retained the existing railway warehouses.'[26]

Plans to replace the goods station with a modern music hall are advanced, but final decisions have not yet been made (in January 2002). There are many in important places who seem to think that the red brick buildings of the goods station established a little over a century ago, are much too modest in the company of the national monuments. Arguments for protecting this railway area are weakened because its history is mostly unwritten. Brief historical references, such as the totally fabricated naming of the buildings as the 'Stables of the Czar', have been used as romantic vignettes to arouse nostalgic feelings. The most widely reported historical documentation has concentrated on the plans made for the area during the last hundred years. These include Eliel Saarinen's Greater Helsinki Plan (1918), Oiva Kallio's winning entry in a planning competition (1927), P. E. Blomstedt's proposal in connection with the Olympic Stadium competition (1933) and Alvar Aalto's plans for the Helsinki City Centre (1960s). All of them projected a future without the railway.[27] While historical accounts of the area have been scarce or non-existent, a multitude of contemporary presentations project the future of the vacated railways area. In these projections, the depictions of the existing buildings customarily lack references to the history of those structures that are evaluated as nondescript, such as railway buildings, even when they have been important elements in the evolution of the area. As a consequence of this, the area has been misleadingly presented as empty and suitable for grand development projects, corresponding to the modernistic ideal of a *tabula rasa* with no historical ties. The fact that these histories still remain unwritten not only reflects contemporary values but also serves to direct present interests by excluding some lines of action and presenting others as normal, thus as the only alternatives available.

Railways as urban memory

The notion of the railway as a prosaic technological element and its unwritten urban history are intertwined. Histories, including urban histories are customarily written about events and places with political and national significance. The history of the railways has traditionally been about the political frame of its initial stages and the effects of its construction on a nation. In the segregated history of transportation, the railway has been seen as a technical system, developed solely for its self-evident specialised purpose that is by definition non-ideological and

[26] *Helsinki Music Center Architectural Competition: Architectural Competitions in Finland*, no. 1, 2001, 10.

[27] The older plans were presented in the material for the competition in 1985, City Planning Department, City of Helsinki, *Kamppi-Töölönlahti aatekilpailun ohjelma* (Kamppi-Töölönlahti idea competition programme) (Helsinki 1985), 24–31.

non-disputable. The underlying presupposition is that the railway belongs to the infrastructure, that is, part of the support system for the real functions of the organisation or society.[28] In relation to built forms in cities, this implies that the railway is invisible not only as a contemporary urban element but also as a historical phenomenon.

I would like to compare the conventions of writing urban histories to those of writing national histories. In the concluding chapter of the impressive three-part *Les Lieux de mémoire*, its editor Pierre Nora describes the idea of the history of France and of the French as one of multiple voices, questioning the concept of a unified national history. Nora replaces the notion of a 'historic' nation (*la nation historique*) where the presence of the past is concentrated in a highly refined system of representations which ignores all the rest, with the notion of a 'memoric' nation (*la nation mémorial*) where the reverse occurs. Things and places regarded in earlier times as commonplace are given meanings beyond their initial context. The private grows into public, the local into national. History understood as national memory becomes a field of discussion and confrontation among different cultural groups, and is constantly being re-evalued.[29] Similarly, conventions of writing histories of cities, particularly those of capitals, present a unified and finalised view of their past. The 'Grand Narrative' of a city is often a story about how the city council with both its political bodies and administrative departments have produced the city as a contemporary monument through the changing times. Nora's notions suggest an alternative where the past of the city is perceived as urban memory and where the identity of the city is generated through multiple voices and multiple perspectives into its past. Instead of a unified history of a city, elements initially perceived as marginal, such as railways in the city centre, may generate valuable insight into the history of the city.

Writing about the history of the railways in the city centre, therefore, does not mean just adding a new subtitle to a pre-existing collection of urban histories. Rather, as I see it, positioning the notion of railways as a fundamental part of the changes in the urban core, proposes a new point of view for the study of cities. The study of railways in the city centre opens a field for more integrated, multidisciplinary approaches in urban histories. In the context of urban histories, the contribution of art history may be useful because it can offer traditions in studying the material and visual reality. The art historical focus on urban spaces, edifices and built forms anchors the social and economic changes of the city and its inhabitants to places documented in texts, in images such as maps, photographs, and film as well as in the three-dimensional built city. Art-historical objects can be used as

---

[28] On the 'invisibility' of technical systems, see, for example, Pär Blomqvist and Arne Kaijser, 'De osynliga systemen (The hidden systems)', in Pär Blomqvist and Arne Kaijser, eds., *Den konstruerade världen, Tekniska system i historisk perspektiv* (The constructed world. Technical systems in historical perspective) (Stockholm 1998), 7–17, esp. 9.

[29] Pierre Nora, 'L'ère de commémoration', in Pierre Nora, ed., *Les Lieux de mémoire*, 3 vols. (Paris 1997, first published 1984–1992), vol. 3, 4687–719, esp. 4713–14.

concrete points of reference to which the non-material aspects of reality are connected. This is related to built forms not only as images or symbols, but also as the products and producers of particular historically evolving societies. The material and spatial histories of a city are also always about the social and economic histories of its various cultures.

For art historians, built forms and spaces are important sources in the writing of urban histories. The interpretation of historical built forms relates to their meanings, what they have been about. These meanings are not characteristics of the built forms themselves, but are produced through the social practices of communities or cultural groups. Built forms, therefore, carry different meanings for different cultures. We may study the built forms as traces of the meanings which various urban cultures have given to them.[30] For example, while members of some urban cultures may regard railway structures as unimportant or even unpleasant, others may, at the same time, see them as significant and exciting. If the notion of culturally dependent meanings is accepted, the destruction of the railways from the city centres becomes a question of whose cultural meanings are protected and whose are demolished. To destroy a goods station in the heart of Helsinki is not only a matter of irrevocably erasing parts of the history of some groups such as those who are, or have become, rooted in the city, but also of replacing the cultural groups for which the place now has meanings, with others.

Demolitions are also issues of the 'historicality' of the city centre. We may read the histories of built forms only if traces of all of its time layers exist, not just the one which in a particular era is seen as valuable and aesthetically coherent. If we only preserve what we appreciate today, other equally authentic, but less understood remains will be destroyed. Railways in the city centre contain our memory. They are invaluable to us as documents of a past bygone but possible for us to understand, if we follow the tracks.

---

[30]   For a more extensive discussion, see Anja K. Nevanlinna, 'Cities as Texts: Urban Practices Represented or Forgotten in Art History', in Wessel Reinink and Jeroen Stumpel, eds., *Memory and Oblivion* (The Hague 1999), 373–7.

CHAPTER THIRTEEN

Political networks, rail networks: public transportation and neighbourhood radicalism in Weimar Berlin

Pamela E. Swett

Berlin's rail era began in 1838 with the opening of Potsdamer Station, followed by other major terminals, including Anhalter, Lehrter and Görlitzer. Local transport was introduced with the building of the ring line in the years between 1871 and 1877 and the construction of an interior East-West connection in 1882. Although the number of passengers on these rail lines rose quickly, their initial purpose was to serve military and commercial needs in the years surrounding the unification of the country in 1871, and the terminals built to service these lines reflected the confidence and grandeur of the monarchy. However, over the last decades of the nineteenth century a number of factors appeared motivating the expansion and improvement of the transportation system throughout Germany, and Berlin in particular.

First, Berlin was becoming an industrial powerhouse. The emergence of large industrial complexes toward the end of the century in the open spaces North and West of central Berlin increased the demand for a faster and more extensive transportation network for commuters. The capital of the new German Empire was already a haven for those looking for an alternative to agriculture. In 1870 only forty per cent of its inhabitants had been born in Berlin. The stream of immigrants continued through the end of the nineteenth century, as men and women flocked from the countryside to take advantage of the growing employment opportunities, such as at the enormous Siemens site, which opened in Spandau in 1898. Thanks to this influx of labourers from the East, the population in Berlin skyrocketed from 700,000 in 1867, to about two million by 1900, and over four million by 1933. Berlin already had one of the few profitable horse-drawn tram systems in Europe, in service since 1865. And there was no reason to think that expansion in this area would not also reap financial reward. Clearly, greater profits could be found in transporting labourers to the manufacturing sites and in running the 'bankers' trains' to bring the growing number of middle class residents from their newly built suburban homes.[1]

Second, Germans recognised that greater rail service and electric tram lines would cut down on the numbers of horses on city streets. Diminishing the number of horses on the roads would mean a more hygienic city, longer-lasting streets, and less mistreatment of the animals. A third motivation set Germany and its capital apart from the rest of Europe. Germany was already the leader in electrical technology as home to the firms Siemens and Halske and *Allgemeine Elektrizitäts-Gesellschaft* (AEG). These two companies, concerned about the threat of competition in transportation technology especially from the United States, wanted to remain innovators in the field and enjoy continued profits. Because powerful domestic firms were among the loudest voices calling for expansion and 'progress' in terms of electrification, underground rail, and other projects in Germany, John McKay argues that city planners and the German public were more willing to accept their proposals than in other European countries, where administrators and citizens remained suspicious of foreign imports.[2]

With these factors encouraging change at the end of the nineteenth century, Berlin was well on its way to developing an extensive, modern transit system. As early as 1891, Berlin was unique in offering special commuting rates for workers on the growing city rail system, allowing labourers for the first time to live in one part of the city, the low rent centre, and work in another. Germany also led the way among European nations in electrifying their urban tramlines, introducing the world's very first electric streetcar in 1881 and virtually completing the task of electrification by the close of 1902.[3] For many new arrivals in Berlin, therefore, a rail station was their first introduction to the city itself and to urban living in general. The grand stations remained etched in the memories of those who passed through them and hold a special place in the fiction of the late Weimar era. In some novels, the rail stations are the quintessential symbol of the urban landscape and play a role as important as any character in the book. In Erich Kästner's satirical look at life for the educated but impoverished middle class, urban transport characterises the modern metropolis and eventually provides an escape from the difficulties of life in Berlin. Down on his luck in love and career during the Depression, the author's protagonist, Jacob Fabian, finally flees the capital for his provincial hometown. In despair over his future and the suicide of his best friend, he wanders to *Anhalter Bahnhof*. Though he had once sought the hustle and bustle of the 'city of millions', he now finds no comfort in its presence or the traffic outside. 'He leaned against the wall, not far from a group of porters, and closed his

---

[1]   For one example of the usage of this phrase, see Gerhard Capelle, 'Hundert Jahre Eisenbahn Berlin – Potsdam, 1938', in Alfred Gottwaldt, ed., *Berliner Fehrbahnhöfe: Erinnerungen an ihre große Zeit* (Düsseldorf 1983), 95–6.

[2]   See John P. McKay, *Tramways and Trolleys: The Rise of Urban Mass Transport in Europe* (Princeton 1976), 108–9.

[3]   Ibid. 73.

eyes. But now the noise tormented him. It was as though the trams and omnibuses were driving right through his body.'[4]

In Irmgard Keun's '*Gilgi – eine von uns*', the train stations of Berlin have a different meaning. They serve as gateways to possibility. Early in the story Gilgi's friend, Olga, single and independent, plans to take the train from Cologne to Berlin to work as a painter, attract American patronage, and perhaps use it as a jumping off point for other adventures. At the end of the story, single and pregnant, Gilgi decides her only chance for survival is likewise to leave depressed and conservative Cologne to join her friend in Berlin, where she presumes all are welcome and work is waiting.[5] These two novels and many more testify to the

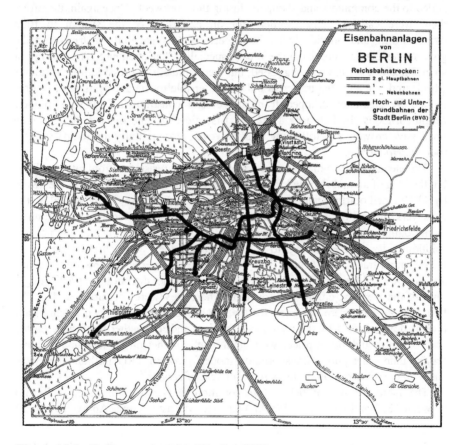

Figure 13.1   Railway network of Berlin, 1930

Source: Remy, *Die Elektrisierung der Berliner Stadt-, Ring- und Vorortbahnen als Wirtschaftsproblem* (Berlin 1931), plate 1.

---

[4]   Erich Kästner, *Fabian: the Story of a Moralist* (Evanston 1993, first edition 1931), 118.
[5]   Irmgard Keun, *Gilgi – eine von uns* (Düsseldorf 1979, first edition 1931), 23, and 252–8.

impact of Berlin's rail system on the ways people imagined the German capital and experienced it on a daily basis. I will argue, however, that between 1900 and 1930 the rail system became much more to working class Berliners than a gateway to the city, a monument to the modern age, or a means of commuting to work. In those years, rail stations, especially the small, local rail, tram, and underground stations, became central to the social and political life of Berlin's neighbourhoods, in ways that challenged the very definition of these transportation sites as public spaces.

In 1905 the Berlin transit system carried 750 million people on buses, streetcars and local rail lines.[6] Those hoping to escape the metropolis on the weekends by travelling to the lakes, garden allotments, and hiking areas surrounding the city added to the commuters and shoppers during the workweek. Once again, therefore, there were calls by city dwellers for an extension of the system to fight overcrowding and provide better links between the inner city districts and the growing residential suburbs of the West, especially Charlottenburg. The concept of an elevated rail system was suggested, but faced immediate pressure from residents who feared that elevated tracks would create terrible traffic accidents, lead to fires ignited by cigarettes dropped from above, and constitute an eye-sore in their neighbourhoods. In February 1902 the first elevated line opened, to less than impressive crowds. The following year, however, close to thirty million passengers rode the *Hochbahn*.

The elevated tracks may have encountered initial resistance from city dwellers, but the idea of an underground transportation network, first advocated in the 1890s by AEG, faced outright rejection. The engineers at AEG were not dissuaded by the naysayers, and set out to prove that it was indeed possible to construct rail tunnels in the damp ground of Berlin. Once they succeeded in finding the engineering solutions, city planners began to warm up to the idea.[7] The chief advantage of underground tracks, or *U-Bahn*, was that, unlike the overhead wires of the trams and the elevated tracks of the *Hochbahn*, they would not disrupt the attractive sight lines of the wealthy, commercial districts where they were first utilised. That the first *U-Bahn* cars were designed for the wealthy patrons who lived around their lines is demonstrated by the mahogany interiors and red leather upholstery on the seats. Even though ticket prices were significantly higher on the new underground service than other public transportation modes, close to thirty million rides were taken on the limited *U-Bahn* in its first full year of service.[8]

The increased use of public transportation in *Groß-Berlin* (Greater Berlin) between 1871 and the end of World War One was astounding. An average of 13

---

[6]   See Peer Hauschild, 'Bahnhöfe in Berlin', in Wolfgang Gottschalk, ed., *Bahnhöfe in Berlin: Photografen von Max Missmann* (Berlin 1991), 5–14, esp. 9.

[7]   Ibid. 10. For a discussion of land usage and the financial side of subway planning in Berlin, see Ute Frank, 'Terrainerschließung und U-Bahn-Bau', in Jochen Boberg, Tilman Fichter, and Eckhart Gillen, eds., *Exerzierfeld der Moderne: Industriekultur in Berlin im 19. Jahrhundert*, 2 vols. (München 1984), vol. 1, 232–9.

[8]   See Goerd Peschken, 'Die Hochbahn', in Boberg, ibid., vol. 1, 132–7, esp. 133, and Heinz Jung and Wolfgang Kramer, 'Die U-Bahn', in ibid., vol. 1, 138–9, esp. 139.

trips on public transportation per person in 1871 had grown to 374 rides per person in 1917.[9] In the years preceding World War One, the city was forced to expand some electric tram stations, which had already become overcrowded. The case of the Beussel Street tram station in the industrial district of Wedding was not uncommon: though between 7.30 and 7.45 a.m. only 184 people boarded the trams at this location, one hour earlier, 3,900 passengers entered the station in the same fifteen minutes span, making commuting a chaotic experience.[10] These statistics for the total number of rides taken per person in Berlin are even more significant when we take into consideration the fact that before 1918 the new elevated and underground lines, which were in the hands of private companies, serviced mainly the wealthy southwestern neighbourhoods and suburbs and were also too expensive for most workers to use on a regular basis.[11] This discrepancy, however, would change in the 1920s.

In the Weimar period, Berlin's transportation system grew along with the population's pride in and dependence on the vast network of trams, trains, and buses. In October 1920 the *Groß-Berlin Gesetz* (Great-Berlin Law) went into effect, adjusting the borders of Berlin to include a number of the previously independent adjoining communities, including Charlottenburg, Neukölln, Wilmersdorf, and Spandau. The passage of this legislation paved the way for the building projects of the 1920s. Though building was limited in the early part of the decade due to the financial crisis that accompanied defeat, the lengthening of existing lines and construction of new lines took off again after the stabilisation of the economy in 1924. In 1927, 4.3 million rides were taken daily on Berlin's public transportation network; 2.3 million of those were taken on electric streetcars, 400,000 on buses, 600,000 on the *S*- and *U-Bahn* lines, and close to one million on the city, ring and regional train lines.[12] By the end of the 1920s all of the city's railway lines, including the most recently constructed suburban lines, were electric, and the Berlin Transport Company (*Berliner Verkehrsgesellschaft*, BVG), uniting the tram, bus, elevated and undrground train companies, was the largest community transit firm in the world.[13] Electrification meant cleaner air and quieter travel compared to steam, and shortened the travel time by one third.[14]

By the beginning of the new decade the city's transit system encompassed 248 stations, 65 of which were either overhead or underground stations. Each year 1.5

9   See the graph of Berlin's growing use of public transportation in Thomas Lindenberger, *Straßenpolitik. Zur Sozialgeschichte der öffentlichen Ordnung in Berlin 1900–1914* (Berlin 1995), 41.

10 Ibid. 48.

11 Brian Ladd, *Urban Planning and Civic Order in Germany, 1860–1914* (Cambridge 1990), 208.

12 Remy, 'Bahnhofsumbauten in Berlin' (1929), excerpted in Alfred Gottwaldt, *Berliner Fernbahnhöfe: Erinnerungen an ihre Große Zeit* (Düsseldorf 1983), 73.

13 Alexandra Richie, *Faust's Metropolis* (New York 1998), 331.

14 Peter Bley, 'Eisenbahnknotenpunkt Berlin', in Jochen Boberg, Tilman Fichter, and Eckhart Gillen, eds., *Exerzierfeld der Moderne: Industriekultur in Berlin im 19. Jahrhundert*, 2 vols. (München 1984), vol. 1, 114–25, esp. 122.

billion passengers, roughly equal to the world's population in the early 1930s, travelled on public transportation in the German capital.[15] The city's mayor, Gustav Böß, was confident that Berlin's transit system provided the proof that it had become a 'world city'. Yet even so, he demanded that more energy and money be put into the system to keep it up to date in terms of efficiency and comfort. In addition to maintaining Berlin's reputation as a world leader, Böß also argued that the rail system was also vital to the economy. In addition to delivering goods, the network was also essential for delivering men and women comfortably to their workplaces prepared to do business and return them home in a hassle-free setting so as to begin their recuperation before the coming day's work. In these and other ways, Berlin's public transportation was believed to be vital both to the 'family and the *Volk* as a whole.'[16]

Though this vast transportation network was a hallmark of the city's importance and modernity, all along the ideological spectrum Berliners eyed the system with political interest. Those on the far left believed that when the proletariat revolution came, securing the capital city's transportation system would be an immediate priority for achieving their goal of overthrowing the republic. This strategy had indeed been used successfully in 1920 by supporters of the republic, who in declaring a general strike brought the city's traffic to a halt and the right-wing Kapp putsch to a speedy end. In the years that followed, the Communist Party even drew diagrams that illustrated the 'belt' revolutionaries could tighten around the city by controlling transportation and utilities. Due to such precedent and hopeful planning, moderates viewed the network at times as the Achilles heel of the capital. In November 1932, for a short time it appeared that perhaps the worst would be realised when both Communist and Nazi workers for the Berlin Transport Company (BVG) united in a strike action. The amount of press coverage and general public attention the strike received was due in part to this fear that a disruption of the transportation system could realistically bring down the government. During the upheaval, one female art student was arrested for passing out a pro-strike pamphlet in Friedrichshain. Though she claimed it was simply Communist election campaign material, the police and judiciary saw the literature as much more threatening. The authorities claimed that the KPD did not see the BVG strike as 'an economic weapon, rather used it for political aims', which were 'to turn this partial strike (*Teilstreik*) into a general or mass strike, in order to lead the way to a revolutionary crisis (…) in order to overthrow the current government and in its place set up a dictatorship (…) on the Russian model.'[17]

When evaluating the impact of urban development on Berlin's inner-city districts, which tended to be workers' neighbourhoods, our initial impulse is to presume that the building of the transportation network – primarily city rail, *S-* and

---

[15] Thomas Friedrich, *Berlin Between the Wars* (New York 1991), 159.

[16] Gustav Böß, *Berlin von Heute: Stadtverwaltung und Wirtschaft* (Berlin 1929), 78. See also page 82 in which Böß pleads for more funding to modernise and expand the system.

[17] Landesarchiv Berlin (hereafter LAB), Rep. 58, No. 1478, Film 740, Concluding report concerning 'Kampf gegen Lohnraub und faschistische Diktatur', November 4, 1932.

U-Bahn lines – weakened the sense of community at the local level. First, we know that the construction of the lines disrupted the built environment of many Berlin neighbourhoods. Indeed, whole blocks of homes were sometimes levelled to make way for elevated and underground tracks and stations. Second, rail lines, once imposed upon the landscape, divided communities, cutting off friends and neighbours from one another. Third, new modes of transportation meant residents could more readily leave their familiar surroundings for work or pleasure. After glimpsing new opportunities, some young people in particular chose not to return to the streets where they had grown up, diluting neighbourhood continuity and loyalty. Fourth, by tying the city districts together, public transportation made it increasingly common for outsiders to enter these neighbourhoods. Some were simply passing through, but others were among the growing number of representatives from various governmental departments coming to investigate life in Berlin's 'slums' – or, in the case of police patrols of public transportation nodes, to control these newly created public spaces.

Though I agree that these four factors challenged the existence of a unique working class culture in Berlin during the Weimar era, in the rest of this short essay I would like to propose an alternative or perhaps a correlative interpretation. I believe that the growth of the city's transportation network, with particular regard to the local rail, *S-* and *U-Bahn* stations and lines, effectively supported and even amplified the sense of neighbourhood identity in Berlin in the 1920s and early 1930s. Evidence for this assertion can be found in the social and commercial uses of transit stations. More importantly for this era of German history, this claim is supported by the ways these stations and even the rail cars themselves became sites of contention in the increasingly violent, radical political culture that developed in Berlin during the last years of the Weimar Republic.

One commonly overlooked reason why transportation hubs were integral in the creation and maintenance of neighbourhood culture is that the unique qualities of the small stations have been overshadowed by the drama of the grand, yet impersonal, terminals. It is true, as Wolfgang Schivelbusch and others have argued, that the large railway stations built in the mid- and late nineteenth century were initially seen as 'alien appendages' that tore up the landscape, often dwarfing the surrounding buildings and stigmatising the industrial districts in which they were located because they attracted prostitutes and vagabonds.[18] But the later, much smaller, local *S-* and *U-Bahn* lines and their stations were more easily integrated in terms of architectural scale into the fabric of the community. Moreover, since many of the *S-Bahn* stations had open sheds or no sheds in the case of many tram stations, one never left the landscape of the surrounding area. Even those *Hochbahn* stations in Berlin with closed halls were designed with light iron skeletons and thin walls, with plenty of windows and light, retaining the visual

---

[18] Wolfgang Schivelbusch, *The Railway Journey* (New York 1986), 171.

connection to the surroundings.[19] A visit to one of the monumental stations offered a much different experience. Once behind their grand façades, these stations offered a concourse hall as a transitional space between the city and the machinery of the tracks and cars located in the shed.[20] Amid the throngs of travellers from outside city limits in the concourse hall, or finding themselves unable to speak over the sounds of the approaching and departing locomotives in the shed, the city dweller at the grand terminal had clearly entered a separate world. At the local station, standing in the open air watching the neighbourhood hustle and bustle, or crowded among familiar faces during the commuting hours, Berliners maintained contact with their communities.

When Berlin's first viaduct-style rail architecture was introduced in 1882 after over six years of construction, it was greeted as a great achievement, a suitable heir to the wall of Babylon and the Roman aqueducts from which it hailed stylistically.[21] For the neighbourhoods in which these stations were built, however, that the space under the elevated tracks would soon house pubs, craftsmen's studios, and market stalls was more important than such adulation. These stations clearly provided more to the local residents than simply the means for travel out of the neighbourhood. The viaduct architectural design of the elevated system brought commerce to the neighbourhood, helping to maintain these communities as self-sufficient entities and drawing more residents to the station on a regular basis. Though on a less dramatic scale, the underground stations too helped to foster community ties, by housing newspaper and snack stands, and in a few cases architects designed passageways to larger stores, such as the underground entrance to Berlin's Karstadt department store which still exists in Neukölln. The above ground entrances of the *U-Bahn* and tram stations also attracted pubs and restaurants, making these stations important meeting spots for friends.

In other words, these transit stations came to serve as landmarks in workers' neighbourhoods. They brought together the inhabitants of the surrounding streets on a regular basis, in a way that allowed for socialising, commerce, and the sharing of information. The rail lines themselves also played a role in the maintenance of local identity, by forming the border separating one neighbourhood from another. This separation could be seen as isolating. However, it also gave the residents of the enclave a sense of location within the 'city of millions'. The Karl-Friedrich neighbourhood was one example of a small workers' community within the

---

[19] See Goerd Peschken, 'Die Hochbahn', in Jochen Boberg, Tilman Fichter, and Eckhart Gillen, eds., *Exerzierfeld der Moderne: Industriekultur in Berlin im 19. Jahrhundert*, 2 vols. (München 1984), vol. 1, 132–7, esp. 133.

[20] See Anthony Raynsford, 'Swarm of the Metropolis: Passenger Circulation at Grand Central Terminal and the Ideology of the Crowd Aesthetic', in *Journal of Architectural Education*, 50, no. 1, 1996, 2–14, esp. 4.

[21] *Nationalzeitung*, February 7, 1882, excerpted in Lothar Binger, 'Stadtbahnbögen', in Jochen Boberg, Tilman Fichter, and Eckhart Gillen, eds., *Exerzierfeld der Moderne: Industriekultur in Berlin im 19. Jahrhundert*, 2 vols. (München 1984), vol. 1, 106–13, esp. 106.

bourgeois district of Tiergarten.[22] Because these workers were physically separated from the surrounding area by rail lines on one side and a commercial thoroughfare on the other, those living there – who were not homogeneous in terms of political loyalties (Communist and Centre Party) or ethnicity (Germans and Catholic Poles) – felt united and at home during the turbulent 1920s.

Beyond creating social cohesion and economic vitality for the neighbourhoods in which they were situated, local stations and rail lines also had a significant political function in late Weimar Berlin. After 1929 the atmosphere in the capital became increasingly violent. As the government proved unable to provide adequate solutions to the increasing unemployment and misery caused by the Great Depression, some in the city joined radical political organisations which, in terms of the official rhetoric espoused by the two main combatants (the Communist and National Socialist parties), sought to bring about an end to republican rule and the creation of either a Soviet style regime or a National Socialist dictatorship. Already by the mid 1920s, these two parties had set up paramilitary organisations, the Communist *Roter Frontkämpferbund* (RFB) and Nazi *Sturmabteilung* (SA). In addition to these organisations, other supporters of these two parties and even members of the moderate Social Democratic *Schutztruppe* the *Reichsbanner* (RB) became entangled with each other on the streets of Berlin. Even after the RFB was banned in 1929 and a number of emergency decrees aimed at limiting political radicalism were issued in the early 1930s, the violence worsened, often involving the police and bystanders.

Continued study of this violent activism at the street level, which weakened the first German republic and prepared the way for Adolf Hitler's appointment as Chancellor in 1933, has shown that the violence of the era reflected local issues rather than the grand ideologies of the competing parties. In other words, participants in the daily riots, brawls and unprovoked attacks were motivated primarily by their own personal concerns about loss of power in their own lives.[23] The recourse to violence was not an overnight occurrence; rather long-term traditions of domestic violence, the experience of World War One and radical politics had already greatly impacted social relationships in Germany. However, the Depression dramatically escalated the tension in neighbourhoods already susceptible to instability and violence. Widespread unemployment was paramount in creating a sense of impotence among workers in Berlin. Long-term unemployment meant more than the loss of a pay cheque. For many men, it also

---

[22] Eva Brücker, 'Soziale Fragmentierung und Kollektives Gedächtnis. Nachbarschaftsbeziehungen in einem Berliner Arbeiterviertel 1920–1980', in Wolfgang Hofmann and Gerd Kuhn, eds., *Wohnungspolitik und Städtebau, 1900–1930* (Berlin 1993), 285–306, esp. 290–2.

[23] On political violence in late Weimar Germany, see James Diehl, *Paramilitary Politics in the Weimar Republic* (Indiana 1977); Conan Fischer, *The German Communists and the Rise of Nazism* (New York 1991); Eve Rosenhaft, *Beating the Fascists?* (New York 1983), and Pamela E. Swett, *Neighborhood Mobilization and the Violence of Collapse: Berlin Political Culture, 1929–1933*, Brown University Providence Ph.D. thesis, 1999.

meant the loss of a daily structure, one's identity as a worker, camaraderie among workmates, and authority in the family as breadwinner.

These changes wrought by the Depression had a dramatic impact on the unemployed man's self-image as well as transforming his relationship to his neighbourhood. On the one hand identification with the neighbourhood increased, because unemployment meant long days spent at local rail and subway stations, on street corners, or at the neighbourhood pub. Men congregated together at these sites to share rumours of employment opportunities, tales of disempowerment, and pass the time. Without the worksite to offer a haven from the feminine home space, men sought to emphasise the existing masculine nature of pubs and streets. They also claimed seemingly gender-neutral sites, such as transport nodes, as their territory through overtly political gestures including rallies, propaganda campaigns, and violence. On the other hand, the financial crisis threatened the self-sufficient culture of Berlin's neighbourhoods. The economic downturn meant the closure of many local shops and social spots as well as the loss of many larger manufacturing concerns. Some residents were forced to leave their neighbourhoods in search of work or move their residence as a way to cut down on rent. Neighbourly assistance waned as more and more families found themselves unable to help others. The political make-up of many of Berlin's workers' neighbourhoods was also changing as the growing support for the Nazi party meant the infiltration of neighbourhoods once held exclusively by the political left. Finally, outsiders – police and welfare workers, in particular – were increasingly present monitoring the growing radicalism and poverty.

What we get here, therefore, is a very complicated and to some extent paradoxical situation. At the very time that some inhabitants felt a greater need to control their neighbourhoods, because of their desire to create a space for themselves by, for example, confronting the changing political landscape of their communities, the elements of neighbourhood cohesion were becoming increasingly less attainable. This combination of factors, I am arguing, led to the extreme volatility of this era. When we look at specific incidents of political violence between Nazi sympathisers and those who supported the traditional workers' parties (the Communists and to a lesser degree the Social Democrats), it becomes clear that in many cases the violence was precipitated by conflicts over space. As one 1932 pamphlet sent out by the underground RFB in the *Helmholzplatz* neighbourhood of *Prenzlauer Berg* declared:

> We call out to all honest workers, the whole population around the Helmholzplatz! Protect your streets, take part in active resistance, fight in the Anti-fascist Action together with all workers of your residential area, through the strongest mass pressure force the closing of this brown Murder-barracks and thereby chase out all Nazi spies and provocateurs from these workers' streets.[24]

---

[24]   LAB, Rep. 58, No. 1357, Film 736, 'Arbeiter und Angestellte den Helmholzplatz', October, 1932. Though this language also reflects the KPD's inability to organise in factories due to high unemployment and surveillance of radical workers, the fact that it

Local transit stations, lines and rail cars were often at the centre of these conflicts. These sites had become important political landmarks to those who lived around them – territory worth fighting over.[25] By laying claim to these ostensibly public spaces, transportation nodes were transformed into semi-public centres of neighbourhood life. By this I mean that at the local *S-* and *U-Bahn* stations residents felt at home, as if they were in a communally-held private space, open only to those in the larger family of the neighbourhood. If these spaces were 'lost' to others from beyond the borders of the community, who in this climate of political polarisation often represented different political views, it meant political defeat. More importantly, in Depression-era Berlin the violation of these semi-

Figure 13.2   Elevated train line at *Gitschiner Straße*, 1930

Source: Photo: Hans Schaller, Bildarchiv Preußischer Kulturbesitze (bpk).

---

was used in these largely independently written neighbourhood newspapers shows that such rhetoric was embraced at the grass-roots level. This was not always the case for party directives and slogans in these years.

[25] Though historians stress the political significance of the pub for working class culture, we should not ignore the politicisation of other community structures. Robert Tittler, in reference to the civic hall in early modern England, makes an important point about how public space can function 'as the 'tangible formulation' of the notion of civic authority.' See Robert Tittler, *Architecture and Power: The Town Hall and the English Urban Community, c. 1500–1640* (Oxford 1991), 93.

private spaces meant that the neighbourhood was no longer an autonomous entity, which signified a further defeat to its struggling inhabitants, especially to some men who felt bound to defend these landmarks as they would their own homes.

In the example of Kreuzberg's Nostiz-area neighbourhood, also often called a *Kiez* – an explicitly political term designating the area as united by its radical leftist politics – a number of physical elements served to mark the boundaries of this semi-public neighbourhood culture. First, there was the *Nostizstraße* itself, a narrow residential street crowded by five-storey apartment buildings built at the turn of the century, with small shops and pubs in the basement and at the ground floor. To escape their overcrowded tenements in suitable weather, many people spent a great deal of time on doorsteps, in the buildings' courtyards, and on the street. Strong Communist party representation among the residents, supported by two Communist pubs on Nostiz itself, made this street the heart of the *Kiez*.[26] Three blocks to the east was a small square, *Marheinekeplatz*, dominated by a market hall dating from the 1880s.[27] The square also served as a meeting place and the market hall included a pub. To the Southwest, *Viktoriapark* served as a recreational area for the workers of the neighbourhood, especially in the summer, and here too one could enjoy a beer in the park's *Biergarten*. Finally, the main thoroughfare through the *Kiez*, *Gneisenaustraße*, was serviced by an electric tram and subway line, the stations of which served the residents in ways already described and also as the territorial boundary to the North, separating the Nostiz-area Communists and Social Democrats from the growing Nazi contingent only a few blocks away around Urban Street.

The tram and *U-Bahn* lines and stations of *Gneisenaustraße* were, therefore, just two among a number of neighbourhood landmarks. However, conflict in and around the stations, here as throughout the city, ranked high among the type of sites which commonly drew violence and bloodshed. Transit stations and lines showed their political importance to the neighbourhood in a number of ways. First, some politicised Berliners who wrote street-newspapers (*Straßenzeitungen*) for

---

[26] The most notorious Communist bar in the *Kiez* was owned by a man named Lorenz. It was the site of a number of brawls and police searches. Toward the end of 1931, the police reported that Lorenz had had a falling out with the local Communists and no longer planned to associate his bar with the party. The unwanted KPD supporters quickly found a home at Lipinski's pub at 63 *Nostizstraße*. There was even a rumour that Lorenz subsequently allowed the growing SA to hold its functions at his pub, but the owner denied the accusation. See Brandenburgisches Landeshauptarchiv (hereafter BLHA), Rep 30, Bln C, Title 95, Sekt. 9, Nr. 164, Report from 112th police station Berlin, 4 August 1931.

[27] The market at *Markeinekeplatz* was built in the 1880s as a part of a city-wide plan to construct 14 small market halls to replace the weekly outdoor markets which supplied fresh food to the population. See Manfred Stürzbecher, 'Stadthygiene', in Jochen Boberg, Tilman Fichter, and Eckhart Gillen, eds., *Exerzierfeld der Moderne: Industriekultur in Berlin im 19. Jahrhundert*, 2 vols. (München 1984), vol. 1, 160–9, esp. 168–9. On Berlin's markets in the Weimar era, see also city mayor Gustav Böß, *Berlin von Heute: Stadtverwaltung und Wirtschaft* (Berlin 1929).

their neighbourhoods, to chronicle daily events and to provide political editorial aimed at encouraging greater activism among the readership, named their papers for the local transit station. For example, by choosing the title *Rund um den Bahnhof Schönholz*, the authors of this KPD paper in Reinickendorf were making it clear that this station was a central landmark of their *Kiez*, belonging to the residents around it and by extension to the KPD.[28] Second, crossing the border, often a subway, tram, or elevated train line into a neighbouring, antagonistic *Kiez* showed bravery and commitment by the venturing group, who risked danger to prove that their opponents did not have control in their neighbourhood. When the SA marched southward across Gneisenau, for example, they were consistently met by an angry crowd of inhabitants from the *Nostizstraße* area, who tried to defend against the invasion of their space. Successful penetration itself, however, allowed for public posturing by the outsiders. For example, even though crowds of inhabitants 'were already on their feet' to meet a large marching contingent of Hitler Youth in the workers' district of Neukölln in December 1930, the Nazi party was quick to emphasise the inability of the neighbourhood to repel their presence. A Nazi newspaper article following the demonstration claimed that 'now the Hitler Youth has conquered red Neukölln' and taunted the residents like a pre-schooler: 'Poor Communist Party!'[29] Third, sometimes less dramatic methods were employed to challenge the authority of *Kiez* territory: a common strategy was for one politicised group to enter a rival neighbourhood's *S- or U-Bahn* station after nightfall and replace the existing political posters with those of their own favoured party. Residents would quickly respond to this affront by removing this 'foreign' propaganda the following day.[30]

These forms of marking territorial landmarks and borders were among many in late Weimar Berlin, though rail stations consistently appear as sites of radical activism. Because of the heavy traffic at these transportation nodes, political parties distributed party literature to commuters and stationed their newspaper salesmen there during the day. Train stations were also frequent sites for physical confrontation. Representatives of one party would cross the path of their opponents, not always coincidently, en route to the countryside for campaigning or military exercises or returning home from a rally somewhere else in the city. We can see how train stations were at the centre of this violent political culture in one example, which involved between fifty and sixty young men and a number of police who were sent to break up the *mêlée*. On one evening in November 1930 a dozen or so members of the Nazi party were returning home together to their

---

[28] LAB, Rep. 59, No. 1695, Film 751, 'Rund um den Bahnhof Schönholz. Häuserblock-zeitung der KPD', Unterbezirk Nord, no. January 12, 1932.

[29] *Völkischer Beobachter*, 'Hitler-Jugend erobert das rote Neukölln', no. 288, December 4, 1930.

[30] For visual illustrations and analysis of the extent of the propaganda war waged in Berlin toward the end of the Republic, see Gerhard Paul, 'Krieg der Symbole. Formen und Inhalte des symbolpublizistischen Bürgerkriegs 1932', in Diethart Kerbs and Henrich Stahr, eds., *Berlin 1932. Das letzte Jahr der Weimarer Republik* (Berlin 1992), 27–55.

Neukölln neighbourhood. When they got off the train at *Köllnische Heide* station, they were attacked by about forty local members of the Communist party. The arriving Nazis were chased into the streets and some were beaten. A police squadron arrived, but of the estimated forty Communists only five were arrested, though another three were identified by witnesses as participants.[31]

In this case a number of factors – found repeated in other violent incidents – lend credence to the assertion that political radicalism was linked to a desire to maintain neighbourhood autonomy, by securing landmarks such as transit stations. First, those arrested and those attacked were locals, living among each other in Neukölln, one of the most politically violent districts in the city. Both groups also clearly linked the train station with their political activities. The Nazis had probably gathered there earlier in the evening to travel to their rally en masse. They would have been in uniform and likely carrying local banners and party flags, making a visual statement to other passengers about the strength of the *Nationalsozialistische Deutsche Arbeiterpartei* (NSDAP) in Neukölln. One of those attacked later claimed that in the tumult his 'briefcase with stamps, lists and various papers' was stolen from him.[32] These were likely party materials, which political opponents frequently sought in order to humiliate and learn more about the activities of the opposition. Moreover, the Communists taken into custody claimed that this was not a premeditated act of violence. Rather they explained that they had gathered at the train station as a key stop in a propaganda campaign, hanging posters for the KPD and guarding those already up on walls in the station and surrounding streets, as evidence that this was their territory. This defence was a believable one and good enough to help some of the young defendants – ages between 19 and 22 years – receive milder sentences or acquittals.[33] Finally, the fact that so many of the alleged assailants were able to escape capture was due at least in part to the fact that so many of the young men lived in the adjoining streets and could quickly find their own homes or those of friends willing to provide cover from the 'intrusive' police.

Brawls on train platforms were also common when speakers would arrive from other cities, to be greeted by supporters and detractors. As a result, police even tried to stay informed of those political groups entering and leaving the city via train in order to keep the peace between passengers. Controlling travel was always a difficult task throughout the summer months, when local radicals would head to the countryside for paramilitary training, but it was especially complicated on the weekend of the annual *Reichsverfassungstag* (Constitution Day) in August. On the tenth anniversary of the Weimar Constitution in 1929, the Berlin-Brandenburg regional leadership of the *Reichsbanner* informed the city's police force that it should expect as many as 100,000 supporters of the republic to arrive for the

---

[31]   LAB, Rep. 58, No. 154, Film 370, Concluding report by the Kriminalassistent, October 16, 1930.

[32]   Ibid.

[33]   LAB, Rep. 58, No. 154, Film 370, Proceedings of the erweiterte Schöffengericht Neukölln, November 21, 1930.

festivities, the vast majority of whom would travel to Berlin by rail. The police were quite concerned about the safety of these visitors. Extra trains (*Sonderzüge*) were scheduled to carry the men, and the police ordered additional protection at all rail stations and requested information regarding arrival times from the RB leadership.[34] In the waning days of the republic, the police lobbied to have all political literature banned from city transit stations in order to defuse the political tension at these theoretically apolitical public spaces.

The importance of rail for understanding the social upheaval and violence in Berlin's neighbourhoods in the early 1930s, therefore, is two-fold. First, a look at local rail stations lends evidence to my argument that the development of Berlin's transit system did not undermine neighbourhood identity. The growing network actually reinforced it in many ways. These stations provided economic and social benefits to their surroundings – so much so in fact that residents of the area felt they owned and were compelled to defend these spaces. In itself, this phenomenon draws our attention to the dangers of considering public and private spaces to be mutually exclusive. Second, the railways remind us that we can better understand the history of daily life, and in this case the collapse of the Weimar Republic, by looking at how people politicised the physical structures around them. Ironically, though the physical struggle for these coveted local landmarks was meant to defend the viability of a way of life, the radicalism and bloodshed in the transportation system served only to weaken further the sense of community needed to weather the deepening political and economic crises. In their desire to control these vital landmarks, radical Berliners created fear among neighbours and encouraged further surveillance by the authorities.

---

[34] BLHA, Rep. 30. Bln. C, Title 90, no. 7531, 297, Reichsbanner Gauvorstand Berlin-Brandenburg to the Polizeipräsident Abteilung II, August 1, 1929 and 318, Memo from the Schupo Kommando, August 8, 1929. For schedules of the *Sonderzüge* see 293–5.

CHAPTER FOURTEEN

The impact of the railway on the lives of women in the nineteenth-century city

Diane Drummond

Introduction

Both John R. Kellett's book, *The Impact of Railways on Victorian Cities* and Wolfgang Schivelbusch's, *The Railway Journey* transformed our understanding of the impact of the railway upon the nineteenth-century city.[1] For Kellett the railway had very direct physical and economic repercussions on the city. Building the railway cut great swathes through existing areas as buildings were demolished to make way for new surface or underground lines. This brought both temporary and permanent chaos and disruption to city life. The city's form and appearance was also totally remade by the railway and the economic forces it instigated or accelerated. This completely remodelled the geography of the modern city. New business zones were established at the city's centre while on its perimeter new suburbs grew up. As a result, work life and home life were physically separated, first of all for members of the middle-class, but, in time, for the working-classes too.

While Kellett's work examined the physical and economic impact of railway building in the nineteenth-century British city, Schivelbusch's book focuses on the 'railway journey' and the role it played in transforming the perception of the modern city. Distances both within the city, and between them, appeared to shrink. The train journey also brought an new understanding of the extent and form of the modern city and nation. For Schivelbusch the experience of travelling on the train completely changed contemporary understanding of time and space. It modernised the contemporary 'mental map' and as a result, a new vision of the spatial dimensions of the city emerged.

However one dilemma with both Kellett's and Schivelbusch's pathbreaking visions of the impact of the railway on the nineteenth-century city is that they only partially suggest that this was not universally the same for all of Britain's

---

[1]   See John R. Kellett, *The Impact of Railways on Victorian Cities* (London 1969), and Wolfgang Schivelbusch, *The Railway Journey: The Industrialization of Time and Space in the Nineteenth Century* (London 1977).

nineteenth-century city dwellers. An individual's location within the city; their class, and of concern here, their gender, might make huge differences to the impact that the railway had on their lives. This is true in regard to both the direct, physical results of the railway (the factors that Kellett explored), and this matter of the railway journey. The following chapter seeks to add some vision of the impact that the railway had for women in the nineteenth-century city to both Kellett's and Schivelbusch's work.

Theory and approaches to 'women and the railway in the nineteenth-century British city'

That both Schivelbusch and the earlier writer Kellett should have failed to bring a 'gender dimension' to their work is, of course, not surprising. They produced their visions of the railway and the city some years before such railway historians as Jack Simmons and Jeffrey Richards and John MacKenzie made comment on the impact of the railway for women.[2] More feminist or indeed post-modern understandings of the city and of space within the city (gendered patterns on the ground) also developed much later. While both Schivelbusch's and Kellett's work shows a keen understanding of the importance of time and change, the idea that nineteenth-century London life was 'an orderly succession of sharply distinct experiences involving movement in space and time', were not yet appreciated.[3] Nor indeed was the concept that these experiences might, in specific circumstances, differ significantly for men and women.

The twenty to thirty years that have elapsed since Kellett's and Schivelbusch's work were first published have seen a huge increase of interest in the areas of 'gender' and 'women'. This is not just in the discipline of history but in other areas such as sociology and geography too. Theoretical understandings of representation and the use of 'urban space' in time have also developed significantly. These are especially significant when reviewing Kellett's work. As will be seen later, such writers as Leonore Davidoff and Catherine Hall in their work on Birmingham have determined the various economic and social factors that led to the separation of home and work.[4] As a result the city suburb developed, with middle-class men and women living significantly different lives during the 'working' day, with the men returning to the domestic ideal of the home at evenings and weekends. In other

---

[2] Jack R. Simmons, *The Victorian Railway* (London 1995), 332–6, and Jeffrey Richards and John M. MacKenzie, *The Railway Station: A Social History* (Oxford 1986), chapter 6.

[3] Donald Olsen, *The Growth of Victorian London* (London 1976), 110.

[4] Leonore Davidoff and Catherine Hall, *Family Fortunes: Men and Women of the English Middle-Class, 1780–1850* (London 1987), and also Leonore Davidoff and Catherine Hall, 'Gender Divisions and Class Formation in the Birmingham middle-class, 1780–1850', in Catherine Hall, ed., *White, Male and Middle-Class: Explorations in Feminism and History* (Cambridge 1992), 94–107.

words men and women used urban space in different ways or at different times, these producing temporal differences in how the genders moved within the city.

More recently, proponents of 'space, place and gender theory' such as Doreen Massey, Shirley Ardener and Lynda Nead have discussed how contemporary social constructs together with the fear of physical or moral danger have created a temporal use of space in the modern city that is different for men and women.[5] These factors not only defined women's identities in the Victorian city, but the extent and location of the spatial environment they were confined within.[6] The symbolic use of city space together with the presence of social surveillance, 'the gaze', further reinforced this process. Fear of both moral and physical danger brought other restrictions on where the urban female might walk or travel. Or indeed the means of travel that she was prepared to take. These are most important factors to take into consideration regarding the impact of the railway for women in the Victorian city.

As a result the nineteenth-century British city became a complex place – and space – of excitement and danger for contemporary women. In contrast, the new city suburbs became their refuge and often their perceived 'proper' place. This differentiation in the temporal use of city space according to gender was clearly the product of far wider forces than the coming of the railway, but the railway arguably played a role both in enabling and accelerating this process.

Other writers on space, place and gender have recorded the impact of other forces upon women's lives and their use of space within the modern city. For most working-class women, while social constructions and conventions unquestionably played a part in determining how and when they used their city and where they lived, labour market forces added a further, very strong dynamic to their spatial experience of the city and therefore to Kelllett's 'patterns on the ground'. Susan Hanson and Geraldine Pratt in their study of early twentieth-century Worcester, Massachusetts, note that not only was the city's labour market segregated on the basis of both race and gender, but that this sexual division of labour was differentiated spatially too.[7] Thus men and women were employed in different workplaces, even very different areas of the city. Labour markets in nineteenth-century British cities might well have some of the same qualities and have included middle- as well as working-class women as they entered employment.

This recent theoretical work on space, place and gender also has important implications for Schivelbusch's vision of the impact of the railway journey on the nineteenth-century perception of time, space and the city. The separation of work and home; the generation of new city suburbs and of labour markets that were not

---

5   Doreen Massey, *Space, Place and Gender* (Cambridge 1994), Shirley Ardener, 'Ground Rules and Social Maps for Women: An Introduction', in Shirley Ardener, ed., *Women and Space: Ground Rules and social mapping* (Oxford 1993), 1–21, and Lynda Nead, *Victorian Babylon: People, Streets and Images in Nineteenth-Century London* (New Haven 2000).

6   Massey, ibid., 180.

7   Susan Hanson and Geraldine Pratt, *Gender, Work and Space* (London 1995), 2.

only sexually-divided, but spatially differentiated too, all this meant that the frequency and length of the railway journey taken might be significantly different for men and women, as well as for members of the different social classes. To use Hanson and Pratt's own words: 'Every story is a travel story (...) a spatial practice.'[8]

Other theorists such as Shirley Ardener argue that the social constraints that restricted women to a specific space and place might also deter them from taking personal or more independent forms of transport. Indeed, the whole nature of women's lives during this time, especially their restriction to specific urban spaces or their different temporal use of space, may have relatively curtailed their use of the railway in comparison to men's. This, in turn might affect women's 'experiences and perceptions' of time, space and the city. The impact of the railway arguably being far more limited for women than men in the nineteenth century-British city.

Many of these ideas on space and place are drawn from an array of writings on 'the separate spheres ideal', especially the arguments forwarded by Jürgen Habermas in *The Structural Transformation of the Public Sphere.*[9] Of course for Habermas the public sphere was one of *discourse* and not of space, but, as will be seen later, many theorists, especially Doreen Massey, maintain that such ideas had a profound impact on women's use of space in time.

Clearly, many of these new ideas and concepts are of importance in making a reconsideration of the impact of the railway for women in the nineteenth-century British city, and with this, a reconsideration of Kellett's and Schivelbusch's work. However, there are problems in actually doing this. Helen Mellor for instances warns that: 'Gender in the urban environment is not a useful conceptual tool. (It is) everywhere and nowhere'.[10]

One minute the various ways in which men and women of the different social classes used space and transport within the city comes into sharp relief, especially when these are compared across a particular time period such as the working day. In other instances their paths become the same or are shared once again. The historical sources available for investigating such factors also present problems.

---

8   Ibid. 1.

9   See Jürgen Habermas, *The Structural Transformation of the Public Sphere* (London 1963). For more on how Habermas's ideas have influenced feminist thought see Geoffrey Eley, 'Public and Political Cultures: Placing Habermas in the nineteenth century' and Nancy Fraser, 'Rethinking the public sphere: A Contribution to the critique of actually existing democracy', both in Craig Calhoun, ed., *Habermas and the Public Sphere* (Cambridge, MA 1996), 289–317, and 109–31.

10 Helen Mellor, Women's History Tutorial: 'Women, Cities and Social change, 1840–1940', History Courseware for Historians CD-Rom (Glasgow 1999), and Helen Mellor, Women's History Tutorial: 'Urbanisation, Civilisation and Society: The Role of Women', Ibid. Here Mellor also cites Louise Tilly on this subject, 'Gender is everywhere; it is like a low-lying mist (...) if we posit gender as everywhere, we have no standpoint from which to explain it or the institutions, processes, experiences it is said to shape'. Ibid.

Often such sources are 'blind' to women's connections with the railway, unconsciously reporting men's direct and indirect involvement with it while neglecting women's. In other instances the documents report on the volume and number of passengers without, understandably, any references being made to the passengers' genders. Thus important British government sources such as the *Railway Returns* and various other reports that railway companies were required to make to the British central government simply record the number of passengers taking various services. Few documents, such as a Board of Trade Inquiry into ladies' carriages made in 1887, give any real idea of how frequently and to what extent women travelled on the train during the nineteenth century.[11] As a result historical sources that are often used for investigating women's history, such as diaries, memoirs, even fictional writing and especially contemporary illustrations, will be used here.

Reviewing Kellett

How might Kellett's ideas and arguments concerning the impact that the railway had upon the nineteenth-century British city be reconsidered in order to include some vision of how these affected women? For Kellett possibly the first result of the railway's arrival in the city came in the form of the destruction and demolition it prompted. Whole areas suffered as the permanent-way or underground tunnel was forced through them as they were completely demolished, their residence being displaced to find shelter elsewhere in the city.

Contemporary drawings and photographs of railway and underground construction in London, dramatically illustrate the impact that this activity had upon nineteenth-century life. For instance, a photograph taken of the demolition taking place at Tothill Street for the construction of the District railway in 1867 – now kept at the London Transport Museum – clearly marks the end of a slum area, while another of a tunnel being built along Praed Street in 1866 shows the close proximity of lower middle-class homes and railway construction.[12] Those living in the Victorian city recorded how it was possible to view railway building without even 'leaving the warm shelter of their drawing-rooms or bed-rooms'.[13]

Railway building and the demolition that it caused affected all members of the family of course, but it is possible to argue that this was worse for the women of the household as they remained at home during the day, suffering the noise and disturbance of railway construction while fathers and husbands were at work somewhere else within the city. Again the photograph of construction at Praed

---

[11] See Parliamentary Papers (1900) vol. 76, Returns of the number of workmen's trains by the railways of Great Britain, and Board of Trade Inquiry into the provision of carriages for ladies by Britain's Railway companies. Accounts and Papers of 1887.

[12] Lynda Nead, *Victorian Babylon: People, Streets and Images in Nineteenth-Century London* (New Haven 2000), 43–4.

[13] Ibid. 42, quoting from John Hollingshead, *Underground London* (London 1871).

Street illustrates this. As navvies work on the construction of the new line a small group of women and children look on from a flat roof of their home – and possibly business – that is right beside the underground tunnel.[14]

The complete demolition of an area resulted in even greater disturbance for its residents as they vacated their homes and their neighbourhood. However, as Kellett points out, this was especially traumatic for the city slum-dwellers, these members of the lower classes being far less likely to receive any form of compensation from the railway companies, which was usually paid to their landlords and not to themselves. For women and children, the impact of this could be worse than for men, especially if these women were single or widowed. While such slum clearance unquestionably improved the life and look of the city, the fact that no working-class housing was erected to make up for the premises lost in this process resulted in a lack of working-class housing. This brought about an increase in rents obliging many, especially the most poorly paid such as women, to either pay higher rents for more inadequate accommodation, or even to begin living on the streets. Thomas Wright the famous journeyman engineer records how railway building in London displaced his family in 1867. They soon found new rooms, but these were far less comfortable than their previous ones. It was Wright's wife who bore the brunt of this as she withstood the fights and foul language of their new neighbours.[15]

Nor was the disturbance over once the railway had been built or the family had moved on. Those, such as the women living on Praed Street, or their working-class counterparts whose homes were in close proximity to the railway or underground, found the noise, dust and stench of the railway continued to affect their daily lives, causing extra housework and frustration. Nineteenth-century illustrations of the town of Stockport clearly show workers' houses located beneath the railway viaduct that still dominates the town. The middle-classes of Victorian Britain also often lived in close proximity to the railway. That famous fictious nobody Charles Pooter noted that one of the inconveniences of moving to the Laurels, Brickfield Terrace, Holloway was the fact that the 'nice little back garden' ran down to the railway. Initially he, his wife Carrie and son Lupin were 'rather afraid of the noise of the trains'. However the landlord reduced their rent by two pounds and after a while they failed to notice anything other than a slight cracking in the garden wall.[16]

Both Kellett and Schivelbusch note another important impact that the railway had upon the nineteenth-century city, that is the development of both the business areas in the city centre and the suburb, located on the outskirts of the city. Suburbanisation and the complementary effect of the separation of home and work were, of course, products of deep social forces and not simply the railway. They are, as Doreen Massey explains, the 'culturally specific distinctions between the

---

[14] Ibid.

[15] Thomas Wright, *Some Habits and Customs of the Working-Classes* (London 1867).

[16] George and Weedon Grossmith, *The Diary of A Nobody* (London 1979).

public and private sphere, and the attempt to confine women to the domestic sphere'.[17] This spatially separated home, and the middle-class male domain of work for the first time. While suburbanisation in Britain, particularly in London, pre-dated the arrival of the railway and could have been sustained without it, there is little doubt that it was the railway that allowed the process to develop to the huge extent that it did. The development of both surface and underground railway networks in cities such as London, and later Glasgow and Liverpool, ensured that this trend not only continued but escalated, the railway acting as a catalyst, allowing the suburbs to become more and more distant from their city centres. Something of the dynamic impetus that the railway provided to suburbanisation is conveyed in Gustave Doré's and Jerrold Blanchard's, *London: A Pilgrimage*:

> The underground railway from Paddington to the City; the Thames Embankment; the Holborn Viaduct; the new Bridges at Westminster and Blackfriars; the broad streets skirted with palatial offices which have been driven through the City, opening up the east and west traffic; the railway through Brunel's Thames Tunnel; and lastly, the extraordinary network of the metropolitan railway system that brings the locomotive almost to every man's door; are salient points of a London that would be as strange to the spirit of the historian.[18]

In London the railway led to the development of such city suburbs as Clapham, Lewisham, Ealing and Crystal Palace which were developed by the 1850s. By the late nineteenth century the distance that those who worked in London commuted between home and work was often considerable, stretching to some thirty miles or so, the 'Home Counties' of Surrey, Middlesex and Buckinghamshire, providing the suburban homes for London's middle-class workers and their families. The commencement of the London underground with the building of the Metropolitan railway between Paddington Station and King's Cross during the 1860s, with lines eventually going out to meet the Eastern Counties Railway Line at Shoreditch in the east, enhanced this process within the city itself. These created a complex of railway connections that were highly significant in allowing the separation of home and work, and therefore often of men and women in their daily working lives. The London underground system, like the surface railway network, expanded throughout the nineteenth and early twentieth centuries, further developing and extending this gendered form of city-suburban life.

Nor was this suburbanisation, and with it the creation of a segregated daily life for men and women, confined to the upper- and middle-classes, as H. J. Dyos's book on the working-class London suburb of Camberwell demonstrates.[19] Suburbanisation also became a feature of many other British cities during the nineteenth and early twentieth centuries. The development of intricate local railway networks, and in the case of cities such as Liverpool and Glasgow, of very

---

[17] Doreen Massey, *Space, Place and Gender* (Cambridge 1994), 179.
[18] Gustave Doré and Jerrold Blanchard, *London: A Pilgrimage* (London 1872), chapter XII: London Under Green Leaves.
[19] H. J. Dyos, *Victorian Suburb: A Study of the Growth of Camberwell* (Leicester 1961).

early underground and overhead railway systems, helped to generate and sustain suburbs and gendered suburban life-styles elsewhere too.

While both contemporaries and, until recently, historians and theorists, were very conscious of the links between the railway and suburbanisation, and of the impact that this had up on contemporary city life, they were often oblivious to the results of this on women. For instance Dionysius Lardner, one of the earlier commentators on the social impact of the railway wrote in 1851:

> It is now not unusual for persons whose places of business is in the centre of the capital to reside with their families at a distance of fifteen to twenty miles from that city. Nevertheless, they are able to arrive at their respective shops, counting Houses or office at an early hour of the morning, to return without inconvenience to their residences at the usual time in the evening.[20]

Only occasionally was the impact of the railway on women's lives made explicit. When it was, it was usually women who made comment. Katharine Chorley's memoirs of life in Alderley Edge in the 1900s for instance, recalls how the Manchester suburb became the preserve of middle-class women and children, domestic servants and service workers after the early morning business trains had taken the men to their work.[21]

The railway was important in helping to produce other changes in the use of city space that promoted further differences in the lives of men and women, here notably amongst the city's working-classes. Hanson and Pratt in their study of early twentieth-century Worcester in Massachusetts argue that the local labour market had become highly segregated by gender and that this had been made possible by the creation of a cheap and efficient transport system, including urban railway or underground railway systems.[22]

Determining the details of both the nature of the labour market, and the involvement of the railway in the nineteenth-century British city, in this case London, presents huge difficulties. Certainly with the continued growth of such areas of middle-class employment as banking, finance, commerce and government occurring in London throughout the nineteenth century, a huge number of middle-class men would have been employed in specific areas of the city, those areas being separated from their home suburbs by the daily railway journey. It is more difficult to ascertain how far the developing labour market was differentiating the use of urban space for middle-class women, let alone the form of such a pattern. There is much to suggest that it was the separation of themselves at home from male members of their family as they commuted to the city that remained the most important spatial dimension for most women of this class. By 1901 most middle-class women in the London area were still recorded as having no particular occupation, and therefore would have stayed at home in the suburb. Only two

---

[20] Dionysius Lardner, *Railway Economy* (London 1851), 36.
[21] Katharine Chorley, *Manchester Made Them* (London 1950), 114–15.
[22] Susan Hanson and Geraldine Pratt, *Gender, Work and Space* (London 1995), 1.

per cent of women of that class found work in the professions by this time.[23] However as the leading areas of employment within those professions were areas such as teaching, where women would have either worked near to their home, or even have taken up residence in the school, relatively few women would have journeyed from the suburb to the city for their work.

Working-class women's labour markets in early twentieth-century London are equally as difficult to reconstruct. While Census reports for nineteenth-century London, including those for 1901, clearly show that male and female employment was centred in very different sectors of the economy, it is difficult to establish the spatial nature of this and the involvement of the railway. Certainly the census indicates that textile manufacturing and the production of dress employed similar numbers of men and women, while other areas of manufacturing, construction and transport were very predominately male sectors. Domestic service was, of course, predominantly female.[24] The dilemma comes however in gaining some idea of how this sexually-segregated labour market actually worked out as a 'pattern on the ground', or a spatially orientated labour market within the nineteenth-century British city. Census reports and returns on the different areas of London, together with more detailed studies of work in specific areas by various historians provide some indication of this. Information of where places of work were located, their activity and how far this was a male or female pursuit, may also be of significance. However it is nearly impossible to recreate fully the sexual segregation of the nineteenth-century city labour market, or indeed to say how far the railway was involved in making this possible.

One final aspect of how the use of space in the city differed for men and women that is not present in Kellett's work is related to the threat and danger for women in the city station or in the dark alleys and areas that the railway so often created. As Lynda Nead notes in her book *Victorian Babylon*, and Judith Walkowitz in *City of Dreadful Delight,* the threat and meaning of the city was very different for men and women, and for middle-class and working-class women and their less respectable sisters.[25] Social convention, approbation and genuine concern for personal safety therefore determined where and often when women could venture, as Doreen Massey has noted. Women abroad in the nineteenth-century city also discovered that walking alone in certain areas automatically brought into question their moral standing and character. The railway station was often the site of all of these dangers, for while the station, especially the major city terminus, was a highly controlled and 'policed' open space, accessible to all, it could also be a very threatening place, especially for women. The nineteenth-century British city station was also filled with the 'symbolic meaning of spaces/places' and 'the

---

[23] Parliamentary Papers (1902) Census Reports for 1901, vol. 2, 77.
[24] Ibid. 89–91.
[25] Judith R. Walkowitz, *City of Dreadful Delight: Narratives of Sexual Danger in Late Victorian London* (London 1992).

gendered messages that they transmit', factors that would lead to women using the station space in a different way to men.[26]

While many of Britain's city railway stations were impressive pieces of architecture, whether they were in a high gothic style such as the Midland Railway Company's St. Pancras station, or the austere 'glass train shed' of nearby King's Cross, others were little more than 'train sheds', dirty industrial spaces where passengers were forced to enter in order to take the train. According to Jack Simmons, many of Britain's stations 'took up any shape left over by the engineers'.[27] Leeds station in Yorkshire for instance accommodated a number of different railway companies, separate structures gradually being merged together in order to form a complex and poorly-built station where underground passageways between the various platforms proved potentially dangerous for the travelling public. Even those stations that had been well designed initially soon had a confusion of underground passages, footbridges and walkways added to them, these bringing further confusion and possible danger to women making a railway journey. These were clearly places of danger and threat to unaccompanied women. Didcot was a rural but important junction on the Great Western Railway, but for those travelling between London and the West Country who had to change trains there, it was particularly confusing. Underground passages provided the links between the different platforms, and these were poorly lit while the way was insufficiently sign-posted, a contemporary stating: 'There were some directions painted on the wall below, which no one appeared to understand.'[28] The press of people gathering to catch the train added to the confusion, and to the difficulty for women in using the railway station as an 'urban space'. This commotion of passengers, stations staff and the general public was added to by the noise and steam of the locomotives, these often letting out shrill, disconcerting whistles, while the sound of trains leaving or entering the station made conversation impossible.

'Taking the train' also brought people of different classes into close proximity, the railway station forcing together men and women of all backgrounds. Clearly first-class passengers, and ladies who wished to use the ladies' waiting rooms that were provided in most stations from the earliest days of the railway in Britain, saw relatively little of the members of the lower orders who frequented the stations.[29] However, as Jeffrey Richards and John MacKenzie argue in their history of the railway station, with its newspaper-sellers, porters and general hawkers: 'the

---

[26] Shirley Ardener, ed., *Women and Space: Ground Rules and social mapping* (Oxford 1993), 182.

[27] Jack R. Simmons, *The Railway in Town and Country* (London 1976), 142.

[28] H. A. Simmons, *Ernest Struggles* (London 1879), 43–4, and quoted in Jack R. Simmons, *Railways: An Anthology* (London 1991).

[29] Jack R. Simmons and Gordon Biddle, *The Oxford Companion to Railway History* (Oxford 1997), 566.

station was one of the few places where the poorest could encounter the better-off'.[30]

The railway station also exposed women to criminality, either through observing criminal acts or arrests, or in becoming victims of such actions themselves. William Powell Frith's famous painting, *The Railway Station*, painted in 1862, reveals some of this contemporary fear of stations in its portrayal of the arrest of a criminal taking place on the platform right beside a group of middle-class men, women and children. City stations also became the haunts of prostitutes, some soliciting on platforms and conducting their trade on trains as they proceeded to their clients' suburban homes. This obviously exposed respectable unaccompanied women to the danger of being seen as fallen women simply because they were in a station on their own.

Reviewing Schivelbusch

Women in the nineteenth-century British city clearly had a different understanding and use of space and place therefore, the railway playing an important but by no means definitive role in producing this gendered use of urban space, especially here the railway station. Recent theory, especially that forwarded by feminists such Ardener, also argues that this differentiated use of urban space together with contemporary social constraints may also have limited women's use of urban transportation, such as the train. This was especially the case for any woman who wished to travel alone. This might therefore have led women to make railway journeys more infrequently, while other factors may well have resulted in women's train journeys tending to be shorter than men's. It is this experience of the railway journey which takes the chapter on to examining how Schivelbusch's ideas might be re-examined in light of primary evidence concerning women and the railway journey in the nineteenth-century city.

A number of factors clearly suggest that women of this period used the train far less frequently than men of a similar social class to their own. However this does not mean that the nineteenth-century woman did not take the train. First of all it should be noted that both the reality of train travel for women and public opinion presented a degree of anxiety and social approbation for the Victorian woman who wished to use the train, especially if she decided to journey alone. This was true not only in the earlier days of the railways and underground, but later, especially after some particular 'outrage' (which could be anything from impropriety on the part of a male passenger to a murder) had taken place. The dangers that railway journeys presented to women were all too apparent for everyone to see, an early author of a guide to using the new railway system writing in the 1840s: 'There is

---

[30] Jeffrey Richards and John M. MacKenzie, *The Railway Station: A Social History* (Oxford 1986), 137.

no place where a young woman is insulted in so bad a fashion as in the railway carriage.'[31]

The possibilities of being 'insulted' were greatly increased in the carriages that were used on Britain's railways throughout the nineteenth century. Ostensibly, for the first-class passenger at least, these were like 'parlours-on-wheels', confined and often highly decorative domestic places where women could feel safe and secure. However, consisting of small individual compartments and lacking connecting corridors these British carriages were far more dangerous than the American open cabs. If a threatening person entered such a carriage at a station there was no means of escaping until the train arrived at the next stop. The dangers of the British railway carriage were even worse before the introduction of the communication chord in 1864, although a peephole was provided between each compartment, railway companies hoping that the possibility of being watched would dissuade passengers from criminal or violent acts.[32]

Nor were the hazards of railway travel restricted to the possibility of male impropriety or assault. A Board of Trade Inquiry 'concerning railway companies' provision of 'Ladies Only' carriages of 1887 was instigated by the murder of a Miss Scragg, a third-class passenger on the London and North Western company line between Wellington and Shrewsbury in August 1886.[33] Death might also come through railway accident, a feature from which women were not immune, as Charles Dickens' description of his own ministrations to a woman mortally injured in the Staplehurst crash in 1865 demonstrate. Other dangers of 'taking the train' were those allegedly presented to health and well-being. Schivelbusch explored the links that contemporary medical doctors made between railway travel and physical and mental health. Fears of such danger emerged strongly during the 1860s, in articles in *The Lancet*, and again in the 1880s, when the idea of 'railway neurosis' was first diagnosed.[34] However, despite the usual Victorian anxieties about women's health, especially concerning reproduction, no disease that was seen to be promoted by the railway was particularly confined to women.

However despite all this, the records of the railway companies which replied to the Board of Trade's Inquiry of 1887 indicate that few women, including the murdered Miss Scraggs, used the carriages provided for their exclusive use. The London and South Western Railway for instance carried out a short survey which showed that only 143 out of the 1,109 seats available in the 'ladies only' carriages were used. This ratio was higher on the Great Western Railway, but it was still rather limited (in all only 248 out of the total number of 1,060 seats in the 'ladies

---

[31] Anonymous, *Drake's Guide to the Grand Junction Railway*, 2 vols. (London 1848), vol. 1, 76.

[32] J. R. Whitbread, *The Railway Policeman* (London 1961), 167.

[33] Board of Trade Inquiry into the provision of carriages for ladies by Britain's Railway companies. Accounts and Papers of 1887. PP 1888 LXXXIX. 97 C.5283.

[34] Wolfgang Schivelbusch, *The Railway Journey: The Industrialization of Time and Space in the Nineteenth Century* (London 1977), chapter three.

only' carriages were used during the time that the GWR took its survey).[35] This was possibly the result of relatively few women travelling on trains alone, or because those who did felt perfectly safe on the railway. After all, British railway companies set great store in their kind and courteous staff, who were instructed to help unaccompanied women, or women with children. Of course, assault and murder on the railway was not confined to women. In fact, the first recorded victim of a 'railway murder' in Britain was a man, Thomas Briggs, a seventy year old chief clerk to a city bank, who was killed in 1864.[36] Quite possibly the female understanding of the level of personal safety that the railway offered changed and developed over the years. Indeed the perception of danger might have been enhanced by the militant women's suffrage movement and its attempts to demonstrate the hypocrisy of the male claim that all men naturally protected the weaker female. Thus the women's suffrage newspaper *The Vote*, called for more women only railway carriages in 1919. Finally there is much evidence to suggest that while contemporary opinion was against women travelling on trains alone, unaccompanied by either a protecting male or a chaperoning female, many women defied this convention.[37] For many Victorian women railway travel was not only

Figure 14.1 Abraham Solomon, *The Meeting*, 1855

Source: National Railway Museum

[35] Ibid.
[36] *Annual Register*, 1864, and J. R. Whitbread, *The Railway Policeman* (London 1961), 117.
[37] This is discussed in Susan Kingsley Kent, *Gender and Power in Britain* (London 2000), 292.

necessary but also highly liberating, Jack Simmons arguing that it gave women their first opportunity to make journeys alone.[38]

This is not to say that such an idea was not shocking to the Victorians. However, historical evidence suggests that often it was contemporary social opinion and male fear of impropriety rather than women's genuine fear that led to a call for unaccompanied women not to take the train. That contemporaries could be amazed by the idea of a woman travelling alone on a railway train is more than evident in the public response to Abraham Solomon's painting, *The Meeting*. A portrait of a fresh-faced young woman alone in a splendid first class railway carriage with a young navy officer, the painting provoked so much controversy when it was first exhibited in 1855 that Solomon was obliged to withdrew it from exhibition. He then added the figure of a kindly, protective father between the two in order to redress propriety. Similarly, the Duke of Wellington heavily castigated his son for being prepared to allow his wife to travel between London and Windsor on her own, the Duke exclaiming: 'I do not like to see her treated otherwise than if she was worth taking care of.'[39]

However, while public concern and fatherly (or fatherly-in-law) protection of the journeying female were very apparent, other less well-motivated reasons for wanting to prevent women travelling alone on a train were also evident. In 1866 an article in *Punch* parodied the dangers for men of inadvertently making a journey with an unaccompanied female, suggesting that these often ended in women making false accusations of improper conduct against the man.[40] Not that such things did not happen on Victorian trains, the famous clergy diary keeper, the Reverend Francis Kilvert describing a journey where:

> A strange wild-looking woman was sitting opposite me. She conceived a mortal dislike to a man who sat in another corner of the carriage and kept on glancing round over her shoulder at me, poking me violently in the ribs, and turning away from him with a shudder and a horrible grimace (said to me),'Do you know this man? He's a wicked man![41]

Despite all this, women of all social classes were more than happy to take the train. Illustrative evidence suggests that women travelled on the train, accompanied by men, in mixed groups, with children or alone from the earliest days of the railway. Indeed, some of Britain's earliest trains, notably on the Liverpool and Manchester Railway, allowed passengers to have their own private carriages loaded on to a train, this affording all concerned maximum privacy and convenience. Thomas Talbot Bury's illustrations of the Liverpool and Manchester Railway made in 1831, not only show this, but also demonstrate the fascination of this new form of transport and its technology for women. One of Bury's drawings shows a woman

---

[38] Jack R. Simmons, *The Victorian Railway* (London 1995), 335.

[39] Quoted in Ibid., 333.

[40] *Punch*, 1865, 70, and quoted in Ibid., 334.

[41] Francis Kilvert, *Diary*, 2 vols. (London 1939), vol. 2, 70–1.

being guided by gaslight into the tunnel leading out of Lime Street station. However women soon travelled by train on their own. In illustrations of Baker Street Station, one of the first underground stations in London opened in 1863, one or two unaccompanied women can be seen. These illustrations are interesting for they not only prove that women were quite happy to travel on the underground alone, but also provide a glimpse of how ordinary a feature of daily life in the city such a form of transport became for middle-class women from its opening.[42]

That city-based railway travel was essential to the middle-class women of the Victorian period is more than evident from other sources. The idea of the suburb could not work without women resorting to the train at some point, whether it was for commuting to the city for leisure, such as a trip to the theatre, or for shopping. Memoirs and even fictional writing makes clear how acceptable and ordinary a feature of life this was for many middle-class women. Indeed many women such as Bessie Raynor Parkes (later Belloc), commuted very regularly from their homes in the suburbs or even in the countryside, in Parkes' case from Roberts-bridge, to London.[43] Similarly Lynda Nead notes an entry made in a young London woman's

Figure 14.2   August Leopold Egg, *The Travelling Companions*, 1860

Source: Birmingham Museum & Art Gallery.

---

[42] Samuel J. Hodson, *Climolithograph of Baker Street Underground Station on the Metropolitan Line* (London 1863), shown in Andrew Emmerson, *Underground Pioneers* (Harrow Weald 2000), 32.

[43] Bessie Raynor Parkes (later Belloc), *In a Walled Garden* (New York 1895), 89.

diary in 1857, where she records that the woman was obliged to walk to town because the train had already left her local station when she arrived there. Clearly the young woman in question felt quite happy and safe to take the train, but when a man offered her a lift in his carriage she felt too bashful to accept![44]

An increasing number of middle-class women may have taken the train in order to go to their work in the city, although in total this would have still been relatively few. While the majority of women of that class living in London had no form of employment and remained at home, the 1901 Census indicates that nearly 40,000 women, some two per cent of all females over the age of ten years who were 'occupied', were employed in some form of professional capacity in the city.[45]

However as many women who were involved in such occupations would have been teachers, employed in schools near to their homes or in boarding schools where they themselves lived, the number of middle-class women who commuted some distance between the city and the suburb still would have been limited when compared with the number of middle-class men who would such a daily journey. Social approbation and convention, as well as the nature of middle-class women's professional employment, also appears to have restricted their use of the train for travelling to work. Again Katharine Chorley's memoirs of life in Alderley Edge demonstrate this:

> The businessmen travelled, of course, in the first-class carriages (...) any wife or daughter who had to travel into Manchester by one of those trains always travelled third; to share a compartment with the 'gentlemen' would have been unthinkable. Indeed the ladies always avoided the business trains if they possibly could. It was highly embarrassing, a sort of indelicacy, to stand on the platform surrounded by a crowd of males who had to be polite but were obviously not in the mood for feminine society.[46]

More distance travel on the overground railway soon became an integral part of this class of women's lives too. In fact such was the ease and level of acceptance of railway travel by women by the 1860s that the British artist, August Leopold Egg, produced a most beautiful portrayal of two young middle-class women travelling unchaperoned and quite contentedly on a continental railway possibly in the south of France near Mentone.[47] These young women are so unconcerned by railway travel that they sit reading or napping in their carriage, disinterested with the lovely scenery that they are passing through.

It is interesting to note however that while the idea that the railway was an essential and an inconspicuous part of the life of middle-class women – and children – as it was for their men was still not always seen to be such by contemporary writers and commentators. For instance the following rhyme published in a

---

[44] Lynda Nead, 'Taking to the Streets', *The B.B.C. History Magazine*, 1, no. 7 (November), 2000, 34–5.
[45] Parliamentary Papers (1902) Census Reports for 1901, vol. 2, 77.
[46] Katharine Chorley, *Manchester Made Them* (London 1950), 114–15.
[47] The painting was *The Travelling Companions,* kept at the Birmingham City Art Gallery.

children's book, *London Town*, of 1883, the writer quite unconsciously accompanies an illustration of a middle-class suburban matron and her children about to board an underground train with the words:

> Wonderful trains! From morn till night,
> Clattering though tunnels without daylight.
> Hither and thither they run, up and down,
> Beneath the streets of London Town.
>
> Many prefer these trains instead
> Of the cabs and 'busses' overhead,
> For they run much faster than horses can,
> Miss Dot's papa is a busy man,
> And goes to the City every day
> By the underground – the quickest way.[48]

This use of the train, as limited as it was, was not confined to middle-class women. The 1901 Census of London shows that some 1,663,431 women, the vast majority of the 1,924,368 females employed in the capital at that time, made a daily journey to work.[49] Of these some 1,623,431 would have been of the working-class. While the length of the journey and the form of transportation taken by these working women is, unfortunately, not recorded, it is quite likely that it was often a short one, women tending to work near home in order to undertake childcare or to look after other relatives. In addition to this, only a limited number of working-class women would have used the train to travel to their work. There is evidence to suggest that working-class women used workmen's trains, provided by Britain's railway companies from the 1840s onwards. Such provision was extended under a government act of 1883, although many companies provided them of their own volition many years prior to this. While only one railway company in the London area, the London, Brighton and South Coast Railway, directly states in its returns to parliament that these trains were used by both 'men and women', there is little doubt that at least some working women took them.[50] For instance, Jack Simmons records that a waiting room for women arriving on workers' early morning trains was provided at one of London's termini stations at Liverpool Street.[51]

However, the only real evidence regarding the number of daily journeys that working women made on these workmen's trains is provided in the 1901 Report on Workmen's trains on the Maryport and Carlisle Railway, a far from urban line! In 1899, out of all the different forms of tickets sold to working people by that railway company only three per cent of them or 1,705 tickets out of a total of 51,264, were bought by the local 'pitbrow women' in order to make their journey

---

[48] Anonymous, *London Town* (London 1883).
[49] Parliamentary Papers (1902) Census Reports for 1901, vol. 2, 77–89.
[50] Parliamentary Papers (1900), vol. 76, part 1, 937, Returns of the number of workmen's trains by the railways of Great Britain.
[51] Jack R. Simmons, *The Victorian Railway* (London 1995), 334.

to work. The use of workmen's trains by working women may have been similarly relatively low in Victorian cities such as London.[52]

Workmen's trains certainly ran early enough to have been used by women needing to get into the city for their work. However returns made by London-based railway companies suggest that cheap early morning fares, even for a short distance, were far from affordable for most working-class women. For instance trains from the London suburb of Clapham leaving between five and seven a.m. cost as little as three pence a day, or one shilling and six pence a week. On the Metropolitan underground line some workers' tickets cost even less, a penny a day. However with women earning less than twenty shillings a week, even this was beyond most of their budgets.[53] Possibly the most likely time for working-class

THE OXFORD AND CAMBRIDGE BOAT-RACE: A METROPOLITAN RAILWAY STATION ON A RACE DAY.

Figure 14.3   A platform on the London Underground on Boat Race Day, 1872

Source: *London News*, March 23, 1872

---

[52] Parliamentary Papers (1900) vol. 76, part 1, 937, Returns of the number of workmen's trains by the railways of Great Britain.
[53] Ibid.

women to have an opportunity to take the train to their work occurred when those engaged in domestic service travelled to the home of their employer, the employer presumably paying for the young servant's journey. Again direct evidence of this is not easy to find, but one illustration from a contemporary magazine, reproduced in Michael Freeman's *The Railway and the Victorian Imagination* shows a girl going to her new employment in a railway carriage.[54]

Working-class women also took railway trips for pleasure from comparatively early in the history of the railway. Special excursions were a common feature of working-class life by the 1850s, the journey to London to see the Great Exhibition being their very first train trip for many working-class families. The use of city-based railway lines, including the London underground, to visit attractions within or near to the metropolis also became a feature of working women's lives. Engravings appearing in the *Illustrated London News* in 1873 show a great crowd of working-class men and women waiting on a platform to catch the underground train to see the Oxford-Cambridge boat race on the river Thames.

In summary therefore, women's railway journeys may have been less frequent, even shorter, but the simple act of taking one railway journey appears to have been enough to change one's perceptions for ever as the actress Frances Anne Kemble's description of her first train ride in 1829:

> You can't imagine how strange it seemed to be journeying on thus, without any visible cause of progress other than the magical machine, with its flying white breath and rhythmical, unvarying pace (...). The engine was set off at its utmost speed, 35 miles an hour, swifter than a bird flies (...). You cannot conceive of what the sensation of cutting the air was (...). When I closed my eyes this sensation of flying was quite delightful and strange beyond description.[55]

---

[54] Michael Freeman, *The Railway and the Victorian Imagination* (Yale 2000).
[55] Frances Anne Kemble, *Memoirs of a Girlhood* (London 1874).

Bibliography

Introduction: The city and the railway in Europe
Ralf Roth and Marie-Noëlle Polino

Agence des Gares AREP, ed., *Parcours 1988–1998* (Diagonale, Rome 1998).

Bade, Klaus J., *Europa in Bewegung: Migration vom späten 18. Jahrhundert bis zur Gegenwart* (Verlag C. H. Beck Verlag, München 2000).

Barker, Theo C., and Robbins, Michael, *A History of London Transport. Passenger Travel and the Development of the Metropolis*, 2 vols. (Allen and Unwin, London 1963–1975).

Bendikat, Elfi, *Öffentliche Nahverkehrspolitik in Berlin und Paris 1890–1914: Strukturbedingungen, politische Konzeptionen und Realisierungsprobleme* (Walter de Gruyter, Berlin/New York 1999).

Bergmann, Gerd, *150 Jahre Eisenbahn in Eisenach* (Eisenacher Geschichtsverein, Eisenach 1997).

Bastian, Till, and Theml, Harald, *Unsere wahnsinnige Liebe zum Auto* (Weinheim 1990).

Bode, Peter M., Hamberger, Sylvia, and Zängl, Wolfgang, *Alptraum Auto. Eine hundertjährige Erfindung und ihre Folgen* (Raben Verlag, München 1986).

Bowie, Karen, *L'Éclectisme pittoresque et l'architecture des gares parisiennes au XIXe siècle*, 3 vols., université de Paris I Ph.D. thesis, 1985.

Bowie, Karen, ed., *Les Grandes Gares parisiennes au XIXe siècle*, exhibition catalogue (Paris 1987).

Bowie, Karen, ed., *Polarisation du territoire et développement urbain: les gares du Nord et de l'Est et la transformation de Paris au XIXe siècle. Une étude sur l'instauration et l'évolution des rapports entre les acteurs des grands aménagements ferroviaires urbains, première étape (1830–1870)*, 2 vols. (AHICF, Paris 1999).

Braunberger, Gerald, 'Der neue TGV lehrt Air France das fürchten', *Frankfurter Allgemeine Zeitung*, June 6, 2001.

Brophy, James M., *Capitalism, Politics, and Railroads in Prussia 1830–1870* (Ohio State University Press, Columbus/Ohio 1998).

Bund Deutscher Architekten and Deutsche Bahn AG, eds., *Renaissance der Bahnhöfe. Die Stadt im 21. Jahrhundert* (vieweg, Stuttgart 1996).

Cronon, William, *Nature's Metropolis. Chicago and the Great West* (W. W. Norton & Comp., Chicago 1992).

Dethier, Jean, ed., *Le Temps des gares*, exhibition catalogue (Centre Georges Pompidou, Paris 1978).

Dupuy, Gabriel, *L'Urbanisme des réseaux, Théories et méthodes*, (Armand Colin, coll. 'U Géographie', Paris 1991).

Flonneau, Mathieu, *L'Automobile à la conquête de Paris, 1910–1977. Formes urbaines, champs politiques et représentations*, 3 vols., Université de Paris I Ph.D. thesis, 2002.

Fourniau, Jean-Michel, *La Genèse des grandes vitesses à la SNCF, de l'innovation à la décision du T.G.V. Sud-Est*, INRETS report no. 60 (Paris 1988).

Fremdling, Rainer, *Eisenbahnen und deutsches Wirtschaftswachstum 1840–1879. Ein Beitrag zur Entwicklungstheorie und zur Theorie der Infrastruktur*, 2nd edn. (Gesellschaft für Westfälische Wirtschaftsgeschichte, Dortmund 1986).

Gall, Lothar, and Pohl, Manfred, eds., *Die Eisenbahn in Deutschland. Von den Anfängen bis zur Gegenwart* (Beck Verlag, München 1999).

Génelot, Paul, *La Gare de Montpellier à travers le temps* (Espace Sud éditions, Montpellier 1993).

Hall, Peter, and Pfeiffer, Ulrich, *Urban 21. Der Expertenbericht zur Zukunft der Städte* (Deutsche Verlagsanstalt, Stuttgart 2000).

Joseph, Isaac et al., eds., *Gare du Nord: mode d'emploi, programme de recherches concertées Plan Urbain-SNCF-RATP*, INRETS report no. 96 (Paris 1994).

Joseph, Isaac, ed., *Les Lieux-mouvements de la ville*, seminar proceedings, 5 vols. (RATP, Paris).

Joseph, Isaac, ed., *Villes en gares* (Ed. de l'Aube, La Tour d'Aigues 1999).

Kaiss, Kurt, *Dresdens Eisenbahn 1894–1994* (Alba Verlag, Düsseldorf 1994).

Kellett, John R., *The Impact of Railways on Victorian Cities* (Routledge & Kegan Paul, London and Henley 1979).

Königl.-preußischer Minister der öffentlichen Arbeiten, ed., *Berlin und seine Eisenbahnen 1846–1896*, 2 vols. (Verlag von Julius Springer, Berlin 1896).

Krings, Ulrich, *Bahnhofsarchitektur: Deutsche Großbahnhöfe des Historismus* (Prestel Verlag, München 1985).

Krings, Ulrich, *Der Kölner Hauptbahnhof* (Prestel Verlag, Köln 1977).

Kubinszky, Mihály, *Bahnhöfe Europas. Ihre Geschichte, Kunst und Technik* (Deutsche Verlagsanstalt, Stuttgart 1969).

Lambert, Michèle, *Les Voies ferrées et les gares dans les villes*, 2 vols. (AHICF, Paris 1992 and 1994).

Larroque, Dominique, Margairaz, Michel, and Zembri, Pierre, *Paris et ses transports, XIXe-XXe siècles* (Ed. Recherches, Paris 2002).

Lepetit, Bernard, Agier, Michel, Roncayolo, Marcel, Pinot, Jean-Luc, Joseph, Isaac, et al., 'La ville des sciences sociales', special issue, *Enquête – anthropologie – histoire – sociologie*, no. 4, 1996.

Leroux, Luc and Scotto, Marcel, 'Hi-tech train link to boost Marseille's fortunes', *Guardian Weekly*, June 14, 2001.

Lisson, Peter, ed., *Drehscheibe des Südens. Eisenbahnknoten München* (Hestra-Verlag, Darmstadt 1991).

Maier, Helmut, *Berlin Anhalter Bahnhof* (Verlag Ästhetik und Kommunikation, Berlin 1984).

Mannone, Valérie, *L'Impact régional du TGV Sud-Est*, 2 vols., Université d'Aix-Marseille II Ph.D. thesis, 1995.

Matzerath, Horst, ed., *Stadt und Verkehr im Industriezeitalter* (Böhlau Verlag, Köln 1996).

Meeks, Carrol L. V., *The Railroad Station. An Architectural History* (Yale University Press, New Haven 1956).

Mitchell, Allan, *The Great Train Race: Railways and the Franco-German Rivalry* (Berghahn Books, New York and Oxford 2000).

Ollivro, Jean, *Essai de modélisation d'une implantation ferroviaire. L'exemple du T.G.V. Méditerranée*, Université de Haute-Bretagne Ph.D. thesis, Geography, 1994.

Ollivro, Jean, 'Le réseau des lignes à grande vitesse: prégnance centralisatrice ou redéfinition de l'espace français?', *Revue d'histoire des chemins de fer* 12–13, 1995, 195–219.

Sabler, S. V., and Sosnovskii, I. V., *Sibirskaia zheleznaia doroga v ee proshlom i nastoiaschem* (St. Petersburg 1903).

Sassen, Saskia, *Metropolen des Weltmarkts. Die neue Rolle der Global Cities* (Campus Verlag, Frankfurt am Main 1997).

Schomann, Heinz, *Der Frankfurter Hauptbahnhof* (Deutsche Verlagsanstalt, Stuttgart 1983).

Schott, Dieter, *Die Vernetzung der Stadt. Kommunale Energiepolitik, öffentlicher Nahverkehr und die 'Produktion' der modernen Stadt. Darmstadt – Mannheim – Mainz 1880–1918* (Wissenschaftliche Buchgesellschaft, Darmstadt 1999).

Siedenbiedel, Christian, 'In 60 Minuten von Frankfurt nach Stuttgart', *Frankfurter Allgemeine Zeitung*, January 25, 2002.

Siedenbiedel, Christian, 'Pendeln im ICE mit Tempo 300. Montabaur und Limburg rüsten auf', *Frankfurter Allgemeine Zeitung*, December 23, 2001.

Simmons, Jack, *The Railway in Town and Country, 1830–1914* (David & Charles, London 1986).

Speer, Albert, *Die intelligente Stadt* (Deutsche Verlagsanstalt, Stuttgart 1992).

Sutcliffe, Anthony, 'Die Bedeutung der Innovation in der Mechanisierung städtischer Verkehrssysteme in Europa zwischen 1860 und 1914', in Horst Matzerath, ed., *Stadt und Verkehr im Industriezeitalter* (Böhlau Verlag, Köln 1996), 231–41.

Térade, Annie, *La Formation du quartier de l'Europe à Paris: lotissement et haussmannisation (1820–1870)*, 2 vols., Université de Paris VIII Ph.D. thesis, 2001.

Térade, Annie, 'Le nouveau quartier de l'Europe et la gare Saint-Lazare', *Revue d'histoire des chemins de fer*, vol. 5–6, 1991/1992, 237–260.

Then, Volker, *Eisenbahnen und Eisenbahnunternehmer in der industriellen Revolution. Ein preußisch/deutsch-englischer Vergleich* (Vandenhoeck und Ruprecht, Göttingen 1997).

Wilson-Bareau, Juliet, *Manet, Monet: La gare Saint-Lazare*, exhibition catalogue (Édition de la Réunion des musées nationaux, Paris 1998).

Wolf, Winfried, *Eisenbahn und Autowahn. Personen und Gütertransport auf Schiene und Straße* (Hamburg 1986).

Ziegler, Dieter, *Eisenbahnen und Staat im Zeitalter der Industrialisierung. Die Eisenbahnpolitik der deutschen Staaten im Vergleich* (Vandenhoeck und Ruprecht, Göttingen 1996).

Interactions between railways and cities in nineteenth-century Germany: some case studies
Ralf Roth

Allekotte, Hans, *Carl Josef Meyer als Eisenbahnunternehmer in Mitteldeutschland um die Mitte des vorigen Jahrhunderts* (Carl Simonowski, Steinheim 1931).

Andresen, Wibke, *Die Darstellung des städtischen Lebens in der deutschen Malerei des späten 19. Jahrhunderts* (tuduv Verlagsgesellschaft, München 1987).

Anonymous, 'Die Concurrenz für den Centralbahnhof zu Frankfurt am Main', *Wochenblatt für Architekten und Ingenieure*, 1881, 69–82.

Anonymous, *Empfangs-Gebäude für den Central-Bahnhof zu Frankfurt am Main. Sammelmappe hervorragender Concurrenz-Entwürfe*, 2 vols. (Verlag von Ernst Wasmuth, Berlin 1881).

Anonymous, 'Ist es für Frankfurt nothwendig, Eisenbahnen anzulegen', *Frankfurter Jahrbücher*, 7, no. 16, 1836, 95–6.

Bendikat, Elfi, *Öffentliche Nahverkehrspolitik in Berlin und Paris 1890–1914: Strukturbedingungen, politische Konzeptionen und Realisierungsprobleme* (Walter de Gruyter, Berlin/New York 1999).

Bergmann, Gerd, *150 Jahre Eisenbahn in Eisenach* (Eisenacher Geschichtsverein, Eisenach 1997).

Bernhardt, Christoph, *Bauplatz Groß-Berlin: Wohnungsmärkte, Terraingewerbe und Kommunalpolitik im Städtewachstum der Hochindustrialisierung, 1871–1918* (Walter de Gruyter, Berlin/New York 1998).

Bley, Peter, '100 Jahre Berliner Nordbahn 10.7.1877 – 10.7.1977', *Berliner Verkehrsblätter*, 24, 1977, 110–72.

Bley, Peter, 'Eisenbahnknoten Berlin', in Jochen Boberg, Tilman Fichter, and Eckhart Gillen, eds., *Exerzierfeld der Moderne: Industriekultur in Berlin im 19. Jahrhundert*, 2 vols. (Verlag C. H. Beck, München 1984), vol. 1, 114–25.

Bley, Peter, *150 Jahre Berlin-Anhaltische Eisenbahn* (Alba Verlag, Düsseldorf 1990).

Bodenschatz, Harald, *'Platz frei für das Neue Berlin!' Geschichte der Stadterneuerung in der 'größten Mietskasernenstadt der Welt' seit 1871* (Transit Verlag, Berlin 1971).

Bogdal, Klaus Michael, *Schaurige Bilder: Der Arbeiter im Blick des Bürgers* (Syndikat Verlagsgesellschaft, Fankfurt am Main 1978).

Bohle-Heintzenberg, Sabine, *Architektur der Berliner Hoch- und Untergrundbahn: Planungen, Entwürfe, Bauten bis 1930* (Verlag Willmuth Arenhövel, Berlin 1980).

Born, 'Die Entwicklung der Königlich Preußischen Ostbahn', *Archiv für Eisenbahnwesen*, 34, 1911, 879–939, 1125–72, and 1431–61.

Brake, Ludwig, *Die erste Eisenbahnen in Hessen: Eisenbahnpolitik und Eisenbahnbau in Frankfurt, Hessen-Darmstadt, Kurhessen und Nassau bis 1866* (Historische Kommission für Nassau, Wiesbaden 1991).

Brunn, Gerhard, 'Berlin (1871–1939) – Megalopolis Manqué', in Theo Barker and Anthony Sutcliffe, eds., *Megalopolis: the Giant City in History* (Hampshire and London 1993), 97–115.

Brunner, Reinhold, *'...die dem Armen hilft, das Wenige, was er besitzt, zu Rathe zu halten...': Die Geschichte der Sparkasse Wartburgkreis 1822 bis 1997* (Deutsche Verlagsanstalt, Stuttgart 1997).

Crew, David, 'Modernität und soziale Mobilität in einer deutschen Industriestadt: Bochum 1880–1901', in Hartmut Kaelble, ed., *Geschichte der sozialen Mobilität in der industriellen Revolution* (Verlag Anton Hain Meisenheim, Königstein im Taunus 1978), 139–85.

Engel, E., 'Die Wohnungsnoth: Ein Vortrag auf der Eisenacher Conferenz am 6. Oktober 1872', *Zeitschrift des kgl. Statistischen Bureaus*, 1872, 392–4.

Engeli, Christian, 'Die Großstadt um 1900: Wahrnehmungen und Wirkungen in Literatur, Kunst, Wissenschaft und Politik', in Clemens Zimmermann and Jürgen Reulecke, eds., *Die Stadt als Moloch? Das Land als Kraftquell? Wahrnehmungen und Wirkungen der Großstädte um 1900* (Birkhäuser Verlag, Basel et al. 1999), 21–51.

Foerster, Heinrich, *Von oeder Heide zur Industrie-Großstadt: Eine wirtschaftliche Studie und Schilderung des Werdens und der Entwicklung der Stadt Oberhausen/Rheinland*, Johann Wolfgang Goethe-Universität Frankfurt am Main Ph.D. thesis, 1922.

Freese, Jens, and Hofmann, Michael, *Der Äbbelwoi-Express: Auf den Spuren der Lokalbahn von Frankfurt nach Offenbach* (Verlag Wolfgang Bleiweis, Schweinfurt 1995).

Gall, Lothar, and Roth, Ralf, *Die Eisenbahn und die Revolution 1848* (Deutsche Bahn, Berlin 1999).

Giedion, Siegfried, *Raum, Zeit und Architektur* (Ravensburg 1965).

Glück, Kurt, and Görlich, Hermann, *150 Jahre Industrie- und Handelskammer Offenbach a. M., 1821–1971* (Industrie- und Handelskammer, Offenbach 1971).

Göbel, Heinz Christian, *Verkehrslage und wirtschaftliche Entwicklung der Stadt Offenbach*, Universtität Heidelberg Ph.D. thesis, 1912.

Halter, Martin, *Sklaven der Arbeit – Ritter vom Geiste: Arbeit und Arbeiter im deutschen Sozialroman zwischen, 1840–1880* (Peter Lang, Fankfurt am Main/Bern 1983).

Hansemann, David, *Die Eisenbahnen und deren Aktionäre in ihrem Verhältnis zum Staat* (Rengersche Verlagsbuchhandlung, Leipzig and Halle 1837).

Harkort, Friedrich, *Die Eisenbahn von Minden nach Cöln* (v. d. Linnepe Verlagsgesellschaft, Hagen 1961).

Hart, Julius, 'Auf der Fahrt nach Berlin', in Waltraud Wende, ed., *Großstadtlyrik* (Reclam Verlag, Stuttgart 1999), 45–6.

Hegemann, Werner, *Das steinerne Berlin: Geschichte der grössten Mietkasernenstadt der Welt* (Verlag von Gustav Kiepenheuer, Berlin 1922).

Henz, Ludwig, *Bericht über Project und Vorarbeiten zu der Anlage einer Eisenbahn von Elberfeld über Hagen nach Witten* (Sam. Lucas, Elberfeld 1836).

Hobrecht, James, *Entwicklung der Verkehrsverhältnisse in Berlin* (Verlag von Wilhelm Ernst, Berlin 1893).

Jakob van Hoddis, 'Morgen', in Waltraud Wende, ed., *Großstadtlyrik* (Reclam Verlag, Stuttgart 1999), 96.

Höwer, Ernst R., 'S-Bahn-Verkehr und Siedlungsentwicklung im Berliner Raum am Bsp. der Zossener Vorortstrecke', in Wolfgang Ribbe, ed., *Berlin-Forschungen* (Colloquium Verlag, Berlin 1989), vol. 4, 179–234.

Jähner, Horst, *Kuenstlergruppe Brücke* (Henschel Verlag, Berlin 1996).

Just, Michael, 'Transitland Kaiserreich: Ost- und südosteuropäische Massenauswanderung über deutsche Häfen', in Klaus J. Bade, ed., *Deutsche im Ausland – Fremde in Deutschland: Migration in Geschichte und Gegenwart*, (Verlag C. H. Beck, München 1992), 295–302.

Kaufhold, Karl Heinrich, 'Strassenbahnen im Deutschen Reich vor 1914: Wachstum, Verkehrsleistung, wirtschaftliche Verhältnisse', in Dietmar Petzina and Jürgen Reulecke, eds., *Bevölkerung, Wirtschaft, Gesellschaft seit der Industrialisierung* (Gesellschaft für Westfälische Wirtschaftsgeschichte, Dortmund 1990), 219–37.

Kemman, Gustav, 'Schnellverkehr in Städten mit besonderer Berücksichtigung von London und Newyork', *Archiv für Eisenbahnwesen*, 16, 1893, 263–72, and 455–71.

Kliem, Peter G., and Noack, Klaus, *Berlin Anhalter Bahnhof* (Verlag Ullstein, Frankfurt am Main et al. 1984).

Köllmann, Wolfgang, ed., *Quellen zur Bevölkerungs-, Sozial- und Wirtschaftsstatistik Deutschlands 1815–1875*, 3 vols. (Boppard 1980).

Königl.-preußischer Minister der öffentlichen Arbeiten, ed., *Berlin und seine Eisenbahnen 1846–1896*, 2 vols. (Verlag von Julius Springer, Berlin 1896).

Krings, Ulrich, *Bahnhofsarchitektur: Deutsche Großbahnhöfe des Historismus* (Prestel Verlag, München 1985).

Kubinszky, Mihály, *Bahnhöfe Europas. Ihre Geschichte, Kunst und Technik* (Deutsche Verlags Anstalt, Stuttgart 1969).

Kühn, Ernst, *Die historische Entwicklung des Deutschen und Deutsch-Oesterreichischen Eisenbahn-Netzes. Vom Jahre 1838 bis einschließlich 1881*, 2 vols. (Verlag des Königlichen Statistischen Bureau's, Berlin 1882).

List, Friedrich, 'Über ein sächsisches Eisenbahnsystem als Grundlage eines allgemeinen deutschen Eisenbahnsystems und insbesondere über die Anlegung einer Eisenbahn von Leipzig nach Dresden', in Erwin Beckerath and Otto Stühler, eds., *Friedrich List: Schriften zum Verkehrswesen*, 2 vols. (Verlag von Reimar Hobbing, Berlin 1929), vol. 1, 155–95.

List, Friedrich, *Das deutsche National-Transport-System in volks- und staatswirtschaftlicher Beziehung* (Transpress Verlag, Berlin 1988).

Maier, Helmut, *Berlin Anhalter Bahnhof* (Verlag Ästhetik und Kommunikation, Berlin 1984).

Marschall, Birgit, *Reisen und Regieren: Die Nordlandfahrten Kaiser Wilhelm II* (Carl Winter Universitätsverlag, Heidelberg 1991).

Matzerath, Horst, ed., *Stadt und Verkehr im Industriezeitalter* (Böhlau Verlag, Köln 1996).

Meeks, Carrol L. V., *The Railroad Station: An Architectural History* (Yale University Press, New Haven 1956).

Meyer, Alfred Gotthold, *Eisenbahnbauten: Ihre Geschichte und Ästhetik* (Esslingen 1907).

Mitchell, Allan, *The Great Train Race. Railways and the Franco-German Rivalry, 1815–1914* (Berghahn Books, New York and Oxford 2000).

Most, Otto, *Die deutsche Stadt und ihre Verwaltung: Eine Einführung in die Kommunalpolitik der Gegenwart*, 3 vols. (G. J. Göschensche Verlagsbuchhandlung, Berlin and Leipzig 1912).

Mumford, Lewis, *The City in History: Its Origins, Its Transformations, and Its Prospects* (Harcourt Brace Jovanovich Book, San Diego et al. 1961).

Neumeyer, Fritz, 'Massenwohnungsbau', in Jochen Boberg, Tilman Fichter, and Eckhart Gillen, eds., *Exerzierfeld der Moderne: Industriekultur in Berlin im 19. Jahrhundert*, 2 vols. (Verlag C. H. Beck, München 1984), vol. 1, 224–31.

Newhouse, Ludwig, *Vorschlag zur Herstellung einer Eisenbahn im Großherzogtum Baden von Mannheim bis Basel und an den Bodensee* (Verlag von Gottlieb Braun, Karlsruhe 1833).

Orth, Peter, *Die Kleinstaaterei im Rhein-Main Gebiet und die Eisenbahnpolitik, 1830–1866* (Limburger Verlagsdruckerei, Limburg a. d. Lahn 1938).

Perels, Christoph, 'Vom Rand der Stadt ins Dickicht der Städte: Wege der deutschen Großstadtliteratur zwischen Liliencron und Brecht', in Cord Meckseper and Elisabeth Schraut, eds., *Die Stadt in der Literatur* (Vandenhoeck und Ruprecht, Göttingen 1983), 57–80.

Peschken, Goerd, 'Wohnen in der Metropole', in Jochen Boberg, Tilman Fichter, and Eckhart Gillen, eds., *Exerzierfeld der Moderne: Industriekultur in Berlin im 19. Jahrhundert*, 2 vols. (Verlag C. H. Beck, München 1984), vol. 1, 132–7.

Radicke, Dieter, 'Öffentlicher Nahverkehr und Stadterweiterung: Die Anfänge einer Entwicklung beobachtet am Beispiel von Berlin zwische 1850 und 1875', in Gerhard Fehl and Juan Rodriguez-Lores, eds., *Stadterweiterungen, 1800–1875: Von den Anfängen des modernen Städtebaues in Deutschland* (Hans Christians Verlag, Hamburg 1983), 345–57.

Reif, Heinz, *Die verspätete Stadt: Industrialisierung, städtischer Raum und Politik in Oberhausen, 1846–1929* (Landschaftsverband Rheinland, Oberhausen 1993).

Reulecke, Jürgen, *Geschichte der Urbanisierung in Deutschland* (Suhrkamp Verlag, Frankfurt am Main 1985).

Reulecke, Jürgen, 'Verstädterung und Binnenwanderung als Faktoren soziokommunikativen Wandels im 19. Jahrhundert', in Dieter Cherubim and Klaus Mattheier, eds., *Voraussetzungen und Grundlagen der Gegenwartssprache: Sprach- und sozialgeschichtliche Untersuchungen zum 19. Jahrhundert* (Berlin 1989), 43–56.

Roth, Ralf, 'Metropolenkommunikation: Einige Überlegungen zum Zusammenhang von Migrationsbewegungen und Ideentransfer am Beispiel von Berlin und Chicago im 19. Jahrhundert', *Rheinisch-westfälische Zeitschrift für Volkskunde*, 46, 2001, 291–318.

Roth, Ralf, *Stadt und Bürgertum in Frankfurt am Main: Ein besonderer Weg von der ständischen zur modernen Bürgergesellschaft, 1760–1914* (Oldenbourg Verlag, München 1996).

Roth, Ralf, 'Der Sturz des Eisenbahnkönigs Bethel Henry Strousberg: Ein jüdischer Wirtschaftsbürger in den Turbulenzen der Reichsgründung', *Jahrbuch für Antisemitismusforschung*, 10, 2001, 86–112.

Roth, Ralf, 'Ab in den Untergrund: Zur Geschichte der Berliner Schnellbahnen', *Damals*, 32, no. 11, 2000, 36–42.

Roth, Ralf, 'Weltausstellung und Eisenbahn: Versuchsfelder der Moderne', *Damals*, 32, no. 6, 2000, 36–42.

Schambach, Karin, *Stadtbürgertum und industrieller Umbruch in Dortmund, 1780–1870* (Oldenbourg Verlag, München 1996).

Scharrer, Johannes, *Deutschlands erste Eisenbahn mit Dampfkraft oder Verhandlungen der Ludwigs-Eisenbahn-Gesellschaft in Nürnberg: von ihrer Entstehung bis zur Vollendung der Bahn* (Riegel und Wießner, Nürnberg 1836).

Scheffler, Karl, *Wandlungen einer Stadt* (Berlin 1931).

Schimpff, Gustav, 'Wirtschaftliche Betrachtungen über Stadt- und Vorortbahnen', *Archiv für Eisenbahnwesen*, 35, 1912, 597–643, 849–73, 1167–1201, 1456–82, and *Archiv für Eisenbahnwesen*, 36, 1913, 20–53, 383–416.

Schivelbusch, Wolfgang, *Geschichte der Eisenbahnreise: Zur Industrialisierung von Raum und Zeit im 19. Jahrhundert* (Hanser Verlag, München and Wien 1977).

Schmied, Wieland, 'Ausgangspunkt und Verwandlungen: Gedanken über Vision, Expressionismus und Konstruktion in der deutschen Kunst, 1905–1985', in Christos M. Joachimides, Norman Rosenthal, and Wieland Schmied, eds., *Deutsche Kunst im 20. Jahrhundert: Malerei und Plastik, 1905–1985* (Prestel Verlag, München 1986), 21–41.

Schomann, Heinz, *Der Frankfurter Hauptbahnhof* (Deutsche Verlagsanstalt, Stuttgart 1983).

Schott, Dieter, *Die Vernetzung der Stadt: Kommunale Energiepolitik, öffentlicher Nahverkehr und die 'Produktion' der modernen Stadt. Darmstadt-Mannheim-Mainz, 1880–1918* (Wissenschaftliche Buchgesellschaft, Darmstadt 1999).

Schubert, Dirk, 'Großstadtfeindschaft und Stadtplanung: Neue Anmerkungen zu einer alten Diskussion', *Die alte Stadt*, 13, 1986, 22–41.

Schulz, Karin, 'Der Auswandererbahnhof Ruhleben: Nadelöhr zum Westen', in Dieter Vorsteher, ed., *Die Reise nach Berlin* (Siedler Verlag, Berlin 1987), 237–41.

Schwabe, Hermann, *Berliner Südwestbahn und Centralbahn, beleuchtet vom Standpunkt der Wohnungsfrage und der Industrie Gesellschaft* (Berlin 1873).

Schwemer, Richard, *Geschichte der freien Stadt Frankfurt am Main, 1814–1866*, 3 vols. (Frankfurt am Main 1910–15).

Sofsky, Wolfgang, 'Schreckbild Stadt: Stationen der modernen Stadtkritik', *Die alte Stadt*, 13, 1986, 1–21.

Steen, Jürgen, *Frankfurt am Main und die Elektrizität, 1800–1914. Die zweite industrielle Revolution* (Historisches Museum, Frankfurt am Main 1981).

Steen, Jürgen, *'Eine neue Zeit ...': Die Internationale Elektrotechnische Ausstellung 1891* (Historisches Museum, Frankfurt am Main 1991).

Then, Volker, *Eisenbahnen und Eisenbahnunternehmer in der industriellen Revolution: Ein preußisch/deutsch-englischer Vergleich* (Vandenhoeck und Ruprecht, Göttingen 1997).

Traitteur, von, *Gutachten über die Anlage einer Locomotiv-Eisenbahn zwischen Mannheim (resp. Frankfurt), Straßburg und Basel* (Buchdruckerein von Hoff und Heuser, Mannheim 1837).

Uslular-Thiele, Christina, 'Die leidigen Bahnangelegenheiten', in Winfried S. Sahm and Christina Uslular-Thiele, eds., *Offenbach: Was für eine Stadt* (Volks-hochschule Offenbach, Offenbach 1998), 150–6.

Weber, Egon, 'Die Entwicklung des Ostseebades Saßnitz bis zum ersten Weltkrieg', *Greifswald-Stralsunder Jahrbuch*, 4, 1964, 117–80, and *Greifswald-Stralsunder Jahrbuch*, 5, 1965, 45–92.

Weinhold, Renate, *Die Eisenbahn als Motiv der Malerei: Eine Studie zur Bildinhaltskunde des 19. und 20. Jahrhunderts*, Universität Leipzig Ph.D. thesis, 1955.

Wittig, Paul, *Die Weltstädte und der elektrisch Schnellverkehr* (Verlag von Wilhelm Ernst, Berlin 1909).

Wolfes, Thomas, *Die Villenkolonie Lichterfeld: Zur Geschichte eines Berliner Vor-ortes, 1865–1920* (Institut für Stadt- und Regionalplanung, Berlin 1997).

Zlotowicz, Jensen, *Villen in Eisenach*, 2 vols. (Rhino Verlag, Weimar 1999).

Cities and railways in The Netherlands between 1830 and 1860
Henk Schmal

Ameshoff, H., *De Nederlandsche Rhijnspoorweg* (Utrecht 1891).

Anonymous, *100 jaar spoorwegen in Nederland. Overzicht van het ontstaan en de ontwikkeling der spoorwegen in Nederland van 1839–1939* (Nederlandsche Spoorwegen, Utrecht 1939).

Anonymous, *Hollandsche IJzeren Spoorweg-Maatschappij 1839–1889* (Ellerman, Harms & Co, Amsterdam 1889).

Boom, S., and Saal, P., 'Spoorwegaanleg en het beeld van de eerste helft van de negentiende eeuw', *Economisch en Sociaal-Historisch Jaarboek*, 46, 1983, 5–25.

Broeke, W. van den, *Financiën en financiers van de Nederlandse spoorwegen 1837–1890* (Waanders, Zwolle 1985).

Brugmans, I. J., *Paardenkracht en Mensenmacht, Sociaal-economische geschiedenis van Nederland 1795–1940* (Martinus Nijhoff, Den Haag 1961).

Carter, H., *An Introduction to Urban Historical Geography* (Edward Arnold, London 1983).

Citters, E. van, and Roosendaal, J. C. A. van, *Verzameling van wetten, besluiten, enz. betreffende de spoorwegen in Nederland* (Van Cleef, 's-Gravenhage 1877–1940).

Copeland, J., *Roads and their traffic, 1750–1850* (David & Charles, Newton Abbot 1968).

Dijksterhuis, R., *Spoorwegtracering en stedenbouw in Nederland: historische analyse van een wisselwerking* (Delft 1984).

Dillen, J. G. van, 'De economische ontwikkeling van Nederland', in J. A. Bartstra, and W. Banning, eds., *Nederland tussen de natiën*, 2 vols. (Ploegsma, Amsterdam 1948), vol. 2, 80–120.

Doedens, A., and Mulder, L., *Een spoor van verandering. Nederland en 150 jaar spoorwegen* (Bosch en Keuning, Baarn 1989).

Doorn, W. Th. C. van, *De Nederlandsche spoorwegwet en de daarbij behorende besluiten en reglementen* (Arnhem 1889).

Duparc, H. J. A., and Pater, A. D. de, 'De archivalia op het gebied van de Nederlandse spoor- en tramwegbedrijven', *Economisch-Historisch jaarboek*, 32, 1969, 269–281.

Faber, J. A., ed., *Het spoor. 150 jaar spoorwegen in Nederland* (Meulenhoff Informatief, Amsterdam and N. V. Nederlandsche Spoorwegen, Utrecht 1989).

Fritschy, W., 'Spoorwegaanleg in Nederland van 1831 tot 1845 en de rol van de staat', *Economisch en Sociaal-Historisch Jaarboek*, 46, 1983, 180–246.

Fuchs, J. H., *Beurt- en wagenveren*, Boucher ('s-Gravenhage 1946).

Griffiths, R. T., *Industrial retardation in the Netherlands, 1830–1850* (Martinus Nijhoff, Den Haag 1979).

Immink, D. A. E., *De Nederlandsche Centraal Spoorweg Maatschappij van 1863–1913* (place unknown 1913).

Jonckers Nieboer, J. H., *Geschiedenis der Nederlandse spoorwegen, 1832–1938* (Nijgh & van Ditmar, Rotterdam 1938).

Kellett, John R., *Railways and Victorian Cities* (Routledge & Kegan Paul, London and Henley 1979).

Kuiler, H. C., *Verkeer en vervoer in Nederland. Schets eener ontwikkeling sinds 1815* (Oosthoek, Utrecht 1949).

Lintsen, H. W., et al., eds., *Geschiedenis van de techniek in Nederland. De wording van een moderne samenleving 1800–1890* (De Walburg Pers, Zutphen 1993).

Maatschappij tot Exploitatie van Staatsspoorwegen 1861–1913 (Mij. Tot Expl. Van Staatsspoorwegen, Utrecht 1913).

Meene, J. G. C. van de, and Nijhof, P., *Spoorwegmonumenten in Nederland. Eindrapport van de werkgroep Spoorwegmonumenten ingesteld door de Koninklijke Nederlandse Oudheidkundige Bond* (KNOB, Amsterdam 1985).

Nusteling, H. P. H., *De Rijnvaart in het tijdperk van stoom en steenkool, 1830–1914* (Holland University Pres, Amsterdam 1974).

Raatgever, J., *100 jaar N. S. 1839–1939* (Algemeen publiciteitskantoor, Amsterdam 1939).

Romers, H., *De spoorwegarchitectuur in Nederland 1841–1938* (De Walburg Pers, Zutphen 1981).

Saal, P., and Spangenberg, F., *Kijk op stations* (Elsevier, Amsterdam 1983).

Schawacht, J. H., *Schiffahrt und Güterverkehr zwischen den Häfen des deutschen Niederrheins und Rotterdam vom Ende des 18. bis zur Mitte des 19. Jahrhunderts* (Rheinisch-Westfälisches Wirtschaftsarchiv, Köln 1973).

Schmal, Henk, 's Rijks groote wegen in de 19e eeuw', in A. P. de Klerk et al., eds., *Historische geografie in meervoud* (Stichting Matrijs, Utrecht 1984), 78–94.

Schmal, Henk, 'Patterns of de-urbanization in the Netherlands between 1650 and 1850', in H. van der Wee, ed., *The Rise and Decline of Urban Industries in Italy and in the Low Countries* (Leuven University Press, Leuven 1988), 287–307.

Schmal, Henk, 'Stedelingen in het Gooi; vestiging van de zeventiende tot de twintigste eeuw', *Amstelodamum*, 84, no. 4, 1997, 99–108.

Sluiter, J. W., *Beknopt overzicht van de Nederlandse spoor- en tramwegbedrijven* (Tweede druk, Brill, Leiden 1967).

Stieltjes, E. H., 'Overzicht van de ontwikkeling van het spoorwegnet in Nederland', in *Gedenkboek, uitgegeven ter gelegenheid van het vijftigjarig bestaan van het koninklijk instituut van ingenieurs 1847–1897* ('s-Gravenhage 1897), 63–71.

Stieltjes, J. J., 'De Spoor- en Tramwegen', *Tijdschrift van het Koninklijk Nederlandsch Aardrijkskundig Genootschap*, 50, 1933, 420–78.

Stuyvenberg, J. H. van, 'Economische groei in Nederland: een terreinverkenning', in P. W. Klein, ed., *Van Stapelmarkt tot Welvaartsstaat: economisch-historische studiën over groei en stagnatie van de Nederlandse volkshuishouding, 1600–1970* (Universitaire Pers Rotterdam, Rotterdam 1970), 52–74.

Veenendaal, A. J., 'Railways in the Netherlands', 1830–1914, *Railroad History* 173, 1995, 5–57.

Veenendaal, A. J., *De IJzeren Weg in een Land vol Water 1834–1958* (De Bataafsche Leeuw, Amsterdam 1998).

Vries, J. de, *Barges and Capitalism: passenger transportation in the Dutch economy, 1632–1839* (HES, Utrecht 1981).

Vries, J. de, *Amsterdam Rotterdam, rivaliteit in economisch-historisch perspectief* (Van Dishoeck, Bussum 1965).

Westerman, J. C., and Greup, G. M., *Gedenkboek samengesteld ter gelegenheid van het 125 jarig bestaan van de Kamer van Koophandel en Fabrieken voor Amsterdam* (Kamer van Koophandel en Fabrieken voor Amsterdam, Amsterdam 1936).

Zappey, W. M., 'Het Kanaal door Holland op zijn langst', *Ons Amsterdam*, 28, no. 8/9, 1976, 234–41.

Railways, towns and villages in Transylvania (Romania): impact of the railways on urban and rural morphology
Michel Tanase

Anonymous, *Joncţiunea Căilor Ferate ale României cu Ungariaşi Transilvanie* (J. Gött, Bucureşti-Braşov 1871).

Anonymous, *Memorialul pentru cel dintâi drum de fier din România unitq* (J. Gött, Braşov 1862).

Anonymous, *Zur Orientirung in der Siebenbürgischen Eisenbahnfrage* (Wien 1863).

Anonymous, *Voies et villes. Les transports routiers, ferroviaires et navals dans le développement des villes, from October 7–8, 1994* (Bistriţa 1994).

Anonymous, *Die Wahrheit in der siebenbürgischen Eisenbahnfrage. Eine Denkschrift an den Reichsrath* (Manz & Comp., Wien 1865).

Becke, Carl-Franz von, *Die Siebenbürger Eisenbahnfrage aus dem Gesichspunckte des österrechischen auswärtige Handels* (J. Gött, Kronstadt (Braşov) 1864).

Bellu, Radu, *Mică monografie a căilor ferate din România*, vol. 1: *Regionala Braşov* (Filaret, Bucarest 1995).

Caron, François, *Histoire des chemins de fer en France*, 2 vols. (Fayard, Paris 1997).

Chevallier, Raymond, *Les Voies romaines* (Picard, Paris 1997).

Friedmann, Otto-Bernharde, *Der gegenwärtige Stand der Eisenbahnfrage in Oesterreich* (Zamarski, Wien 1865).

Iordănescu, D., and Georgescu, C., *Construcţii pentru transporturi în România* (Constructions for the transport system in Romania) (Bucarest 1986).

Köpeczi, Béla, ed., *Histoire de la Transylvanie* (Akadémiai Kiado, Budapest 1992).

Lamming, Clive, *Les Grands Trains de 1830 à nos jours* (Larousse, Paris 1989).

Merlin, Pierre, ed., *Morphologie urbaine et parcellaire* (Presses Universitaires de Vincennes, Saint-Denis 1988).

Miller, Karl, *Die Peutingersche Tafel des Weltkartes des Castorius* (Stuttgart 1929).

Mureşan, Hilde, 'Proiecte privind construirea primelor căi ferate în Transilvania', *Anuarul Institutului de Istorie şi Arheologie*, 17, 1974, 268–79.

Tanase, Michel, 'La substitution du réseau routier romain en Transylvanie', in *L'homme et la route en Europe occidentale au Moyen Age et aux Temps modernes* (Centre culturel de l'abbaye de Flaran, Auch 1982), 289–94.

Tanase, Michel, 'Contribuţie la studiul evoluţiei drumurilor în Transilvania. Continuitateşi substituiri în partea meridională', *Historia Urbana*, 3, no. 1, 1995, 79–104.

The advent of transport and aspects of urban modernisation in the Levant during the nineteenth century
Vilma Hastaoglou-Martinidis

Anonymous, *Actes de la concession des chemins de fer de la Turquie d'Europe* (Constantinople 1874).

Arnaud, Jean-Luc, *Le Caire; mise en place d'une ville moderne* (Sindbad, Arles 1998).

AFR (Association of the Friends of Railways), *The Greek Railways* (in Greek) (Militos, Athens without date).

Awad, M. F., 'Le modèle européen: l'évolution urbaine de 1807 à 1958', *Revue de l'Occident Musulman et de la Méditerranée*, 46 (special issue: Alexandrie entre deux mondes), 1987, 93–109.

Birault, C., 'Le port d'Alexandrie. Historique et travaux en cours d'exécution', *Le Génie Civil*, 46, no. 6, 1904, 81–5.

Canpolat, Emin, *Izmir, kurulusundan bugüne kadar* (Istanbul Teknik Universitesi, Istanbul 1953).

Çelik, Zeynep, *The Remaking of Istanbul: Portrait of an Ottoman City in the Nineteenth Century* (University of California Press, Berkeley 1993).

Davie, May, *Beyrouth et ses faubourgs, 1840–1940* (Cahiers du Centre d'Etudes et des Recherches sur le Moyen-Orient Contemporain, Beyrouth 1996).

Debbas, Fouad, *Beirut, our memory* (Folios, Beirut 1986).

D'Eichthal, Gustave, *Economic and Social Situation in Greece after the Revolution* (Greek transl.) (Byron, Athens 1974).

Engin, Vahdettin, *Rumeli demiryollari* (Eren, Istanbul 1993).

Guide Joanne, *De Paris à Constantinople. Hongrie-Balkans-Asie Mineure* (Librairie Hachette, Paris 1912).

Godard, Louis, 'L'irrigation en Turquie', *Le Génie Civil*, 56, no. 15 (12 Février) 1910, 282–5.

Godard Louis, 'Les chemins de fer en Turquie', *Le Génie Civil*, 55, no. 12–14 (3 Juillet), 1909, 189–93.

Gounaris, Basil, 'Salonica', *Review*, 16, no. 4, 1993, 499–518.

Hansen, Jens, 'Ottomanizing Beirut under Sultan Abdülhamid II, 1876–1909', in P. Rowe and H. Sarkis, eds., *Projecting Beirut* (Prestel Verlag, New York 1998), 41–67.

Hastaoglou-Martinidis, Vilma, 'Les villes-ports du bassin oriental de la Méditerranée à la fin du XIXe siècle: travaux portuaires et transformations urbaines', in C. Vallat, ed., *Petites et grandes villes du bassin méditerranéen* (Ecole Française de Rome, Rome 1999), 507–25.

Hastaoglou-Martinidis, Vilma, 'The harbour of Thessaloniki, 1896–1920', in A. Jarvis and K. Smith, eds., *Albert Dock: Trade and Technology* (Merseyside Maritime Museum, Liverpool 1999), 133–41.

Ilbert, Robert, *Alexandrie, 1830–1930* (Institut Français d'Archéologie Orientale, Le Caire 1996).

Issawi, Charles, *The Economic History of Turkey, 1800–1914* (The University of Chicago Press, Chicago 1980).

Kasaba, Resat, 'Izmir', *Review*, 16, no. 4, 1993, 387–410.

Kotea, Marianthi, 'The industrial zone of Piraeus, 1860–1900', in Chr. Loukos, ed., *The city in the modern era* (in Greek) (Society for Contemporary Greek Studies, Athens 2000), 115–23.

Kütükoglu, Mübahat, 'Izmir rihtimi insaati ve isletme imtiyäzi', *Tarih Dergisi*, 32, no. 3, 1979, 495–558.

Leontidou, Lila, *Cities of Silence. Working-class colonization of urban space, Athens and Piraeus 1909–1940* (in Greek) (Cultural Technical Foundation of the Greek Bank for Industrial Development, Athens 1989).

Lorin, Henri, *L'Egypte aujourd'hui. Le pays et les hommes* (Imprimerie de l'Institut Français d'Archéologie Orientale, Cairo 1926).

Micheli, Liza, *Piraeus: From Porto-Leone to Manchester of the Orient* (in Greek) (Dromena, Athens 1988).

Morsy, Magaly, *Les Saint-Simoniens et l'Orient* (Edisud, Aix-en-Provence 1989).

Mouratoglous, Ar., 'The railways in Asia Minor' (in Greek), *Archimides*, no. 9, 1908, 56–8, and *Archimides*, no. 10, 1908, 105–9.

Özveren, Y. Eyüp, 'Beirut', *Review*, 16, no. 4, 1993, 467–97.

Papadimitriou, Dimitrios, and Kalemkeris Christos, *The trains in Northern Greece* (in Greek) (Reprotime, Thessaloniki 2000).

Quataert, Donald, 'Workers, peasants and economic change in the Ottoman Empire, 1730–1914', in H. Batu and J. L. Bacqué-Grammont, eds., *L'Empire Ottoman, la République de Turquie et la France* (ISIS, Istanbul 1986), 159–73.

Quataert, Donald, 'The age of Reforms, 1812–1914', in H. Inalcik and D. Quataert, eds., *An Economic and Social History of the Ottoman Empire, 1300–1914* (Cambridge University Press, Cambridge 1994), 759–823.

Svoronos, Nikos, *The commerce of Salonica in the eighteenth century* (in Greek) (Themelio, Athens 1996).

Storari, Luigi, *Guida di Smirne* (Stamperia de l'Unione Tipografico, Torino 1857).

Tekeli, Ilhan, 'The transformation in the settlement pattern of the Aegean region in the nineteenth century', in *Three Ages of Izmir* (Yeni Kredi Yayinlari, Istanbul 1993), 125–41.

Tekeli, Ilhan, *The Development of the Istanbul Metropolitan Area: Urban Administration and Planning* (International Union of Local Authorities, Eastern Mediterranean and Middle East Region, Istanbul 1994).

The impact of The Trans-siberian Railway on architecture and urban planning of Siberian cities

Ivan V. Nevzgodine

Andersson, H. O., and Bedoire, F., 'Fjodor Ivanovitj Lidvall – ett rysk-svenskt arkitektöde', *Arkitekturmuseet. Årsbok*, Stockholm 1980, 6–19.

Anonymous, *XVI Soveschatel'nii s'ezd inzhenerov sluzhby puti russkih zheleznih dorog: protokoly zasedanii, trydi* (St. Petersburg 1898).

Anonymous, *Al'bom chertezhei Zapadno-Sibirskoi, Zlatoust-Cheliabinskoi i Ekaterinburg-Cheliabinskoi zheleznyh dorog. 1891–1896gg.* (St. Petersburg 1897).

Anonymous, *Al'bom tipovih i ispolnitel'nyh chertezhei Krugobaikal'skoi zheleznoi dorogi. 1900–1905gg.* (St. Petersburg 1907).

Anonymous, 'D. A. Lebedev', *Zodchij* (The Architect), 19, 1904, 225–6.

Anonymous, *Sibirskiy Torgovo-Promyshlennii Kalendar' na 1911g.* (St. Petersburg 1911).

Anonymous, *Sibirskie tserkvi i shkoli fonda imeni imperatora Aleksandra III k 1 ianvaria 1903g.* (St. Petersburg 1903).

Anonymous, *Sibirskie tserkvi i shkoli: K desiatiletiyu fonda imeni imperatora Aleksandra III (1884–1904)* (St. Petersburg 1904).

Anonymous, *Sooruzhenie Sredne-Sibirskoi zheleznoi dorogi 1893–1898: Sbornik technicheskih uslovii, instruktsii i poiasnitel'nih zapisok* (St. Petersburg 1901).

Anonymous, *Ves' Novonikolaevsk. Adresno-spravochnaia kniga na 1924–1925 gody* (Novonikolaevsk 1924).

Anonymous, *Vysochajshii Reskript na immia ministra putei soobscheniia, po sluchayu 25-letiia pristupa k postroike Sibirskoi zheleznoi dorogi*, May 19, 1916 (St. Petersburg 1916).

Azadovskii, M. K., Anson, A. A., and Basov, M. M., eds., *Sibirskaia sovetskaia entsiklopedia* (Siberian Soviet encyclopaedia), 4 vols. (Sibirskoe kraevoe izdatel'stvo, Novosibirsk 1929).

Belelubsky, N. A., 'Zum Brückenbau in Rußland: Neuere Brückenbelastungen, Brückenmaterial, freie Querträger', *Zentralblatt der Bauverwaltung*, 28, no. 51, 1908, 349–50.

Belelubsky N. A., and Boguslavskiy, N. B., *Most cherez reku Ob otverstiem 327, 50 sazh. Konsol'noi sistemi. Proletnoe stroenie* (Zapadno – Sibirskaya zheleznaya doroga) (Tipografiia Yu. N. Erlih, St. Petersburg 1895).

Borisova, E. A., and Kazdan, T. P., *Russkaia arkhitektura kontsa XIX – nachala XX veka* (Nauka, Moscow 1971).

Chan-Magomedov, Selim O., 'Die Konstruktivisten und die Stilbildung der sowjetischen Architektur-Avantgarde', in Rainer Graefe, Murat Gappoev, and Ottmar Pertschi, eds., *Vladimir G. Šuchov 1853–1939: die Kunst der sparsamen Konstruktion* (Deutsche Verlags-Anstalt, Stuttgart 1990), 168–72.

Cooke, Catherine, 'Activities of the Garden City movement in Russia', in *Transactions of the Martin Centre For Architectural and Urban Studies*, 2 vols. (University of Cambridge, Cambridge 1976).

Cooke, Catherine, 'Russian responses to the Garden City idea', *Architectural Review*, 6, 1978, 353–63.

Dmitriev-Mamonov, A. I., and Zdziarski, A. F., *Guide to the Great Siberian Railway, 1900* (Drake publishers, New York 1972).

Endiminov, A. F., 'Proshloe russkogo mostostroeniia', *Stroitel'naia promyshlennost'*, 11, 1926, 778–81.

Glinka, G. V., ed., *Aziatskaia Rossiia, Luidi i poriadki za Uralom*, 2 vols. (Izdanie pereselencheskago upravleniya Glavnogo upravleniya zemleustroystva i zemledelia, St. Petersburg 1914).

I., P., 'Obzori i zametki, Prof. Lavr Dmitrievich Proskuriakov (14 sentiabria 1926 g.)', *Stroitel'naia promyshlennost'*, 9, 1926, 665–6.

Kann, S. K., 'Opyt zheleznodorozhnogo stroitel'stva v Amerike i proektirovanie Transsiba', in: L. M. Goriushkin, ed., *Zarubezhnye ekonomicheskie i kulturnye sviazi Sibiri (XVIII – XX vv.)* (Sb. nauch. tr., In-t istorii SO RAN, Novosibirsk 1995), 114–36.

Kovel'man, G. M., *Tvorchestvo pochetnogo akademika inzhenera Vladimira Grigor'evicha Shukhova* (Gosudarstvennoe izdatel'stvo literatury po stroitel'stvu, arhiteture i stroitel'nym materialam, Moscow 1961).

Mameev, S. N., *Bibliografiia zheleznodorozhnogo voprosa Sibiri* (Tobol'skii gubernskii muzei, Tobol'sk 1895).

Nashchokina, M. V., 'Gradostroitel'naia politika Rossii kontsa XIX – nachala XX veka v deiatel'nosti S. Yu. Witte i P.A. Stolypina', in I. A. Bondarenko, ed., *Arhitektura v istorii russkoi kul'turi. Vypusk 4: Vlast' i tvorchestvo* (Era, Moscow 1999), 138–45.

Paton, E. O., 'Metall i nagruzki zh.-d. mostov za sto let', *Stroitel'naia promyshlennost'* (The Building Industry), 2, 1926, 85–9.

Patton, E. O., 'Neuere bemerkenswerte Brückenbauten in Rußland', *Zentralblatt der Bauverwaltung*, 28, no. 99, 1908, 657–9.

Petrov, A. I., 'Mr. Howard's Ideals in Siberia', *Garden cities and town-planning*, 15, no. 4, 1925, 94.

Sabler, S. V., and Sosnovskii, I. V., *Sibirskaia zheleznaia doroga v ee proshlom i nastoiaschem* (St. Petersburg 1903).

Smirnova, E. A., 'Iz opita formirovaniya prizheleznodorozhnih kompleksov transsibirskoy magistrali', *Izvestiya vysshih uchebnih zavedeniy: Stroitel'stvo i arhitektura*, 6, 1984, 60–4.

Sostavil, S. N., *Bibliografiia zheleznodorozhnogo voprosa Sibiri* (Mameev, bibliotekar' Tobol'skogo gubernskogo muzeia, Tobol'sk 1895).

Starr, S. Frederick, 'The revival and schism of urban planning in twentieth-century Russia', in Michael F. Hamm, ed., *The city in Russian history* (The University Press of Kentucky, Lexington 1976), 222–42.

Stolypin, P. A., *Nam nuzhna velkaia Rossiia: polnoe sobranie rechei v Gosudarstvennoi Dume i Gosudarstvennom Sovete. 1906–1911* (Moscow 1991).

Sytenko, N. A., 'Obschiy vzgliad na sostoianie zheleznodorozhnoy seti v Rossiyskoy imperii, sovremennoe St.-Peterburgskoy sessii mezhdunarodnogo zheleznodorozhnogo kongressa', Stantsii, Glava IV, Otdel 1, in *Ocherk seti russkih zheleznih dorog, ee ustroistva, soderzhaniia i deyatel'nosti po 1892 god*, 2 vols. (St. Petersburg 1896).

Threadgold, Donald Warren, *The great Siberian migration: government and peasant resettlement from emancipation to the First World War* (Princeton University Press, Princeton 1957).

Tsarev, V. I., and Grinberg, Yu. I., *Achinsk: gradostroitel'naia istoriia* (Stroiizdat, Krasnoyarskoe otdelenie, Krasnoyarsk 1992).

Wagner, Rosemarie, 'Der Brückenbau', in Rainer Graefe, Murat Gappoev, and Ottmar Pertschi, eds., *Vladimir G. Šuchov 1853–1939: die Kunst der sparsamen Konstruktion* (Deutsche Verlags-Anstalt, Stuttgart 1990), 136–49.

Zhurin, Nikolai P., 'Gradostroitel'nye idei arkhitektora D. A. Lebedeva v sviazi so stroitel'stvom Transsibirskoi zheleznodorozhnoi magistrali', in *Problemy istorii, teorii i praktiki russkoi i sovetskoi arhitekturi* (Leningrad 1978), 123–6.

Portuguese cities and railways in the nineteenth and twentieth century
Magda Pinheiro

Alegria, Maria Fernanda, 'O tráfego de passageiros e mercadorias', in Maria Filomena Mónica, Magda Pinheiro, Fernanda Alegria, and José Barreto, eds., *Para a História do caminho de Ferro em Portugal* (Estudos Históricos, Lisbon 1999), 62–87.

Anonymous, *Censo da Populaçao 1911*, 2 vols. (IN, Lisbon 1917).

Anonymous, *Atlas Escolar Português* (Gotha, Lüddecke 1897).

Carvalho, Luciano, 'Caminhos de ferro de Minho e Douro. A linha urbana do Porto', *Revista de Obras Públicas e Minas*, 27, 1897, 128–52.

Companhia dos caminhos de Ferro Portugueses, *Relatório do Conselho de administração parecer do Conselho fisca- Exercício de 1955* (Lisbon 1956).

Correia Fino, Gaspar, *Legislação sobre Caminhos de Ferro*, 4 vols. (IN, Lisbon 1884–1904).

Guichard, François, *Porto, la ville dans sa région*, 2 vols. (F.G. Gulbenkian, Paris 1992).

Guichard, François, 'O Porto no século XX', in *História do Porto* (Porto Editora, Porto 1994), 524–637.

Justino, David, *A Formação do Espaço Económico Nacional, Portugal 1810–1913*, 2 vols. (Lisbon 1988).

Martins, João Maria de Oliveira, *Estudos Ferroviários – A Questão Ferroviária* (CP, Lisbon 1996).

Marques, Antonio de Oliveira, 'Meios de Comunicaçao' in *Historia da Primeira Republica* (Lisbon 1978).

Nunes, Anabela, 'Portuguese Urban System: 1890–1991', in Pedro Telhado Pereira and Maria Eugénia Mata, eds., *Urban Dominance and Labour Market Differentiation of a European Capital City, Lisbon 1890–1910* (Kluwer Academic Publishers, Boston et al. 1996), 7–47.

Pereira, Miriam Halpern, 'Niveis de Consumo e Niveis de Vida em Portugal, 1874–1922', in *Das Revoluçoes Liberais ao Estado Novo* (Presença, Lisbon 1994), 162–203.

Pimentel, Frederico, *Apontamentos para a História dos Caminhos de Ferro Portugueses* (Tipografia Universal, Lisbon 1892).

Pinheiro, Magda, 'Lisboa e os caminhos de ferro: os caminhos de ferro da capital', *Ler História*, 25, 1994, 77–91.

Pinheiro, Magda, 'Transportes e Vias de Comunicação', in Nuno Valério, ed., *Estatísticas Históricas Portuguesas*, 2 vols. (INE, Lisbon 2001), vol. 1, 357–96.

Pinheiro, Magda, 'Crescimento e modernização das cidades no Portugal oitocentista', *Ler História*, 20, 1990, 79–107.

Pinheiro, Magda, *Chemins de Fer, Structure Financière de L'État et Dépendance Extérieure au Portugal, 1852–1890*, 3 vols., University Paris I Ph. D. thesis, 1986.

Salgueiro, Teresa Barata, *A Cidade em Portugal* (Afrontamento, Oporto 1994).

Tomás, Ana, 'As cidades', in Nuno Valério, ed., *Estatísticas Históricas Portuguesas*, (INE, Lisbon 2001), vol. 1, 127–48.

Downtown by the train: the impact of railways on Italian Cities in the nineteenth century – case studies
Andrea Giuntini

Angeleri, G., and Bianchi, U. Mariotti, *I cento anni della vecchia Termini* (Edizioni della Banca Nazionale delle Comunicazioni, Roma 1974).

Angelini, I., et al., *Prime stazioni a Milano* (Editrice Bbe, Torino 1987).

Anonymous, *Milano nell'Italia liberale 1898–1922* (Cariplo, Milano 1993).

Anonymous, *La stazione Centrale di Milano. Mostra del Cinquantenario* (Di Baio, Milano 1981).

Anonymous, *La stazione e la città. Riferimenti storici e proposte per Roma* (Gangemi editore, Roma 1990).

Bellinazzi, A., and Giuntini, A., eds., *In treno a Firenze. Stazioni e strade ferrate nella Toscana di Leopoldo II* (Edizioni Polistampa, Firenze 1998).

Bernardello, A., 'L'origine e la realizzazione della stazione ferroviaria di Venezia 1838–1866', *Storia Urbana*, 9, no. 33, 1985, 3–45.

Berti, P., and Firenze, V., eds., *La nuova stazione di Firenze. Struttura e architettura* (Edifir, Savi 1993).

Boriani, M., and Rossari, A., eds., *La Milano del Piano Beruto (1884–1889). Società, urbanistica e architettura nella seconda metà dell'Ottocento* (Guerini e associati, Milano 1992).

Cioni, P., 'La ferrovia e le stazioni', in *Il disegno della città. L'urbanistica a Firenze nell'Ottocento e nel Novecento* (Alinea, Firenze 1986), 131–47.

Ciucci, G., et al., 'L'architettura dei fabbricati viaggiatori negli anni del razionalismo', *Ingegneria Ferroviaria*, 40, no. 4, 1985, 140–78.

De Finetti, G., *Milano costruzione di una città*, ed. by G. Cislaghi, M. De Benedetti, and P. Marabelli (Etas Kompass, Milano 1969).

Falco, L., 'La società degli ingegneri e degli architetti in Torino e il dibattito sulle stazioni nella città', *Storia Urbana*, 14, no. 50, 1990, 199–245.

Ferrarini, A., *Forme e icone del moderno. La stazione e i treni nell'immaginario collettivo* (Edizioni Pendragon, Bologna 1999).

Finetti, G. de, *Milano costruzione di una città* (Etas Kompass, Milano 1969).

Fontana, V., 'Il concorso per la Stazione centrale di Milano', in V. Fontana, *Il nuovo paesaggio dell'Italia giolittiana* (Laterza, Roma-Bari 1981), 98–105.

Gabetti, R., and Olmo, C., 'Discontinuità e ricorrenze nel paesaggio industriale italiano', in C. De Seta, ed., *Storia d'Italia. Annali 8. Insediamenti e territorio* (Einaudi, Torino 1985), 113–154.

Giuntini, Andrea, *Leopoldo e il treno. Le ferrovie nel Granducato di Toscana, 1824–1861* (ESI, Napoli 1991).

Giuntini, Andrea, 'Les gares de chemin de fer dans l'historiographie italienne récente', *Revue d'histoire des chemins de fer*, 5–6, 1992, 137–47.

Gottarelli, E., 'La Stazione Ferroviaria di Bologna', *Il carrobbio*, 8, 1982, 149–62.

Indovina, F., ed., *La città di fine millennio. Firenze, Genova, Milano, Napoli, Roma, Torino* (Franco Angeli, Milano 1990).

Karrer, F., and Luigi, Cosenza eds., *Effetti territoriali delle infrastrutture di trasporto* (Luigi Pellegrini editore, Cosenza 1995).

Lombardi, F., *Firenze nord-ovest. Formazione, sviluppo e trasformazioni, 1848–1986* (Le Monnier, Firenze 1987).

Mazzoni, Angiolo, *Architetto nell'Italia tra le due guerre* (Grafis Edizioni, Bologna 1984).

Meyers Konversations-Lexikon. Eine Enzyklopädie des allgemeinen Wissens, vol. 6, 11, and 13 (Leipzig and Wien 1890).

Penzo, P. P., 'Alle origini della periferia urbana. L'area intorno alla stazione di Bologna nella seconda metà dell'Ottocento', *Il carrobbio*, 11, 1985, 209–34.

Petti, R., 'L'architetto Angiolo Mazzoni e la nuova stazione di Siena', *Bullettino Senese di Storia Patria*, 98, 1991, 227–60.

Pucci, P., *I nodi infrastrutturali: luoghi e non luoghi metropolitani* (Franco Angeli, Milano 1996).

Savi, V., *De auctore* (Edifir, Firenze 1985).

Selvafolta, O., 'I progetti e la realizzazione della Stazione Centrale di Milano', in O. Selvafolta and A. Castellano, eds., *Costruire in Lombardia 1880–1980. Rete e infrastrutture territoriali* (Electa, Milano 1984), 207–42.

Stella, A., 'Architecture de la technique ou architecture de la ville? Les gares projetées par Angiolo Mazzoni dans les années 1930 et 1940', *Revue d'histoire des chemins de fer*, 10–11, 1994, 306–22.

Ventura, F., 'Genesi e progetti di un ingrandimento di città nella prima metà dell'800: il nuovo quartiere presso il Forte da Basso a Firenze', *Storia Urbana*, 9, no. 33, 1985, 47–66.

Ventura, F., 'Le trasformazioni urbanistiche della Firenze pre-unitaria', in *Il disegno della città. L'urbanistica a Firenze nell'Ottocento e nel Novecento* (Alinea, Firenze 1986), 21–38.

Zanni, F., 'Attori della morfogenesi: il sistema delle vie ferrate in Milano', in *Quaderni del dipartimento di progettazione dell'architettura*, 5, 1987, 69–74.

Railway development in the capital city: the case of Paris
François Caron

Anonymous, 'La traction électrique sur le prolongement du chemin de fer d'Orléans à Paris', *Revue générale des chemins de fer*, 21–2, no. 5 (November) 1898, 384–7.

Auphan, Etienne, 'L'espace et les systèmes à grande vitesse', *Cahiers du Centre de recherches et d'études sur Paris et l'Île-de-France (CREPIF)*, no. 61 (special issue: Les impacts du TGV sur l'organisation de l'espace en France et en Corée), 1997, 9–38.

Bordas, Claude, and Gayda, Marc, *De Saint-Germain-en-Laye à Marne-la-Vallée* (Editions de l'Ormet, Valignat 1992).

Bowie, Karen, ed., *Polarisation du territoire et développement urbain: les gares du Nord et de l'Est et la transformation de Paris au XIXe siècle. Une étude sur l'instauration et l'évolution des rapports entre les acteurs des grands aménagements ferroviaires urbains, première étape, 1830–1870*, 2 vols. (AHICF, Paris 1999).

Carrière, Bruno, *L'Aventure de la Grande Ceinture* (La Vie du rail, Paris 1991).

Carrière, Bruno, *Les Trains de banlieue*, vol. 1: *1837–1938* (La Vie du rail, Paris 1998).

Clozier, René, *La Gare du Nord* (Baillère, Paris 1940).

Commission des embellissements de Paris, 'Rapport à l'empereur Napoléon III', in Pierre Casselle, ed., *Cahiers de la Rotonde*, vol. 23 (Paris 2000), 1–205.

Lartilleux, *Géographie des chemins de fer français*, 2 vols. (Chaix, Paris 1962).

Meyers Konversations-Lexikon. Eine Enzyklopädie des allgemeinen Wissens, vol. 12 (Leipzig and Wien 1890).

Ollivro, Jean, 'Le réseau des lignes à grande vitesse: prégnance centralisatrice ou redéfinition de l'espace français?', *Revue d'histoire des chemins de fer*, 12–13 1995, 196–219.

Picard, A., *Les Chemins de fer français*, 2 vols. (Rothschild éditeur, Paris 1883).

Pumain, Denise, 'Chemins de fer et croissance urbaine en France au XIXe siècle', *Annales de géographie*, no. 507 (Septembre–Octobre), 1982, 529–48.

Sauvigny, Guillaume de Bertier de, *Nouvelle histoire de Paris: La Restauration* (Hachette, Paris 1977).

SNCF, *Contribution à l'élaboration d'un nouveau schéma directeur de l'Île de France* (Paris 1992).

Varlet, Jean, *Géographie des relations ferroviaires en France*, Université de Clermont II Ph.D. thesis, 1987.

Wolkowitsch, Maurice, *L'Économie régionale des transports dans le Centre et le Centre ouest de la France* (SEDES, Paris 1960).

Railway stations and planning projects in Prague, 1845–1945
Alena Kubova

Anonymous, 'Le cubisme tchèque', in Alena Kubova, ed., *L'Avant-garde architecturale en Tchécoslovaquie 1918–1939* (Pierre Mardaga, Liège 1992), 37–50.

Capek, Karel, 'Idealni Velka Praha', in Karel Capek, ed., *Spisy o umeni a kulture*, 2 vols. (CS, Prague 1985), vol. 2, 46–50.

Kohout, Jiri, and Vancura, Jiri, *Praha 19. a 20. stoleti: Technicke promeny* (SNTL, Prague 1986).

Kubova, Alena, 'Les fondements de ma modernité tchèque', in Alena Kubova, ed., *L'Avant-garde architecturale en Tchécoslovaquie 1918–1939* (Pierre Mardaga, Liège 1992), 11–34.

Masaryk, T. G., *Ceska otazka* (The Czech Question) (Cin, Prague 1936).

Pechar, Josef, *Ceskoslovenska architektura 1945–1977* (Odeon, Prague 1979).

Pecirka, J., *Alois Wachsman* (NCSVU, Prague 1963).

Piernitz, Alexandre, ed., 'Czechoslovakia. Documents of contemporary architecture, *L'Architecture d'aujourd'hui* (Architecture of today), 9, no. 10, October 1938.

Poche, Emanuel, et al., eds., *Praha narodniho probuzeni* (Panorama, Prague 1980).

Stary, Oldrich, ed., *Ceskoslovenska architektura od nejstarsi doby po soucasnost* (NCSVU, Prague 1985).

Wagner, Otto, *Architecture moderne et autres écrits* (Pierre Mardaga, Liège 1980).

Urban Form, social patterns and economic impact arising from the development of public transport in London, 1840–1940
Neil McAlpine and Austin Smyth

Aldcroft, D. H., 'Urban Transport Problems in an Historical Perspective', in A. Slaven and D. H. Aldcroft, eds., *Buisness Banking and Urban History: Essays in Honour of S. G. Checkland* (Donald, Edinburgh 1982), 156–178.

Bagwell, Philip, *The Transport Revolution from 1770* (Batsford, Oxford 1974).

Barker, Theo C., and Robbins, Michael, *A History of London Transport. Passenger Travel and the Development of the Metropolis*, 2 vols, (Allen and Unwin, London 1963–1975).

Binford, H., *The Profitability and Performance of British Railways* (Oxford 1978).

Cain, P. J., *Railways 1870–1914: The Maturity of the Private System* (Ian Allan, Shepperton 1983).

Collins, Paul, *London Trams. A View from the Past* (Hersham 2001).

Dyos, H. J., 'Some Social Costs of Railway Building in London', *Journal of Transport History*, 11, 1955, 23–30.

Dyos, H. J., *Railways and Housing in Victorian London* (London 1959).

Glover, J., *Glory Days, Metropolitan Railway* (Hersham 1998).

Habermas, Jürgen, *An ambitious connection with the past: modernity* (Frankfurt am Main 2001).

Hamilton, Ellis C., *British Railway History*, 2 vols. (Allen and Unwin, London 1957).

Houses of Parliament Record Office, Royal Commisions, *Royal Commission on the Housing of the Working Classes*, 4 vols. (London 1874).

Kellett, John R., *Railways and Victorian Cities* (Routledge & Kegan Paul, London 1979).

Koselleck, Reinhart, *Futuro Pasado. Para una semantica de los tiempos historicos* (Barcelona 1993).

Langlois, Charles V., *Introduction to the study of History* (Duckworth, Buenos Aires 1972).

Mee, A., *The King's England London North of The Thames except the City and Westminster* (London 1972).
Meyers *Konversations-Lexikon. Eine Enzyklopädie des allgemeinen Wissens*, vol. 10 (Leipzig and Wien 1890).
Pollins, H., *Britain's Railways: An Industrial History* (David & Charles, Newton Abbot 1971).
Turnock, D., *Essays in Comparative History* (Ashgate, Aldershot 1998).
Ville, S., *Transport and the Industrial Revolution*, University College, London Ph.D. thesis, 1992.

Railways plans and urban politics in nineteenth-century Dublin
Hugh Campbell

Anonymous, *Industries of Dublin* (Dublin 1890).
Benjamin, Walter, *Paris – The Capital of the Nineteenth Century in Charles Baudelaire* (Verso, London 1997).
Briggs, Asa, *Victorian Cities* (Penguin, Harmondsworth 1990, first published 1963).
Butt, Isaac, *A Speech delivered at the Mansion House, February 13, 1840* (Dublin 1840).
Campbell, Hugh, *Contested Territory, Common Ground: Architecture and Politics in Nineteenth Century Dublin*, University College Dublin Ph.D. thesis, 1998.
Conroy, J. C., *A History of Railways in Ireland* (Longmans, London 1928).
Corcoran, Michael, *Through Streets Broad and Narrow: A history of Dublin Trams* (Midland Publishing, Athlone 2000).
Craig, Maurice, *Dublin 1660–1860* (Penguin, Harmondsworth 1992, first published 1952).
Daly, Mary, *Dublin, the Deposed Capital* (Cork University Press, Cork 1985).
Dickens, Charles, *Dombey and Son* (Penguin, Harmondsworth 1985, first published 1848).
Edgeworth, Maria, *The Absentee* (Oxford University Press, Oxford 1988, first published 1812).
Foster, Roy, *Modern Ireland 1600–1982* (Penguin, London 1988).
Lee, Joseph, *The Modernisation of Irish Society* (Gill and Macmillan, Dublin 1983).
McCullough, Niall, *Dublin – an Urban History* (Anne Street Press, Dublin 1989).
Meyers *Konversations-Lexikon. Eine Enzyklopädie des allgemeinen Wissens*, vol. 5 (Verlag des bibliographischen Instituts, Leipzig and Wien 1890).
Sennett, Richard, *Flesh and Stone: The Body and the City in Western Civilization* (Faber and Faber, London and New York 1994).
Simmons, Jack, 'The Power of the Railway', in H. J. Dyos and M. Wolff, eds., *The Victorian City: Images and Realities*, 2 vols. (Routledge & Kegan Paul, London 1973), vol. 1, 277–310.
Wright, G. N., *An Historical Guide to the City of Dublin* (London 1821).

Following the tracks – railways in the city centre of Helsinki: bygone past or unwritten urban history?
Anja Kervanto Nevanlinna

Anonymous, 'Frågan om ny stadsplan för Skatudden', in *Tekniska Föreningens i Finland Förhandlingar* (Helsinki 1883), 1–15.
Åström, Sven-Erik, *Samhällsplanering och regionsbildning i kejsartidens Helsingfors* (Helsinki 1957).

Blomqvist, Pär, and Kaijser, Arne, 'De osynliga systemen', in Pär Blomqvist and Arne Kaijser, eds., *Den konstruerade världen, Tekniska system i historisk perspektiv* (Brutus Östlings Bokförlag Symposium, Stockholm 1998), 7–17.

Bonillo, Jean-Lucien, et al., *Marseille, Ville & Port* (Parenthèses, Marseille 1991).

Briggs, Asa, *Victorian Cities* (Penguin, Harmondsworth 1990, first published 1963).

Erävuori, Jukka, *Helsingin sataman ja satamahallinnon historia* (Helsingin kaupunki, Helsinki 1981).

Fierro, Alfred, *Histoire et dictionnaire de Paris* (Robert Laffont, Paris 1996).

Helsingin kaupunki, *Kamppi-Töölönlahti aatekilpailun ohjelma* (Kamppi-Töölönlahti idea competition programme) (Helsinki 1985).

Helsingin kaupunki, *Kamppi-Töölönlahti* (Kamppi-Töölönlahti Ideas Competition Results) (Helsinki 1986).

Helsingin kaupunkisuunnitteluviraston kaavoitusosasto, *Töölönlahden asemakaavan muutoksen selostus, January 4, 2001* (Helsinki 2001).

Hietala, Marjatta, *Innovaatioiden ja kansainvälistymisen vuosikymmenet* (Knowledge, know-how, professionalism. Helsinki as part of European development, 1875–1917), vol. 1 of Marjatta Hietala, ed., *Tietoa, taitoa, asiantuntemusta: Helsinki eurooppalaisessa kehityksessä 1875–1917*, 3 vols. (Suomen Historiallinen Seura & Helsingin kaupungin tietokeskus, Helsinki 1992).

Hobsbawm, Eric J., *The Age of Capital 1848–1875* (Abacus, London 1977).

Jackson, Gordon, *The History and Archeology of Ports* (World's Work, Kingswood 1983).

Jensen, Sigurd, and Smidt, Claus M., *Rammerne spraenges*, vol. 4: *Köbenhavns historie, 1830–1900* (Gyldendal, Copenhagen 1982).

Kajander, Lasse, 'Rautatiet Pasilassa 1862–1997', in Harry Schulman and Mikael Sundman, eds., *Pasila, Helsingin uusi keskus* (Helsingin kaupungin tietokeskus, Helsinki 1998), 83–8.

Kallenautio, Jorma, 'Kunnallistalous, yhdyskuntatekniikka, liikelaitokset ja joukkoliikenne 1875–1917', in Päiviö Tommila, ed., *Suomen kaupunkilaitoksen historia* (The history of the town institution in Finland), 2 vols. (Suomen kaupunkiliitto, Helsinki 1983), vol. 2, 271–330.

Kostof, Spiro, *A History of Architecture* (Oxford University Press, Oxford 1985).

Kovero, Martti, 'Helsinki liikennekeskuksena', in *Helsingin kaupungin historia* (The history of the City of Helsinki), 5 vols. (Helsingin kaupunki, Helsinki 1950–1967), vol. 3/1, 255–365, and vol. 4/1, 211–71.

Kuisma, Markku, 'Europe's Wood Basket Transformed. Finnish Economic History in a Long Perspective', in Tuomas M. S. Lehtonen, ed., *Europe's Northern Frontier. Perspectives on Finland's Western Identity* (PS-Kustannus, Jyväskylä 1999), 50–85.

Laati, Iisakki, 'Kunnalliselämä', in *Helsingin kaupungin historia* (The history of the City of Helsinki), 5 vols. (Helsingin kaupunki, Helsinki 1950–1967), vol. 4/2, 335–434.

Lindberg, Carolus, *Helsingfors, Nordens vita stad* (Werner Söderström, Helsinki 1931).

Martinsen, Rolf, 'Maapoliittinen sopimus ja kaavoituksen pallomylly', in Rolf Martinsen, ed., *Uhattu Helsinki, Kirja Helsingin kaupunkisuunnittelun kriisistä* (Helsingin kaupunkisuunnitteluseura, Helsinki 2000), 81–105.

Mumford, Lewis, *The City in History* (Harcourt, Brace & World, New York 1961).

Nevanlinna, Anja K., 'Cities as Texts: Urban Practices Represented or Forgotten in Art History', in Wessel Reinink and Jeroen Stumpel, eds., *Memory and Oblivion* (Kluwer Academic Publishers, The Hague 1999), 373–7.

Nikula, Riitta, *Yhtenäinen kaupunkikuva, 1900–1930. Suomalaisen kaupunkirakentamisen ihanteista ja päämääristä, esimerkkeinä Helsingin Etu-Töölö ja Uusi Vallila. Bidrag till kännedom av Finlands natur och folk* (Finska Vetenskaps-societeten, Helsinki 1981).

Nora, Pierre, 'L'ére de la commémoration', in Pierre Nora, ed., *Les Lieux de mémoire*, 3 vols. (Quarto Gallimard, Paris 1997, first published 1984–1992), vol. 3, 4687–719.

Pevsner, Nikolaus, *A History of Building Types* (Thames and Hudson, London 1976).

Roncayolo, Marcel, ed., *Histoire de la France urbaine*, vol. 5: *La ville aujourd'hui* (Seuil, Paris 1985).

Roncayolo, Marcel, *Histoire du Commerce et de l'industrie de Marseille, XIXe – XXe siècles*, vol. 5: *L'Imaginaire de Marseille, Port, Ville, Pôle* (Chambre de Commerce et d'Industrie de Marseille, Marseille 1990).

Schivelbusch, Wolfgang, *Junamatkan historia*, (orig.: Geschichte der Eisenbahnreise. Zur Industrialisierung von Raum und Zeit im 19. Jahrhundert) (Vastapaino, Tampere 1996).

Simmons, Jack, 'The Power of the Railway', in H. J. Dyos and Michael Wolff, eds., *The Victorian City: Images and Realities*, 2 vols. (Routledge & Kegan Paul, London 1973), vol. 2, 277–310.

Smeds, Kerstin, *Helsingfors – Paris, Finland på världsutställningarna 1851–1900* (Svenska litteratursällskapet i Finland & Finska Historiska Samfundet, Helsinki 1996).

Strengell, Gustaf, *Kaupunki taideluomana* (Otava, Helsinki 1923).

Sundman, Mikael, 'Kauppatori kunniaansa', *Arkkitehti*, 91, no. 2/3, 1994, 78–9.

Tanner, Väinö, *Näin Helsingin kasvavan* (Tammi, Helsinki 1947).

Volkov, Solomon, *Pietari, eurooppalainen kaupunki* (orig. St.Petersburg: A Cultural History) (Otava, Helsinki 1999).

Waris, Heikki, 'Helsinkiläisyhteiskunta', in *Helsingin kaupungin historia* (The history of the City of Helsinki), 5 vols. (Helsingin kaupunki, Helsinki 1950–1967), vol. 3/2, 7–211.

Political networks, rail Networks: public transportation and neighbourhood radicalism in Weimar Berlin
Pamela E. Swett

Binger, Lothar, 'Stadtbahnbögen', in Jochen Boberg, Tilman Fichter, and Eckhart Gillen, eds., *Exerzierfeld der Moderne: Industriekultur in Berlin im 19. Jahrhundert*, 2 vols. (Verlag C. H. Beck, München 1984), vol. 1, 106–13.

Bley, Peter, 'Eisenbahnknotenpunkt Berlin', in Jochen Boberg, Tilman Fichter, and Eckhart Gillen, eds., *Exerzierfeld der Moderne: Industriekultur in Berlin im 19. Jahrhundert*, 2 vols. (Verlag C. H. Beck, München 1984), vol. 1, 114–25.

Böß, Gustav, *Berlin von Heute: Stadtverwaltung und Wirtschaft* (Gsellius, Berlin 1929).

Brücker, Eva, 'Soziale Fragmentierung und Kollektives Gedächtnis. Nachbarschaftsbeziehungen in einem Berliner Arbeiterviertel 1920–1980', in Wolfgang Hofmann and Gerd Kuhn, eds., *Wohnungspolitik und Städtebau, 1900–1930* (Technische Universität, Berlin 1993), 285–306.

Capelle, Gerhard, 'Hundert Jahre Eisenbahn Berlin – Potsdam, 1938'', in Alfred Gottwaldt, ed., *Berliner Fernbahnhöfe: Erinnerungen an ihre große Zeit* (Alba Verlag, Düsseldorf 1983), 95–6.

Diehl, James, *Paramilitary Politics in the Weimar Republic* (Bloomington, Indiana University Press, Indiana 1977).

Fischer, Conan, *The German Communists and the Rise of Nazism* (St Martin's Press, New York 1991).

Frank, Ute, 'Terrainerschließung und U-Bahn-Bau' in Jochen Boberg, Tilman Fichter, and Eckhart Gillen, eds., *Exerzierfeld der Moderne: Industriekultur in Berlin im 19. Jahrhundert*, 2 vols. (Verlag C. H. Beck, München 1984), vol. 1, 232–9.

Friedrich, Thomas, *Berlin Between the Wars* (Vendome Press, New York 1991).

Gottwaldt, Alfred, *Berliner Fernbahnhöfe: Erinnerungen an ihre Große Zeit* (Alba Verlag, Düsseldorf 1983).

Hauschild, Peer, 'Bahnhöfe in Berlin', in Alfred Gottschalk, ed., *Bahnhöfe in Berlin: Photografen von Max Missmann* (Argon, Berlin 1991), 5–14.

Jung, Heinz, and Kramer, Wolfgang, 'Die U-Bahn', in Jochen Boberg, Tilman Fichter, and Eckhart Gillen, eds., *Exerzierfeld der Moderne: Industriekultur in Berlin im 19. Jahrhundert*, 2 vols. (Verlag C. H. Beck, München 1984), vol. 1, 138–9.

Kästner, Erich, *Fabian: the Story of a Moralist* (Northwestern University Press, Evanston 1993).

Keun, Irmgard, *Gilgi – eine von uns* (Claassen, Düsseldorf 1979, first edition 1931).

Ladd, Brian, *Urban Planning and Civic Order in Germany, 1860–1914* (Harvard University Press, Cambridge 1990).

Lindenberger, Thomas, *Straßenpolitik. Zur Sozialgeschichte der öffentlichen Ordnung in Berlin 1900–1914* (Dietz, Berlin 1995).

McKay, John P., *Tramways and Trolleys: The Rise of Urban Mass Transport in Europe* (Princeton University Press, Princeton 1976).

Paul, Gerhard, 'Krieg der Symbole. Formen und Inhalte des symbolpublizistischen Bürgerkriegs 1932', in Diethart Kerbs and Henrich Stahr, eds., *Berlin 1932: Das letzte Jahr der Weimarer Republik* (Hentrich, Berlin 1992), 27–55.

Peschken, Goerd, 'Die Hochbahn', in Jochen Boberg, Tilman Fichter, and Eckhart Gillen, eds., *Exerzierfeld der Moderne: Industriekultur in Berlin im 19. Jahrhundert*, 2 vols. (Verlag C. H. Beck, München 1984), vol. 1, 132–7.

Raynsford, Anthony, 'Swarm of the Metropolis: Passenger Circulation at Grand Central Terminal and the Ideology of the Crowd Aesthetic', *Journal of Architectural Education*, 50, no. 1, 1996, 2–14.

Remy, 'Bahnhofsumbauten in Berlin', in Alfred Gottwaldt, *Berliner Fernbahnhöfe: Erinnerungen an ihre Große Zeit* (Alba Verlag, Düsseldorf 1983), 73.

Remy, *Die Elektrisierung der Berliner Stadt-, Ring- und Vorortbahnen als Wirtschaftsproblem* (Verlag von Julius Springer, Berlin 1931).

Richie, Alexandra, *Faust's Metropolis* (Carroll and Graf, New York 1998).

Rosenhaft, Eve, *Beating the Fascists?* (Cambridge University Press, New York 1983).

Schivelbusch, Wolfgang, *The Railway Journey* (Berg, New York 1986).

Stürzbecher, Manfred, 'Stadthygiene', in Jochen Boberg, Tilman Fichter, and Eckhart Gillen, eds., *Exerzierfeld der Moderne: Industriekultur in Berlin im 19. Jahrhundert*, 2 vols. (Verlag C. H. Beck, München 1984), vol. 1, 160–69.

Swett, Pamela E., *Neighborhood Mobilization and the Violence of Collapse: Berlin Political Culture, 1929–1933*, Brown University Providence Ph.D. thesis, 1999.

Tittler, Robert, *Architecture and Power: The Town Hall and the English Urban Community, c. 1500–1640* (Clarendon Press, Oxford 1991).

The impact of the railway on the lives of women in the nineteenth-century city
Diane Drummond

Anonymous, *Drake's Guide to the Grand Junction Railway*, 2 vols. (London 1848).

Anonymous, *London Town* (London 1883).

Ardener, Shirley, 'Ground Rules and Social Maps for Women: An Introduction', in Shirley Ardener, ed., *Women and Space: Ground Rules and social mapping* (Berg, Oxford 1993), 1–21.

Chorley, Katharine, *Manchester Made Them* (Faber and Faber, London 1950).

Davidoff, Leonore, and Hall, Catherine, 'Gender Divisions and Class Formation in the Birmingham middle-class, 1780–1850', in Catherine Hall, ed., *White, Male and Middle-Class: Explorations in Feminism and History* (Polity, Cambridge 1992), 94–107.

Davidoff, Leonore, and Hall, Catherine, *Family Fortunes: Men and Women of the English Middle-Class, 1780–1850* (Routledge, London 1987).

Doré, Gustave, and Blanchard, Jerrold, *London: A Pilgrimage* (Grant & Co., London 1872).

Dyos, H. J., *Victorian Suburb: A Study of the Growth of Camberwell* (Leicester University Press, Leicester 1961).

Eley, Geoffrey, 'Public and Political Cultures: Placing Habermas in the nineteenth century', in Craig Calhoun, ed., *Habermas and the Public Sphere* (MIT Press, Cambridge, MA 1996), 289–317.

Emmerson, Andrew, *Underground Pioneers* (Capital Transport, Harrow Weald 2000).

Fraser, Nancy, 'Rethinking the public sphere: A Contribution to the critique of actually existing democracy', in Craig Calhoun, ed., *Habermas and the Public Sphere* (MIT Press, Cambridge, MA 1996), 109–31.

Freeman, Michael, *The Railway and the Victorian Imagination* (Yale University Press, Yale 2000).

Grossmith, George and Weedon, *The Diary of A Nobody* (Penguin, London 1979).

Habermas, Jürgen, *The Structural Transformation of the Public Sphere* (London 1963).

Hanson, Susan, and Pratt, Geraldine, *Gender, Work and Space* (Routledge, London 1995).

Hodson, Samuel J., *Climolithograph of Baker Street Underground Station on the Metropolitan Line* (London 1863).

Hollingshead, John, *Underground London* (London 1871).

Kellett, John R., *The Impact of Railways on Victorian Cities* (Routledge & Kegan Paul, London and Henley 1969).

Kemble, Frances Anne, *Memoirs of a Girlhood* (London 1874).

Kent, Susan Kingsley, *Gender and Power in Britain* (Routledge, London 2000).

Kilvert, Francis, *Diary*, 2 vols. (Jonathan Cape, London 1939).

Lardner, Dionysius, *Railway Economy* (London 1851).

Massey, Doreen, *Space, Place and Gender* (Polity, Cambridge 1994).

Mellor, Helen, Women's History Tutorial: 'Urbanisation, Civilisation and Society: The Role of Women', History Courseware for Historians CD-Rom (University of Glasgow, Glasgow 1999).

Mellor, Helen, Women's History Tutorial: 'Women, Cities and Social change, 1840–1940', History Courseware for Historians CD-Rom (University of Glasgow, Glasgow 1999).

Nead, Lynda, 'Taking to the Streets', *The B.B.C. History Magazine*, 1, no. 7 (November), 2000, 34–5.

Nead, Lynda, *Victorian Babylon: People, Streets and Images in Nineteenth-Century London* (Yale University Press, New Haven 2000).

Olsen, Donald, *The Growth of Victorian London* (Penguin, London 1976).

Parkes (later Belloc), Bessie Raynor, *In a Walled Garden* (Holmes & Meier, New York 1895).

Richards, Jeffrey, and MacKenzie, John M., *The Railway Station: A Social History* (Oxford University Press, Oxford 1986).

Schivelbusch, Wolfgang, *The Railway Journey: The Industrialization of Time and Space in the Nineteenth Century* (London 1977).

Simmons, H. A., *Ernest Struggles* (London 1879).

Simmons, Jack R., and Biddle, Gordon, *The Oxford Companion to Railway History* (Oxford University Press, Oxford 1997).

Simmons, Jack R., *Railways: An Anthology* (Collins, London 1991).

Simmons, Jack R., *The Railway in Town and Country* (David & Charles, London 1976).

Simmons, Jack R., *The Victorian Railway* (Thames and Hudson, London 1995).

Walkowitz, Judith R., *City of Dreadful Delight: Narratives of Sexual Danger in Late Victorian London* (Virago, London 1992).

Whitbread, J. R., *The Railway Policeman* (G. G. Harrap, London 1961).

Wright, Thomas, *Some Habits and Customs of the Working-Classes* (Tinsley Brothers, London 1867).

Index